Trust and Power

Trust and Power argues that corporations have faced conflicts with the very consumers whose loyalty they sought. The book provides novel insights into the dialogue between modern corporations and consumers by examining automobiles during the 20th century. In the new market at the turn of the century, automakers produced defective cars, and consumers faced risks of physical injuries as well as financial losses. By the 1920s, automobiles were sold in a mass market in which state agencies intervened to monitor, however imperfectly, product quality and fair pricing mechanisms. After 1945, the market matured as most U.S. families came to rely on auto transport. Automakers sold a product suited to the unequal distribution of income. Again, the state intervened to regulate relations between buyers and sellers in terms of who had access to credit, and thus the ability to purchase expensive durables like automobiles.

Sally H. Clarke is Professor of History at the University of Texas at Austin. She specializes in the political economy of the United States during the 20th century and is the author of *Regulation and the Revolution in United States Farm Productivity.*

Trust and Power

Consumers, the Modern Corporation, and the Making of the United States Automobile Market

SALLY H. CLARKE

The University of Texas at Austin

CAMBRIDGE UNIVERSITY PRESS

CAMBRIDGE UNIVERSITY PRESS
Cambridge, New York, Melbourne, Madrid, Cape Town, Singapore, São Paulo

Cambridge University Press
32 Avenue of the Americas, New York, NY 10013-2473, USA

www.cambridge.org
Information on this title: www.cambridge.org/9780521868785

First published 2007

Printed in the United States of America.

A catalog record for this publication is available from the British Library.

Library of Congress Cataloging in Publication Data
Clarke, Sally H.
Trust and Power : consumers, the modern corporation, and the making of the
United States automobile market / Sally H. Clarke.
p.   cm.
Includes bibliographical references and index.
ISBN-13: 978-0-521-86878-5 (hardback)
ISBN-10: 0-521-86878-5 (hardback)
1. Automobile industry and trade – United States – History.   I. Title.
HD9710.U52C53   2006
338.4′762920973 – dc22   2006018742

ISBN   978-0-521-86878-5 hardback

For my mother and in memory of my father

Contents

List of Tables and Figures

TABLES

FIGURES

Acknowledgments

It is with great pleasure that I thank the many scholars who have made this book possible. Jack Brown, Peter Jelavich, Naomi R. Lamoreaux, Jeffrey L. Meikle, and Steven Tolliday read and commented on the entire manuscript. The final product is much improved because of their contributions. At the risk of omitting someone who has offered advice on this project, I wish to extend many thanks to Christopher Bailey, Nelson Bowers, Roy Church, Lizabeth Cohen, Daniel R. Ernst, John Franz, Patrick Fridenson, Andrew Godley, Sally Griffith, Louis Galambos, Bruce Hunt, Alice Kessler-Harris, Scott G. Knowles, Pamela Laird, Glenn Porter, Daniel M. G. Raff, Mark Rose, Leonard Rosenband, Christopher L. Tomlins, Andrea Tone, Steven W. Usselman, Barbara Welke, and Marjorie Woods, as well as the members of seminars or meetings at the Georgia Institute of Technology, the Radcliffe Institute for Advanced Study at Harvard University, the Hagley Museum and Library, the Shelby Cullom Davis Center for Historical Studies at Princeton University, the University of Pennsylvania, the Johns Hopkins University, the Economic History Group of the Research Triangle, the University of California – Los Angeles, the Organization of American Historians, the International Business History Conference, the Business History Conference, the Economic History Association, the Society for the History of Technology, and the American Historical Association.

I explored some of my ideas for this book in articles that appeared as "Consumers, Information, and Marketing Efficiency at GM, 1921–1940," *Business and Economic History* 25 (Fall 1996): 186–95; "Consumer Negotiations," *Business and Economic History* 26 (Fall 1997): 101–22; "Managing Design: the Art and Colour Section at General Motors, 1927–1941," *Journal of Design History* 12 No. 1 (1999): 65–79; "Closing the Deal: GM's Marketing Dilemma and Its Franchised Dealers, 1921–41," *Business History* 45 (January 2003): 60–79 (http://www.tanf.co.uk); and "Unmanageable Risks: *MacPherson v. Buick* and the Emergence of a Mass Consumer Market," *Law and History Review* 23 (January 2005): 1–52. I received some of the most valuable criticism from the aforementioned journals' anonymous referees and am deeply grateful to all of these scholars who commented on my work. I include material, in revised form, from these journals thanks to the permission of the Business History Conference, the Design History Society, and the American Society for Legal History and the University of Illinois Press.

Historical scholarship is rooted in archival research. I wish to thank the archivists at the Henry Ford, especially Linda Skolarus, who introduced me to the legal records of the Ford Motor Company, David White of the Richard P. Scharchburg Archives of Kettering University, Sarah Roberts at Michigan State University, Mark Patrick and Barbara Thompson at the National Automotive History Collection of the Detroit Public Library, James R. Sahlem and Jo Ann Mattingly of the Supreme Court Library at Buffalo, and Jon Bill at the Auburn Cord Duesenberg Museum. I wish to express my thanks as well to the librarians and archivists of the Archives and Records Preservation of the Supreme Judicial Court of Massachusetts, the Baker Library of the Harvard Business School, the Bentley Historical Library of the University of Michigan, the California State Archives, the Free Library of Philadelphia, the Georgia Archives, the Hagley Museum and Library, the Kansas State Historical Society, the Kentucky Department for Libraries and Archives, the Iowa State Law Library, the Library of Congress, the Missouri State Library, the National Agricultural Library, the National Archives at College Park, the National Archives – Northeast Region, the National Archives – Great Lakes Region, the National Archives – Southwest Region, the New York State Library, the Special Collections Library of the University of Michigan, the Social Law Library, the South Carolina Department of Archives and History, the University of Michigan Law Library, the University of Texas at Austin Law Library, the University of Texas at Austin Perry–Castaneda Library, the Virginia State Law Library, the Widener Library of Harvard University, the Wisconsin Historical Society, and the Wisconsin State Law Library.

Financial support has been critical in allowing me to research and write this book. I wish to thank the Hagley Museum and Library, the National Endowment for the Humanities, the Shelby Cullom Davis Center for Historical Studies at Princeton University, the Radcliffe Institute for Advanced Study at Harvard University, the Alfred P. Sloan Foundation, and the University of Texas at Austin. I am grateful to many individuals who administered this financial support, including Glenn Porter at Hagley; Gail Pesyna at the Sloan Foundation; Drew Gilpin Faust, the Dean of the Radcliffe Institute; Judith Vichniac, the director of Fellows at the Radcliffe Institute; William C. Jordan at Princeton University; and Alan Tully, the Chair of the History Department at the University of Texas at Austin.

The American Council of Learned Societies (ACLS) provided a unique opportunity for the publication of an electronic version of this book in their History E-Book Project. The electronic version can be found at the ACLS website: http://www.hebook.org/xml-titlelist.html. I wish to thank Ronald Musto and Eileen Gardner, my editors at the ACLS, for their enthusiastic support. I also wish to thank the ACLS for its generous book subvention.

More friends and colleagues helped along the way. I very much appreciate the advice of L. B. Boyce, Tristram Hewitt, Peter Jelavich, Martha Newman, Joey Walker, Tom Whatley, and Leslie S. Walker. At Cambridge University Press, my manuscript received the careful attention of Cathy Felgar. I wish to express my gratitude to the editor of my book, Frank Smith.

Abbreviations: Archives, Collections, and Libraries

1. THE HENRY FORD COLLECTIONS

HF	Benson Ford Research Center, The Henry Ford, Dearborn, MI.
Acc. 1	The Fair Lane Papers, Accession 1.
Acc. 2	Henry Ford Office Papers, Accession 2.
Acc. 75	Ford Motor Company Legal Records, 1912–31, Accession 75.
Acc. 85	Ford Motor Company Minute Books, Accession 85.
Acc. 94	Engineering – Dearborn Laboratories, Accession 94.
Acc. 140	Secretary's Office – Contracts and Agreements, Accession 140.
Acc. 297	Ford Motor Company Legal – Cases and Claims, Accession 297.
Acc. 390	Purchasing – A. M. Wibel, Accession 390.
Acc. 483	Office of the Treasurer – General, 1903–1933, Accession 483.
Acc. 1673	Automotive Design Oral Histories, Accession 1673.
Acc. 1750	Frank C. Armstrong Papers, Accession 1750.

2. ARCHIVES AND COLLECTIONS (OTHER THAN THE HENRY FORD)

ADL	Arthur D. Little, Inc. Collection, Manuscripts Division, LC.
BHL	Bentley Historical Library, UM.
Chapin Papers	Roy D. Chapin Papers, BHL, UM.
CFK	Charles F. Kettering Archives, KU.
Cox	Claude E. Cox Collection, Accession 15, DPL.
DPL	National Automotive History Collection, Detroit Public Library, Detroit, MI.
GM Files	General Motors Company Files, DPL.
GMC/Proving Ground	GMC/Proving Ground Collection, KU.
GMC/History Collection	GMC/History Collection, KU.
Hagley	Hagley Museum and Library, Wilmington, DE.

HBS	Baker Library, Harvard Business School, Boston, MA.
Hudson Papers	Hudson Motor Company Papers, BHL, UM.
King Collection	Charles Brady King Collection, Accession 34, DPL.
KU	Richard P. Scharchburg Archives, Kettering University, Flint, MI.
LC	Library of Congress, Washington, D.C.
Leland Collection	Henry and Wilfred Leland Collection, Accession 27, DPL.
Mott Papers	Charles Stewart Mott Papers, KU.
MSU	Michigan State University Archives and Historical Collections, East Lansing, MI.
NA	National Archives, College Park, MD.
NA, Chicago	National Archives, Great Lakes Region, Chicago, IL.
NA, NY	National Archives, Northeast Region, New York, NY.
NBC	National Broadcasting Company, Inc., 1921–1969, Records, Accession 17AF, WHS.
Olds Papers	Ransom E. Olds Papers, MSU.
RG 122	"Economic Investigations File, Motor Vehicles 1915–1938," Entry 7, Record Group 122, NA.
RG 122 BC	Federal Trade Commission, Bureau of Corporations, Record Group 122, NA.
RG 276	Records for the U.S. Circuit Court of Appeals, Record Group 276, National Archives.
RG 82	Records of the Board of Governors of the Federal Reserve System, Entry 1, Record Group 82, NA.
SCL	Special Collections Library, UM.
UM	University of Michigan, Ann Arbor, MI.
WHS	Wisconsin Historical Society, Madison, WI.
Wilkerson Collection	Daniel C. Wilkerson Collection, KU.

3. RECORDS AND BRIEFS OF COURT CASES

Note: Part of my analysis in Chapter 2 is based on a database of automobile dealer agreements. In the Appendix, I provide citations for all the automobile dealer agreements. Here I provide abbreviations for the records and briefs cited throughout the book.

Records and Briefs for *Buick*	*Buick Motor Car Co. v. Reid Mfg. Co.*, 150 Mich. 118 (1907), Records of the Supreme Court of Michigan, University of Michigan Law Library, Ann Arbor, MI.
Records and Briefs for *Cadillac*	*Cadillac Motor Car Co. v. Johnson*, 221 F. 801 (2d Cir. 1915), Transcript of Record, Case No. 157, RG 276, NA, NY.
Records and Briefs for *Columbia*	*Columbia Motor Car Co. et al. v. C. A. Duerr & Co. et al.*, 184 F. 893 (1st Cir. 1911), Transcript of Record, Case No. 4058-60 (consolidated numbers), RG 276, NA, NY.
Records and Briefs for *Garfield*	*Garfield v. Peerless Motor Car Company*, 189 Mass. 395 (1908), Massachusetts Reports Papers and Briefs, Volume 189, Social Law Library, Boston, MA.
Records and Briefs for *General Motors*	*United States v. General Motors Corporation et al.*, 121 F.2d 376 (7th Cir. 1941), Transcript of Record for the U.S. Court of Appeals for the Seventh Circuit, Case No. 7146, Box 1003, RG 276, NA, Chicago.
Records and Briefs for *Joslyn*	*Joslyn v. Cadillac Motor Car Co.*, 177 F. 863 (6th Cir. 1910), Case No. 1998, Records of the U.S. Court of Appeals, Sixth Circuit, Record Group 276, NA, Chicago.
Records and Briefs for *MacPherson*	*Donald C. MacPherson v. Buick Motor Company*, Court of Appeals of the State of New York, March 14, 1916, *MacPherson v. Buick*, 217 N.Y. 382, 111 N.E. 1050 (N.Y. 1916), Supreme Court Library at Buffalo, Buffalo, NY.
Records and Briefs for *Masters*	*Masters & Another v. Wayne Automobile Company & Others*, 198 Mass. 25 (1908), Massachusetts Reports Papers and Briefs, Volume 198, Supreme Judicial Court of Massachusetts, Suffolk, Social Law Library, Boston, MA.

Records and Briefs for *Neale*	*Neale v. American Electric Vehicle Company*, 186 Mass. 303 (1904), Case No. 2411, Massachusetts Reports Papers and Briefs, Volume 186, Supreme Judicial Court of Massachusetts, Suffolk, Social Law Library, Boston, MA.
Records and Briefs for *Oakland*	*Oakland Motor Car Co. v. Indiana Automobile Co.*, 201 F. 499 (7th Cir. 1912), Transcript of Record, Case No. 1891, RG 276, NA, Chicago.
Records and Briefs for *Studebaker*	*Studebaker Corporation of America v. George J. Gollmar & LeRoy Messenger (co-partners doing business as Gollmar & Messenger Auto Company)*, 159 Wis. 336 (1915), Records of the Supreme Court of Wisconsin, Wisconsin State Law Library, Madison, WI.
Records and Briefs for *Welch*	*Welch Motor Car Company of New York v. P. Brady & Son Company*, 149 A.D. 945 (1912), Supreme Court of New York, Appellate Division, First Department, New York State Library, Albany, NY.
Records and Briefs for *Wheaton*	*Wheaton v. Cadillac Automobile Co.*, 143 Mich. 21 (1906), Records of the Supreme Court of Michigan, University of Michigan Law Library, Ann Arbor, MI.
Records and Briefs for *White*	*White Company v. American Motor-Car Co.*, 11 Ga. App. 285 (1912), Court of Appeals of Georgia, Case No. 4159, Box 80, The Georgia Archives, Morrow, GA.

Introduction

Markets are distinctive products of what Adam Smith called the human "propensity to truck, barter, and exchange one thing for another." After all, he noted: "Nobody ever saw a dog make a fair and deliberate exchange of one bone for another with another dog. Nobody ever saw one animal by its gestures and natural cries signify to another, this is mine, that yours; I am willing to give this for that."[1] In his examination of the human capacity to create markets, Smith took up the question of fairness when he argued that self-interest worked to the benefit of buyers and sellers – an insight that has since been captured in the phrase "mutually beneficial exchange." Yet Smith balanced his enthusiasm for markets with the concern that powerful interests would grab at whatever opportunities presented themselves to try to inflate their profits. Businesses, for instance, would readily exercise power through market relationships to enlarge their profits at consumers' expense.[2] Smith thus tempered his faith in the capacity of self-interest to foster trust in market relations with the explicit concern about the power firms exercised through market transactions.

This book examines a different economy, place, and time: it traces the evolution of a modern market, that for automobiles, in the United States during the twentieth century. But my approach follows Smith's study of political economy. For what was entailed in the process of exchange? Was it "fair and deliberate"? At the heart of my study is the premise that although in many industries managers wanted and indeed cultivated consumers' trust, in the automobile market this was not the case. Unable to coordinate consumers' buying habits with a firm's internal operations, managers sought to shape consumers' behavior and impose social costs on car buyers. From the market's start, private and public entities – the courts, insurance underwriters, engineering societies, state motor vehicle administrations, the Justice Department, the Federal Trade Commission (FTC), and the Board of Governors of the Federal Reserve System – regulated relations between buyers

---

[1] Adam Smith, *The Wealth of Nations*, ed. Edwin Cannan (1776; repr., New York: Modern Library Paperback, 2000), 14.

[2] Ibid., 148–49, 287–88, 715–17; and Amartya Sen, *Development as Freedom* (New York: Anchor Books, 1999), 271.

and sellers. The contests between consumers and corporations and the roles played by regulators meant that the development of this modern consumer market was almost at every turn a study in political economy.

I trace the market's evolution from a new market to a mass market and, finally, to a mature market.[3] The new market for automobiles emerged between the mid-1890s and the mid-1910s. In this era – prior to the market's consolidation around the "Big Three" automakers – numerous firms populated the field. It is conventional for business historians to focus on entrepreneurs who assumed considerable risks as they perfected a complex mechanical device. Without denying the roles of the early entrepreneurs, I posit that the market's first car buyers also assumed considerable risks. Innovation in a market context meant that firms initially sold crude machines even as they worked to better their products.[4] Car buyers thus incurred financial losses and physical injuries born out of technological defects inherent in these rudimentary rigs. In other words, they absorbed social costs as an inherent part of the process of market innovation. Although some consumers accepted the costs, others sued manufacturers. In the Progressive era, as Americans redefined the causes of accidents, the courts took up the question: Who should assume the risks of market innovation?[5] What was the corporation's responsibility to consumers for a new product's quality?

[3] As readers will see, my periodization follows from my focus on the market's evolution, but readers will find alternative frameworks among other automobile historians. See for example, James J. Flink, "Three Stages of American Automobile Consciousness," *American Quarterly* 24 (October 1972): 451–73; and John M. Staudenmaier, "The Politics of Successful Technologies," in *In Context: History and the History of Techonology: Essays in Honor of Melvin Kranzberg*, ed. Stephen H. Cutcliffe and Robert C. Post (Bethlehem, PA: Lehigh University Press, 1989), 150–71.

[4] In addition, products posed risks simply through their poor design. In the case of the bicycle, risks of accidents (such as tumbling head-first over the handlebars of a high-wheeler) followed from the design of the vehicle rather than from defects. In other cases aside from automobiles, defects also marred the product. In the mid-nineteenth century, boiler explosions on the nation's steamboats were frightening events, as Louis Hunter long ago explained to readers. On bicycles, see Wiebe E. Bijker, *Of Bicycles, Bakelites, and Bulbs: Toward a Theory of Sociotechnical Change* (Cambridge, MA: MIT Press, 1995), 37–41, 73–77, 97–100. On steamboats, see Louis C. Hunter, *Steamboats on the Western Rivers: An Economic and Technological History* (Cambridge, MA: Harvard University Press, 1949), 271–304.

[5] Arthur F. McEvoy, "The Triangle Shirtwaist Factory Fire of 1911: Social Change, Industrial Accidents, and the Evolution of Common-Sense Causality," *Law and Social Inquiry* 20 (Spring 1995): 621–51; Barbara Young Welke, *Recasting American Liberty: Gender, Race, Law, and the Railroad Revolution, 1865–1920* (New York: Cambridge University Press, 2001); John Fabian Witt, "Speedy Fred Taylor and the Ironies of Enterprise Liability," *Columbia Law Review* 103 (January 2003): 1–49; idem, *The Accidental Republic: Crippled Workmen, Destitute Widows, and the Remaking of American Law* (Cambridge, MA: Harvard University Press, 2004); Scott Gabriel Knowles, "Lessons in the Rubble: The World Trade Center and the History of Disaster Investigations in the United States," *History and Technology* 19 (2003): 9–28; and Sarah S. Lochlann Jain, "'Dangerous Instrumentalities': The Bystander as Subject in Automobility," *Cultural Anthropology* 19, no. 1 (2004): 61–94. On social costs, see R. H. Coase, "The Problem of Social Cost," *Journal of Law & Economics* 3 (October 1960): 1–44; and Cornelius W. Gillam, *Products Liability in the Automobile Industry: A Study in*

Between 1910 and 1930, cars became more reliable and car ownership increased from one percent of U.S. households to sixty percent (before slipping to fifty-five percent during the Great Depression).[6] Alfred P. Sloan, Jr., the president of General Motors (GM), outlined in his autobiography the steps the modern bureaucratic firm took to establish the institutions and policies needed to efficiently produce and effectively market automobiles on a mass scale.[7] The modern research laboratory, methods of mass production, the coordination of production and distribution, and bureaucratic measures of efficiency represented one side of a mass market. Sloan also called attention to innovations in marketing, such as installment credit and automobile styling (the annual model change).[8] GM managers combined these business institutions in their effort to secure loyal customers. In a mass market, a firm's success in sustaining a large market share required that it win and keep repeat car buyers. Yet this goal proved elusive, because managers could never chart a clear path for maintaining their profits and cultivating loyal consumers. Engineering safe vehicles, for instance, added manufacturing costs and slowed the introduction of new features used to market vehicles.[9] Aesthetic creativity in a car's design also threatened to drive up the cost of production.[10] Unable to synchronize production with consumers' tastes, managers confronted dealers and consumers in the market as they negotiated each transaction that set a car's price. Facing competing goals, managers sought to shift costs of

---

Strict Liability and Social Control (Minneapolis, MN: University of Minnesota Press, 1960), 196–210. See also Arthur F. McEvoy, *The Fisherman's Problem: Ecology and Law in the California Fisheries, 1850–1980* (New York: Cambridge University Press, 1986).

[6] Stanley Lebergott, *Pursuing Happiness: American Consumers in the Twentieth Century* (Princeton, NJ: Princeton University Press, 1993), 130.

[7] Alfred P. Sloan, Jr., *My Years with General Motors*, ed. John McDonald with Catherine Stevens (Garden City, NY: Doubleday & Company, Inc., 1964).

[8] Stuart W. Leslie, *Boss Kettering: Wizard of General Motors* (New York: Columbia University Press, 1983); and David A. Hounshell, *From the American System to Mass Production, 1800-1932: The Development of Manufacturing Technology in the United States* (Baltimore: Johns Hopkins University Press, 1984). The literature about GM is extensive. See also Arthur J. Kuhn, *GM Passes Ford, 1918-1939: Designing the General Motors Performance-Control System* (University Park, PA: Pennsylvania State University Press, 1986); and Robert F. Freeland, *The Struggle for Control of the Modern Corporation: Organizational Change at General Motors, 1924-1970* (New York: Cambridge University Press, 2001).

[9] For the tradeoffs engineers faced in designing vehicles, see in general Joel W. Eastman, *Styling vs. Safety: The American Automobile Industry and the Development of Automotive Safety, 1900-1966* (New York: University Press of America, 1984).

[10] David Hounshell applied the notion of a "productivity dilemma" to his study of a series of markets as engineers and managers faced tradeoffs between increasing efficiency in the short term or pursuing long-term innovations. Hounshell followed the example of William Abernathy in referring to the "productivity dilemma," but he used the concept in a broader context to open the firm to various outside forces that might cause managers to face the tradeoff between short-term efficiency and long-term innovation. Hounshell, *From the American System to Mass Production*, 13; and William J. Abernathy, *The Productivity Dilemma: Roadblock to Innovation in the Automobile Industry* (Baltimore: Johns Hopkins University Press, 1978).

defective products or simply unpopular products to consumers; and during the 1920s and 1930s, several public and private agencies, including the courts, insurance underwriters, engineering societies, state regulatory agencies, the Justice Department, and the FTC, regulated market relations between buyers and sellers by asking what constituted fair market practices in terms of product quality and pricing policies.

By the time the United States entered World War II, leading automakers had formulated a set of institutions for a modern automobile market; however, the market matured in a different regard after the war's end. Whereas in 1945 nearly half of all U.S. families did not own an automobile, by the mid-1960s eight in ten families owned at least one car (nearly a quarter owned at least two cars).[11] The market's expansion meant selling vehicles to consumers further down the income ladder. This process posed a conflict between consumers and automakers in terms of the kind of car sold and its financing. One possible solution was the sale of small vehicles in keeping with consumers' smaller budgets – but this did not happen. Alternatively, it was possible that the postwar prosperity increased Americans' incomes enough to facilitate the market's growth. Yet although Americans prospered on average after World War II, the rising incomes did not by themselves support the market's development. Instead, auto manufacturers counted on generous finance terms. Liberalized credit financing allowed dealers to sell large, expensive cars to buyers further down the income ladder. Yet, during these same years, credit discrimination excluded many potential buyers from the market. Lenders acted as gatekeepers of the postwar world of consumption and filtered consumers through their prevailing notions of financial acceptability, but also through their social identity. Numerous groups of consumers, including women, persons over the age of sixty-five, and persons of color, were denied access to credit and thus to the purchase of what had become an essential item of daily life. In 1974, when Congress passed the Equal Credit Opportunity Act (ECOA), it called on the Board of Governors of the Federal Reserve System to establish fair lending guidelines and monitor lenders.[12]

Tracing the market's development, I pursue three interrelated themes. First, I examine how managers' efforts to develop the auto market resulted in contests over consumers' welfare in terms of personal injury, fair market practices, and credit discrimination. Second, I examine how conflicts between buyers and sellers affected the modern corporation in terms of the structure of the modern firm; its methods of research; its policies for efficiently coordinating production and distribution; and its marketing strategy for broadening the market. Third, I assess the state's varied roles in conditioning relations between buyers and sellers.

[11] Lebergott, *Pursuing Happiness*, 130.
[12] For a general review of credit discrimination, see National Consumer Law Center, *Credit Discrimination*, 3rd ed. (Boston: National Consumer Law Center, Inc., 2002).

My study necessarily differs from the market as it is pictured by one of the most influential intellectual traditions – neoclassical economics. That theory's primary goal has been to explain market outcomes: how supply intersects with demand to determine equilibrium prices and quantities.[13] To accomplish this goal, economists invoked a set of narrow behavioral assumptions about firms and consumers. All firms were said to maximize profits and have "perfect" information to respond to market signals. Moreover, assuming that their primary job was to produce goods most efficiently, firms were pictured, as one economic study reported, "as little more than equation-solving entities that, given market prices, determined output by equalizing marginal revenue and marginal costs."[14] On the demand side of the market, the theory assumed that all consumers varied as "individuals" in their "tastes" for goods. Although no one's tastes could be measured in a definitive way, each person was assumed to make tradeoffs among goods to maximize his or her utility. These assumptions enabled buyers and sellers to be expressed as abstractions; to create supply and demand curves, defined in mathematical terms; and to solve a market's equilibrium price and quantity.

This process of abstracting firms and consumers has been the basis of neoclassical theory's influence: its behavioral assumptions have permitted theoretical principles to be applied to most markets in many societies for various historical eras. But the neoclassical rendering of the market has had important shortcomings. It pictured the market as an ideal, and its assumptions about firms and consumers were unrealistic – that is, divorced from historically specific contexts. That is why many economists have found the theory inadequate. New institutional economists have replaced the image of the firm as a two-dimensional cost function with an appreciation of the modern corporation as a complex, as well as a porous, social organization. The new information economists began to emerge in the 1970s on the fringe of the economics profession. When Joseph E. Stiglitz, A. Michael Spence, and George A. Akerlof won the Nobel Memorial Prize in Economic Science in 2001, the award signaled the arrival of a new way of thinking about the

[13] Economic textbooks offer an introduction to the abstract concepts of supply and demand and the market's equilibrium. The shift from classical to neoclassical models is described in William Breit and Roger L. Ransom, *The Academic Scribblers*, 3rd ed. (Princeton, NJ: Princeton University Press, 1998), 7–11. The intellectual history of the economics profession in the United States is traced in Dorothy Ross, *The Origins of American Social Science* (New York: Cambridge University Press, 1991); and Michael A. Bernstein, *A Perilous Progress: Economists and Public Purpose in Twentieth-Century America* (Princeton, NJ: Princeton University Press, 2001). On the accomplishments and intellectual constraints characterizing the field of economic history, see Naomi R. Lamoreaux, "Economic History and the Cliometric Revolution," in *Imagined Histories: American Historians Interpret the Past*, ed. Anthony Molho and Gordon S. Wood (Princeton, NJ: Princeton University Press, 1998), 59–84.

[14] Naomi R. Lamoreaux, Daniel M. G. Raff, and Peter Temin, eds., *Learning by Doing in Markets, Firms, and Countries*, National Bureau of Economic Research (Chicago: University of Chicago Press, 1999), 6–7.

modern firm and markets, one in which universal notions of optimal efficiency proved false, and the existence of information problems called for state intervention in markets in a variety of roles: directly regulating product quality, requiring that firms disclose information about products, and providing medical insurance (among other activities).[15] Knowledge of information economics has helped me execute this study, because by offering a new conceptual portrait of the firm, this scholarship has opened the door to seeing the multiple ways actors on the market's demand side engaged managers in their primary tasks of engineering, producing, and selling goods. It has meant as well that I have found the history of technology, political and legal history, and social history essential for the study of a market's evolution.

In a series of essays and books, Naomi Lamoreaux, Daniel Raff, and Peter Temin chronicled the shift taking place among economists in their study of the modern corporation.[16] Three changes were critical in this regard. First, economists replaced the neoclassical assumption of perfect information with an appreciation that information was imperfect, costly, and subject to manipulation. It is hard to overstate the import of this one assumption. Stiglitz wrote: "The competitive paradigm is an artfully constructed structure: when one of the central pieces (the assumption of perfect information) is removed, the structure collapses."[17] Second, Lamoreaux, Raff, and Temin recognized that the interests of many different groups of people within firms differed: the concerns of stockholders differed from those of top managers, which in turn differed from those of middle managers, sales agents, foremen,

---

[15] The *New York Times* quoted the economist Alan Krueger as saying, "The three of them really pioneered the view that markets, when confronted with imperfections, may not be the best way to allocate resources." Louis Uchtelle, "3 Americans Awarded Nobel for Economics," *New York Times* (October 11, 2001): C1, C10. The literature about information economics is vast. For a review of the literature see John C. Riley, "Silver Signals: Twenty-five Years of Screening and Signaling," *Journal of Economic Literature* 39 (June 2001): 432–78. Pioneering works include George A. Akerlof, "The Market for 'Lemons': Quality Uncertainty and the Market Mechanism," *Quarterly Journal of Economics* 84 (August 1970): 488–500; Michael Spence, "Consumer Misperceptions, Product Failure and Producer Liability," *Review of Economic Studies* 44 (1977): 561–72; idem, "Information Aspects of Market Structure: An Introduction," *Quarterly Journal of Economics* 90 (November 1976): 591–97; and Joseph E. Stiglitz, "Information and Economic Analysis: A Perspective," *The Economic Journal* 95, Supplement: Conference Papers (1985): 21–41.

[16] The three authors have compiled a large collection of essays and books. See Peter Temin, ed., *Inside the Business Enterprise: Historical Perspectives on the Use of Information* (Chicago: University of Chicago Press, 1991); Naomi R. Lamoreaux and Daniel M. G. Raff, eds., *Coordination and Information: Historical Perspectives on the Organization of Enterprise* (Chicago: University of Chicago Press, 1995); Naomi R. Lamoreaux, Daniel M. G. Raff, and Peter Temin, "New Economic Approaches to the Study of Business History," *Business and Economic History* 26 (Fall 1997): 57–79; idem, *Learning by Doing in Markets, Firms, and Countries*; and idem, "Beyond Markets and Hierarchies: Toward a New Synthesis of American Business History," *American Historical Review* 108 (April 2003): 404–33.

[17] Stiglitz, "Information and Economic Analysis," 26.

and workers. Third, they shifted their focus from accounting for market outcomes to explaining managers' actions and, thus, to the inherently uncertain process of coordinating activities within small and large organizations. Depending on the task at hand, managers often confronted situations in which they needed to devise policies for their subordinates. In the language of this new institutional economics, superiors, known as principals, crafted rules or policies intended to induce the maximum effort of their subordinates or agents. Principals and agents changed depending on the particular relationship. Stockholders acted as principals when instructing top managers as their agents; top executives acted as principals in setting policies for managers, their agents, further down the corporate hierarchy.[18]

In their focus on social relationships within the firm, Lamoreaux, Raff, and Temin placed the firm's drive for efficiency in a much broader organizational environment.[19] Rather than a universal measure of optimal performance, they linked efficiency in coordinating activities in the modern firm to the power managers exercised through their policies, rules, and routines. The trio instructed: "To understand how decisions are made, one has to take into account the technology employed by the firm, the way in which power is distributed within the organization, the knowledge structures at the disposal of different groups within the enterprise, the goals and aspirations of these various economic actors, and the way in which their concerns link up with broad intellectual movements in the larger society."[20]

In moving away from neoclassical theory, this new conceptual portrait of the modern corporation invited questions about how managers translated the abstract concept of demand into information problems about

---

[18] Lamoreaux, Raff, and Temin, "New Economic Approaches to the Study of Business History," 62–64.

[19] In their 2003 article, Lamoreaux, Raff, and Temin "subsume" the model of Alfred Chandler within their own framework. Two critical premises are at stake. First, although Chandler recognized the importance of managers in coordinating mass production and mass distribution, he assumed managers acted rationally and thus failed to consider how the process of coordination was undertaken. Second, Lamoreaux, Raff, and Temin charge that Chandler offered no evidence to sustain the claim that large-scale corporations, thanks to their scale and scope, were more efficient than their smaller rivals. I find both complaints persuasive, and more importantly, I find the new institutional economics opens up the question of efficiency, because the problem managers faced in coordination could not be separated from the power they exercised in their policies intended to motivate and monitor subordinates. Lamoreaux, Raff, and Temin, "Beyond Markets and Hierarchies." Chandler's work dominated the study of business history, as reflected in his three monumental works. Alfred D. Chandler, Jr., *Strategy and Structure: Chapters in the History of the American Industrial Enterprise* (Cambridge, MA: MIT Press, 1962); idem, *The Visible Hand: The Managerial Revolution in American Business* (Cambridge, MA: Harvard University Press, 1977); and idem, *Scale and Scope: The Dynamics of Industrial Capitalism* (Cambridge, MA: Harvard University Press, 1990).

[20] Lamoreaux, Raff, and Temin, "New Economic Approaches to the Study of Business History," 68.

consumers. Business historians (often with no particular interest in economics) framed questions about consumers and the firm in novel ways. Historians of design and technology, including Adrian Forty, Jeffrey Meikle, Regina Lee Blaszczyk, and Glenn Porter, addressed the role industrial designers played in the cultural process of developing goods in business contexts.[21] Blaszczyk, in particular, cataloged numerous individuals, whom she collectively called "fashion intermediaries." Sales agents, home economists, and market researchers, as market intermediaries, offered cultural portraits of consumers that in turn shaped the design of goods.[22] Nancy F. Koehn addressed not mediators, but entrepreneurs. She emphasized that entrepreneurs, based on their "firsthand experience," processed information about the demand and supply sides of the market to identify opportunities – that is, ways to add value to goods to build consumers' trust and profit through a product's brand identity.[23] Glenn Porter singled out market research.[24] Industrial designers and marketing executives routinely surveyed consumers in an attempt to identify their living patterns and buying habits. The designer Raymond Loewy, for example, tried to entice consumers with something new – but not so new as to startle his clients' shoppers. Market research helped determine what consumers thought of as comfortable or conventional, and, given their conventions, Loewy claimed to design products in keeping with his principle of being "the Most Advanced Yet Acceptable."[25]

Although their particular analytical questions and techniques varied, these scholars documented numerous ways in which information problems about

---

[21] Regina Lee Blaszczyk, *Imagining Consumers: Design and Innovation from Wedgwood to Corning* (Baltimore: Johns Hopkins University Press, 2000). See also Adrian Forty, *Objects of Desire: Design and Society since 1750* (London: Thames and Hudson, 1986); Jeffrey L. Meikle, *American Plastic: A Cultural History* (New Brunswick, NJ: Rutgers University Press, 1995); Glenn Porter, "Cultural Forces and Commercial Constraints: Designing Packaging in the Twentieth-Century United States," *Journal of Design History* 12, no. 1 (1999): 25–44; and idem, *Raymond Loewy: Designs for a Consumer Culture* (Wilmington, DE: Hagley Museum & Library, 2002).

[22] Whereas Blaszczyk studied several mediators, Carolyn Goldstein examined in detail the ambiguities and nuances of one group of mediators, home economists. Blaszczyk, *Imagining Consumers*, especially 11–13; and Carolyn M. Goldstein, "Mediating Consumption: Home Economics and American Consumers, 1900–1940" (Ph.D. diss., University of Delaware, 1994).

[23] Nancy F. Koehn, *Brand New: How Entrepreneurs Earned Consumers' Trust from Wedgwood to Dell* (Boston: Harvard Business School Press, 2001).

[24] Porter, *Raymond Loewy*, 13, 24–25, 42, 69, 102, 111–13; and idem, "Cultural Forces and Commercial Constraints," 25–43. On the topic of market research, see also Daniel J. Robinson, *The Measure of Democracy: Polling, Market Research, and Public Life, 1930-1945* (Toronto: University of Toronto Press, 1999); and Gerben Bakker, "Building Knowledge about the Consumer: The Emergence of Market Research in the Motion Picture Industry," *Business History* 45 (January 2003): 101–27.

[25] Porter, *Raymond Loewy*, 7–8, 17, 42, 44, 114, 150.

consumers influenced activities inside the firm. It was not just that firms conducted consumer surveys for the purposes of marketing their products, but that information about consumers impinged on managers' pursuit of efficiency and innovation. Koehn, for instance, explained that Michael Dell tabulated consumers' complaints voiced through his toll-free hotline and used the data to monitor the quality of work on his production lines. Maintaining his products' high quality was critical to Dell's ability to convince consumers to purchase PCs by mail order.[26] Edwin Perkins argued that Charles Merrill's impression of consumers helped him rethink his stock brokerage business. Because consumers in a survey voiced distrust of brokers who bought and sold stocks to earn commissions from the trades ("churning accounts"), Merrill switched brokers from a payment system based on commissions to a fixed salary. He also redistributed clients among brokers to keep costs low while he overcame potential clients' distrust in the stock investment process. Whether the survey was accurate is impossible to ascertain. What was important was that his perception of consumers as being distrustful of a commission-based system prompted Merrill to redefine the method of rewarding and organizing his sales force.[27]

Although these scholars translated the abstract image of supply intersecting with demand into a body of scholarship about the ways that consumers intruded on managers' authority and a firm's operations, they did not pursue the reverse question: how have corporations exercised their authority in relationships with consumers? Economists traced the exercise of corporate power to two general conditions: first, as Smith already recognized, a violation of competitive markets in which firms were able to raise prices; and second, uncertainty surrounding product prices and quality, which permitted firms to exploit market situations in which they claimed information about products that consumers lacked. If business historians responded to any literature about corporate power, it was that of a distinctly different group of colleagues: historians intent on demonstrating corporate hegemony.[28] Blaszczyk, for example, argued against this perspective in framing

---

[26] Koehn, *Brand New*, 257–305, especially 288–90.

[27] Merrill undertook other changes in an effort to attract new accounts. For example, Perkins found that he advocated the diffusion of information about stocks to all clients. The intent was to build customers' confidence, but the reports also served to attract new customers. Edwin Perkins, *Wall Street to Main Street: Charles Merrill and Middle-Class Investors* (New York: Cambridge University Press, 1999), 144–80.

[28] T. J. Jackson Lears, "The Concept of Cultural Hegemony: Problems and Possibilities," *American Historical Review* 90 (June 1985): 567–93. See also idem, *Fables of Abundance: A Cultural History of Advertising in America* (New York: Basic Books, 1994). The literature concerning consumer culture is surveyed in my essay, "Consumer Negotiations," *Business and Economic History* 26 (Fall 1997): 101–22. See also Susan Strasser, "Making Consumption Conspicuous: Transgressive Topics Go Mainstream," *Technology and Culture* 43 (October 2002): 755–70.

her study of glass and ceramics markets. She also examined intensely competitive markets. As neoclassical economists would expect and she found, firms that failed to respond to consumers and to lower prices, maintain quality, and introduce attractive styles risked losing profits if not being driven out of business altogether. She declared: "Make no mistake: supply did not create demand in home furnishings, but demand determined supply."[29] Many markets, however, never passed for close approximations of perfect competition. What were the implications for relations between corporations and consumers in cases where firms subverted competitive pressures?

The uncertainty surrounding product prices and quality posed a second set of problems between a market's buyers and sellers. Akerlof noted that firms could take steps to "counteract the effects of quality uncertainty. One obvious institution is guarantees. Most consumer durables carry guarantees to ensure the buyer of some normal expected quality.... A second example of an institution which counteracts the effects of quality uncertainty is the brand-name good."[30] Both guarantees and brand names acted as "signals," according to economists, telling consumers about the product's quality.[31] Koehn both illustrated and developed Akerlof's insight in her study of entrepreneurs. These unusual men and women escaped the rigors of competition by building consumers' trust through the value they added to their products. Michael Dell, for example, offered money-back guarantees to help overcome consumers' distrust of buying computers by mail order; he also made certain that the technicians answering consumers' complaints were carefully trained to communicate quickly and effectively with computer users.[32] Koehn charted processes by which firms created successful brands, and, in doing so, dealt with an important subset of cases. But there were other markets in which uncertainty about products persisted. What happened in cases where the prices and quality of goods were difficult for consumers to assess? Porter hinted at this problem in his study of market research. As firms pursued more and more ways to track consumers, he mused that in "the whirling squirrel cage of capitalism," consumers "proved to be elusive, moving, mutating targets."[33] His point bears emphasis for the study of managers' efforts to coordinate activities efficiently. Because consumers were so hard to track, managers necessarily used inaccurate information about consumers to coordinate activities inside the firm. Those inaccuracies represented costs (unpopular products or goods of poor quality), and,

---

[29] Blaszczyk, *Imagining Consumers*, 353–55, quote 13.

[30] Akerlof, "The Market for 'Lemons,'" 499–500.

[31] Spence, "Information Aspects of Market Structure," 592; and Riley, "Silver Signals," 438.

[32] Koehn, *Brand New*, 286–96.

[33] An ad man made this point when he complained: "consumers 'are like roaches – you spray them and spray them and they get immune after a while.'" Glenn Porter, "Cultural Forces and Commercial Constraints," quote 27, 38 n.58, 42; and "Marketers Seek the 'Naked' Truth in Consumer Psyches," *Wall Street Journal* (May 30, 1997): B1.

depending on market conditions, the costs were internalized or transferred to parties on the market's demand side.

Spence identified precisely this problem in his account of "product failure" or product defects. In cases where consumers lacked sufficient understanding "about the probabilities of product failure," he argued that producers would not necessarily "supply" reliability or safety in their products to the degree that consumers wanted. In other words, in markets where consumers did not fully understand or could not obtain adequate information about products, manufacturers could impose costs of defects on consumers. Without appropriate warning of a good's likely chance of being defective and causing injury, Spence argued that the government should intervene in the market by regulating the product's design, initiating public safety campaigns to "inform consumers," and holding the manufacturer liable for defects.[34] Put in broader terms, Spence and other information economists recognized that information problems, such as product defects, resulted in "market failures" and required government intervention.[35]

Historians, perhaps unaware of this economic literature, have long recognized the tension residing in the links among corporate power, economic development, and the role of the state. In their respective studies of railroad accidents, Thomas K. McCraw, Steven W. Usselman, and Barbara Young Welke each identified the effects of corporate power as seen in the personal injuries passengers suffered as a result of unsafe equipment.[36] Railroads

---

[34] Spence further qualified these options. "Direct regulation," he postulated, "may be preferable when the loss to the consumer exceeds the seller's ability to pay. Informing the consumer may be an ineffective strategy if the information is highly technical." Spence, "Consumer Misperceptions, Product Failure and Producer Liability," 561, 566.

[35] George Akerlof explained this problem in terms of the automobile market, choosing this example for its clarity but not its uniqueness. Lamoreaux, Raff, and Temin, "Beyond Markets and Hierarchies," 6, 8; and Akerlof, "The Market for 'Lemons,'" 488–500.

[36] Thomas K. McCraw, *Prophets of Regulation: Charles Francis Adams, Louis D. Brandeis, James M. Landis, Alfred E. Kahn* (Cambridge, MA: Harvard University Press, 1984); Steven W. Usselman, *Regulating Railroad Innovation: Business, Technology, and Politics in America, 1840–1920* (New York: Cambridge University Press, 2002); and Welke, *Recasting American Liberty*. For the topic of accidents in the Progressive era, see Lawrence Friedman and Jack Ladinsky, "Social Change and the Law in Industrial Accidents," in *American Law and the Constitutional Order: Historical Perspectives*, ed. Lawrence M. Friedman and Harry N. Scheiber (Cambridge, MA: Harvard University Press, 1988), 269–82; Lawrence Friedman, *Total Justice* (New York: Russell Sage Foundation, 1985); Lawrence Friedman and Thomas D. Russell, "More Civil Wrongs: Personal Injury Litigation, 1901–1910," *American Journal of Legal History* 34 (July 1990): 295–314; Witt, *The Accidental Republic*; Christopher L. Tomlins, "A Mysterious Power: Industrial Accidents and the Legal Construction of Employment Relations in Massachusetts, 1800–1850," *Law and History Review* 6 (Fall 1988): 375–437; McEvoy, "The Triangle Shirtwaist Factory Fire of 1911," 621–51; Peter Temin, *Taking Your Medicine: Drug Regulation in the United States* (Cambridge, MA: Harvard University Press, 1980); and Price V. Fishback and Shawn Everett Kantor, *A Prelude to the Welfare State: The Origins of Workers' Compensation*, National Bureau of Economic Research (Chicago: University of Chicago Press, 2000).

accounted for perhaps the most glaring source of injuries for workers and consumers at the turn of the century, but many products before and after 1900 put consumers at risk of injury because of their defects – among them glass bottles, guns, medicines, wooden wheels, steam boilers, cosmetics, chemical-based products, and electric tools.[37] Reevaluating the New Deal, historian Meg Jacobs argued that reformers such as Robert Lynd, Gardiner Means, and Paul Douglas saw corporate power as not only lowering workers' wages but also raising consumers' prices and degrading the quality of goods.[38] Carolyn Goldstein found that home economists from their base at the U.S. Department of Agriculture could not convince manufacturers to disclose information about products such as refrigerators so that consumers could make informed decisions.[39] Demands for both transparent standards and restraints on corporate power to raise prices, Jacobs found, were themes that resonated among many New Dealers.[40] Examining credit discrimination, Martha Olney identified the economic context in which creditors withheld particular types of loans from African American borrowers.[41] Lizabeth Cohen similarly wrote of the credit discrimination women faced, which she considered part of a broad pattern. Cohen maintained that despite the state's claim to provide for economic prosperity on a mass scale in the years after World War II, it actually worked to perpetuate inequalities inherent in the U.S. economy, not only in terms of the distribution of income but also in terms of hierarchies based on race and gender that skewed access to credit, jobs, education, and, thus, to the basic resources for economic opportunity.[42]

These contests between consumers and corporations, I argue, were not byproducts of, but figured directly in the auto market's creation and evolution. In a new market, consumers' injuries were inherent in the process of innovation. Though manufacturers worked to better their products, they initially sold highly imperfect or defective vehicles that put consumers at risk

---

[37] Edward H. Levi, *An Introduction to Legal Reasoning* (Chicago: University of Chicago Press, 1949), 6–19; Friedman and Ladinsky, "Social Change and the Law of Industrial Accidents," 269–82; Friedman and Russell, "More Civil Wrongs," 295–314; Tomlins, "A Mysterious Power," 375–437; McEvoy, "The Triangle Shirtwaist Factory Fire of 1911," 621–51; and Witt, *The Accidental Republic.*

[38] Meg Jacobs, "'Democracy's Third Estate': New Deal Politics and the Construction of a 'Consuming Public,'" *International Labor and Working-Class History* 55 (Spring 1999): 27–51. See also idem, *Pocketbook Politics: Economic Citizenship in Twentieth-Century America* (Princeton, NJ: Princeton University Press, 2005), 95–135.

[39] Goldstein, "Mediating Consumption," 142–77.

[40] Jacobs, "'Democracy's Third Estate,'" 27–51. See also Jacobs, *Pocketbook Politics.*

[41] Martha Olney, "When Your Word is Not Enough: Race, Collateral, and Household Credit," *Journal of Economic History* 58 (June 1998): 408–31.

[42] Lizabeth Cohen, *A Consumers' Republic: The Politics of Mass Consumption in Postwar America* (New York: Knopf, 2003).

of injury. In a burgeoning mass market, consumers' difficulty in discerning the quality and prices of vehicles was linked to managers' problems in trying to establish efficient and profitable firms. Unable to achieve the perfect coordination of activities inside the firm, managers tried to transfer the costs of their inaccuracies to buyers – both dealers and consumers. As the market for automobiles matured in the years after World War II, automakers employed credit as a tool for shaping consumers' purchases to enlarge the market in keeping with the skewed distribution of income and wealth. However, given prevalent discriminatory attitudes, not all borrowers could obtain the credit needed for the purchase of expensive durables.

Just as these contests conditioned market relations between buyers and sellers, so did the idea of trust. Koehn, for example, made the central question in her study: how did entrepreneurs acquire consumers' trust through the design of their products, as well as their methods of production and distribution?[43] Lamoreaux, Raff, and Temin paid close attention to trust as it applied to the role of firms in the economy. In contrast to the image of market participants engaging in the immediate exchange of goods, they found that on-going relationships proved critical to the economy throughout the nineteenth and twentieth centuries. Merchants' extended family networks were familiar examples in the nineteenth century which may be contrasted with technological networks, or what Louis Galambos called "networks of innovation," in the twentieth century.[44] Legal historian Robert W. Gordon put trust at the center of a body of scholarship initiated by Stewart Macaulay and Ian Macneil. Whereas discrete transactions referred to an immediate market exchange by two parties who may not know one another, relational contracting referred to long-term relations based on trust between two or more parties.[45] Gordon emphasized that, more so than their self-interest, market participants' "mutual trust" encouraged the long-term projects that sustained the "successful operation of capitalist economies."[46] Yet, he also worried about a "dark side" in relational contracting: "In the messy and

---

[43] Koehn, *Brand New*.

[44] Lamoreaux, Raff, and Temin, "Beyond Markets and Hierarchies: Toward a New Synthesis of American Business History," 404–33; and Louis Galambos with Jane Sewell, *Networks of Innovation: Vaccine Development at Merck, Sharp & Dohme, and Mulford, 1895–1995* (New York: Cambridge University Press, 1995).

[45] Robert W. Gordon, "Macaulay, Macneil, and the Discovery of Solidarity and Power in Contract Law," *Wisconsin Law Review* (May/June 1985): 569.

[46] Ibid., quote 570, and 578–79. Several economic scholars have recognized, albeit in different ways, the significance of trust (as opposed simply to self-interest) in promoting economic development. See Oliver E. Williamson, "Transaction-Cost Economics: The Governance of Contractual Relations," *Journal of Law and Economics* 22 (October 1979): 233–61, especially 240–41; Sen, *Development as Freedom*; and Albert O. Hirschman, *Exit, Voice, and Loyalty: Responses to Decline in Firms, Organizations, and States* (Cambridge, MA: Harvard University Press, 1970).

open-ended world of continuing contract relations, where the contours of obligation are constantly shifting, the effects of power imbalances are not limited to the concessions that parties can extort in the original bargain. This is the potential of the dark side of continuing contract relations, as organic solidarity is the bright side: what starts out as a mere inequity in market power can be deepened into persistent domination on one side and dependence on the other." Where one firm makes a large investment, and thus has "sunk costs" in the relationship, Gordon concluded "that the trauma of abandoning a relationship . . . can keep it tied into a dependence that its members experience as all the more corrupting because it is in some sense voluntary."[47]

The tension residing between the trust upon which actors form bonds that allow them to foster an economy's development and the power that actors may execute through market relationships was particularly felt in the case of the automobile market. Taking Gordon's point seriously, I do not assume manufacturers' efforts to win car buyers' loyalty fell simply under the category of cultural hegemony. Certainly, automakers engaged in marketing campaigns to attract and keep loyal car buyers. There is no doubt that those campaigns, combined with several other efforts often executed through cultural media, notably advertising, shaped the modern world of consumption.[48] My point is that these marketing campaigns did not alone secure viable market relationships between firms and consumers. Trust among market participants endured in the product and the market relations surrounding the product. As Koehn found, many entrepreneurs succeeded in instilling integrity in their goods. Michael Dell represented an exemplary case. In many other markets, however, managers found it difficult to create trustworthy products, and automobiles represented one distinctive example. Unable to build consumers' trust in a straightforward way through the product's integrity, automakers exercised power in their market relations to both impose costs on car buyers and shape their behavior. The tension between trust and power in market relations thus forms the basis of this book's narrative.

Recognizing the contests between consumers and corporations directs our attention to the state. When I speak of regulation, I do not mean to focus on it, as institutional economists have done, as a straightforward response to market failures. Recalling the contributions of Stewart Macaulay and Ian Macneil, Gordon emphasized that markets and "state and non-state

---

[47] Gordon, "Macaulay, Macneil, and the Discovery of Solidarity and Power in Contract Law," quote 570.

[48] Historians have varied in the claims they have made for cultural hegemony. See especially Lears, "The Concept of Cultural Hegemony," 567–93; Roland Marchand, *Advertising the American Dream: Making Way for Modernity, 1920–1940* (Berkeley: University of California Press, 1985); and idem, *Creating the Corporate Soul: The Rise of Public Relations and Corporate Imagery in American Big Business* (Berkeley, CA: University of California Press, 1998).

regulation" always have been embedded in broad "social landscapes."[49] This revised starting point allows for many possible formulations of the relationship between the state and the market. In some cases, as Macaulay explained, actors may have worked out solutions without resorting to the state's intervention.[50] Macaulay identified the "bright side" of relational contracts in the informal bonds automakers developed with their dealers.[51] Alternatively, the state may have played an integral part in the market's formation, and given rise to inequities between buyers and sellers.[52] The significance of credit in fostering the auto market's development after World War II, as induced by the Fed's policies, offered one illustration. Further, various historians emphasized the independent voice the state claimed in economic disputes.[53] Rather than picture the state as addressing a market failure, I examine the state's influence in shaping market relations between buyers and sellers while drawing no single conclusion about the impact of regulation.

[49] Gordon, "Macaulay, Macneil, and the Discovery of Solidarity and Power in Contract Law," 578. Especially important were Stewart Macaulay, *Law and the Balance of Power: The Automobile Manufacturers and Their Dealers* (New York: Russell Sage Foundation, 1966); idem, "Non-Contractual Relations in Business: A Preliminary Study," *American Sociological Review* 28 (February 1963): 55–67; and Ian Macneil, "Contracts: Adjustment of Long-Term Economic Relations Under Classical, Neoclassical, and Relational Contract Law," *Northwestern Law Review* 72 (1978): 854–905. An economist's response to these legal insights comes in Williamson, "Transaction-Cost Economics," 233–61. See also Gillian K. Hadfield, "Problematic Relations: Franchising and the Law of Incomplete Contracts," *Stanford Law Review* 42 (April 1990): 927–92. But also read Gordon, "Macaulay, Macneil, and the Discovery of Solidarity and Power in Contract Law," 575, n.27. The law and society scholars followed, as Gordon noted, in the footsteps of legal realists. For automobiles, see especially Friedrich Kessler, "Automobile Dealer Franchises: Vertical Integration by Contract," *Yale Law Journal* 66 (July 1957): 1135–90. An introduction to legal realists and their empirical research is found in John Henry Schlegel, *American Legal Realism and Empirical Social Science* (Chapel Hill, NC: University of North Carolina Press, 1995).

[50] Gordon, "Macaulay, Macneil, and the Discovery of Solidarity and Power in Contract Law," 571–72; and Macaulay, "Non-Contractual Relations in Business," 55–67.

[51] Macaulay, *Law and the Balance of Power.*

[52] Several examples may be found at the crossroads of social and political history. See especially Cohen, *A Consumers' Republic*; Thomas J. Sugrue, *The Origins of the Urban Crisis: Race and Inequality in Postwar Detroit* (Princeton, NJ: Princeton University Press, 1996); and Christopher L. Tomlins, *The State and the Unions* (New York: Cambridge University Press, 1985).

[53] Among business historians, Lamoreaux offers an example in her study of antitrust policy and the merger movement. See Naomi R. Lamoreaux, *The Great Merger Movement in American Business, 1895–1904* (New York: Cambridge University Press, 1987), 159–86. Legal historians made this point in reaction to the notion of law as a mere reflection or "mirror" of powerful interests in society. See Michael Grossberg, "Legal History and Social Science: Friedman's *History of American Law*, the Second Time Around," *Law and Social Inquiry* 13 (Spring 1988): 359–83; and Christopher L. Tomlins, "A Mirror Crack'd? The Rule of Law in American History," *William and Mary Law Review* 32 (Winter 1991): 353–97.

My narrative proceeds in three parts. Part I, Chapters 1 and 2, takes up the question of who bore the costs of innovation in a new market. Rather than count on consumers' trust to start this new market, manufacturers succeeded, in part, because the market's very early buyers evinced a risk-taking spirit similar to that of entrepreneurs – often couched in cultural terms as a male sense of mechanical know-how and adventure. The drivers may not have fully understood the risks they took. When those who suffered accidents and injuries sued manufacturers, firms deflected lawsuits onto dealers through their choice in the firm's structure. By defining mass distribution through the franchise sales contract, firms sold cars to dealers, who resold the cars to consumers. Therefore, consumers lacked privity of contract upon which to sue manufacturers. This legal standard was not the whole story, however. Automakers sought to improve their products to broaden the market, and they initiated relational contracts with their dealers and suppliers. Manufacturers counted on suppliers as trustworthy or reputable sources for their parts while also using them as an alternative source of responsibility for defects. Yet, as the courts rethought where trust and responsibility resided for a product's safety, they limited the ability of manufacturers to use the privity requirement to block suits as delineated in the landmark case, *MacPherson v. Buick* (N.Y. 1916).[54]

Part II examines why the development of a mass market between 1916 and 1941 resulted in challenges to fair market practices in the way prices were set and quality determined. The mass market for automobiles could have been a straightforward story of innovation as firms adopted mass production to lower car prices and marketing techniques to captivate consumers. As Ford, GM, and Chrysler each claimed a quarter- or a third-stake in the market, their future profits depended on sustaining consumers' repeat purchases or loyalty. This market structure thus promoted manufacturers' efforts to win consumers' trust and, as part of this effort, managers invested in several business institutions to design, produce, distribute, and market their vehicles. Still, as I argue in Chapter 3, the assumptions managers, such as Alfred Sloan, invoked about the demand side of the market dissolved into information problems about and conflicts with their customers, or what I call consumer dilemmas, concerning engineering, aesthetics, and market transactions. Chapter 4 explores one dilemma about engineering quality. Although managers wanted to make vehicles safer as a way to attract loyal

---

[54] *MacPherson v. Buick*, 111 N.E. 1050 (N.Y. 1916). On Cardozo and his landmark ruling, see Andrew L. Kaufman, *Cardozo* (Cambridge, MA: Harvard University Press, 1998); Steven P. Croley and Jon D. Hanson, "Rescuing the Revolution: the Revived Case for Enterprise Liability," *Michigan Law Review* 91 (February 1993): 683–797; John C. P. Goldberg and Benjamin C. Zipursky, "The Moral of *MacPherson*," *University of Pennsylvania Law Review* 146 (August 1998): 1733–1847; and William E. Nelson, *The Legalist Reformation: Law, Politics, and Ideology in New York, 1920–1980* (Chapel Hill, NC: University of North Carolina Press, 2001), 93–107, 187–88.

car owners, they also wanted to lower production costs and rush new engineering features to market. How they balanced these choices could promote or degrade a vehicle's safety. And, in response, management's approach to product quality was shaped by a broad network of public and private oversight entities, including insurance underwriters, engineering societies, federal agencies, and state regulators. Chapter 5 examines the quality of vehicles in terms of a car's aesthetics.[55] Design posed a dilemma for managers because styling obviously sold cars, but it proved difficult for managers to determine which styles sold. As the Big Three automakers came to dominate the market, manufacturers used styling as a competitive weapon wielded to make other firms' cars appear outdated even as GM managers limited their own brands' aesthetic possibilities. Chapter 6 treats the role of franchised car dealers and the pricing of automobiles. The mass market was characterized by the sale of cars on installments, the pattern of trading in used cars to bargain down a new car's price, and the annual model change's year-end close-out (or the liquidation of old models). The three features posed a dilemma inasmuch as each market transaction meant that one party (the firm, the franchised dealer, or the consumer) gained at the expense of the other two. Unable to smoothly translate consumer demands into the production of cars, managers, dealers, and consumers squared off over the question of who should bear the costs of inaccuracies. Just as manufacturers pressed their dealers to take unordered cars, dealers and manufacturers pursued pricing strategies to negotiate better deals with their consumers. During the 1930s, the FTC and the Justice Department actively shaped the structure of the market with respect to mundane but still important issues such as the clarity of information about car prices and the role of credit. By the start of World War II, automakers had created the business institutions critical for a mass market: the industrial research laboratory, the styling department, and the franchised car dealer. Yet, because of their very inability to resolve consumers' dilemmas, the state had regulated vehicles' quality and methods for pricing

---

[55] I follow the example of design historians in this chapter, but with two distinctions. First, in contrast to Blaszczyk, my interest is not to detail how mediators reported consumers back to manufacturers. She concluded: "Although these liaisons viewed the marketplace through tinted lenses, most of them fully recognized the importance of reporting consumer wants, needs and desires with a high degree of accuracy. Distorting the evidence by peppering it with personal opinion could undermine fashion brokerage, causing the product development system to collapse." My interest is to examine how management responded to the problem of designing vehicles where they could never completely claim an accurate read on consumers' "tastes." My interpretation is closer to Porter's, who wrote of designers' "constrained creativity" in the modern firm, but I locate those constraints in terms of the power firms like GM acquired in the market. Second, I differ more explicitly with design historians in my focus on how GM exercised power through the role of aesthetics in its effort to limit competition, which affected both car prices and the possibilities of aesthetic creativity. Blaszczyk, *Imagining Consumers*, quote 274; and Porter, "Cultural Forces and Commercial Constraints," 38. See also Meikle, *American Plastic*.

vehicles. And, because the state's own role proved imperfect, transactions in the auto market had fostered a modern basis of distrust between buyers and sellers.

Part III (Chapter 7) examines the development of a mature or entrenched market for automobiles in the years between 1945 and 1965. Compared to the Depression or World War II, by the mid-1960s automobile ownership had become a fact of life for most families (Table 7.1). The new-found prosperity after World War II did not alone explain the market's expansion. One additional factor was the change in credit markets. Since the 1930s, as scholars like Kenneth Jackson and Lizabeth Cohen argued, New Deal agencies redefined the terms for financing home mortgages.[56] These changes, I argue, applied as well to consumer loans. Using the Survey of Consumer Finances, conducted by the Fed, I argue that in postwar America credit made possible a particular type of consumer market for automobiles. Rather than dealers selling low-priced vehicles (or consumers relying on mass transit), the availability of credit facilitated the sale of big, expensive cars. Manufacturers thus pursued a marketing strategy focused on selling new vehicles to the richest third of Americans. As those families traded in their old cars for new machines, credit again facilitated the sale of used cars to households further down the income ladder. Americans took out bigger loans, but stretched out their payments so that monthly obligations remained within their budgets. That said, General Motors Acceptance Corporation (GMAC), commercial banks, and other lenders still offered loans based on their prevailing ideas of creditworthiness. Using the Fed's data, I argue that although auto loans expanded the market along class lines, credit nevertheless reinforced patterns of dependency as well as exclusion for different groups of Americans. With the ECOA of 1974, the Fed established policies, known as Regulation B, to regulate credit discrimination and monitor lenders.[57]

Although my study concerns another time and place, my interest in trust and power follows from the writings of Adam Smith. Smith's many admirers, including those who make their pilgrimage to his grave in the cemetery of Canongate Church, Edinburgh, celebrate a moral philosopher who advocated much more than the "free market." Smith concerned himself with markets' beneficial as well as oppressive effects. Today's readers are most familiar with Smith's discussion of their benefits. The economist Amartya Sen, for example, acknowledged that the human attribute of self-interest, as Smith emphasized, could be taken as a sole motivation for "mutually beneficial exchange."[58] "It is not from the benevolence of the butcher, the

---

[56] Kenneth Jackson, *Crabgrass Frontier: The Suburbanization of the United States* (New York: Oxford University Press, 1985), 172–218; and Lizabeth Cohen, *Making a New Deal: Industrial Workers in Chicago, 1919–1939* (New York: Cambridge University Press, 1990).

[57] National Consumer Law Center, *Credit Discrimination*.

[58] Sen, *Development as Freedom*, 271.

brewer, or the baker, that we expect our dinner," Smith wrote, "but from their regard to their own interest."[59] Sen emphasized: "The butcher sells bread to the consumer, not because he intends to promote the consumer's welfare, but because he wants to make money." Conversely, Sen wrote, the buyer purchases goods out of his or her own interest and not the interest of the seller. Together, by pursuing their own interests, consumers and producers benefit one another. Quoting Smith, Sen reiterated that it was by "an invisible hand" that a buyer or a seller reached a beneficial outcome that "was no part of his intention."[60] Self-interest was not the sole motivation Smith identified for well-functioning markets, however. Sen cited other motivations. "The development and use of trust in one another's words and promises," Sen declared, "can be a very important ingredient of market success."[61] Further, in contrast to self-interest, Smith called attention to "humanity, generosity, and public spirit," as Sen emphasized, as attributes vital in addressing questions of distribution and equity.[62]

Emma Rothschild wrote that in the wake of the political backlash and the sedition trials of the 1790s, *The Wealth of Nations* was reinterpreted in terms of the single theme of free trade and freedom from government regulation, and in the process many of Smith's cherished ideas were "disregarded" or "submerged."[63] She took pains to explain that Smith had been "critical of religious establishments, of war, of poverty, and of the privileges of the rich."[64] In other words, he opposed many forms of oppression, or what he called "vexations."[65] Further, he objected to most public policies for the obvious reason that they benefited a few well-situated producers. This did not mean he unilaterally opposed market regulation.[66] Sen cautioned that Smith did not invite any "jumping to policy conclusions from some 'pro' or 'anti' attitude to markets."[67] Smith's study of the attributes of self-interest, power, and trust, as well as the state's intervention in the economy, provide a point of departure for my study of a very different market, but one still conditioned by these same concerns.

---

[59] Ibid., 256; and Smith, *The Wealth of Nations*, 15.

[60] Sen, *Development as Freedom*, 256; and Emma Rothschild, "Adam Smith and Conservative Economics," *Economic History Review* 45 (February 1992): 74–96.

[61] Sen, *Development as Freedom*, 262–65, 269–72, and quote 261.

[62] Ibid., 272. The quote is from Adam Smith, *Theory of Moral Sentiments*, ed. D. D. Raphael and A. L. Macfie, (1976; repr., Indianpolis: Liberty Fund, 1982), 189.

[63] Rothschild, "Adam Smith and Conservative Economics," 74–96, especially 91–94. See also idem, *Economic Sentiments: Adam Smith, Condorcet, and the Enlightenment* (Cambridge, MA: Harvard University Press, 2001), chapter 2.

[64] Rothschild, *Economic Sentiments*, 64–71, quote 71.

[65] Ibid., 27.   [66] Ibid., 11–12, 150–51, and 225–26.

[67] Sen, *Development as Freedom*, 126.

PART I

A NEW MARKET, 1896–1916

The automobile market began as little more than an experiment. A familiar starting date is the Chicago *Times-Herald* Thanksgiving Day race of 1895.[1] Charles and J. Frank Duryea won the race on that snowy and slippery day, when just two cars crossed the finish line and just six posted out of a field of eighty-three.[2] Still, the race challenged entrepreneurs to take their chances in the new market. Within a decade, many inventors and mechanics had tried their hand at assembling and selling motor cars, often naming their cars after themselves – Stanley, Buick, Olds, Winton, and Ford.[3] Whereas sales came to an estimated fifteen in 1896, and 4,000 in 1900, they jumped to 187,000 machines in 1910, a year in which government officials estimated that one percent of U.S. households owned an automobile.[4]

It seems natural to focus on the market's many entrepreneurs when we speak of the creation of the automobile market. Of Ransom Olds, historian Peter Hugill wrote that he "spun off even more companies when he subcontracted the parts for his 1901 model to Henry Leland (who founded first Cadillac, then Lincoln), the Dodge brothers (who backed Ford, then went

---

[1] Automotive historians have offered several perspectives on the seemingly simple question: when can we date the start of the automobile market? Consider Richard P. Scharchburg's account of the Duryea brothers, *Carriages without Horses: J. Frank Duryea and the Birth of the American Automobile Industry* (Warrendale, PA: Society of Automotive Engineers, Inc., 1993). Clay McShane discussed early steam-powered autos and their perils in *Down the Asphalt Path: The Automobile and the American City* (New York: Columbia University Press, 1994). James J. Flink offered a very readable account of the auto market's early years in *America Adopts the Automobile, 1895–1910* (Cambridge, MA: MIT Press, 1970). An encyclopedic book with numerous details of the auto industry, including brief notes on nearly all automobile companies, is Editors of Automobile Quarterly, *The American Car since 1775: the most complete survey of the American automobile ever published*, 2nd ed. (New York: L. Scott Bailey, 1971).

[2] *Horseless Age* 1 (November 1895): 52–55; and *Horseless Age* 1 (January 1896): 29–33. A description is also provided by Flink, *America Adopts the Automobile*, 23–25.

[3] Interested readers are encouraged to review the automobile manufacturers described in Editors of Automobile Quarterly, *The American Car since 1775*.

[4] U.S. Federal Trade Commission, *Report on Motor Vehicle Industry*, 76th Cong., 1st sess., House Document No. 468 (Washington, D.C.: U.S. Government Printing Office, 1939), 22; and Stanley Lebergott, *Pursuing Happiness: American Consumers in the Twentieth Century* (Princeton, NJ: Princeton University Press, 1993), 130.

on to their own), and Fred Fisher (later to merge Fisher Body into General Motors)."[5] Roy Chapin also got his start with Ransom Olds, dropping out of the University of Michigan to try his hand in the new field. Chapin went on to found the Hudson Motor Company and to introduce a reasonably priced closed body Essex touring car at the end of World War I. Henry Leland came to Detroit after having worked for Brown and Sharpe, a machine tool shop in Providence, Rhode Island. True to his Yankee background, he dedicated himself to interchangeability and instilling high quality in parts. Leland's hard work was rewarded in 1909 when he won the Dewar Trophy, given by the Royal Automobile Club of London, for his demonstration of the interchangeability of three Cadillacs. The cars were taken apart; their parts mixed together; and upon rebuilding the three cars, they each were driven 500 miles and earned "perfect scores."[6] In 1912 Charles Kettering earned his fame as the inventor who developed a reliable electric self-starter, the one Cadillac used in its cars.[7]

Peopled by so many entrepreneurs, any study of the early auto market may be framed in the intellectual tradition of Joseph Schumpeter. The Austrian economist singled out the role of entrepreneurs in accounting for the dynamic process of economic growth. In contrast to inventors who developed new ideas, entrepreneurs, according to Schumpeter, often did not invent new products or processes, but had the distinctive capacity to see beyond daily routines, fight entrenched interests, and introduce new ideas into the economy.[8] Economic scholars have modified Schumpeter's theory. For example, Stuart Leslie found in the imaginative career of Charles "Boss" Kettering examples of an inventor capable of marketing ideas on his own as well as within a giant corporation. He defied any simple picture of an inventor

---

[5] Peter J. Hugill, "Technology and Geography in the Emergence of the American Automobile Industry, 1895–1915," in *Roadside America: The Automobile in Design and Culture*, ed. Jan Jennings (Ames, IA: Iowa State University Press, 1990), 29–39, quote 30.

[6] Flink, *America Adopts the Automobile*, 262–65, 291, quote 265; and idem, *The Automobile Age* (Cambridge, MA: MIT Press, 1988), 36.

[7] On Kettering's self-starter, see Stuart W. Leslie, *Boss Kettering: Wizard of General Motors* (New York: Columbia University Press, 1983), 49–50.

[8] Joseph Schumpeter, *Capitalism, Socialism and Democracy* (1942; repr., New York: Harper & Brothers, 1976); and idem, "The Creative Response in Economic History," *Journal of Economic History* 7 (1947): 149–59. Many scholars have revised parts of Schumpeter's conceptual framework, and their contributions have varied given their areas of specialization. An effort to revise Schumpeterian notions of innovation by economists is found in Richard R. Nelson and Sidney G. Winter, *An Evolutionary Theory of Economic Change* (Cambridge, MA: Harvard University Press, 1982). See also Richard R. Nelson, *The Sources of Economic Growth* (Cambridge, MA: Harvard University Press, 1996), 85–119. A business historian's revisions may be found in Nancy F. Koehn, *Brand New: How Entrepreneurs Earned Consumers' Trust from Wedgwood to Dell* (Boston, MA: Harvard Business School Press, 2001). For a valuable study of a government agency as an entrepreneurial entity, read Arthur L. Norberg and Judy E. O'Neill, *Transforming Computer Technology: Information Processing for the Pentagon, 1962-1986* (Baltimore: Johns Hopkins University Press, 1996).

unable to innovate.[9] Reviewing the coming of mass production, David Hounshell emphasized Henry Ford's good fortune in bringing together, in part
by chance, such an imaginative and complementary group of mechanics.[10]
Nancy Koehn argued that entrepreneurs often evinced a common attribute
of acquiring experiences early in their careers that they used to exploit opportunities at a future time.[11] Walter P. Chrysler illustrated this quality. He went
to work for Buick in 1912 and soon earned a salary of a half-million dollars
and the reputation as a boy wonder for his work in getting the assembly line
moving at Buick. In the process, Chrysler acquired, as sociologist Michael
Schwartz observed, "a trust in the integrity and resourcefulness of outside
suppliers."[12] Chrysler's ties to suppliers became the entrepreneur's critical
asset in transforming the two giants into the "Big Three" automakers during the halcyon 1920s and crisis-ridden 1930s.

As just recounted, innovation in the early auto market meant risks were
assumed on the market's supply side by inventors, entrepreneurs, managers,
mechanics, and other individuals who worked inside firms.[13] Economist
Ronald Coase, nevertheless, invited a different point of departure for assessing the emergence of a mass market. Coase identified social costs as those
costs not associated with the actual production process, such as the cost of
raw materials or labor, but the resources society lost through the production
and sale of goods. Writing about autos, Cornelius Gillam included among
social costs the death and injury of persons as a result of defective vehicles,
the value of their labor that was lost, the cost of any medical care required,
plus the resources that went into the vehicles that were lost as a result of
their defects.[14] Autos were not unusual in this regard. Several technological
innovations – including bicycles, boilers, guns, glass bottles, machine tools,

[9] Leslie, *Boss Kettering*.
[10] David A. Hounshell, *From the American System to Mass Production, 1800-1932: The Development of Manufacturing Technology in the United States* (Baltimore, MD: Johns Hopkins
University Press, 1984), 217–61.
[11] Koehn, *Brand New*, 320–21.
[12] Michael Schwartz, "Markets, Networks, and the Rise of Chrysler in Old Detroit, 1920-
1940," *Enterprise & Society* 1 (March 2000): 63–99, 78.
[13] My point is not meant as a criticism. Much of the best scholarship in the field examines innovation from this perspective. See for instance Louis Galambos with Jane Sewell, *Networks
of Innovation: Vaccine Development at Merck, Sharp & Dohme, and Mulford, 1895-1995*
(New York: Cambridge University Press, 1995); David A. Hounshell and John K. Smith,
Science and Corporate Strategy: Du Pont R&D, 1902-1980 (New York: Cambridge University Press, 1988); W. Bernard Carlson, *Innovation as a Social Process: Elihu Thomson
and the rise of General Electric* (New York: Cambridge University Press, 1991); and Thomas
J. Misa, *A Nation of Steel: The Making of Modern America, 1865-1925* (Baltimore, MD:
Johns Hopkins University Press, 1995).
[14] R. H. Coase, "The Problem of Social Cost," *Journal of Law & Economics* 3 (October 1960):
1–44; and Cornelius W. Gillam, *Products Liability in the Automobile Industry: A Study in
Strict Liability and Social Control* (Minneapolis, MN: University of Minnesota Press, 1960),
196–210, especially 196–97.

coffee urns, chemical products, and pharmaceuticals – proved dangerous when defective.[15] Existing studies about market innovation, however, have paid little attention to consumers' risks of injury or the impact of liability rules on a new market's development.[16] Although the literature about automobiles is vast, scholars have overlooked liability for defects in terms of who bore the costs of innovation.[17] Without disputing the fact that actors on the market's supply side faced risks, the premise underpinning my analysis is that actors on the market's demand side incurred social costs in the form of financial losses and physical injuries as an inherent part of the process of innovation in a market context.[18]

A brief review of the early automobile's technology makes the point that the machines were crude and dangerous.[19] At the turn of the century, three

---

[15] Among legal writers, see Edward H. Levi, *An Introduction to Legal Reasoning* (Chicago: University of Chicago Press, 1949), 7–19.

[16] Although not focused on innovation, a valuable account of automobile safety is Joel W. Eastman, *Styling vs. Safety: The American Automobile Industry and the Development of Automotive Safety, 1900-1966* (New York: University Press of America, 1984). See also Sarah S. Lochlann Jain, "'Dangerous Instrumentalities': The Bystander as Subject in Automobility," *Cultural Anthropology* 19, no. 1 (2004): 61–94.

[17] Automobile historians typically have focused on the many ingredients with which manufacturers produced a complex machine on a mass scale. They have asked how producers improved devices or marketed goods, rather than who bore the costs of those innovations. There are a few exceptions. Economist Michael Spence called attention to liability as an information problem. Cornelius W. Gillam in his review of appellate cases involving automobiles argued that consumers absorbed social costs in the form of injuries born out of defective vehicles. Among excellent scholarly accounts of the automobile market, see Alfred D. Chandler, Jr., *Strategy and Structure: Chapters in the History of the American Industrial Enterprise* (Cambridge, MA: MIT Press, 1962); Donald Finlay Davis, *Conspicuous Production: Automobiles and Elites in Detroit, 1899-1933* (Philadelphia, PA: Temple University Press, 1988); Hounshell, *From the American System to Mass Production*; Arthur J. Kuhn, *GM Passes Ford, 1918-1939: Designing the General Motors Performance-Control System* (University Park, PA: Pennsylvania State University Press, 1986); and Leslie, *Boss Kettering*. On liability for defects, see Michael Spence, "Consumer Misperceptions, Product Failure and Producer Liability," *Review of Economic Studies* 44 (1977): 561–72; Gillam, *Products Liability in the Automobile Industry*, 196–210; and Jain, "'Dangerous Instrumentalities,'" 61–94.

[18] Business historians and historians of design, in particular, have written about managers' efforts to respond to consumers, but have not examined consumers' lawsuits. Two valuable studies are Koehn, *Brand New*; and Regina Lee Blaszczyk, *Imagining Consumers: Design and Innovation from Wedgwood to Corning* (Baltimore, MD: Johns Hopkins University Press, 2000). Economic historians have studied accidents, but as a byproduct rather than as a central element of the economy's development. See Peter Temin, *Taking Your Medicine: drug regulation in the United States* (Cambridge, MA: Harvard University Press, 1980); and Price V. Fishback and Shawn Everett Kantor, *A Prelude to the Welfare State: The Origins of Workers' Compensation*, National Bureau of Economic Research (Chicago: University of Chicago Press, 2000).

[19] Reviews of the industry's early development include Flink, *The Automobile Age*; idem, *America Adopts the Automobile*; Ralph C. Epstein, *The Automobile Industry: Its Economic and*

technologies vied for the auto market. The steam-powered auto was one competitor. In 1900, the Locomobile Company of America ranked first in auto sales with its steamer. Two other makers of steam-powered autos were the White Sewing Machine Company and Stanley. However, in 1903, Locomobile switched from making steam-powered vehicles to gasoline-powered autos. In 1910, the White Company also switched.[20] Among its shortcomings, the steam vehicles were known to explode, and indeed, during the late nineteenth century, vehicles so frightened residents that they were banned from some towns.[21] The vehicles also were hampered by the need to be close to a good water supply. Although Stanley continued to make steamers, the market shrank in size.[22]

The second competing technology was the electric car. Similar to early gas-powered autos, electric-powered vehicles also housed defects. Historian David Kirsch noted, for example, that a "hot wheel bearing could result in excessive energy usage and ultimately lead to battery failure." One report focused on acid, noting "one of the greatest sources of trouble in the cabs is the slopping of acid on the working parts."[23] When the New York Transportation Company switched from electric to gas automobiles, its manager based part of the decision on safety. As Kirsch explained, "the gasoline cabs, despite their higher speed, were easier to control and resulted in fewer damage claims against the company."[24] In addition, the demise of the electric vehicle was tied to the layout of urban spaces and the underlying infrastructure. Among trucks, electric vehicles claimed a niche of eleven percent of commercial vehicles in 1909, but as World War I shifted focus to gasoline trucks and as the flexibility of gas vehicles made them popular, the electric car declined to just one percent of the output of commercial vehicles in 1919.[25] The third remaining technology was the gasoline automobile.

Commercial Development (1928; repr., New York: Arno Press, 1972); John B. Rae, *American Automobile Manufacturers: The First Forty Years* (Philadelphia: Chilton Company, 1959); Allan Nevins with Frank Ernest Hill, *Ford: The Times, the Man, the Company* (New York: Charles Scribner's Sons, 1954); Davis, *Conspicuous Production*; and McShane, *Down the Asphalt Path.*

[20] Flink, *The Automobile Age*, 6–7.   [21] McShane, *Down the Asphalt Path*, 81–101.

[22] Flink, *The Automobile Age*, 7.

[23] David A. Kirsch, *The Electric Vehicle and the Burden of History* (New Brunswick, NJ: Rutgers University Press, 2000), 40, quote 45.

[24] Ibid., 79. See also Gijs Mom, *The Electric Vehicle: Technology and Expectations in the Automobile Age* (Baltimore, MD: Johns Hopkins University Press, 2004), 136–37.

[25] Kirsch, *The Electric Vehicle and the Burden of History*, 164, 129–66. In addition, Gijs Mom singled out the importance of technological developments associated with gasoline vehicles. In particular, the coming of a more reliable rubber tire made the gasoline vehicle a more appealing choice for motorists. As Mom recounted, with the 1910 introduction of the improved tire, "one of the most important functional obstacles to the adoption of the gasoline car as a universal vehicle seemed to have been removed." Mom, *The Electric Vehicle*, 107–12, quote 111.

Hugill grouped the gas-powered auto's development into four categories covering the years between 1895 and 1915.[26] One was the gas-buggy. After the Duryeas' initial foray into the auto business, Alexander Winton produced the gas-buggy in quantity. Other entrepreneurs tried their hand at making and selling buggies, including Ransom E. Olds and James Packard. A key problem, however, was their vehicles' lack of power. According to Hugill, the 1901 curved-dash Oldsmobile's "weight-to-power ratio was abysmal: 157 pounds per horsepower." Further, the vehicles' high center of gravity made for "poor handling."[27] Gas-buggies, Hugill observed, disappeared with the coming of a second type of car first illustrated by Mercedes at the 1902 New York Motor Show. The Mercedes automobile had a four-cylinder engine with thirty-five horsepower. The car cleared the ground by about "eight or nine inches" and its "low center of gravity made for excellent handling." The shift to the Mercedes-style vehicle was well under way by 1905.[28] Concurrently, two other vehicle types appeared. Citing the poor quality of western roads, Hugill wrote that the western buggy or high wheeler replaced the gas-buggy in rural areas with poor roads. The fourth car prior to the coming of the Model T was the "cyclecar." It relied on wire-wheels and a small, one-cylinder engine. Although it was cheap, selling for around $500, the cars lacked any substantial power and seated only two passengers. The market for this vehicle peaked in the mid-1910s and collapsed soon thereafter.[29]

The Model T, introduced in 1908, incorporated its predecessors' strengths. Hugill observed: "High-quality steels made for a strong, yet light, chassis. Given a lightweight chassis, a relatively light, economical engine could still give a weight-to-power ratio as good as all but the very best Mercedes-style automobiles, thus ensuring that the Model T could usually pull itself clear of all but the worst mudholes. Ford gave his T almost the ground clearance of a high wheeler and a suspension design that kept the wheels in contact with the road in almost any condition."[30]

In technical terms, early automobiles such as the Model T, much like today's vehicles, consisted of many critical parts – the engine, carburetor, ignition, clutch, gears, bumpers, transmission, axles, shock absorbers, steering mechanism, brakes, wheels, tires, bodies, and headlights. The assembled vehicle was often thought of in terms of its systems: brakes, cooling, electrical, exhaust, fuel, ignition, suspension, and starting and charging (batteries). The parts and systems could be impaired by several possible defects. First, the materials used for components, such as wood for wheels, could be defective owing to natural causes. The materials could also lack the strength, flexibility,

---

[26] Hugill, "Technology and Geography in the Emergence of the American Automobile Industry, 1895-1915," 29-39, quote 29.
[27] Ibid., 30.   [28] Ibid., 33-34.
[29] Ibid., 36-37.   [30] Ibid., 38.

or other mechanical properties required of the component. Second, the factory could treat the materials in such a way as to make them defective. The improper drying of wood or the improper heat treatment of metal resulted in cracked wood or brittle metal parts. Third, components could be badly designed or could be assembled hastily. Henry Ford's biographer, Allan Nevins, recalled that the 1904 Model A's brakes "were good if assembled with great care," but that the rush to assemble resulted in defects.[31] Adding further difficulties to the manufacturing process prior to the coming of interchangeability, one part could vary in its quality from the next. As a fourth worry, even if all the parts were properly manufactured and assembled, their final construction mattered: depending on the size and weight of vehicles, the movement of one part could exert enough force on another part to cause it to wear out or break. Finally, automobiles frequently caught fire owing to several possible causes, such as exposed electrical wires; leaks in gas tanks, carburetors, or valves; and backfiring in carburetors, attributable to a sticky valve or an improper mixture of gas and air.[32]

Two questions followed from the recognition of the social costs of innovation. First, why did consumers enter the new market? This is the subject of Chapter 1. To get the market started, would-be manufacturers needed consumers who were willing to pay high prices for defective products. Having purchased the imperfect vehicles and suffered injuries or losses, consumers responded in different ways. One was to sue the dealer or manufacturer. Doing so, they prompted a second question: Who should bear the social costs of innovation in a new market? Company managers offered a partial answer in the structure of their young firms, but the question was as much political as economic. It mattered, therefore, that the auto market emerged during the Progressive era. As Americans rethought the power corporations exercised, including the power corporations held over a product's safe design, they changed their ideas about corporate responsibility and safety, and, in turn, held automakers to a new standard of accountability.[33]

---

[31] Nevins added, "Dealers then had to take the rear axle to pieces and remove the brake bands to get at the trouble." Nevins with Hill, *Ford: The Times, the Man, the Company*, 247–49, quote 247.

[32] N. B. Pope, "The Automobile as a Fire Hazard," *Weekly Underwriter* 86 (February 3, 1912): 117–19. Automotive writers recognized the problem of leaks early on. See "Leaky Tanks," *Horseless Age* 10 (July 9, 1902): 28.

[33] Naomi R. Lamoreaux, *The Great Merger Movement in American Business* (New York: Cambridge University Press, 1987); and Thomas K. McCraw, *Prophets of Regulation: Charles Francis Adams, Louis D. Brandeis, James M. Landis, Alfred E. Kahn* (Cambridge, MA: Harvard University Press, 1984).

1

Risks of Innovation, Risks of Injury

In 1904, as the nation adjusted to a new economic landscape now dotted
with giant mergers, some of its wealthy celebrities took to the new sport
of motoring. Andrew Carnegie was one. He purchased two electric vehicles, but found both cars disappointing. Carnegie complained to the Electric
Vehicle Company's (EVC) sales manager, a Mr. James Joyce, and EVC spent
several weeks fretting over how to make the vehicles "give a satisfactory
speed and mileage to Mr. Carnegie."[1] Carnegie's new associates at U.S. Steel
encountered similar troubles. H. W. Marsh wrote to EVC in 1904 noting
that "[s]everal gentlemen connected with the Steel Company...have been
comparing experiences on these electric rigs, when lunching at the Club, and
we are keeping carefully the cost of our repairs and I can assure you that
up to date they are no advertisement for your vehicles." Marsh closed his
missive: "You must certainly admit that 457 hours, over 74 days to keep a
vehicle in shape for another season's use, that has been run less than five
months is not an advertisement that you would care to circulate widely."[2]
   Having made their money by paying attention to the cost of things,
Carnegie and Marsh were well positioned to comment on the expense of
repairs. They could count their blessings, however, for not having to report
accidents. In September 1902, Caspar Miller recounted one misadventure to
readers of *Horseless Age*, the industry's premier trade journal. A husband
and wife went out for a ride, and while motoring up a hill the vehicle's chain
broke. They put on the brakes, but "[t]he forward brake was of course inoperative, and it was found that the brake on the differential also did not hold."
The car rolled back down the declivity, and across "a steep bank....the
occupants were thrown over the back of the seat." Luckily, no one was hurt.
Even so, Miller instructed: "let us have them [the brakes] on the wheels, or

---

[1] The problem in both machines apparently was the battery. Andrew Carnegie (dictated) to
F. C. Armstrong, Electric Vehicle Co., November 4, 1904; H. W. Alden, Memorandum to
Mr. Joyce, January 26, 1905; and James Joyce to Electric Vehicle Company, January 30,
1905, all in Folder 4-3, Box 4, Acc. 1750, HF. An excellent account of electric vehicles is
found in David A. Kirsch, *The Electric Vehicle and the Burden of History* (New Brunswick,
NJ: Rutgers University Press, 2000).
[2] H. W. Marsh to Manager, The Electric Vehicle Co., November 23, 1904, Folder 4-10, Box
4, Acc. 1750, HF.

some part directly attached to them. The above accident occurred because the brakes on the differential were not properly adjusted. They might just as well have been caused by failure of the differential pinions or differential crown gear keys. Differential brakes are cheap to the manufacturer, but dear to the user."[3] *Horseless Age* reported other accidents. Two motorists from Arkansas were "seriously injured" when "[t]he steam gave out near the top of a hill, the brake failed to hold and the machine dashed down the hill into a ravine."[4] In another case, a chain broke, "lodged" itself in the vehicle, thus halting the machine "so suddenly" as to throw the driver out of his seat.[5] Some accidents were simply attributed to vehicles becoming "unmanageable," as reported when "the wife of United States Senator W. M. Stewart, of Nevada, was thrown out violently against the curb and killed."[6] From Maine came the account of a car diving into the Kennebec River when its steering apparatus became "unmanageable."[7]

Many buyers lost money and injured their bodies, that is, absorbed social costs, as a result of purchasing highly imperfect or defective vehicles.[8] In some cases, the defect was as simple as a loose wire or a failed spark plug; in others, as serious as an axle that broke because it had been improperly heat treated. Henry Ford built his first auto in 1896, and inventors, entrepreneurs,

---

[3] Caspar W. Miller, "Accident Due to Defective Brakes," (letter to the Editor), *Horseless Age* 10 (September 10, 1902): 274.

[4] "Auto Accidents," *Horseless Age* 10 (July 23, 1902): 95.

[5] "Automobile Accidents," *Horseless Age* 10 (September 17, 1902): 309.

[6] Ibid.   [7] Ibid.

[8] R. H. Coase, "The Problem of Social Cost," *Journal of Law & Economics* 3 (October 1960): 1–44. See also Cornelius W. Gillam, *Products Liability in the Automobile Industry: A Study in Strict Liability and Social Control* (Minneapolis, MN: University of Minnesota Press, 1960), 196–210, especially 196–97. Arthur F. McEvoy examined social costs in *The Fisherman's Problem: Ecology and Law in the California Fisheries, 1850–1980* (New York: Cambridge University Press, 1986). Barbara Welke found that advances in technology plus the increased speed of trains created new risks of injury for passengers and bystanders. Barbara Young Welke, *Recasting American Liberty: Gender, Race, Law, and the Railroad Revolution, 1865–1920* (New York: Cambridge University Press, 2001), 27–28. Scott Knowles focused on dangerous products and the risks of injury stemming especially from fire hazards. Knowles examined how private oversight entities, notably the Underwriters' Laboratories, developed bodies of knowledge and the authority to influence corporate managers and shape their markets. Scott Gabriel Knowles, "Inventing Safety: Fire, Technology, and Trust in Modern America" (Ph.D. diss., Johns Hopkins University, 2003). Sarah S. Lochlann Jain examined injuries borne by bystanders in the early auto market in "'Dangerous Instrumentalities': The Bystander as Subject in Automobility," *Cultural Anthropology* 19, no. 1 (2004): 61–94. Albert O. Hirschmann studied the dynamics between buyers and sellers in mature markets when product quality deteriorates in *Exit, Voice, and Loyalty: Responses to Decline in Firms, Organizations, and States* (Cambridge, MA: Harvard University Press, 1970). On the subject of workmen's accidents, see John Fabian Witt, *The Accidental Republic: Crippled Workmen, Destitute Widows, and the Remaking of American Law* (Cambridge, MA: Harvard University Press, 2004); and idem, "Speedy Fred Taylor and the Ironies of Enterprise Liability," *Columbia Law Review* 103 (January 2003): 1–49.

and managers spent the next twenty years solving many technological problems.[9] This chapter begins with the idea that social costs followed from a process of innovation in a market context. Provided demand remained strong, automakers did not need to wait till they perfected the technology before selling machines. Instead, they sold imperfect or defective vehicles. Although consumers incurred social costs in the short term, manufacturers reinvested their profits to better their machines and broaden the market.

Because vehicles were such crude and expensive devices, why did the first buyers enter the market? In *Exit, Voice and Loyalty*, economist Albert Hirschman considered the question of a product's quality for established markets.[10] When firms let their products' quality slip, Hirschman proposed that consumers could elect one of two options: they could simply stop doing business with the firm or leave the market (exit); alternatively, they could communicate their complaints however they saw fit (voice). In a new (rather than a mature) market, the problem is the reverse: how did consumers enter a market, and what consequences followed from their having to pay good money for rudimentary machines? Following Hirschman's example, I characterize consumers' actions in terms of two options. First, many of the very first car buyers voluntarily assumed risks associated with new, highly imperfect vehicles. For those car owners who absorbed costs, many pursued a second option: they voiced their complaints about defects, just as Hirschman expected. But what proved most important for the development of the auto market were the actions of a smaller number of buyers so agitated by their products' defects that they sued retailers and manufacturers.

PROLOGUE: THE AUTO MARKET IN THE 1890S

Boasting that "thousands of people in this broad land are besieging inventors for the coveted improvement [automobiles]," *Horseless Age* called on capitalists in the spring of 1896 to "come to the inventor's assistance and bridge the gulf between demand and supply."[11] Automobile racing offered one potential source of capital, although not the best. The Detroit inventor, Charles B. King, estimated the cost of designing a new vehicle at $1,000 in

---

[9] One of the first automobile historians, Ralph Epstein, wrote that through the year 1910 "the expense occasioned by the rapid breaking and wearing out of parts...often either equaled or exceeded the annual cost of operation." Ralph C. Epstein, *The Automobile Industry: Its Economic and Commercial Development* (1928; repr., New York: Arno Press, 1972), 85. On Ford's first experimental auto, see Allan Nevins with Frank Ernest Hill, *Ford: The Times, the Man, the Company* (New York: Charles Scribner's Sons, 1954), 148–57. Pamela Walker Laird outlined the efforts of automakers to reassure motorists about their products' quality in "'The Car without a Single Weakness': Early Automobile Advertising," *Technology and Culture* 37 (October 1996): 796–812.

[10] Hirschman, *Exit, Voice, and Loyalty*.

[11] "To the Capitalist," *Horseless Age* 1 (April 1896): 6.

1896 and wanted large prizes to entice inventors to devote their energy to motor cars.[12] In 1896, he complained to Charles Duryea that the *Cosmopolitan Magazine* as sponsor of the upcoming New York race should raise its prizes from $3,000 to $5,000, stating: "This industry cannot be stimulated by half-hearted faith."[13] Other inventors were not forced to raise capital through races. Alexander Winton, for instance, had been a bicycle manufacturer and Ransom E. Olds had maintained a profitable gasoline engine business. At first they funded their auto projects by piggy-backing off their main enterprises. Olds then raised capital through local sources in Lansing, Michigan; Winton similarly raised capital in his hometown of Cleveland, Ohio. Still, these inventors also looked for ways to publicize motor vehicles. In 1896, a Duryea rig, *Horseless Age* noted, was featured in the Barnum & Bailey circus as well as the Franklin Bros. circus.[14] In 1897, Alexander Winton won "national recognition" when he completed an automobile trip from Cleveland to New York. He repeated the journey in 1899, carrying a journalist who wrote articles and attracted so much attention that, when they drove into New York, an estimated million people gathered to see the inventor's machine. Winton's trip helped convince the public of the car's viability.[15] Winton and Henry Ford also followed King's example in seeing auto racing as a tool for promoting their vehicles. In 1901 the two faced each other in a duel that Ford won and which he would later claim set him apart and on the course to his future success.[16]

Aside from racing, King promoted the nascent market by calling for a trade association devoted to the interests of the motor vehicle. He declared in the first issue of *Horseless Age* the need for "a national organization which will have as its object the furtherance of all details connected" to the motor vehicle.[17] He proposed the new organization be named the "American Motor League" (AML) and, within a year, the journal reported that the AML had been formed with help from inventors such as King and Duryea, as well as from wealthy citizens like Truman Newberry and Henry B. Joy

---

[12] "Communications," *Horseless Age* 1 (April 1896): 23. Charles B. King to Charles E. Duryea, March 19, 1896; and Charles B. King to John Brisben Walker, Editor, Cosmopolitan Magazine, March 23, 1896, both in Book 3, Letter Press Books, Box 2.3, King Collection, DPL.

[13] Charles B. King to Charles E. Duryea, March 19, 1896, Box 2.3, Book 3, King Collection, DPL.

[14] *Horseless Age* 1 (March 1896): 16; *Horseless Age* 1 (May 1896): 30; and James J. Flink, *America Adopts the Automobile, 1895-1910* (Cambridge, MA: MIT Press, 1970), 47.

[15] James J. Flink, *The Automobile Age* (Cambridge, MA: MIT Press, 1988), 23, 30; and Flink, *America Adopts the Automobile, 1895-1910*, 25, 36–37.

[16] John B. Rae, *American Automobile Manufacturers: The First Forty Years* (Philadelphia: Chilton Company, 1959), 13, 33.

[17] Charles B. King to Editor, *Horseless Age* 1 (November 1895): 8. See also Flink, *America Adopts the Automobile, 1895-1910*, 144.

of Detroit.[18] The AML, although small in size (with 27 members in 1896), still used its political might to promote the new trade. Its mission statement declared a commitment to foster horseless carriages through lectures, new legislation, improved roads, and "the defense" of vehicles in court. That year, it claimed two victories: it stopped a bill in the Ohio state legislature that would have prohibited the use of all motor carriages on Ohio roads, and it opened Chicago's parks to motor carriages.[19]

In addition to his promotions, King aided the market directly with his regular correspondence with other mechanics and potential buyers. To Mr. Skiff of Syracuse, NY, he declared that the King "engine is perfectly balanced and runs at the highest speed without vibration, is perfectly reliable, can always be started and only stops when the gasoline is exhausted." Compared to the French machines (a point he could make thanks to his correspondence with foreign makers), he added: "It is lighter and more powerful and has less vibration." To William Macklin of Dinsmore, PA, he promoted his machine by claiming it "was the well known Duryea type which won first prize in the Chicago Times Herald Race." Although he lacked any sales literature, he offered to send a blueprint. To W. D. & J. W. Packard of Warren, Ohio, King defended his motor, saying it "is in no way an experiment...." He would sell his machine for $410, which included the "five horse power motor, complete with batteries, coil, starting handle and muffler."[20]

King's correspondence yields an interesting picture of inventors, would-be manufacturers, and car buyers communicating across considerable distance within the United States and to participants who at the time had developed the technology in France and Germany. Elwood Haynes had earned engineering degrees from two leading educational institutions in the United States and had studied German to keep apprised of the findings of two automakers, Gottfried Daimler and Karl Benz. Haynes was assembling the Haynes Apperson car from his home in Kokomo, Indiana, and Alfred Sloan met him in 1899 in his efforts to drum up business for the Hyatt Roller Bearing Company. As a supplier of roller bearings to both auto assemblers and auto parts makers, notably axle makers like the Weston-Mott Company, Sloan met several men in the trade, including Billy Durant, Charles Stewart Mott, Henry Leland, and Walter Chrysler. Though Hyatt was based in New Jersey,

---

[18] Donald Finlay Davis discusses the wealth of Joy and other early promoters of the auto industry in *Conspicuous Production: Automobiles and Elites in Detroit, 1899-1933* (Philadelphia, PA: Temple University Press, 1988), 57–58.

[19] *Horseless Age* 1 (January 1896): 15; and *Horseless Age* 1 (February 1896): 34. Charles B. King to S. Skiff, February 28, 1896; and "List of Members to Date in A. M. L.," March 16, 1896, both in Box 2.3, Book 3, King Collection, DPL.

[20] Charles B. King to William Macklin, February 18, 1896, Box 2.3, Book 3; Charles B. King to S. Skiff, February 18, 1896, Box 2.3, Book 3; and Charles B. King to W. D. & J. W. Packard, February 15, 1896, Box 5.6, Correspondence: Packard Letters: 1896, all in King Collection, DPL.

FIGURE 1.1. A Curved-Dash Oldsmobile, 1902. Manufacturers conducted many stunts during the early 1900s. The events served different purposes which ranged from displaying vehicles' novelty to convincing potential car buyers of the machines' sound operation. Courtesy of the Detroit Public Library, National Automotive History Collection.

Sloan and his key sales associate, Peter Steenstrup, traveled frequently to the Detroit area. He also traveled to auto shows, where Sloan was said to have first met Henry Ford in 1901 at Hyatt's booth at the Madison Square Garden. Many other suppliers and automakers made connections at auto shows or through trips to cities in Michigan and other states. In the case of Hyatt, Steenstrup typically attracted potential customers to the Hyatt booth and then Sloan, according to his biographer David Farber, "would figure out how to design Hyatt bearings into the auto manufacturer's assemblage."[21]

The combination of efforts – the work of the AML, the ability to raise local sources of capital, promoting automobiles in races, tours, or stunts, and the auto shows – succeeded in getting the market started. A few companies had achieved commercial production by 1898 and sold their rigs to individuals who typically were mechanically inclined and well-off (although not necessarily wealthy). William Metzger, fabled to have opened the first automobile store in Detroit, reported his customers in 1898–99 included four capitalists, two manufacturers, four doctors, a few businessmen, a printer, and a plumber. Ralph Epstein had surveyed Metzger and a few other individuals

[21] David R. Farber, *Sloan Rules: Alfred P. Sloan and the Triumph of General Motors* (Chicago: University of Chicago Press, 2002), 7–19, quote 13–14. On auto shows and suppliers, see also Flink, *The Automobile Age*, 30; and idem, *America Adopts the Automobile*, 47–49.

for his 1928 study of the automobile industry. Alexander Winton sold a vehicle, priced at roughly $1,000, to a similar list of clients: engineers, manufacturers, a brewer, a flour miller, and two merchants. In 1898, Waverly Electric sold twenty vehicles in Detroit; distinctive among its buyers were six "ladies," including "two wives of bankers."[22] Records for 1898, though just estimates, placed Winton's sales at twenty-two vehicles, and the Stanley brothers' sales at a hundred steam-powered rigs. By 1900, federal record keepers tabulated annual production at 4,192 vehicles, with Locomobile and Columbia producing slightly more than half the output.[23] By then, the press used the term "automobile" to describe horseless carriages, a term adopted from the French in 1899 (Fig. 1.1).[24]

INNOVATION IN A NEW MARKET: RISK-TAKERS

Prior to 1910, most potential buyers did not enter the market, being prudent or short of the $650 for a new Oldsmobile in 1902, $750 for a Cadillac in 1903, or $850 for a Ford Model A runabout in 1903 or 1904.[25] Although companies like Oldsmobile advertised automobiles as reliable in order to give buyers the confidence to enter the market, they still counted on car owners being willing to face the task of making their rigs stand up. Indeed, because motor vehicles were so crude, it is hard to image the market getting off the ground had consumers not absorbed many costs born out of defective machines.

In 1901, Ransom Olds took the market's lead spot with his one-cylinder engine runabout, simple to operate and priced to sell at $650. He advertised his agile gas-buggy as "Odorless, Noiseless, Safe."[26] The Olds Motor Works

---

[22] Epstein, *The Automobile Industry*, 95–97. See also Flink, *America Adopts the Automobile*, 70–74.

[23] Flink, *The Automobile Age*, 13. For figures on production by individual automakers, see Editors of Automobile Quarterly, *The American Car since 1775: the most complete survey of the American automobile ever published*, 2nd ed. (New York: L. Scott Bailey, 1971), 138–39. Estimates of total vehicle production are found in U.S. Federal Trade Commission, *Report on Motor Vehicle Industry*, 76th Cong., 1st sess., House Document No. 468 (Washington, D.C.: U.S. Government Printing Office, 1939), 22.

[24] Clay McShane, *Down the Asphalt Path: The Automobile and the American City* (New York: Columbia University Press, 1994), 128.

[25] For the price of the Ford Model A and other Ford vehicles, see Nevins with Hill, *Ford: The Times, the Man, the Company*, Appendix V, 646. Oldsmobile advertised its price in "The Oldsmobile," *Motor Age* 1 (February 27, 1902), Advertisements, 41. In early 1903, the same price applied as described in "The Oldsmobile: The Best Thing on Wheels," *Motor Age* 3 (March 25, 1903), Advertisements, 26. For Cadillac, see "Agents Big and Little (That is Wise Ones) All Have Their Eyes Turned Towards The Cadillac," *Motor Age* 3 (January 22, 1903), Advertisements, 26.

[26] "The Oldsmobile," *Motor Age* 1 (February 27, 1902), Advertisements, 41; and Flink, *The Automobile Age*, 31–32. See also Editors of Automobile Quarterly, *The American Car since 1775*, 138–39.

sold 2,500 rigs in 1902, giving the firm revenues of $1.6 million and roughly a quarter of the market; and then in 1903 some 4,000 vehicles passed out of Olds's factory, yielding $2.3 million in revenues and accounting for about a third of the market.[27] As sales increased, so did the firm's dealer network, and by 1903, the Olds Motor Works had forty-one agencies in cities from Boston to San Francisco, as well as smaller metropolises like Texarkana, Ark., and Tucson, Ariz.[28] The firm gladly advertised its runabout's virtues in a 1903 brochure that testified to the rig's "absolute reliability." It was "ideal" for tackling "a crowded street"; it could climb steep hills, even those with a thirty percent grade; it would travel more than twenty-five miles on a gallon of "common stove gasoline"; and, with its four-gallon tank, a motorist could cover 100 miles at a cost of three-eighths of a penny per mile. Only the best parts had been used: the front axle was made of a "very heavy steel tube," and the steering lever was "attached solid to the body, being connected to the front wheels by a spring which absorbs all vibration." The motor consisted of "one cylinder, one piston, one connecting rod and crank, one balance wheel, and two valves." So pleased with the car's simple construction, the brochure challenged: "Any one who can understand a sewing machine can drive an Oldsmobile."[29]

Writing from the Southwest, a dealer by the name of J. B. Spragro offered a different picture. He grumbled that the cars had not been shipped properly and needed "doctoring by a carragemaker [sic] to make them presentable." One car's sparking coil proved defective: it had not been "tampered with" but "simply gave out as far as the induced currents making a spark." Many of the new machines at first ran "beautifully," but then "cutting set in" and he fumed, "I have had the devil to pay since with irate customers." In two clients' vehicles, he located "the trouble in the main sprocket gear which does not get sufficient oil through the small oil tube. I am using the best grade of castor oil and am now experimenting with other lubricants."[30] Spragro went on for twelve pages in this tone. He wrote of tracing a water leak to "a crack in the cylinder," having stud bolts break on a machine's front shaft bearing,

---

[27] Cash sales and profits were reported in "An Established Business Paying Dividends. The Olds Motor Works, Manufacturing the Oldsmobile," 1–2, Folder 8, Box 5, Olds Papers, MSU. Flink, *The Automobile Age*, 31–32. See also Editors of Automobile Quarterly, *The American Car since 1775*, 138–39.

[28] "Metzger Sold 10,000 Cadillacs: Great Record for Detroit's Pioneer Steam Automobile Man," File "Cadillac Motor Car Co., Newspaper Clippings, 1909–1922," Box 8, Leland Collection, DPL. "The Oldsmobile: The Best Thing on Wheels," *Motor Age* 3 (March 26, 1903): 26. Cadillac offers a useful comparison with 21 agents advertised in "Agents Big and Little (That is Wise Ones)," 26.

[29] "The Oldsmobile manufactured by Olds Motor Works," (1903), 11–13, 17–21, Folder 11, Box 5, Olds Papers, MSU. Davis writes of Olds's commitment to a car simple to operate and easily repaired in an owner's garage. See Davis, *Conspicuous Production*, 55.

[30] Jas. B. Spragro to unknown [F. L. S. (Fred)], page 1 missing, no date [1902], 2–3, Folder 15, Box 4, Olds Papers, MSU.

and having as his "greatest nuisance" on a recent trip the "constant breaking
or loosening of battery wires."[31] He wanted a good handle to replace the
"bare metal" on the steering lever; he asked the factory to bolt bodies to their
frames since screws "work loose in but a few weeks"; he further requested
that Olds make cars easy to dismantle as the "ease of making repairs means
a very great deal to users of the machines" and that "low cost of repairs is
everything to a business man."[32]

The dealer listed the sort of problems one might imagine associated with a
new, complex mechanical device. Industry observers blamed their products'
poor quality on the speed with which automakers tried to make and sell
their products in the booming market. In 1901, Albert Clough directed his
anger at axles. "If a manufacturer finds that the axles of his machine are
giving way [breaking] the next lot of vehicles are provided with axles of
a slightly larger diameter and so on, until they begin to stand up pretty
well." This approach ultimately improved axles, but he went on: "it is in no
sense mechanical engineering and is fraught with danger and dissatisfaction."
From this example, Clough drew the general conclusion: car drivers were
"too often" just an "unrecompensed and unwilling 'testing department' for
manufacturers who have hurried into the market with a crude and imperfect
product."[33] In 1907, Harry Dey echoed Clough in his general complaint,
but focused his particular attention on the lack of adequate research in the
nascent industry: "One great deficiency of the American factories is that
they are not conducting any experimental research." Carburetors, valves,
spark plugs, cams, lubricating systems, clutches, brakes, tires, metal alloys –
these and other parts and systems, Dey felt, could benefit from targeted
research. Where a "regular system of experiments" would identify which
practices to adopt, Dey blamed the "almighty dollar" for slowing research
as manufacturers rushed their cars to market.[34]

Aside from the lack of research and testing, the rush to get products to
market affected relations with suppliers. Suppliers had been critical to the
market's start. As Allan Nevins recounted: "Nearly all the early automobile
works in America, like most in Europe, still did little more than assemble
engines, wheels, bodies, and other parts made for them by various dealers."
He further observed that "few companies in the United States had the skill,
facilities, and capital to build an automobile complete, and even those with
the requisite resources for such a task were patronizing the parts makers,

[31] Jas. B. Spragro to unknown [F. L. S. (Fred)], page 1 missing, no date [1902], 5–6, Folder 15,
Box 4, Olds Papers, MSU.

[32] Jas. B. Spragro to unknown [F. L. S. (Fred)], page 1 missing, no date [1902], 7–8, Folder 15,
Box 4, Olds Papers, MSU.

[33] Albert L. Clough, "The Question of Axles," *Horseless Age* 8 (November 6, 1901): 672.

[34] Harry E. Dey, "Experimental Departments," *Horseless Age* 20 (October 2, 1907): 455–56.
See also "Need of Testing Laboratories," *Horseless Age* 17 (May 9, 1906): 657–58.

particularly for engines, bearings, bodies, wheels, and tires."[35] Among suppliers, Nevins credited the Dodge brothers as critical to helping Ford get his new firm off to the right start. Ford's 1903 contract with Horace and John Dodge for engines and transmissions was a blessing because engines were so critical to the quality of early autos and the Dodges ran a good machine shop.[36] Aside from Ford's reliance on the Dodge brothers for engines and transmissions, he also contracted with the C. R. Wilson Company for car bodies and with the W. K. Prudden Company for wooden wheels.[37] Ford (like other assemblers) in turn faced problems over their parts' quality. Nevins reported examples in which Ford faulted the Dodge brothers for shoddy work, and blamed the Dodges' "system of paying employees by the piece" which "resulted in much hasty, botched work."[38] On the other hand, it did not help, as Nevins observed for 1904–05, that Detroit was a boom town where "[m]achinists, moulders, foundrymen, carpenters, lathe-operators, brass-workers, veneer-men – all were in keen demand. In the busiest months even ordinary laborers were hard to find."[39]

At times, suppliers created problems for automakers. In one memorable case, the young Alfred Sloan learned from his senior, Henry Leland, about the importance of high tolerances. Farber, in his biography of Sloan, drew two lessons from this episode. First, it testified to Leland's high standards. Thus, even though products were in general rudimentary, some automakers clearly worked hard to make their machines stand up. Second, the encounter revealed Sloan's desire to listen and learn from experienced mechanics. Farber explained: "Sloan, as both a young man and a man of middle age, was skilled at working with men older than himself as well as with men of his own generation." Sloan took lessons from the inventor, John Wesley Hyatt, whose company he eventually ran, and received important "postgraduate work" from Leland about quality in manufacturing.[40]

Henry Ford also sought to improve quality with each new model, especially his Model T. Nevins claimed that the first notices of the Model T in the spring of 1908 "evoked a dithyrambic response" among Ford's dealers. The car had many attractive features. Its body was raised to allow for plenty of clearance when traveling along bad roads; its four-cylinder engine provided twenty horsepower; its gas tank held ten gallons (for touring models); magnetos replaced dry batteries; the "entire power-plant and transmission were completely enclosed"; and vanadium steel had been employed for "crankshafts, axles, gears, and springs." Nevins observed that the vehicle's price "was not

[35] Nevins with Hill, *Ford: The Times, the Man, the Company*, 222.
[36] Ibid., 230.   [37] Ibid., 233, 239–40; on wheels, see also ibid., 399.
[38] Ibid., 247.   [39] Ibid., 269.
[40] Susan Helper, "Strategy and Irreversibility in Supplier Relations: The Case of the U.S. Automobile Industry," *Business History Review* 65 (Winter 1991): 781–824; and Farber, *Sloan Rules*, 14–15.

spectacularly low, ranging from $825 up."[41] Nor could Ford marketers claim in all sincerity that the T was perfect in all regards. So-called "Babbitt metal" had been used to make bearings for the rear axle, and Nevins recounted that "pounding on the road elongated them, requiring frequent replacements." In 1909 Ford switched to roller bearings. The lining inside transmission bands, he reported, "easily burned out until a better fabric was employed." Rivets did not always hold. Cranking the Model T was difficult, causing "endless profanity" and leading officials to tell "owners with cold garages [to] attach an electric light to a long cord and keep it burning under the hood to keep the motor warm."[42]

Even with its faults, the Model T's selling point was the quality it offered at its price: it impressed buyers as being better built than many more expensive vehicles.[43] Several developments contributed to this price/quality equation. One was vanadium steel. It resisted the many bumps along a road and did not "fatigue," or become brittle and break; and it had the virtue, as Nevins noted, of being "easier to machine than nickel steel." So important was vanadium steel that Ford advertised its virtues for nearly a decade after its first use in 1907.[44] The transmission was designed to make shifting gears easier. It often was the case that because "the metal in the transmission was soft," novice drivers would strip the gears. It did not help that "many clutches were heavy and sticky," which made shifting all the more an effort. Thus, Nevins concluded: "Much of the public was eager for a transmission which could be easily handled without damaging the mechanism, and it found the well-designed planetary system of the Model T a refreshing change." The three-point suspension, Nevins continued in his inventory of improvements, "avoided the distortion of the motor base common with a two-point suspension" when run over bumpy and gutted roads. Finally, the T's springs did not provide a soft ride, but "did free the entire body and chassis from the racking torsions then common in most cars."[45]

That the 1908 Model T marked a decided improvement over earlier vehicles was clear. One proxy of the changing quality of vehicles was the state of motorists' insurance policies. The policies both gauged improvements in vehicles, but also spoke to the dangers autos posed to people (car drivers, passengers, and bystanders) and property. In the 1890s, all an owner could obtain was fire insurance, and this coverage was limited to a car's storage – "when at rest in the owner's stable."[46] Car owners were required

---

[41] Nevins with Hill, *Ford: The Times, the Man, the Company*, 387–88.

[42] Ibid., 394.   [43] Ibid., 388.

[44] Ibid., 349. On advertising vanadium steel, see also David L. Lewis, *The Public Image of Henry Ford: An American Folk Hero and His Company* (Detroit, MI: Wayne State University Press, 1976), 36.

[45] Nevins with Hill, *Ford: The Times, the Man, the Company*, 391–92.

[46] "Automobile Insurance," *Automobile* 11 (July 18, 1903): quote 62; and Dixie Hines, "The Insuring of Automobiles," *Automobile* 11 (August 15, 1903): 160–61. On the history of

to fill gas tanks in "daylight only" and not to allow "a blaze or artificial light" in the room when filling the tank.[47] In 1902, auto fires prompted Boston underwriters to raise rates, as *Horseless Age* reported: "rates are high everywhere, and yet the companies are not at all anxious to secure the business."[48] In 1903, *The Automobile* noted that insurance companies "do not find [liability coverage] a profitable class of business, and a large number of them have, from time to time, withdrawn from the field, leaving the demand much greater than the supply."[49] Not until 1906 did underwriters offer coverage for "damage sustained by the machine itself, as well as against any liability of the owner for damage to other property arising from the collision."[50] Even in 1908, the *Eastern Underwriter* found that for coverage of liability and property damage, Fidelity & Casualty, Frankfort Casualty, Casualty Company of America, Pennsylvania Casualty, and United States Casualty, as well as other underwriters, were "leaving it strictly alone."[51]

By 1908, the quality of vehicles had improved, but the average level of reliability did not ensure that the products were sound or that manufacturers had developed methods to systematically test materials and components. One sign of the ambiguity was the insurance market. Insurers covered many more risks in 1908 than they had in 1901. Still, as noted earlier, some insurance companies remained on the sidelines in 1908, and in 1909, others reported raising rates for collision insurance.[52] In 1911, underwriters reported heavy losses in the Southeast, and two years later, one firm "stopped writing insurance in Missouri because of heavy losses."[53] Occasionally a state, such as Iowa in 1909, prohibited liability coverage.[54] The standard warranty, as outlined by the auto manufacturers' trade association, offered another gauge of the vehicle's quality. Although vehicles were much improved since 1902,

---

automobile insurance, see in general Eugene F. Hord, "History and Organization of Automobile Insurance." Speech Delivered before the Insurance Society of New York, November 11 and 18, 1919, part II, Widener Library (stacks), Harvard University, Cambridge, MA.

[47] *Weekly Underwriter* 64 (May 18, 1901): 359.

[48] "Difficulties of Automobile Insurance," *Horseless Age* 9 (June 4, 1902): 667.

[49] Hines, "The Insuring of Automobiles," quote 160.

[50] *Weekly Underwriter* 74 (January 6, 1906): 4. Prior to 1906, articles noted the demand for property coverage. See "Automobile Insurance Notes," *Automobile Topics* 1 (October 27, 1900): 48; Hines, "The Insuring of Automobiles," 160; "Automobile Insurance," 62; "Automobile Insurance Rates," *Automobile* 11 (September 19, 1903): 284; "Automobile Housing and Insurance," *Automobile* 11 (November 28, 1903): 570; and "Blanket 'Floater' Insurance Rate," *Automobile* 11 (November 28, 1903): 577.

[51] "Automobile Liability," *Eastern Underwriter* 9 (December 24, 1908): 14.

[52] *Weekly Underwriter* 81 (October 16, 1909): 289.

[53] *Weekly Underwriter* 84 (March 18, 1911): 239; and *Weekly Underwriter* 88 (February 1, 1913): 116.

[54] In 1909, the state of Iowa prohibited insurers from "protecting automobile owners from suits resulting from injuries inflicted by their cars." *Weekly Underwriter* 81 (August 28, 1909): 139; and *Weekly Underwriter* 81 (October 16, 1909): 289.

the warranty was not generous. As adopted by the auto manufacturers' trade association in 1913, the warranty covered defects in parts for ninety days after a car's delivery to its owner, thirty days more than in 1902, but still a modest length of time. Accessories not made by the manufacturer were expressly excluded, including obvious items such as batteries and tires, but also devices that were integral to the car's operation, such as the ignition apparatus.[55]

IMAGES OF RISK-TAKING AND OTHER MOTIVES FOR BUYING CARS

Underwriters may have been relieved to know that in 1910 just one percent of households owned automobiles. Yet, when viewed in terms of the early market's development, the numbers, albeit tiny, were important for their rate of growth. Because demand grew rapidly relative to the supply of vehicles, consumers created a market boom and a "cushion" for automakers to better their products' quality.[56] On one hand, manufacturers tried to assert their machines' reliability, despite evidence to the contrary. On the other, advertisers and the auto press portrayed motorists as risk-takers, often couched in terms of male daring. Whether it was a desire for risk-taking or some other motive, what proved important were desires other than the expectation of a reliable vehicle that drew the first motorists into the market.

The problem of a car's mechanics and its other attributes were the subject of early advertisements.[57] In a 1903 ad, nicely trimmed with art nouveau

---

[55] Maxwell Motor Cars, Trade Catalog, 1916, back page, Unprocessed Automobile Catalogs, Historical Collections, HBS. "A. C. of C. Adopts Standard Warranty," *Automobile* 29 (December 18, 1913): 1174. Articles still appeared calling for the careful maintenance of cars. "Daily Care of the Car is Essential," *Automobile* 29 (September 4, 1913): 421. On warranties in 1902, see "Guarantees," *Horseless Age* 9 (May 21, 1902): 598, and the description of warranties in Chapter 2.

[56] Hirschman, *Exit, Voice, and Loyalty*, 24.

[57] As historian Pamela Laird has written, advertisements "featured technical discussions appropriate to a new and expensive, exciting but intimidating technology." Although Laird treats the "early" auto industry, the date for her oldest advertisement is 1912. Her main point is that automobile manufacturers advertised their vehicles in terms of their mechanical features. Certainly, as Laird indicates, one can find many such ads of this sort. However, print advertisements were not the only way in which autos were advertised, and not all print advertisements focused on mechanics. I take her argument as an interesting reminder that the emotional advertisements associated with the 1920s did not appear from the start for automobiles. Those appeals found their way into the press in terms of stories, poems, and songs. Compare, for example, James Flink's study of the many appeals of automobiles to the advertisements treated in Laird, "'The Car without a Single Weakness,'" 796–812. Flink, *America Adopts the Automobile*, 100–12. For the 1920s, compare Laird's advertisements with those in Roland Marchand, *Advertising the American Dream: Making Way for Modernity, 1920-1940* (Berkeley, CA: University of California Press, 1985), 22, 104–105, 122, 128–29, 141, 157, 161–62, 179–81, 220, 236–37, 277–78, 304–308, 326–27, 338.

lines, Cadillac claimed its car had all the "essentials of the serviceable and safe automobile." The copy did not describe its parts, but testified to their quality: "The engine is very compact and very powerful; the transmission gear a triumph of mechanics; the steering wheel very sensitive – and absolute in its control; the brakes reliable under all conditions of grade and speed." In another advertisement with a photo of the Cadillac climbing the steps of the nation's capitol, the copy used the emphatic "most" to describe its parts: "[m]ost powerful engine; most sensitive steering device; most reliable brakes; most flexible running gear – strong and graceful body."[58] Manufacturers also ran ads intended to play up a motor car's other attributes. In 1905, Olds ran a full-page color advertisement on the back cover of the *Saturday Evening Post* claiming that its car was "An office on wheels." It advised: "The city salesman trying to do business without an Oldsmobile is like a merchant trying to do business without a telephone."[59] Appealing to sociability, Olds ran a second full-page color advertisement on the back cover of the *Post* picturing one lady in an Olds chatting to another lady standing next to her; the ad explained that the little car had "endeared itself to the feminine heart just as it has established itself in the business world."[60] Neither ad went into the details of the car's mechanics. Some simple phrases became very popular. At the Ford Motor Company, in 1907 E. LeRoy Pelletier promoted the jingle, "Watch The Fords Go By." It suited the industry's number one producer, and along with Packard's "Ask the Man who Owns One," became one of the most famous slogans in the marketing of automobiles.[61]

While the value of races, reliability runs, and other contests dimmed after 1910, Ford and other automakers received good press in the early years. Allan Nevins wrote: "The company liked to publish photographs of the indomitable little rattletrap climbing a high set of steps, chugging through a wheel-high creek, or perching itself atop some Western mountain. . . . Even in

---

[58] "Power and Control – Cadillac," *Saturday Evening Post* 175 (March 28, 1903): 19; and "The Cadillac: Up the Steps of the National Capitol," *Saturday Evening Post* 175 (May 9, 1903): 21.

[59] "An Office on Wheels – the Oldsmobile," *Saturday Evening Post* 177 (February 11, 1905), back cover.

[60] "Makes Everyone your Neighbor – the Oldsmobile," *Saturday Evening Post* 177 (March 4, 1905), back cover.

[61] Lewis, *The Public Image of Henry Ford*, 36–37, 39. Nevins with Hill, *Ford: The Times, the Man, the Company*, 345–46. A 1903 ad played on a car owner's desire to defend his or her decision to buy a Packard: "Ready to defend it enthusiastically, aggressively against attacks." This ad indirectly acknowledged the problem that many cars were not sturdy or reliable, and thus subject to criticism. Having chosen one make over other possible choices, the car buyer faced scrutiny from friends and family. See "Ask the Man who Owns One," *Saturday Evening Post* 175 (June 20, 1903): 24.

speed races on level courses the little car won its victories."[62] The prizes often were cited in advertisements as a way of proving the car's ability to stand up. Without necessarily going into the details of the mechanics, the awards presumably testified that the vehicles were sturdy and durable enough to justify the expenditure. Word circulated as well in the vast auto press. By 1910, not only did several automobile clubs publish their own journals (i.e., Hartford, Philadelphia, Washington, D.C.), but motorists could choose from a wide variety of publications devoted to the technical side of the automobile market.[63]

Apart from these appeals to reliability, historical records indicate that the vehicles' many other attributes led to a car buyer's decision to spend from $700 to $2,500 (Fig. 1.2).[64] One motivation was novelty: H. G. Buschman declared to an Olds dealer in 1903 his desire to be the first motorist in Prescott, Wisc.[65] Automobiles also offered a measure of status, and some journals catered to their high-class readership with columns such as *Automobile Topics*'s "The Automobile in Society." It reported the events of New York society elites, noting for instance that, in 1900, Andrew Carnegie had been "learning how to operate a Locomobile with great success." Events at Newport and other social happenings, such as Alfred G. Vanderbilt's marriage, were also covered.[66] Romance offered another appeal thanks to the automobile's combined attributes of privacy and mobility. Some journals

---

[62] Nevins with Hill, *Ford: The Times, the Man, the Company*, 404–406. Noting the large drop in the number of vehicles entered in the famous Glidden contest from forty-nine in 1907 to thirteen in 1909, Flink dated the end of the reliability runs to 1909 or 1910. See Flink, *America Adopts the Automobile*, 51.

[63] Among club journals, see for example, *Automobile Club of Hartford Bulletin*, *Automobile Club of Philadelphia Monthly Bulletin*, the Automobile Club of America (based out of New York) *Club Journal*, *Auto News of Washington*, *Automobile Journal* (which became *New England Automobile Journal*), and *Empire State Motorist* (for New Yorkers, which changed its name to *Motordom*). Some journals tried to satisfy all readers, such as *Horseless Age*, *American Automobile*, and *Motor Age*. Some journals focused on topics of keen interest to motorists, such as the *Good Roads Magazine*, and others focused on specific audiences, such as *Motor Body*, and *Dealer and Repairman*. Many journals are housed at the Library of Congress and the Special Collections Department of the University of Michigan, where the interested reader can spend weeks or months reviewing the many journals.

[64] Peter J. Hugill, "Technology and Geography in the Emergence of the American Automobile Industry, 1895–1915," in *Roadside America: The Automobile in Design and Culture*, ed. Jan Jennings (Ames, IA: Iowa State University Press, 1990), 33–34; and Flink, *The Automobile Age*, 33–37.

[65] H. G. Buschman, General Merchandise, to "Friend Olds," May 10, 1903, Folder 7, Box 6, Olds Papers, MSU.

[66] "The Automobile in Society," *Automobile Topics* 1 (November 3, 1900): 81–83, quote 83; and "The Automobile in Society," *Automobile Topics* 1 (January 19, 1901): 499. In the first decade of motoring, several auto journals appealed to wealthy buyers. For examples, read articles in *Automobile*, *The Automobile Magazine*, and *The American Automobile*.

FIGURE 1.2. Michelin Tire Twins, New York Automobile Carnival, 1909. Not only New Yorkers, but automobilists in cities across the United States liked to show off their cars in parades. Courtesy of the Detroit Public Library, National Automotive History Collection.

offered songs for the romance of motoring. One verse from "Love in an Automobile" read:[67]

> A society man with a mint of rocks
> Fell in love with a stately maid,
> But she loved him not, though at her
> feet
> His heart and his wealth he laid.
> At last he bought an automobile,
> For this he heard it told
> Brought Cupid's darts to feminine hearts
> When they couldn't be touched by gold.

Many other songs similarly focused on automobiles and romance. The "Ford March & Two-Step" was performed at President Taft's inaugural ball, and Ford appeared in other songs: "It's a Rambling Flivver," "The Packard and the Ford," "The Scandal of Little Lizzie Ford," and "On the Old Back Seat

[67] "Love in an Automobile," *Motor Age* 1 (June 12, 1902): 9.

of the Henry Ford," which was said to have the moon glow, as historian David Lewis observed, "on couples spooning in flivvers."[68]

Speed was another source of attraction. The press was filled with angry stories about motorists who drove too fast, but the industry thrived on racing. Long after the Winton-Ford contest, manufacturers promoted cars through reliability runs and hill climbing contests along with automobile races. Nevins recalled the events in his history of the Ford Motor Company this way: "the countless contests in hill-climbing power, distance endurance, and speed held during these years were played up in advertising, sometimes *ad nauseam*. In these years half the cities of the land seemed to be staging automobile tournaments of some kind."[69] The contests no doubt encouraged auto sales by promoting the unsafe activity of racing. The one exception to this equation were the benefits of speed for doctors, who claimed to reach their patients more quickly by car than by horse and carriage. Indeed, the proportion of doctors buying automobiles outranked the proportion of all other professions (Fig. 1.3).[70]

Another distinctive attribute among early car buyers was their sex: the vast majority were male.[71] In 1903, *Automobile* counted fifty women among Boston's 3,500 licensed motorists (who were not chauffeurs). Six years later, Alice Ramsey became the first woman to drive across the United States (Fig. 1.4). Her biography told of fixing broken axles, broken springs, busted tires, and a bad ignition coil.[72] Although she had some heavy lifting to do, historian Virginia Scharff observed that her sponsor, the Maxwell Motor Company, used the trip to say cars were tough enough to win "any man's respect, gentle enough for the daintiest lady."[73] The marketing of Alice

---

[68] Lewis, *The Public Image of Henry Ford*, 52.

[69] Nevins with Hill, *Ford: The Times, the Man, the Company*, 404–405.

[70] Flink, *America Adopts the Automobile*, 71, 99–100. See for example, W. H. Coe, "The Motor Car for Physicians and Professional Men," *Motor Car* 2 (May 1905): 212–16, SCL, UM; and "What *The* Doctors Say. A Few Brief Letters from Physicians who Think the Horse a Back Number. . . . Containing Information of Value to all Motor Car Owners," *Motor Car* 1 (December 1904): 455–60, SCL, UM. See also Gijs Mom, *The Electric Vehicle: Technology and Expectations in the Automobile Age* (Baltimore: Johns Hopkins University Press, 2004), 106–107.

[71] In the case of electric vehicles, Gijs Mom also found that few women were car owners. Mom, *The Electric Vehicle*, 59, 62, 105–106.

[72] Curt McConnell, *"A Reliable Car and A Woman Who Knows It": The First Coast-to-Coast Auto Trips by Women, 1899–1916* (Jefferson, NC: McFarland & Company, Inc., 2000), 56–57.

[73] "Four Thousand Boston Men and Women Licensed Motorists," *Automobile* 11 (October 10, 1903): 362. Virginia Scharff reported that in Tuscon, Ariz., for the year 1914, out of 425 owners of automobiles listed in the city's directory, twenty-three were women. In Houston, Texas, she found that 5.5 percent of people owning cars in the city's auto directory were women. In Los Angeles, the county's directory of auto owners reported that in 1914 "fifteen percent of new cars registered in the county appeared under women's names." Scharff noted that more women in all likelihood drove cars, but were not necessarily listed as such in

FIGURE 1.3. Eagle Rock Hill Climb, 1904. Automobile clubs conducted numerous tours and contests, including hill-climbing competitions, to promote their vehicles. Large crowds watched the events. The racer was James L. Breese; the car was a Mercedes. Courtesy of the Detroit Public Library, National Automotive History Collection.

FIGURE 1.4. Alice Ramsey, New York to Philadelphia Run, 1909. Alice Ramsey was the first woman to drive an automobile from coast to coast. Ramsey received considerable press because most drivers were male during the early 1900s. Although she encountered various mishaps, the company sponsor used the journey to tout the car's reliability. Courtesy of the Detroit Public Library, National Automotive History Collection.

Ramsey's trip fit well with distinctions the press and marketers drew along gender lines. Images of women typically communicated the expectation that the vehicle was easy to operate. Winton advertised its 1905 machine with the slogan "The Car of Simplest Control." Picturing a woman intently steering her car, the copy dwelt on the theme of simplicity (Fig. 1.5): "She can *slow* that speed down to *four* miles an hour, by simply *lightening* her foot pressure, on the same pedal. / Isn't that easy to *remember* and hard to forget?" Echoing the Oldsmobile brochure, the advertisement suggested she could run the machine as she "might run a sewing machine." Cheerfully, the text confided, "Everything that could inspire nervousness has been cut out of it."[74] Reliance Motor Car Company pictured a young woman driving its 1905 vehicle for

directories. Virginia Scharff, *Taking the Wheel: Women and the Coming of the Motor Age* (New York: Free Press, 1991), 25–26, 77. For a detailed examination of gendered distinctions in risk-taking among railroad passengers, see Welke, *Recasting American Liberty*, 84–105.
[74] "The Car of Simplest Control," *Saturday Evening Post* 177 (May 13, 1905): 23.

the advertisement, "Perfectly safe – always under absolute control of foot pedal."[75]

The contrast between male and female images was predictable for the time, as the trade press celebrated a sense of male risk-taking, replaying stories of men who achieved great feats – new hills climbed, distances covered, and mechanical puzzles solved. When the Cleveland automobile club sponsored its first hill climbing contest in 1905, *Auto Advocate* reported that the rough road and deep gulleys made "the driving doubly dangerous" and, although Harry Save finished second, "he displayed an amount of daring at dangerous points equal to that of" the contest's winner.[76] Being rugged, drivers also proved to be daredevils or "scorchers," as *Horseless Age* declared they had more money than brains and drove too fast for the safety of pedestrians, other vehicles, and their own bodies.[77] Even when it came to the subject of touring, the drivers dared to take their vehicles on near-impossible routes. *Motor Car* recounted an expedition in Nevada where the drivers forded difficult streams, placed tarp over the desert's sand in order to gain traction, and climbed mountain paths studded with boulders.[78] On a few occasions, the press pictured females competing against males. *The American Automobile* featured on the cover of its July 1900 issue a woman firmly in control of her car's levers. Graced with a pretty hat and flowing scarf, she raced past another car whose driver was made visible mostly by his Stetson, and past the bicyclists and horses.[79] Focusing on the Model T's "graces and gaucheries," Nevins went so far as to picture the owners of the early Model T this way: they "cherished an intimate affection of the unpredictable creature. No two cars were quite alike. Mastery of any one involved highly personal qualities of courage, skill, intuition, and luck. As of Cleopatra, it could be said that time could not wither nor custom stale the infinite variety of the flivver; with all its superior dependability and simplicity it combined an arch and mercurial eccentricity. It was more like a human being (of feminine gender) than any other car every known to man. To buy one was to embark on a great adventure[.]"[80]

---

[75] "Reliance Detroit," *Saturday Evening Post* 177 (February 18, 1905): 20. Gijs Mom found similar advertisements for electric vehicles in which advertisers claimed the car was easy for women to maintain. Mom, *The Electric Vehicle*, 221.

[76] "General Club News," *Auto Advocate and Country Roads* (June 1905): 21, SCL, UM.

[77] "Record Breaking Tours," *Horseless Age* 10 (July 23, 1902): 82.

[78] Grandon Nevins, "The Automobile Roughing It," *Motor Car* 2 (May 1905): 217–26, SCL, UM. Gijs Mom in his study of electric vehicles found that early buyers of gasoline vehicles were drawn to this particular technology in part because of its sense of adventure. "While electric proponents boasted about the greater reliability of their propulsion alternative, the gasoline car seemed to escape all engineering rationality by embedding itself in a male sports culture of technical challenge and adventure." Mom, *The Electric Vehicle*, 107.

[79] *The American Automobile* 1 (July 1900), cover page.

[80] Nevins with Hill, *Ford: The Times, the Man, the Company*, 395.

The Car of Simplest Control

No car in the world is so simply and reliably controlled. This is one reason why no car is so well adapted to be driven by Women as " The Winton of 1905."

There are seven other reasons why, but Winton positive Air-Control is the best of all.

Let us explain how and why this Winton Control operates so promptly and infallibly.

We will tell you all about it, and detail the other reasons why if you will drop us a line today saying you are interested.

Note the long graceful lines of the 1905 Winton Car, in picture below.

And, remember that the name "Winton" has never been identified with a "cheap" nor with an unreliable Car.

There is Prestige, as well as Safety, Comfort, and Ease of Mind, in owning a "Winton" Automobile.

A NY Woman can drive a "Winton" the first time she tries.

Because it is as simple to run as a sewing machine.

Everything that could inspire nervousness has been cut out of it.

She can start it speeding up to 60 miles an hour with the same foot she might run a sewing machine with.

She simply presses that foot on a spring pedal for Speed.

She can slow that speed down to four miles an hour, by simply lightening her foot pressure, on the same pedal.

Isn't that easy to remember and hard to forget?

The Winton Car is as sensitive to Control as a well trained horse, and ten times as reliable.

Because the horse might get scared at sight of a Motor Car, but the Winton can't get scared nor get tired.

Yet $1,800 will buy the latest improved Model C, as shown in picture below, 16-20 Horse-power.
Model B has 24-30 H. P., price $2,500.
Model B, Limousine, 24-30 H. P., $3,500.
Model A has 40-50 H. P., price $3,500.
Model A, Limousine 40-50 H.P., $4,500.
Write today for our 1905 Catalog.

THE WINTON MOTOR CARRIAGE CO.
Department M   Cleveland, O.

$1800

The ·WINTON· of 1905

FIGURE 1.5. "The Car of Simplest Control," *Saturday Evening Post* 177 (May 13, 1905): 23. This advertisement reflected a common distinction based on gender. Whereas the press celebrated a male sense of risk-taking, women were frequently pictured in advertisements as content companions or calm drivers to convey the impression that the car was easy to operate. Courtesy of the University of Texas Libraries, The University of Texas at Austin.

Above all, car owners celebrated their mechanical ingenuity.[81] In 1902, an anonymous motorist reported a near mishap. Out for a ride, the car's steering wheel suddenly could "turn freely upon the column without doing any steering." Had the vehicle been traveling at a high speed, the writer felt sure a horrible accident would have ensued. Yet rather than threaten a lawsuit, the owner explained how to fix this machine. The wheel had been attached to the column "by a left hand jam nut, but the threads in the aluminum wheel had stripped, and thus put the gear in a most dangerous state." The driver's solution: "I put a good, honest steel key into the wheel hub and column, and it has not yet become corrupted by the company it keeps."[82] Perhaps less thrilling or romantic, but also indicative of the daily trials of a motorist was the experience of F. H. Briggs. He complained in a letter to Henry Ford that his Model N gave him so many problems in 1906 that he got rid of the machine after having driven it just 500 miles. Briggs declared that it was next to "impossible to keep sufficient oil in the crank case." Bolts that held the body to the frame worked loose and demanded "practically daily care" to keep tight. He reported a "bad short-circuit" just a few days after purchasing the car, and found that the emergency brake was "absolutely worthless." Briggs nevertheless gave Ford's Boston dealer high marks for being "courteous and helpful." Still an enthusiast, he told Ford that he had "refrained from telling these facts to anyone, not wishing to do anything which might in any way tend to injure the sale of your cars." If Ford could better design his autos, Briggs confided that he would buy another one.[83]

In contrast to the problem of a product's poor quality in a mature market, as Hirschman explained, in a new market firms wanted to attract car buyers who would spend a good sum of money for a highly unreliable machine. Why did consumers enter this market? Part of the answer apparently was that many thrills substituted for product quality in drawing the very first buyers into the market – the car's novelty, its speed, its possibilities for romance, its mechanical puzzles, its opportunities for touring and adventure, or simply its symbol of high-class status. Car buyers' willingness to assume risks, and indeed their celebration of their mechanical skills, figured directly in their purchases.

THE VIRTUES OF SOCIABILITY

Celebrating their mechanical prowess meant that motorists also coped with their machines' technological shortcomings. In the new market, manufacturers who sold unreliable vehicles counted on car buyers to find the means to keep their machines running. Motorists, in turn, counted on their sociability.

---

[81] Mom also identifies this feature in *The Electric Vehicle*, 57.
[82] Anonymous, "Diary Notes of a User, Part III," *Horseless Age* 10 (October 1, 1902): 353.
[83] F. H. Briggs to Henry Ford, September 19, 1906, Folder 17, Box 181, Acc. 1, HF.

By sociability, I mean a variety of activities car buyers undertook to acquire the knowledge to operate and maintain their vehicles. The auto press, for instance, blossomed along with the booming new market. The wide variety of journals offered a form of communication among all the market's participants. In addition, motorists sought advice from car dealers, suppliers, and fellow car owners. Moreover, motorists formed local auto clubs to share advice and promote the new industry.

The auto press offered one valuable source of information. Begun in 1895, *Horseless Age* carried a "Beginner's Page" futuring topics focused on the muffler's operation, the shifting of gears, the nature of the transmission, and the regulation of fuel. *Motor Age* included a similar column along with sections for communications, questions and answers, reports of recent legislation, and patents.[84] *Motor Car* devoted several articles in 1904 to a glossary of automobile parts and terms.[85] Automobile suppliers also dispensed advice and sold auto manuals. In 1903, the supplier Andrew Lee Dyke published *Diseases of a Gasolene [sic] Automobile – and – How to Cure Them*. Dyke provided detailed descriptions of ignition systems, spark plugs, batteries, valves, tires, and other parts. He included elaborate diagrams, common problems, useful precautions, and lists of the necessary tools for a repair kit. Also sprinkled through the book were owners' queries and brief answers. Dyke's was one of the first but not the only publication intended to encourage new and would-be automobilists.[86]

Motorists also appealed to the persons who had sold them their cars. Correspondence survives for E. W. Olds, Ransom Olds's brother, who was a car dealer in Milwaukee, Wisc. In March 1903, C. H. Farnum of Baraboo, Wisc., reported soldering holes in a gas tank. The car "seems to start all right but only goes a few explosives and begins to smoke and stops." Farnum added "no instructions come with mixor [carburetor] and wish you would give me what information you can." To another car owner with carburetor problems, Olds wrote, "the gasoline mixture is a very delicate thing, a little rich, and the mixture will cause loss of power and waste of gasoline, so that a quarter of an inch turn on your needle valve means a good deal."[87]

---

[84] "Beginner's Page," *Horseless Age* 10 (July 2, 1902): 23; "Beginner's Page," *Horseless Age* 10 (July 23, 1902): 91; "Beginner's Page," *Horseless Age* 10 (October 29, 1902): 469; "Recent Automobile Patents," *Motor Age* 3 (January 1, 1903): 18; and "Useful Tips on Motor Operation," *Motor Age* 3 (January 15, 1903): 10. Flink emphasized the efforts the automobile press made to encourage the market in *America Adopts the Automobile*, 128–42.

[85] Herbert L. Towle, "The Motorists [sic] Glossary," *Motor Car* 1 (July 1904): 245–71; and idem, "The Motorists' Glossary," *Motor Car* 1 (October 1904), 367–373, both in SCL, UM.

[86] Andrew Lee Dyke, *Diseases of a Gasolene [sic] Automobile – and – How to Cure Them* (St. Louis, MO: A. L. Dyke Automobile Supply Co., 1903), HBS.

[87] W. E. Bristol, Cashier, Bank of Oakland, to E. W. Olds, March 3, 1903, Folder 3, Box 6; C. H. Farnum to Oldsmobile Co., March 6, 1903, Folder 3, Box 6; and E. W. Olds to B. C. Dinsmore, April 22, 1903, Folder 6, Box 6, all in Olds Papers, MSU.

It is difficult to determine the social standing or simply the income bracket of the market's car owners circa 1905 or 1910. That new vehicles cost, at a minimum, roughly $600 no doubt barred the vast majority of households in the lower part of the income distribution from purchasing a vehicle, save the most determined individuals. Yet, this threshold did not mean that vehicle purchases were confined to the richest one percent of families. Allan Nevins noted: "Nothing delighted Henry Ford so much as the rapid acceptance of the Model T by the rural population."[88] James Flink identified doctors, as well, and the broad, vague category of "middle class" families as early buyers.[89] Yet, the automobile press made clear that many of these early motorists were wealthy or well-connected. They used their clubs or simply their social standing to promote the market.

The Automobile Club of America (ACA) was formed in the summer of 1899 in New York, and by 1901, clubs dotted major cities like Baltimore, Chicago, San Francisco, Buffalo, and Providence, and soon thereafter they had appeared in small cities like Rockford, Ill., and Janesville, Wisc. Motorists founded nearly one hundred clubs by 1904.[90] By pooling their resources, the clubs' members were especially important in promoting automobiles during the market's very early years. First, the clubs offered technical lectures on all aspects of automobiles, and more important, provided hands-on advice with their many outings. Second, the clubs further encouraged touring by erecting sign posts along roads and writing guides listing garages and hotels in their vicinities.[91] Third, the clubs sponsored automobile shows. The shows served as valuable events where automakers could meet potential customers. In 1900, the ACA and the National Association of Automobile Manufacturers sponsored the auto show in New York, offering many spectators "their first trip on an automobile in the ring at Madison Square Garden."[92] As a fourth activity, the clubs frequently lobbied legislatures especially for better roads. In 1904, just seven percent of U.S. roads were surfaced and by 1909 the figure was just nine percent.[93] The clubs actively sought to have states allocate funds for road building, assisting

---

[88] Nevins with Hill, *Ford: The Times, the Man, the Company*, 396.

[89] Flink, *America Adopts the Automobile*, 70–74.

[90] "Club Directory," *American Automobile* 11 (April 1901): 436; and "Club News," *Auto Advocate and Country Roads* (August 1905): 23–35, SCL, UM. The subject of clubs is addressed in detail in Flink, *America Adopts the Automobile*, 144–63.

[91] "Club News," *Auto Advocate and Country Roads* (September 1905): 40, SCL, UM; "Sign Posts," *American Automobile* 11 (March 1901): 395; and Flink, *America Adopts the Automobile*, 210.

[92] "The American Automobile Industry to Date and the Show of the Automobile Club of America at Madison Square Garden," *Automobile Topics* 1 (November 10, 1900): 115–29; "The Last Day of the Show of the Automobile Club of America at Madison Square Garden," *Automobile Topics* 1 (November 17, 1900): 151–56, quote 153; "Influence of Shows on Automobile Industry," *American Automobile* 2 (February 1901): 367; and Flink, *The Automobile Age*, 30, 49.

[93] Flink, *America Adopts the Automobile*, 203, 210.

FIGURE 1.6. New York Automobile Show, 1905. During the market's very early years, auto shows helped to bring together manufacturers and potential car buyers. Courtesy of the Detroit Public Library, National Automotive History Collection.

all citizens but especially themselves. "It is obvious," one auto press writer observed, "that a club of wealthy and influential members would wield a power in stimulating legislation favorable to the interests of good roads."[94] The allocation of state resources also entailed the use of convict labor: in 1906, twenty-two states used convict labor for crushing stone. Southern states stood out; their Jim Crow policies exploited convict labor to build roads but, as one writer put it bluntly, many white southerners supported the system of chain-gang labor "because it gave them good roads."[95] In 1906 the work of the clubs had only begun. In the next two decades, members put substantial pressure on state and then federal legislatures to build roads and highways (Fig. 1.6).[96]

[94] "Automobile Clubs," *Automobile* 1 (November 1899): 11.

[95] "Convict Labor in Road Making," *Good Roads Magazine* 7 (November 1906): 897; "Convict Labor for Road Improvement," *Good Roads Magazine* 7 (February 1906): 116–18; and Alexander Lichtenstein, *Twice the Work of Free Labor: the political economy of convict labor in the New South* (New York: Verso, 1996).

[96] See for example, Flink, *The Automobile Age*, 169–87; and Owen D. Gutfreund, *20th-Century Sprawl: Highways and the Reshaping of the American Landscape* (New York: Oxford University Press, 2004), 7–59.

In celebrating their risk-taking spirit, motorists had taken the prudent step of forming social bonds with fellow motorists, dealers, and suppliers as a way to cope with the problems that they were sure to face. In one sense, their actions fit Hirschman's "voice" option, but their relations were not confined to expressing their complaints. The early motorists sought to acquire the knowledge from and develop connections with other market participants as a means for fixing existing defects. Even with these social networks, the technology got the best of many car buyers: they bore costs in money lost and injuries suffered. And yet, to the extent they kept their machines running and shouldered start-up costs, they nurtured the new market.

RISK-TAKERS AND LITIGATION

However much car buyers formed clubs and established social networks to outfox their machine's mechanical shortcomings, many buyers concluded that their vehicles failed to live up to being a reasonable commercial product. From the market's start, buyers voiced complaints to dealers such as Spragro. Often they expected dealers to fix their vehicles, but no matter how skilled the mechanic, not all problems could be remedied.[97] At the extreme of Hirschman's "voice" option, many buyers became sufficiently exasperated with their horseless carriages and decided to sue automakers. Even if car buyers were not among the very wealthiest, they could be sufficiently well off to fund protracted legal battles, and lawsuits involved all market participants – automakers, car buyers, dealers, and suppliers. The cases fell into different legal categories, but they shared a common denominator in the problem of defects.[98]

Defects rendered the most serious damage in the form of personal injury. In 1902, for example, a dealer reported to *Motor Age* that after having sold a defective steering apparatus to a car owner, he found himself "uncomfortably near a law suit" when the part broke, damaging the machine and causing the passengers to be "terribly injured."[99] Although many accidents were not due to defects, vehicle defects contributed to numerous accidents. When the Electric Vehicle Company ran a cab service in 1900, a driver complained that a short circuit had caused his machine to catch fire; in another case, two buses collided owing to one vehicle's defective brakes.[100] Automakers also

---

[97] Efforts by Ford's management to control automobile repairs are examined in Stephen L. McIntyre, "The Failure of Fordism: Reform of the Automobile Repair Industry, 1913–1940," *Technology and Culture* 41 (April 2000): 269–99.

[98] The growing variety and number of cases are reflected in new editions of treatises devoted to automobiles. See, for example, C. P. Berry, *The Law of Automobiles*, 4th ed. (Chicago: Callaghan and Company, 1924); and Xenophon P. Huddy, *The Law of Automobiles*, 5th ed., ed. Arthur F. Curtis (Albany, NY: Matthew Bender & Co., 1919).

[99] P. J. Dasey, "Dealer Corroborates Complaint of User," *Motor Age* 1 (February 6, 1902): 12.

[100] Harry Phelps and H. C. Becker, two untitled descriptions of accident, July 30, 1900, and William [illegible], untitled description of accident, September 13, 1900, Folder 5-1,

acknowledged their general concern about liability in terms of testing vehicles. After Ford testers were involved in car accidents, the company's board of directors decided in January 1906 to obtain "a liability policy ... covering the Company against damage suits or claims for personal injury caused by any of its employes [sic] while driving automobiles in any part of the United States or Canada" with the "premium not to exceed $5,000,000."[101]

More common than personal injury, however, were the many frustrations car buyers voiced about trying to get their machines to operate properly. In 1905 and 1906, Ford owners spoke of both their continued patience, but also their exasperation. W. Benton Crisp complained to Ford's New York branch manager that within two months of ownership his 1905 car had required two new axles. He heard that Ford had had so much trouble with its supplier that officials "had either commenced or were about to commence an action against" the supplier "for breach of contract in supplying the faulty axles." Crisp concluded: "if the Ford Company [was] damaged by that transaction, each of its customers must likewise have been damaged."[102] Morton E. Duncan was sufficiently exasperated with his Model B that, in 1905, he sued Ford on account of the car's "defective construction." His settlement required that Ford install new "cooling apparatus, new steering column, steering wheel and new dash-board." Provided Ford carried out these requests, Duncan agreed to "use his best influences to promote the sale of Ford Motor Company's cars in the City of Philadelphia and vicinity."[103]

Other car buyers were not as charitable as Duncan. Many lawsuits finding their way to the appellate courts concerned breach of warranty and efforts to recover the full sum buyers had paid for their vehicles. In *Beecroft v. Van Schaick* (N.Y. 1907), Edgar Beecroft had purchased a car with an express warranty but found that despite "repeated attempts to remedy the defects" the car failed to perform satisfactorily. He sued for the return of $685 that

Box 5, Acc. 1750, HF. In his study of electric vehicles, David A. Kirsch reported that many New Yorkers applauded the Electric Vehicle Company's cab service but "[a] handful of complaints about 'incompetent and reckless' drivers was accompanied by lawsuits" in 1899. In some cases what consumers took as the bus drivers' "recklessness" had been conditioned by the vehicles' defects. Kirsch, *The Electric Vehicle and the Burden of History*, 48.

[101] Ford Motor Company Minute Books, September 29, 1904, 54, November 8, 1904, 64, and January 9, 1906, 84, Book #1, Box 1, Acc. 85, HF. See also settlements from these years as reported in Folder "General Legal Records – Claim Releases – Damage Suits – 1903–1926," Box 1, Acc. 483, HF. Among cases involving testers, see *Roach v. Hinchcliff; Roach v. Winton Motor Carriage Co.*, 101 N.E. 383 (Mass. 1913); *Parker v. Matheson Motor Car Company*, 88 A. 653 (Pa. 1913); and *Oakland Motor Co. v. American Fidelity Co.*, 155 N.W. 729 (Mich. 1916).

[102] W. Benton Crisp to Mr. Plantiff, May 26, 1906, Box 37, Acc. 2, HF.

[103] Settlement between Morton E. Duncan and the Ford Motor Company, November 23, 1905, Folder "General Legal Records – Claim Releases – Damage Suits – 1903–1926," Box 1, Acc. 483, HF; and Directors' Minutes, November 17, 1905, 82, Book #1, Box 1, Acc. 85, HF.

he had originally paid for the vehicle.[104] After a car owner in Wisconsin attempted several times to have the dealer make his car operate properly, he also sued to recover the purchase price.[105] In 1906, Morris Osburn acquired a vehicle from Ford's Chicago branch. At the trial, the municipal judge observed: "the machine when received by the plaintiff, and subsequently thereto, did not operate properly, and we do not understand this to be denied by the defendant." The judge added, "nothing seemed radically wrong with it," and thought a good mechanic could put the car in proper order. Yet, the good mechanic did not fix the machine, and instead Osburn shipped the vehicle from Wisconsin back to Chicago. The car burned in a fire, and its destruction set the stage for the lawsuit. Although Ford won the case, the firm could have avoided this conflict had it manufactured a vehicle free of serious defects.[106]

Like Osburn, other buyers lost cases even when they felt the product was defective. One group of cases in which the courts granted a good deal of leeway to sellers concerned the legal doctrine of "seller's talk."[107] In *Morley v. Consolidated Mfg. Co.* (Mass. 1907) the buyer complained to the court that he bought a car when the sales agent had said it "was in first class condition, and all right" and two months later the crankshaft broke. The court found no express or implied warranty, however. At the time of purchase, the car was in good working order; the plaintiff knew the car had been a demonstration car; he also paid half the price of a new vehicle. Judge Hammond called the sales agent's remarks "mere seller's talk."[108] Claude Alfred, a U.S. mail carrier, sued a dealership in 1912 when a used car did not fulfill the seller's claim that it "would give swifter and better service than the horse" Alfred rode. The court ruled against Alfred, finding that the vendor's statement amounted to an opinion and not a fact. The court further noted that the buyer named no specific defect in the car, other than it often failed to work.[109]

---

[104] *Beecroft v. Van Schaick*, 104 N.Y.S. 458 (1907). C. P. Berry, *A Treatise on the Law Relating to Automobiles* (Chicago: Callaghan, 1909), 209.

[105] *Greene v. Curtis Automobile Company*, 129 N.W. 410 (Wis. 1911).

[106] *Ford Motor Company v. Morris R. Osburn*, 140 Ill. App. 633 (1908). Other cases followed from a car's defects and a buyer's efforts to recover the price paid for a new or used vehicle. See, for example, *Pitcher v. Webber*, 68 A. 593 (Me. 1907); *Boulware v. Victor Automobile Manufacturing Company*, 134 S.W. 7 (Mo. Ct. App. 1911); *Bedford v. The Hol-Tan Company*, 128 N.Y.S. 578 (1911); and *Klock v. Newbury*, 114 P. 1032 (Wash. 1911).

[107] "Seller's talk" predated the automobile. Consider one case involving mules who were claimed to be "sound as a dollar." *Robinson v. Harvey*, 82 Ill. 58 (1876). See also *Duffany v. Ferguson*, 66 N.Y. 482 (1876). Both Berry and Huddy cited cases involving seller's talk. See Berry, *A Treatise on the Law Relating to Automobiles*, 209; and Xenophon P. Huddy, *The Law of Automobiles*, 3rd ed., ed. Howard C. Joyce (Albany, NY: Matthew Bender & Company, 1912), 348.

[108] *Morley v. Consolidated Mfg. Co.*, 81 N.E. 993 (Mass. 1907).

[109] *Farris and Barger v. Alfred and Alfred*, 171 Ill. App. 172 (1912).

In contrast to these two cases, George Joslyn linked his vehicle's defects to the legal question of product misrepresentation. Joslyn paid $3,218 for a new Cadillac and discovered that the machine would not climb the hills of Omaha, Nebraska. He complained that its engine never met the advertised rating of thirty horsepower.[110] In other words, Joslyn charged that Cadillac had misrepresented the engine's horsepower in its mass advertising. In court, witnesses for Cadillac testified that thanks to the interchangeability of parts, all engines with the same 4-3/8 bore and five-inch stroke met a thirty h.p. rating. Testifying for the plaintiff, however, Mortimer Cooley, a professor of mechanical engineering at the University of Michigan, noted that "a jig and templet [sic] is commonly employed in manufacturing machines." Although the parts are identical or uniform, they must be "fitted exactly" when put together.[111] As such, many possible deviations could reduce the engine's actual power. Because interchangeability for mass production had yet to be perfected, Cooley testified that Cadillac could not use a theoretical standard to claim the car met its advertised rating.

Defects figured as well in conflicts between dealers and manufacturers, especially regarding lost sales. On June 29, 1904, a Ford dealer in Los Angeles wrote to Henry Ford complaining about the vehicles' brakes, clutch cones, carburetors, and transmission gears. "Rectify[ing]" these defects would not "cost" Ford "one cent," the dealer continued, but it would cost himself a great deal. "Your guarantee includes workmanship as well as material and if you do not intend to re-imburse us for making these things right, how are we to interpret that clause in your guarantee, as you certainly would not expect us to ship these new machines back to the factory in order to have these little defects in workmanship made right."[112] Arthur F. Neale sued the American Electric Vehicle Company in 1902, complaining that he had been unable to sell a vehicle to the Jordan, Marsh Company because it was defective. He further contended that the loss of this sale so tainted his products he could not sell any EVC vehicles in the local Boston market.[113] In 1905, two dealers similarly complained that the Wayne Automobile Company sold them such defective vehicles that they failed to make nearly as many sales as they thought they should have.[114] In 1904, the Reid Manufacturing Company refused to pay its supplier, Buick Motor Company, claiming the parts were defective. Reid managers pointed to costly repairs their Oakland dealer

---

[110] Records and Briefs for *Joslyn*, 4–5, 19, 23, RG 276, NA, Chicago.
[111] Records and Briefs for *Joslyn*, 65, RG 276, NA, Chicago.
[112] G. T. Stamm to Henry Ford, June 29, 1904, Folder 4, Box 181, Acc. 1, HF. On the general problem of repairs, see McIntyre, "The Failure of Fordism."
[113] Plaintiff's Bill of Exceptions, 1–2, and Brief for Plaintiff, 1, Records and Briefs for *Neale*.
[114] Bill of Complaint, 1–3, Master's Report, 16–26, Plaintiff's Objections to the Master's Report, 29–30, Records and Briefs for *Masters*.

undertook as well as sales they lost to their New York agent.[115] In 1909, a Georgia dealer canceled his 1908 contract, explaining to the manufacturer that "several White Steamers belonging to Atlanta owners have been badly damaged or destroied [sic] by fire during the past few years, which fact seems to have created considerable local prejudice against your car."[116]

By the time Henry Ford introduced his Model T and Billy Durant organized General Motors, automakers had faced a host of complaints about their vehicles. Even if many consumers shouldered the costs associated with their vehicles' defects, they also demanded satisfaction from dealers and manufacturers, and a minority of car buyers sued them. Some dealers and suppliers likewise sued automakers over defects. Even in cases where the seller won the dispute in court, the outcome did not reflect well on the manufacturer or the market. Indeed, unable to sell reliable and durable machines, manufacturers found themselves promoting a market without a clear basis for inviting consumers' trust. The lack of trust was fostered by the products' poor quality, and exacerbated by dealers' seller's talk and by automakers' legal strategies.

CONCLUSION

Purchasing a product of which the defects hardly seemed to warrant its high price, the first car buyers played critical roles in getting the market started. Whereas Hirschman had coined the concepts "exit" and "voice" to characterize consumers' options when faced with a product's poor quality in a mature market, the problem of product quality had different implications for consumers in a new market. It did not matter that most potential car buyers could not afford or chose not to spend money on what they may well have perceived to be an extravagance – or worse, a losing proposition. What mattered were those buyers who did choose to purchase vehicles, and that enough of them wanted cars to keep demand running ahead of supply. That the market's first buyers spent large sums for defective machines, in turn, invites a set of propositions about their role in the creation of this new market.

First, spending large sums of money for imperfect machines, car buyers suggested that desires other than reliability and durability had motivated their purchases. A vehicle's mechanical puzzles, the thrill of driving fifteen or twenty-five miles per hour, a sense of adventure, novelty, and social status

[115] Testimony of Harmon J. Hunt, 63–64, 77–81, 103–10, Testimony of David D. Buick, 65–66, Exhibit 79, The Irgens Auto Co. to Reid Manufacturing Company, June 16, 1904, 225–28, Exhibit 97, 236–38, Records and Briefs for *Buick*.
[116] American Motor Car Co. to White Company, April 16, 1908, Exhibit A, 26, Records and Briefs for *White*.

attracted a small number of buyers to the market. Whatever reason compelled the market's first consumers to purchase vehicles, once having done so, they became risk-takers. That is, they now owned highly imperfect machines that put themselves, other travelers, and pedestrians at risk of injury and financial losses.

Second, rather than deal with this risk-taking directly, the auto press and manufacturers tried to reassure buyers about the vehicles' reliability; at the same time, they promoted daring images of risk-taking. From the market's start, car racing was a popular sport. The auto press toadied to male motorists promoting tales of adventure and mechanical know-how. Female motorists often served to illustrate the dubious claim that cars were reliable. Exceeding the boundaries of convention, the press occasionally pictured a female racer passing her male rival, and conversely the press poked fun at a male driver's mishaps. But the dominant themes served to reinforce the image of men taking risks and succeeding in their motor cars.

A third characteristic concerned buyers' willingness to cope with their machines' defects. In his account of established markets, Hirschman spoke of consumers exercising their "voice" option, but in the case of an early market, the role of buyers fixing their machines was not simply a matter of voicing complaints to dealers and automakers, which of course they did. By "coping," I mean to emphasize that car owners also relied on fellow motorists to keep their machines running. Hirschman wrote of the importance of "alert" and "inert" consumers. "The alert customers provide firms with a feedback mechanism which starts the effort at recuperation while the inert customers provide it with the time and dollar cushion needed for this effort to come to fruition."[117] Something analogous applied in the case of autos. Many buyers, though not inert, were patient and resourceful. Rather than expect a viable commercial market with a sound product, they counted on their sociability to cope with their machines. They corresponded with each other through the auto press, joined auto clubs, purchased how-to books, and wrote to dealers, suppliers, and other motorists. Indeed, because vehicles were so rudimentary, it is hard to imagine the market getting started had it not been for consumers who sought out the advice of other market participants. Even as they absorbed many costs and even incurred substantial losses and injuries, they nurtured the new market.

A fourth characteristic associated with the early automobile market was the lack of trust among market participants fostered by the product's defects. In many markets, entrepreneurs had made good on their pledge to build consumers' loyalty through their dedication to the product's quality.[118] Yet,

---

[117] Hirschman, *Exit, Voice, and Loyalty*, 24.
[118] See especially the cases discussed in Nancy F. Koehn, *Brand New: How Entrepreneurs Earned Consumers' Trust from Wedgwood to Dell* (Boston: Harvard Business School Press, 2001).

in the early automobile market, the wide range of possible imperfections resulted in disputes among all the participants – car buyers, dealers, manufacturers, and suppliers. The disputes fell under different legal categories, not only or even mostly personal injury, but also product misrepresentation, breach of warranty, and seller's talk.

A fifth distinctive characteristic among car buyers was their willingness to sue sellers. In comparison to Hirschman's alert customers, what proved important in the development of the auto market was a small number of car buyers so put out by their products' poor quality that they took retailers and manufacturers to court. Their lawsuits had two important consequences. First, in suing retailers and manufacturers, these buyers proved important for asking: who should bear the social costs of innovation? Their cases called attention to the legal platform upon which inventors and entrepreneurs developed the novel device and fostered a commercial market. Second, by filing lawsuits, the plaintiffs forced the issue: how should small firms in a struggling market cope with their products' defects? Both questions are addressed in the next chapter, and both remind us that innovation is political.

2

New Firms and the Problem of Social Costs

On May 17, 1910, Donald C. MacPherson purchased a Buick runabout from the Close Brothers dealership of Schenectady, New York.[1] The new rig sported a "four cylinder, twenty-two and a half horse power" engine, allowing it to reach a speed of fifty miles per hour. Its body had been painted "French gray" and a similar gray color coated the wooden wheels. The runabout accommodated two passengers in the front seat and one in the rumble seat. Though smaller and slower than other cars on the market in 1910, the Buick served MacPherson's purposes. During the summer and fall, he drove the machine to various places in the vicinity of Saratoga Springs for his business as a stone cutter who specialized in making gravestones. Like many motorists in this early market, he stored his runabout in a barn that winter and put it back into service the following May. The auto gave him no serious trouble until July 25. Then, while traveling at a moderate speed along a road leading into Saratoga Springs, the car's left rear wheel collapsed; the machine overturned and trapped MacPherson beneath the rear axle.[2] He later testified that his "eye (right eye) [had] torn apart entirely, [and] laid down from the eye brow," and that his right arm "had broken at the wrist." He suffered such great pain in his right wrist that for many months he could not perform his work as a stone cutter because he lacked the strength to grip his tools. His eyes deteriorated: first his right eye and then his left eye began failing, making it difficult for him to identify clients and friends.[3]

---

[1] MacPherson appeared to have made a good buy, paying $825, well below the asking price of $1,000. The dealer reported: "Mr. MacPherson paid us a check of $750 and we took a second hand car from him valued at $75, making a total of $825." George H. Close, testimony, 36–37, quote 37, Records and Briefs for *MacPherson*. The 1910 Buick runabout is illustrated and its specifications are described in Francois Therou, *Buick "The Golden Era" 1903–1915* (Brea, CA: Decir Publishing Company, 1971), 132–50.

[2] MacPherson's accident is described in *MacPherson v. Buick Motor Co.*, 138 N.Y.S. 224 (N.Y. 1912), 225. Details about testimony and briefs for the case can be found in Complaint, 3–7, and Donald C. MacPherson, testimony, 15–20, Records and Briefs for *MacPherson*. The accident is also described in David W. Peck, *Decision at Law* (New York: Dodd, Mead & Company, 1961), 41–42.

[3] Donald C. MacPherson, testimony, 21–24, quote 21, Records and Briefs for *MacPherson*; and Complaint, 5, Records and Briefs for *MacPherson*.

Soon after his accident, Macpherson sued the Buick Motor Company (a division of General Motors) for negligence. Believing that the hickory spokes used for the car's left rear wheel were rotten, and that this defect had caused his accident and injuries, he asked: Who should bear the costs born out of an imperfect machine in a new market? Who was responsible for the social costs of innovation? Between 1900 and 1916, automakers worked on two answers to these questions. First, they invested in business activities as part of the modern firm, including mass production, industrial research, and a system of dealer franchises. Such undertakings fostered a commercial market and helped produce safer machines, but they took effect slowly. During these years, autos still presented serious defects. As a second answer, automakers adopted the franchise sales contract as their method of mass distribution. This arrangement let managers take advantage of the legal concept of privity of contract and impose many costs of innovation on buyers.

How automakers balanced their conflicting inclinations may be understood in terms of what legal historian Robert Gordon called the "bright" and "dark" sides of relational contracting.[4] On the bright side, automakers fostered long-term bonds with dealers, suppliers, and research entities. These actors made possible the design of sturdier and safer vehicles. Stewart Macaulay and Ian Macneil observed that, despite the neoclassical image of markets as "discrete transactions," economic actors formed on-going relations as a critical part of their efforts to develop markets. Macaulay called particular attention to the auto dealer's franchise contract as an example of this effort at long-term relations. Yet, on the dark side, manufacturers counted on their relations with suppliers and dealers to deflect many costs associated with a new market. In particular, firms took advantage of the legal concept of privity of contract – the requirement that the plaintiff have a contract with the party being sued. Because car buyers purchased vehicles from a franchised car dealer, who in turn had purchased the machines from a manufacturer, the consumer lacked a contract upon which to sue the manufacturer. Viewed from a market perspective, the manufacturer and the dealer had engaged in a discrete transaction. As such, the manufacturer was not liable for its retailers' actions and not liable to consumers as third parties.[5] Writing before Macaulay, Friedrich Kessler studied the power corporations

---

[4] Robert W. Gordon, "Macaulay, Macneil, and the Discovery of Solidarity and Power in Contract Law," *Wisconsin Law Review* (May/June 1985): 565–79.

[5] Stewart Macaulay, *Law and the Balance of Power: The Automobile Manufacturers and Their Dealers* (New York: Russell Sage Foundation, 1966); Ian Macneil, "Economic Analysis of Contractual Relations: Its Shortfalls and the Need for a 'Rich Classificatory Apparatus,'" *Northwestern University Law Review* 75 (February 1981): 1018–61; idem, "Bureaucracy and Contracts of Adhesion," *Osgoode Hall Law Journal* 22 (Spring 1984): 5–28; Gordon, "Macaulay, Macneil, and the Discovery of Solidarity and Power in Contract Law," 565–79; and Gillian K. Hadfield, "Problematic Relations: Franchising and the Law of Incomplete Contracts," *Stanford Law Review* 42 (April 1990): 927–92.

exercised through the franchise sales contract rather than an agency relationship. I offer an explanation for why they chose the franchise contract in terms of the social costs of innovation in a newly emerging market.[6]

As a cautionary note, I do not argue that liability for defects was the sole factor leading to the adoption of auto franchising. Rather, liability represented one important factor among others.[7] Moreover, although vehicles, being crude, advertised their defects in the market's first five to ten years, as time passed and cars worked reasonably well, they still contained defects,

---

[6] Friedrich Kessler, "Automobile Dealer Franchises: Vertical Integration by Contract," *Yale Law Journal* 66 (July 1957): 1135–90; Macaulay, *Law and the Balance of Power*; Macneil, "Economic Analysis of Contractual Relations," 1018–61; idem, "Bureaucracy and Contracts of Adhesion," 5–28; Hadfield, "Problematic Relations," 927–92; and Gordon, "Macaulay, Macneil, and the Discovery of Solidarity and Power in Contract Law," 565–79. Steven P. Croley and Jon D. Hanson singled out Kessler's impact on "the first generation of product liability scholars and judges" in "Rescuing the Revolution: the Revived Case for Enterprise Liability," *Michigan Law Review* 91 (February 1993): 691 n. 29, quote 708–709. Friedrich Kessler, "Contracts of Adhesion – Some Thoughts About Freedom of Contract," *Columbia Law Review* 43 (1943): 629–42. On Kessler's influence, see also George L. Priest, "The Invention of Enterprise Liability: A Critical History of the Intellectual Foundations of Modern Tort Law," *Journal of Legal Studies* 14 (December 1985): 461–527. In his studies of corporate power, Hanson combined the insights of legal realists and critical legal scholars. See Jon D. Hanson and David Yosifon, "The Situation: An Introduction to the Situational Character, Critical Realism, Power Economics, and Deep Capture," *University of Pennsylvania Law Review* 152 (November 2003): 129–346. John Henry Schlegel explored realists' empirical studies in *American Legal Realism and Empirical Social Science* (Chapel Hill, NC: University of North Carolina Press, 1995).

[7] My complaint is that economic and business historians have overlooked liability, in general, and defects, in particular, as factors in managers' decisions. Of most importance, liability for defective products (or other problems) is omitted in the major works in the field. See especially, Alfred D. Chandler, Jr., *The Visible Hand: The Managerial Revolution in American Business* (Cambridge, MA: Harvard University Press, 1977); idem, *Scale and Scope: The Dynamics of Industrial Capitalism* (Cambridge, MA: Harvard University Press, 1990); and Oliver E. Williamson, *The Economic Institutions of Capitalism: Firms, Markets, Relational Contracting* (New York: Free Press, 1985). Economists have written at length about franchising, but in my survey of the literature I did not find that they had examined the impact of liability on a firm's structure. See, for example, Antony W. Dnes, "The Economic Analysis of Franchise Contracts," *Journal of Institutional and Theoretical Economics* 152 (June 1996): 297–324; Paul Rubin, "The Theory of the Firm and the Structure of the Franchise Contract," *Journal of Law and Economics* 21 (April 1978): 223–33; and Patrick J. Kaufmann and Francine LaFontaine, "Costs of Control: The Source of Economic Rents for McDonald's Franchisees," *Journal of Law and Economics* 37 (October 1994): 417–53. The business historian Thomas S. Dicke identified liability as a factor in Ford's reliance on the franchise contract, but did not explore the implications of liability for autos or firms in other industries. Dicke relied on the scholarship of Charles Mason Hewitt, Jr., who traced the evolution of dealer agreements, but his treatment of defects was flawed. Thomas S. Dicke, *Franchising in America: The Development of a Business Method, 1840-1980* (Chapel Hill, NC: University of North Carolina Press, 1992), 66–67; and Charles Mason Hewitt, Jr., *Automobile Franchise Agreements* (Homewood, IL: Richard D. Irwin, Inc., 1956), 37–38.

though they were not as readily apparent to auto owners. Under these market conditions, the privity requirement served to block many consumer lawsuits and, in doing so, left unquestioned the ways in which corporations had designed the vehicles causing the accidents (Fig. 2.1).

It mattered then that MacPherson's lawsuit came during the Progressive era. As Americans questioned the power corporations exercised in the market place, the courts began to find more and more exceptions to the privity requirement.[8] MacPherson offered one important example of the issues at stake. His first trial ended when the judge dismissed the complaint. He appealed, and the state's Appellate Division for the Third Department reversed the judgment and granted a new trial. In March 1913, the jury rendered a verdict for MacPherson amounting to $5,025.[9] Buick then appealed, but in January 1914 the Appellate Division affirmed the judgment for MacPherson. Justice John M. Kellogg found that Buick "owed a duty to all purchasers of automobiles to make a reasonable inspection and test to ascertain whether the wheels purchased and put in use by it were reasonably

---

[8] In their analysis of the privity requirement as it related to product liability, legal scholars typically have singled out the English case, *Winterbottom v. Wright*, 10 M. & W. 109 Eng. Rep. 402 (Ex. 1842), in which a mail coach's driver was injured when the coach broke and overturned. The driver sought compensation not from his employer, the Postmaster General, but instead from the company that had contracted with the postmaster for maintaining the coach. The court declared that the plaintiff could not recover because he was not in privity of contract with the coach's manufacturer. In the United States, the courts soon began finding exceptions to the privity requirement. In 1858, in a New York case in which the defendant had mislabeled a bottle of belladonna (a poison) as a bottle of dandelion extract, a safe liquid, and sold the bottle to a druggist, who in turn sold the bottle to another retailer, who sold the bottle to the ultimate user, who was injured when she consumed the contents, the court, recognizing that the sale of the poison had been made to a druggist, reasoned: "The injury therefore was not likely to fall on him, or on his vendee who was also a dealer; but much more likely to be visited on a remote purchaser, as actually happened." Finding that the defendant's actions put the plaintiff's "life in imminent danger," the court took exception to *Winterbottom* and affirmed the judgment for the plaintiff. *Thomas v. Winchester*, 6 N.Y. 397 (1852), 409. The courts spent several decades enlarging exceptions to the privity requirement. See for example, *Devlin v. Smith*, 89 N.Y. 470 (1882); *Huset v. J. I. Case Threshing Mach. Co.*, 120 F. 865 (8th Cir. 1903); *Kuelling v. Roderick*, 75 N.E. 1098 (N.Y. 1905); and *Statler v. Ray Manufacturing Company*, 88 N.E. 1063 (N.Y. 1909). Among legal reviews of this topic, see Edward H. Levi, *An Introduction to Legal Reasoning* (Chicago: University of Chicago Press, 1949), 7–19; Jonathan Luri, "Lawyers, Judges, and Legal Change, 1852–1916: New York as a Case Study," *Working Papers from the Regional Economic History Research Center*, vol. 3, ed. Glenn Porter and William H. Mulligan, Jr. (Wilmington, DE: Eleutherian Mills-Hagley Foundation, 1980), 31–56; Croley and Hanson, "Rescuing the Revolution," 695–97; and John C. P. Goldberg and Benjamin C. Zipursky, "The Moral of *MacPherson*," *University of Pennsylvania Law Review* 146 (August 1998): 1750–52.

[9] *MacPherson* (1912); and Statement, 1–2, and Judgment of March 10, 1913, 12, Records and Briefs for *MacPherson*.

FIGURE 2.1. Although Donald Macpherson's accident had been caused by a rotten wooden wheel, defects took many forms. A broken axle caused this automobile accident, circa 1912. Courtesy of the Detroit Public Library, National Automotive History Collection.

fit for the purposes for which it used them."[10] Buick appealed again, but Judge Benjamin Cardozo upheld the lower court's ruling. In *MacPherson v. Buick* (N.Y. 1916), Cardozo built on earlier cases when he ruled for the Court of Appeals of New York that Buick "was not at liberty to put the finished product on the market without subjecting the component parts to ordinary and simple tests."[11]

[10] *MacPherson v. Buick*, 145 N.Y.S. 462 (N.Y. 1914), 465.
[11] *MacPherson v. Buick*, 111 N.E. 1050 (N.Y. 1916), 1055. The legal literature concerning Cardozo is abundant. Levi, *An Introduction to Legal Reasoning*, 7–19; Croley and Hanson, "Rescuing the Revolution," 683–797; Goldberg and Zipursky, "The Moral of *MacPherson*," 1733–1847; Andrew L. Kaufman, *Cardozo* (Cambridge, MA: Harvard University Press, 1998), 265–85; Lurie, "Lawyers, Judges, and Legal Change, 1852-1916," 31–56; and William E. Nelson, *The Legalist Reformation: Law, Politics, and Ideology in New York, 1920–1980* (Chapel Hill, NC: University of North Carolina Press, 2001), 93–107, 187–88. Distinctly valuable for its extensive review of automobile cases is Cornelius W. Gillam, *Products Liability in the Automobile Industry: A Study in Strict Liability and Social Control* (Minneapolis, MN: University of Minnesota Press, 1960). Valuable in linking Cardozo's ruling to engineers' ideas about managers and industrial accidents is John Fabian Witt, "Speedy Fred Taylor and the Ironies of Enterprise Liability," *Columbia Law Review* 103 (January 2003): 1–49.

When MacPherson filed his lawsuit against Buick in 1911, as part of its defense Buick claimed that the plaintiff had sued the wrong party. The automaker was not liable, its lawyers contended, since it had sold the car to a franchised dealer, the Close Brothers, and the dealer in turn had sold the car to MacPherson.[12] E. Wells Johnson brought a similar complaint, claiming Cadillac was negligent in the sale of a car whose defective wheel caused his accident and injuries. Relying on its 1908 dealer franchise agreement, Cadillac contended that the car buyer lacked a contract upon which to bring his lawsuit.[13] During much of the nineteenth century, consumers lacked a contract upon which to sue manufacturers simply because most corporations were not integrated. Companies typically distributed their wares through wholesalers, jobbers, or other middlemen who peddled their goods to local retailers – grocers, druggists, dry goods merchants – who in turn sold products to consumers.[14] This relationship changed when, for the sake of achieving new gains in efficiency, managers integrated distribution within the modern firm. Retailers became a firm's sales agents and the firm became liable for their sales agents' actions. Automakers, by contrast, placed concerns about liability for defects ahead of gains in efficiency. Although they were young firms in a new market, by 1909 most automakers had settled on a method of distribution as a system of franchises (Fig. 2.2).

As Alfred Chandler explained in *The Visible Hand*, the integration of mass distribution and mass production was distinctive to the modern firm. It constituted a critical link in a chain of business activities from the acquisition of raw materials to a good's final sale, a process Chandler called "vertical integration." Precisely because of their products' technological complexity, managers wanted to integrate distribution within the firm. That is, they wanted specialized sales agents to market and service their products. Examples included Remington, a maker of office machinery, and manufacturers of heavy machinery, such as the Otis Elevator Company, Western Electric, and Babcock & Wilcox.[15] Charles McCurdy similarly noted that the sewing machine manufacturer, Singer, replaced independent retailers with

---

[12] George H. Close, testimony, 36, Records and Briefs for *MacPherson*.

[13] *Johnson v. Cadillac Motor Car Co.*, 261 F. 878 (2nd Cir. 1919).

[14] Glenn Porter and Harold C. Livesay, *Merchants and Manufacturers: Studies in the Changing Structure of Nineteenth-Century Marketing* (Baltimore: Johns Hopkins University Press, 1971).

[15] Ibid; Chandler, *The Visible Hand*, 302–14, 403, quote 308–309; Harold C. Passer, "Development of Large-Scale Organization: Electrical Manufacturing Around 1900," *Journal of Economic History* 12 (Autumn 1952): 378–95; and Michael Massouh, "Technological and Managerial Innovation: The Johnson Company, 1883-1898," *Business History Review* 50 (Spring 1976): 46–68.

its own retail outlets as of 1879.[16] Between the 1880s and the early 1900s, many corporations established marketing systems based on salaried sales agents. Although Chandler did not explore the legal ramifications of these decisions, firms that relied on salaried agents were liable for their agents' actions (Fig. 2.3).[17]

When automakers defined their relations with dealers through a franchise sales agreement, Friedrich Kessler called this method of distribution "vertical integration by contract."[18] Auto dealers, much like the retailers Chandler cited, sold a complex machine and sunk large investments in their local markets. Although manufacturers did not make dealers salaried employees, they wanted on-going relations with their retailers. They chose between two different arrangements – an agency contract or a franchise sales contract. The courts ruled that where cars were sold outright to a dealer (not on commission) and where a dealer was prohibited from making a contract with car buyers in the company's name, the contract was treated as a sales (not an agency) contract. The distinction mattered to a firm's administrative control and its liability. With an agency contract, the manufacturer, as the principal, directly controlled its dealers as its agents. Further, the manufacturer as principal was liable for its dealers' actions. A sales contract, however, implied an immediate exchange: firms sold cars to dealers at a discounted price and dealers resold cars to consumers at a retail price. As such, manufacturers held no direct control over dealers. They also were not liable for their retailers' actions, and not liable to consumers as third parties.[19]

---

[16] Charles McCurdy, "American Law and the Marketing Structure of the Large Corporation, 1875–1890," *Journal of Economic History* 38 (September 1978): 636–37. See as well, Chandler, *The Visible Hand*, 303–307; and Dicke, *Franchising in America*, 32–45.

[17] Looking at distribution systems, Chandler did not distinguish between franchises or salaried agents. The examples I noted were cases where firms relied on salaried agents. I cited Chandler because his work has been so influential. Other automobile historians did not pursue the question of liability except for Epstein's brief note. See, for example, Edward D. Kennedy, *The Automobile Industry: The Coming of Age of Capitalism's Favorite Child* (Clifton, NJ: Augustus M. Kelley, Publishers, 1972), 62–64, 127, 138–45; John B. Rae, *American Automobile Manufacturers: The First Forty Years* (Philadelphia: Chilton Company, 1959), 46–47, 136–38; and Ralph C. Epstein, *The Automobile Industry: Its Economic and Commercial Development* (1928; repr., New York: Arno Press, 1972), 140, and in general, 136–52. Dicke, relying on Hewitt's study, noted the implications of liability for Ford. Hewitt misread *Joslyn v. Cadillac*, 177 F. 863 (6th Cir. 1910). The plaintiff (car buyer) contended that the dealer made false statements only in the sense that the product, being so defective, failed to live up to its advertised representations. Dicke, *Franchising in America*, 66–67; and Hewitt, *Automobile Franchise Agreements*, 19 n. 27, 24 n. 4, 25, 37–38, 45.

[18] He found that by the 1950s franchising applied to many complex goods – autos, tractors, farm implements, tires, and electronics. Kessler, "Automobile Dealer Franchises," 1135–36.

[19] At least by 1912 the courts had established two features important for separating the agency and sales contracts. The Illinois Appeals Court heard a case in which the dealer claimed his 1909 contract constituted an agency relationship. Even when called an "Agency Agreement,"

FIGURE 2.2. Oldsmobile Automobile Dealership, circa 1905. As a franchise, dealers purchased cars from manufacturers and resold them to consumers. As such, the consumer lacked privity of contract with the manufacturer. (Note the sign on the second floor advertising *Motor* magazine.) Courtesy of the Detroit Public Library, National Automotive History Collection.

On which contract did manufacturers rely? To answer this question, I compiled a database of automobile dealer contracts from the early 1900s (see the Appendix). Excluding companies that operated for just one or two years, my collection includes twenty-one out of eighty-three commercial producers through 1909, and thirty-two out of 115 firms between 1900 and 1914 (a quarter of all commercial producers).[20] Put another way, I have

and even though the dealer was given an exclusive sales territory, the court declared that most parts of the contract were "wholly inconsistent with, and repugnant to, any theory of agency." Vincent Bendix was prohibited from selling cars in the "name of the defendant" and had to pay for the cars "cash on delivery." *Bendix v. Staver Carriage Company*, 174 Ill. App. 589 (1912), 595. See also *Banker Brothers Company v. Commonwealth of Pennsylvania*, 222 U.S. 210 (1911). The many cases regarding sales and agency contracts are reviewed in C. P. Berry, *The Law of Automobiles*, 4th ed. (Chicago: Callaghan and Company, 1924), 1365–89, especially 1367; and Xenophon P. Huddy, *The Law of Automobiles*, 5th ed., ed. Arthur F. Curtis (Albany, NY: Matthew Bender & Co., 1919), 1001–21, especially 1002–3. Although Hewitt did not review these two cases, he discussed many legal issues surrounding dealer contracts in *Automobile Franchise Agreements*.

20 Ralph Epstein compiled a list of "commercial" automakers, but did not define "commercial basis." I added a few firms to his list. The Thomas B. Jeffery Company, for example, operated on a "commercial basis" because it ranked among the leading five producers in 1906; the

FIGURE 2.3. Buick Automobile Dealership, circa 1909. This photograph was taken around the time when Donald MacPherson purchased his Buick runabout. Courtesy of the Detroit Public Library, National Automotive History Collection.

contracts (spanning the years 1900 to 1908) for twelve out of fifty-seven commercial producers that remained in the market in 1908, and seventeen out of seventy-three automakers remaining in the market in 1909.[21] Although several companies entered and exited the early auto market,

Metz Company placed twelfth among the leading manufacturers in 1914. In the case of a few other firms not on Epstein's list, the records and briefs of their court cases indicate that the companies operated beyond their immediate vicinity. These firms include the Wayne Company, the Reliable Dayton Motor Car Company, Reid Manufacturing Company, and the Monarch Motor Car Company. One last firm not on Epstein's list was the Anderson Carriage Company. This Detroit firm made electric carriages, and, as Nevins reported, sold one to Henry Ford for his wife's use. I added six firms (all except Monarch) to the list of commercial producers through 1908 and 1909, and seven for the years through 1914. (I did not count firms for which I have incomplete contracts.) For Epstein's list, see Epstein, *The Automobile Industry*, chart 28, 176, 377–82. On Wayne, see Editors of Automobile Quarterly, *The American Car since 1775: the most complete survey of the American automobile ever published*, 2nd ed. (New York: L. Scott Bailey, 1971), n.p. For Anderson, consult Allan Nevins with Frank Ernest Hill, *Ford: The Times, the Man, the Company* (New York: Charles Scribner's Sons, 1954), 624 n. 33.

[21] The number of firms remaining in the market in 1908 and 1909 is reported in Epstein, *The Automobile Industry*, chart 28, 176. I added five firms (Anderson, Jeffery, Metz, Reliable Dayton, and Wayne) to his figure of fifty-two for 1908 and four for 1909 (the same firms except for Wayne). Information about the dates of operation for almost all firms was reported

roughly five to ten firms sold the majority of cars each year. Table 2.1 lists the firms that at some time ranked among the top five or top ten producers for three time periods between 1903 and 1916. Olds, for example, held on to first place from 1903 through 1905, and between 1903 and 1905, the Ford Motor Company (organized in 1903) ranked among the top four producers before becoming the number one producer in 1906.[22] As another measure of the database's value, I have dealer agreements for five out of the nine firms that ranked among the leading five producers, and six out of the sixteen firms that ranked among the top-ten producers between 1905 and 1909 (or eleven among the nineteen top-ten producers between 1905 and 1914).[23]

My database lets me trace the development of the dealer franchises between 1900 and 1914. Ford's experience may have been sui generis: Its managers adopted the franchise between 1903 and 1904, shortly after they became embroiled in the Selden patent lawsuit and wrote to their dealers, saying they wanted to protect them from liability arising out of the lawsuit.[24] Except for Ford's dealer contract, Tables 2.2 and 2.3 indicate that prior to 1906 firms wrote short dealer agreements or contracts with few provisions. In 1903 or 1904 many firms that would go on to become major producers had just been organized: Ford (1903), Buick (1904), Cadillac (1903) plus its forerunner the Henry Ford Company (1901), Thomas B. Jeffery Company (1902), and Reo (1904), as well as small firms like Peerless (1901) and Wayne (1904).[25] Without a clear understanding of sales relationships, managers at Ford and other companies wrote a variety of contracts. Ford, for example, had sold cars through traveling salesmen and

in Editors of Automobile Quarterly, *The American Car since 1775*, n.p. I did not include Reid, because I could not locate information about the firm's years of operation.

[22] Editors of Automobile Quarterly, *The American Car since 1775*, 138–41.

[23] Between 1905 and 1908, firms that ranked among the top-ten producers were Ford, Cadillac, Jeffery, Reo, Maxwell, Olds Motor Works, the White Company, Buick, Franklin, Packard, Stoddard-Dayton, Studebaker, Stanley, and the Hupp Motor Company. In 1909, Willys-Overland and Brush entered the ranks of the top-ten producers. I have a 1910 contract for Hupp Motor. I do not count Buick's 1909 contract with the Georgia dealer in my estimates, because the contract was unusual. If Dodge is included since it ranked third in 1915, then I have agreements for twelve of the twenty top-ten producers. For production figures, see Editors of Automobile Quarterly, *The American Car since 1775*, 138–39.

[24] In response to the Selden patent, on October 2, 1903, Ford gave its New York dealer a "guarantee," to "hold" the agent and "their customers...free and harmless from any loss, cost, damage and expense, to which they may be put while acting as selling agents for said Ford Motor Company by reason of any suit or legal proceedings brought for the purpose of enforcing the claims of the association [which controlled the patent]." Ford fought this massive legal battle, which in reality represented an attempt by members of the patent club to limit entry to the market, and won in 1911. See Nevins with Hill, *Ford: The Times, the Man, the Company*, 246, 284–322; and Ford-Duerr Guarantee of October 2, 1903, Exhibit 11, vol. 2, 493–94, Records and Briefs for *Columbia*.

[25] Editors of Automobile Quarterly, *The American Car since 1775*, especially 218–372.

Table 2.1. *Leading Automobile Manufacturers, 1903–1916*

Brands that ranked among the top-ten manufacturers in terms of the number of
automobiles produced

1903–1905	1906–1909	1910–1912	1913–1916
Baker	Brush	Brush	Buick
Buick	Buick*	Buick*	Cadillac*
Cadillac*	Cadillac*	Cadillac*	Chevrolet
Ford*	Chalmers	Ford*	Dodge*
Franklin*	Ford*	Hudson	Ford*
Knox	Franklin	Hupmobile	Jeffery
Maxwell	Hudson	Maxwell*	Hudson
Packard	Hupmobile	Oakland	Hupmobile
Pope Hartford*	Maxwell*	Reo	Maxwell*
Oldsmobile*	Packard	Studebaker*	Oakland
Overland	Oakland	Willys-Overland*	Reo
Rambler*	Oldsmobile		Saxon
Reo	Rambler*		Studebaker*
Stanley	Reo*		Willys-Overland*
Stevens-Duryea	Stoddard-Dayton		
White	Studebaker*		
Winton	White		
	Willys-Overland*		

Notes: Overland became Willys-Overland in 1908. An asterisk (*) indicates that the brand
ranked among the top five automobile manufacturers during a given time period.
Source: Editors of Automobile Quarterly, *The American Car since 1775: the most complete
survey of the American automobile ever published*, 2nd ed. (New York: L. Scott Bailey, 1971),
138–39.

through the Wanamaker department store.[26] And, in spite of its use of the
sales contract in 1904, managers also wrote agency contracts with salaried
managers.[27] Cadillac acknowledged the early period of uncertainty in dealer
relations when its sales manager noted in 1902 that the firm had "no regular
contract."[28]

[26] Hewitt, *Automobile Franchise Agreements*, 19.
[27] The managers were paid a salary, but purchased cars at a discount as did other dealers. See, for example, Memorandum of Agreement between Thomas J. Hay and the Ford
Motor Company, October 11, 1906, Folder 1, Box 1, Acc. 140, HF. Hewitt described other
sales arrangements during Ford's early years in *Automobile Franchise Agreements*, 19. See
also Nevins, *Ford: The Times, the Man, the Company*, 264–65; and Dicke, *Franchising in
America*, 59.
[28] W. E. Metzger to W. J. Stewart, December 18, 1902, Exhibit 5, 10–11, Records and Briefs
for *Wheaton*.

Table 2.2. *Clauses in Dealer Agreements Indicating Method of Sales, Automaker's General Liability, and Liability for Delays in Shipping Vehicles, 1900–1914*

Name of Manufacturer	Dealer to Buy Cars at a Discount	Dealer not Mfr.'s Agent	Mfr. not Liable for Delays Beyond Its Control
1900–1905			
Amer. EVC, 1900	commission	no clause	no clause
Peerless, 1902	20%*	no clause	yes
Ford, 1903	20%*	no clause	no clause
Peerless, 1903	15%*	no clause	yes
Reid, 1903	20%	no clause	no clause
Ford, 1904	20%	yes	no clause
Ford, 1905	20%	yes	no clause
Pierce, 1905	yes	no clause	no clause
Wayne, 1905	20%*	no clause	no clause
White, 1905	20%	no clause	no clause
1906–1908			
Ford, 1906	yes	yes	yes
Jeffery, 1906	20%	yes	yes
Reo, 1906	yes	yes	yes
Anderson, 1907	20%	no clause	no clause
Ford, 1907	yes	yes	no clause
Reliable, 1907	20%	yes	yes
Cadillac, 1908	20%	yes	no clause
Ford, 1908	15%	yes	yes
Oakland, 1908	25%	yes	yes
Welch, 1908	20%	no clause	no clause
White, 1908	20%	no clause	yes
1909			
Buick, 1909	unclear	no clause	no clause
Chalmers, 1909	yes*	yes	yes
Ford, 1909	15%	yes	yes
Haynes, 1909	20%*	no clause	yes
Locomobile, 1909	20%	yes	no clause
Pierce, 1909	wholesale	no clause	no clause
Pope Mfg., 1909	no statement	no clause	no clause
Staver, 1909	30%	yes	incomplete
Studebaker, 1909	15%	yes	yes
Velie, 1909	"net prices"	no clause	yes
1910–1911			
Ford, 1910–11	15%	yes	yes
Hupp, 1910	15%	yes	yes
Inter-State, 1910	20%	no clause	yes
Kissel, 1910	yes	no clause	yes
Ford, 1911–12	15%	yes	yes
Hudson, 1911	15%	no clause	yes
Pullman, 1911	unclear	yes	yes
Studebaker, 1911	incomplete	yes	incomplete

(Continued)

Table 2.2 *(Continued)*

Name of Manufacturer	Dealer to Buy Cars at a Discount	Dealer not Mfr.'s Agent	Mfr. not Liable for Delays Beyond Its Control
1912–1914			
Alco, 1912	yes	yes	no clause
Cole, 1912	yes	yes	yes
Ford, 1912–13	15%	yes	yes
Ford, 1913–14	pay 85%	limited-agent	yes
Metz, 1913	net $375	yes	yes
Chalmers, 1914	20%	yes	yes
Dodge, 1914	yes	no clause	no clause
Maxwell, 1914	incomplete	yes	incomplete
Monarch, 1914	yes	yes	yes
Packard, 1914	net prices	yes	yes
Studebaker, 1914	yes	yes	yes

Notes: The second column indicates whether the dealer sold cars on a commission or purchased vehicles at a discount to the list (retail) price. When the contract specified a uniform discount rate, I report that rate. In some cases, the language was ambiguous. Peerless offered its dealer in 1903 "a commission or discount of 15% from the party of the first part's list prices." I have placed an asterisk next to those cases which included the word "commission" in the clause outlining the dealer's payment. The courts sometimes referred to a dealer's lost profit on the sale of a vehicle as his or her commission, but in this context the term could mean the dealer's discount or a commission. The third column reports whether or not dealer agreements included a clause declaring that the dealer was not the manufacturer's agent or "legal representative" (as stated in Ford's 1904 agreement). The fourth column reports whether the automaker included a clause exempting itself from liability for delays "beyond its control," typically strikes and fires (as noted in the 1903 Peerless contract).

"Incomplete" means that I do not have a complete contract upon which to determine whether a manufacturer included the particular clause in its dealer agreement.

Ford's contracts require a few comments. Management altered its 1912–13 agreement to read: "The Limited Dealer-Licensee is in no way the legal representative or agent of The Manufacturer-Licensor." Its 1913–14 agreement made dealers "limited-agents." They earned a "commission" equivalent to 15 percent of the price of a vehicle, and paid for the rest of the car's list price. The contracts still maintained a provision limiting the manufacturer's liability. The 1913–14 and 1914–15 contracts both declared the dealer "shall have no authority or power or duty whatsoever, except as herein expressly conferred." The contracts further declared the dealer was "to save the first party [Ford] harmless against any and all claims made against first party by any person or persons not parties hereto for damages arising out of the conduct of second party's said business or Limited Agency whether from accident or injury or collision or loading or unloading or driving or theft or fire or from any cause of any and every nature whatsoever."

Sources: Memorandum between the Peerless Motor Car Company and Dr. R. M. Garfield, March 12, 1903, Exhibit A, 9–10, *Garfield v. Peerless Motor Car Company*, 189 Mass. 395 (1908), Massachusetts Reporter Papers and Briefs, Volume 189, Social Law Library, Boston, Mass.; Ford Motor Company agreements, 1904, 1905, 1906, 1907, 1908, and 1912–13, File # 7222-68-2, Box 871, RG 122, NA; Limited Agency Contract between the Ford Motor Company and F. O. Henizer, October 31, 1913, Folder 75-30-16, Box 30, Acc. 75, HF; Ford Motor Company Limited Agency Contract, blank form, 1914–15, Folder 75-39-3, Box 39, Acc. 75, HF; Ford's "1913 – Buyer's Order & Agreement – 1914," Folder 75-31-30, Box 31, Acc. 75, HF; Agreement between Maxwell Motor Sales Corporation and W. O. Barnes, May 18, 1915, 5–14, *Barnes v. Maxwell Motor Sales Corporation*, 172 Ky. 409, 189 S.W. 444 (1916), Records of the Court of Appeals of Kentucky, Case No. 44884, Kentucky Department for Libraries & Archives, Frankfort, Ky.; and the Appendix.

Table 2.3. *Clauses in Dealer Agreements Relating to Defects and Repairs,*
1900–1914

Name of Manufacturer	Replace Defective Parts	Length of Time Defective Parts Were Warranted	Mfr. Not Liable for Defects in Suppliers' Parts	Dealer Repair Vehicles
1900–1905				
Amer. EVC, 1900	no clause			no clause
Peerless, 1902	no clause			yes
Ford, 1903	yes	60 days	no clause	yes
Reid, 1903	no clause			no clause
Peerless, 1903	no clause			yes
Ford, 1904	yes	60 days (see notes)	no clause	yes
Ford, 1905	yes	60 days (see notes)	no clause	yes
Pierce, 1905	no clause			no clause
Wayne, 1905	yes	60 days		yes
White, 1905	no clause			no clause
1906–1908				
Ford, 1906	yes	60 days	no clause	yes
Jeffery, 1906	yes	no statement	no clause	no clause
Reo, 1906	no clause			yes
Anderson, 1907	no clause			see notes
Ford, 1907	yes	90 days	no clause	yes
Reliable, 1907	yes	60 days	yes	yes
Cadillac, 1908	yes	60 days	yes	yes
Ford, 1908	yes	90 days	no clause	yes
Oakland, 1908	yes	60 days	yes	no clause
Welch, 1908	no clause			no clause
White, 1908	not clear (see notes)		not clear	no clause
1909				
Buick, 1909	no clause			no clause
Chalmers, 1909	yes	not say	yes	yes
Ford, 1909	yes	90 days	no clause	see notes
Haynes, 1909	yes	60 days	yes	no clause
Locomobile, 1909	yes	60 days	yes	yes
Pierce, 1909	no clause			no clause
Pope Mfg., 1909	yes	60 days	yes	no clause
Staver, 1909	incomplete	incomplete	incomplete	incomplete
Studebaker, 1909	yes	not say	no clause	yes
Velie, 1909	yes	one year	yes	yes
1910–1911				
Ford, 1910	yes	90 days (see notes)	no clause	see notes
Hupp, 1910	yes	60 days	yes	yes
Inter-State, 1910	yes	60 days	yes	no clause
Kissel, 1910	yes	one year	no clause	no clause

(*Continued*)

Table 2.3 *(Continued)*

Name of Manufacturer	Replace Defective Parts	Length of Time Defective Parts Were Warranted	Mfr. Not Liable for Defects in Suppliers' Parts	Dealer Repair Vehicles
Ford, 1911–12	yes	normal use	no clause	yes
Hudson, 1911	no clause			yes
Pullman, 1911	yes	not stated	no clause	yes
Studebaker, 1911	yes	"one full year"	incomplete	incomplete
1912–1914				
Alco, 1912	no clause			no clause
Cole, 1912	yes	one year	yes	yes
Ford, 1912–13	yes	normal use	no clause	yes
Ford, 1913–14	(buyer's order)	normal use	no clause	yes
Metz, 1913	yes	one year	no clause	yes
Chalmers, 1914	yes	90 days	yes	yes
Dodge, 1914	yes	90 days	yes	yes
Maxwell, 1914	yes	(see notes)	incomplete	incomplete
Monarch, 1914	yes	90 days	yes	yes
Packard, 1914	yes	90 days	yes	yes
Studebaker, 1914	yes	90 days	yes	yes

Notes: "Incomplete" means that I do not have a complete contract upon which to determine whether a manufacturer included the particular clause in its dealer agreement. Because the 1908 White contract did not report its warranty, I cannot determine its qualifications for suppliers' parts.

In its 1904 and 1905 agreements, Ford indicated that it was reprinting the "standard warranty" adopted by the National Association of Automobile Manufacturers on August 12, 1902. The entire warranty read as follows:

We, The Ford Motor Company, of Detroit, Mich., warrant all goods furnished by us for sixty days following the date of their shipment, based upon the date of invoice covering the goods, this warranty being limited to the replacement in our factory of all parts giving out under normal service in consequence of defect of material or of workmanship.

If the circumstances do not permit that the work shall be executed in our factory this warranty is limited to the shipment, without charge, of the parts intended to replace those acknowledged to be defective.

It is, however, understood that we make no warranty whatever regarding pneumatic tires or the batteries.

We cannot accept any responsibility in connection with any of our motor cars when they have been altered outside our factory.

We are not responsible to the purchaser of our goods for any undertakings and warranties made by those selling cars manufactured by us beyond those expressed above.

We wish it distinctly understood that we make no warranty of our goods except as stated above, but desire and expect that customers shall make a thorough examination of our goods before purchasing.

Ford added the following two clauses:

(a)The party of the second part shall send to the said party of the first part at Detroit, Mich., such part or parts as are claimed to be defective promptly on the discovery of the claimed defect; transportation to be prepaid by party of the second part and said part or parts to be properly cased for shipment and clearly marked with the name and full address of the sender, and with the number of the automobile from which such part or parts were taken.

(b)The party of the second part shall mail to said party of the first part at Detroit, Mich., on or before shipment to said first party of such part or parts claimed to be defective, a full and complete description of the claim and reasons therefor.

(Footnote continued)

Among other notes on its warranty, Ford's 1908 contract added that the manufacturer's "judgment" regarding defects was "final and conclusive." From 1908 through 1912–13, similar statements appeared in Ford agreements. Beginning with its 1910–11 contract, Ford no longer covered parts for 90 days, but warranted "all such parts as shall under normal use and service appear to have been defective in workmanship or material." In its 1911–12 contract, Ford required that the car buyer had "registered his name, address and date of purchase and number of car and model" with Ford in order to be covered by the warranty. Its 1912–13 agreement and its 1913–14 "Buyer's Order" form carried similar requirements. Ford's warranty was printed in the buyer's order rather than its contract for 1913–14. This warranty was shorter than earlier warranties, but included the stipulation that the car buyer have registered his or her car, and like warranties in earlier contracts, stated that Ford took no responsibility for cars "altered outside of its own Factories or Branch Shops."

In regard to suppliers' parts, Studebaker's 1911 contract, clause I, specifically guaranteed all parts for one year "as a means of increasing the sales of E. M. F. '30' and Flanders '20' cars." The clause declared: "This guaranty includes all material and all equipment (tires excepted) used in connection with the construction of such automobile."

I report information for the 1914 agreement between Maxwell's distributor and its Oklahoma dealer. This agreement instructed that "[e]ach purchaser" be "given the standard warranty of the National Automobile Chamber of Commerce." Chalmers offered the same guarantee in its 1914 agreement, but did not explain the terms of this standard warranty. The National Automobile Chamber of Commerce was the industry's trade association.

For repairs, manufacturers frequently included general statements instructing dealers to maintain repair facilities. I found one Ford 1909 contract (NA) in which the clause was omitted, but four Ford contracts from that year in which it was included. For 1910, Ford included its repair clause in its "1910 – Dealer's License & Agreement – 1911" but not in its "1910 – Limited Dealer's License & Agreement – 1911." Ford contracts for dealers and limited dealers included a repair clause during the next three years. Dodge's 1914 agreement carried a statement to encourage the creation of "Dodge Bros. Service Stations," which received an added discount in the purchase of repair parts and were intended to better serve Dodge customers.

Sources: Agreement between Ford Motor Company and C.A. Duerr, August 7, 1903, Exhibit 10, vol. 2, 493–94, *Columbia Motor Car Co. et al. v. C. A. Duerr & Co. et al.,* 184 F. 893 (1st Cir. 1911), Transcript of Record, Case No. 4058–60 (consolidated numbers), RG 276, NA, NY; Ford Motor Company agreements, 1904–1909, and 1912–13, File # 7222-68-2, Box 871, RG 122, NA; Dealer's License & Agreement between the Ford Motor Company and Wm. Warnock Co., September 2, 1909, File L36, Box 2, Acc. 297, HF; Limited Agency Contract between the Ford Motor Company and F. O. Henizer, October 31, 1913, Folder 75-30-16, Box 30, Acc. 75, HF; Limited Agency Contract, blank form, Folder 75-39-3, Box 39, Acc. 75, HF; "1913 – Buyer's Order & Agreement – 1914," Folder 75-31-30, Box 31, Acc. 75, HF; Agreement between Maxwell Motor Sales Corporation and W. O. Barnes, May 18, 1915, 5–14, *Barnes v. Maxwell Motor Sales Corporation,* 172 Ky. 409, 189 S.W. 444 (1916), Records of the Court of Appeals of Kentucky, Case No. 44884, Kentucky Department for Libraries & Archives, Frankfort, Ky.; Agreement between the Dodge Brothers and Pegram Motor Car Company, no date [expired June 30, 1915], reprinted in *Ellis v. Dodge Bros.,* 237 F. 860 (N.D. Ga. 1916), 860–63; and the Appendix.

Within a brief period of time – by 1909 – most companies had adopted the franchise and declared that the dealer was not the firm's agent. That managers opted to rely on a sales contract did not mean that they chose one for the sole reason of defects. Indeed, in this new market, managers may have opted to rely on the sales contract initially for reasons unrelated to consumers or defects. The franchise may have motivated dealers to sell cars better than a flat salary.[29] In addition, at a time when automakers sold a small number of cars to consumers dispersed over vast geographic territories, a franchised dealer was responsible for servicing and repairing vehicles. From the market's

---

[29] Nevins with Hill, *Ford: The Times, the Man, the Company,* 264–65.

very early years, franchise contracts included a clause holding dealers responsible for repairs (as I note later). There were also issues relating to retailers where it did not matter if the retailer was a franchised dealer or an agent. Consumers placed deposits on new cars, for example, and retailers in turn placed deposits with manufacturers, many of whom used the deposits to help maintain the cash flow of young firms.[30] In contrast to these examples, legal scholars called attention to different types of liability that had little relation to defects. Suppliers' delays in shipping parts threatened to halt production and delay shipment of cars from the factory to dealers. The Deere-Clark Motor Car Company, for instance, began making cars in 1906, but after a labor strike stopped production, lawsuits were filed for failure to deliver cars, and the firm declared bankruptcy in 1907.[31] Ford's 1908 agreement accepted a dealer's orders "subject to any delays occurring in the manufacture of its product."[32] By 1909, several companies had adopted clauses exempting them from any costs resulting from delays due to unforeseen events, typically strikes or fires.[33]

Although managers may have worried about their liability for delays in shipping cars, they may also have wanted to limit their liability in selling defective products. What is important is that soon after firms had been organized, managers quickly learned the consequences of selling faulty cars. Managers did not necessarily worry specifically, or even mostly, about liability for personal injury, but automakers were sued by dealers and consumers for reasons that at root were prompted by their machines' defects. Ford, Cadillac, Buick, Reid, EVC, Wayne, and Pope all faced lawsuits prompted by defects soon after their organization.[34] They could limit their liability

---

[30] In addition to the consumers' deposits, early contracts requested dealers' deposits in some cases. In one case, a dealer placed a deposit of $1,000. Epstein, *The Automobile Industry*, 137–40; and Hewitt, *Automobile Franchise Agreements*, 15, 16 n. 23, 21.

[31] Leslie J. Stegh, "Putting America in the Driver's Seat: The Deere-Clark Motor Car Company," *Illinois Historical Journal* 81 (Winter 1988): 242–54; and Susan Helper, "Strategy and Irreversibility in Supplier Relations: The Case of the U.S. Automobile Industry," *Business History Review* 65 (Winter 1991): 781–824, especially 792–93.

[32] Ford Motor Company 1908 agreement, blank form, File L36, Box 2, Acc. 297, HF.

[33] This clause was similar to the non-delivery clause, which is discussed in Hewitt, *Automobile Franchise Agreements*, 42; Kessler, "Automobile Dealer Franchises," 1147, 1149; and U.S. Federal Trade Commission, *Report on Motor Vehicle Industry*, 76th Cong., 1st sess., House Document No. 468 (Washington, D.C.: U.S. Government Printing Office, 1939), 142. Information is reported in Table 2.2.

[34] *Ford Motor Company v. Morris R. Osburn*, 140 Ill. App. 633 (1908), *Joslyn v. Cadillac*, 177 F. 863 (6th Cir. 1910), *Buick Motor Car Co. v. Reid Mfg. Co.*, 150 Mich. 118 (1907), *Neale v. American Electric Vehicle Company*, 186 Mass. 303 (1904), *Masters & another v. Wayne Automobile Company & others*, 198 Mass. 25 (1908), and *Levis v. Pope Motor Car Company*, 95 N.E. 815 (N.Y. 1911). Jain examined other types of agency relationships in her study, arguing that as early as 1907 the courts limited the ability of bystanders to receive compensation for personal injuries sustained in auto accidents. In my study of manufacturer–dealer relations, I find that prior to 1908 a number of problems prompted by an auto's

through agency and sales agreements, but the two options presented trade-offs as firms discovered in a set of cases decided between 1904 and 1908, as well as other cases initiated during these years.

In two early cases against dealers, managers tried to defend themselves by claiming that they were not responsible for defects or delays in shipping vehicles when their dealers were their agents. In *Neale v. American Electric Vehicle Company* (Mass. 1904), Arthur F. Neale sued EVC, complaining that its vehicles never lived up to the warranty claimed to exist in the contract. The manufacturer first denied that the contract contained a warranty, and second declared that it owed no responsibility for making the machines "merchantable" to the dealer as its agent. Its lawyers reported that the dealer was "paid a commission of 20 per cent of the purchase price." Further, they wrote: "It is a novel legal proposition that a principal in a contract of agency for the sale of chattels is under a duty to his agent, implied by law, to have the chattels merchantable. . . . If no such duty is owed, it is plain that the defendant is not liable for not performing it."[35] By contrast, in *Masters v. Wayne Automobile Company* (Mass. 1908), the plaintiff's brief drew the careful distinction between an agent and a vendee: "the Court holds that a man may be an agent as to some things, and, at the same time, an individual contractor as to others." Where the dealer acted as a vendee in this instance, "the defendant company is liable upon its implied warranty that its automobiles were of merchantable quality. The Master finds and cites certain instances where said cars as delivered by the defendant company were defective and that some would not run without fixing nor climb hills as other automobiles ordinarily do."[36] The plaintiff's attorneys thus persuaded the court to accept their interpretation. A similar distinction applied in *Wheaton v. Cadillac Automobile Company* (Mich. 1906). The dealer sued the manufacturer for failure to deliver goods, but Cadillac succeeded in claiming an agency relationship for which it was not liable to its agent for not having shipped the cars.[37]

Although an agency relationship offered manufacturers a defense against cases rooted in the twin problems of defects and delays, it also left automakers open to other types of lawsuits. Ford's experience was instructive. Although the company wrote a sales contract with dealers in 1904, officials also wrote contracts with branch managers in which the manager was a salaried employee. Thomas Hay held one such contract as Ford's Chicago

---

defects, not just personal injury, gave automakers reason to elect the sales contract over the agency contract. Managers also added clauses to sales contracts limiting their obligations to dealers. Sarah S. Lochlann Jain, "'Dangerous Instrumentalities': The Bystander as Subject in Automobility," *Cultural Anthropology* 19, no. 1 (2004): 67–74.

[35] Brief for Defendant, 1, 4, Records and Briefs for *Neale*.

[36] Plaintiff's brief, 5, Records and Briefs for *Masters*.

[37] *Wheaton v. Cadillac Automobile Co.*, 143 Mich. 21, 106 N.W. 399 (1906), Records and Briefs for *Wheaton*. See also Hewitt, *Automobile Franchise Agreements*, 39 n. 34.

branch manager, and it was upon this contract that Morris Osburn sued Ford instead of Hay. While Ford ultimately prevailed in the 1908 case, officials could have avoided the lawsuit altogether had the branch manager not been the firm's agent.[38] George Joslyn gave Cadillac managers a similar lesson when he sued the company for product misrepresentation. Joslyn did not charge that the dealer had made false statements about the vehicle, but instead maintained that the car was defective. In court, Cadillac tried without luck to shift liability to its sales agent, arguing that the sales manager was in fact a dealer like any other.[39]

In contrast to the agency contract, the sales contract allowed managers both to sidestep lawsuits with disgruntled consumers and to cope with potential lawsuits from dealers over vehicles' defects. By 1909, most automakers had opted to write sales contracts in which the manufacturer sold vehicles to their dealers at a discount from their list prices, but they also added clauses explicitly declaring that the dealer was not the manufacturer's "legal representative" or agent. Ford's 1904 contract explained: "It is hereby expressly agreed and understood by and between the parties hereto that the party of the second part is in no way the legal representative or agent of the party of the first part and has no right or authority from said first party to assume any obligations of any kind, express or implied, on behalf of said first party, or to bind said first party thereby."[40] Along with Ford, Cadillac, Jeffery, Oakland, and Reo included this clause by 1908.[41] In the years between 1906 and 1908, five of the six top-ten producers included a clause declaring the dealer was not the firm's agent. By 1909, seven of the eight major producers, including Studebaker and Chalmers, subscribed to the clause (Table 2.2).[42]

Most automakers also added two clauses further restricting their liability (Table 2.3). One clause concerned the limited nature of warranties. Ford led the way: its 1904 agreement reprinted the industry trade association's standard warranty (adopted in 1902). The company would replace defective parts only for the first sixty days after the car buyer received the vehicle.[43] Further, many contracts limited the manufacturer's liability to replacing the part (not covering the cost of labor), and stipulated that the manufacturer's decision as to whether the part was defective was "final and conclusive." Should any car be altered without the manufacturer's approval, then it was

---

[38] *Ford Motor Company v. Osburn.*

[39] *Joslyn v. Cadillac.* See also Hewitt, *Automobile Franchise Agreements*, 37. The court discussed the vehicle's defects in its lengthy opinion.

[40] Ford Motor Company agreement, 1904, File # 7222-68-2, Box 871, RG 122, NA.

[41] Table 2.2 indicates whether a firm included a clause in its dealer agreement declaring that the dealer was not its agent.

[42] Based on *MacPherson*, Buick could also be included in the list. Table 2.1 lists the top commercial producers. Editors of Automobile Quarterly, *The American Car since 1775*, 138–39.

[43] Ford Motor Company 1904 agreement, File # 7222-68-2, Box 871, RG 122, NA.

no longer backed by the sixty-day warranty.[44] Although not as detailed as Ford's warranty, many firms, such as Jeffery, Reo, Cadillac, and Oakland, added clauses after 1905. Studebaker made the link between defects and sales explicit when it wrote in its 1911 contract that its one-year warranty was so attractive that it would act as "a means of increasing the sales" of its models.[45]

As a second limitation, contracts denied the manufacturer's obligation for defects in suppliers' parts. According to Cadillac's 1908 agreement, the manufacturer's warranty "does not apply to parts not made by the Manufacturer" and directed the dealer to "make all claims" to the supplier.[46] Oakland's 1908 contract carried a similar stipulation, and did "not cover defective tires, rims, coils, radiators, and other equipment not manufactured" by the company. Velie's 1909 agreement offered an unusually long one-year warranty for defective parts, but did "not guarantee tires, batteries, coils, magneto, lamps, or plugs as we use only standard makes guaranteed by the manufacturers of same."[47]

Even as automakers limited their liability, they included from the earliest years clauses stating their dealers' obligation to repair vehicles (Table 2.3).[48] For instance, Wayne's 1905 contract called on the dealer "to keep on hand an

[44] On the general topic of warranties, see Gillam, *Products Liability in the Automobile Industry*, 174–79, 189–93. Ford Motor Company 1904 agreement, File # 7222-68-2, Box 871, RG 122, NA. Warranty information is reported in Table 2.3. Ford Motor Company 1908 agreement, blank form, File L36, Box 2, Acc. 297, HF; and Agreement between Reliable Dayton Motor Car Company and F. E. Sparks, May 28, 1907, Copy of Exhibit A, 27–30, *Sparks v. Reliable Dayton Motor Car Company*, 85 Kan. 29 (1911), Records of the Mitchell district court appealed to the Supreme Court of Kansas, Kansas State Historical Society, Topeka, Kans.

[45] Studebaker selected clauses of 1911 agreement, partial copy of agreement between Studebaker Corporation of America and George J. Gollmar and LeRoy Messenger, September 1, 1911, Exhibit 3, 29–32, quote 30, Records and Briefs for *Studebaker*.

[46] Memorandum of Agreement between Cadillac Motor Car Company and the Utica Motor Car Co., July 22, 1908, Defendant's Exhibit 2, 61–64, Records and Briefs for *Cadillac*.

[47] Memorandum of Agreement, between Cadillac Motor Car Company and the Utica Motor Car Co., July 22, 1908, Defendant's Exhibit 2, 61–64, Records and Briefs for *Cadillac*; Memorandum of Agreement between the Oakland Motor Car Company and the Indiana Automobile Co., September 16, 1908, Plaintiff's Exhibit 1, 49–51, Records and Briefs for *Oakland*; and Agreement between Velie Motor Car Company and Kopmeier Motor Car Co., September 23, 1909, Exhibit A, 6–9, *Velie Motor Car Co. v. Kopmeier Motor Car Co.*, 194 F. 324 (7th Cir. 1912), Transcript of Record, Case No. 1765, RG 276, NA, Chicago.

[48] Hewitt singled out the problem of repairs as one of the six issues shaping manufacturers' approach to dealers in the early years of the auto industry, but he did not offer any systematic analysis of dealer contracts or cite specific cases beyond his reference to the three cases concerning the Peerless 1903 agreement. Hewitt, *Automobile Franchise Agreements*, 17–18, 24–25. I report specific details about the Peerless contract, including its clause on repairs, in Tables 2.2 and 2.3. On the general topic of dealer repairs, see Stephen L. McIntyre, "The Failure of Fordism: Reform of the Automobile Repair Industry, 1913–1940," *Technology and Culture* 41 (April 2000): 269–99.

assortment of parts and make repairs promptly." He also would "carefully and thoroughly instruct all purchasers how to operate said automobiles." Reo's dealer agreed in 1906 to maintain "at all times . . . one workman who shall throughly [sic] understand the different types or styles of REO Motor cars and be specially conversant with the means of adjusting and repairing the same." Reliable Dayton's 1907 contract specified that the dealer "maintain in addition a well equipped repair shop within [sic] a competent mechanic in charge at all times so that purchasers of Reliable Dayton Motor Car Co. cars can have same repaired and adjusted promptly and at reasonable rates."[49]

The auto contracts were noteworthy for a few additional features. As legal scholar Charles Hewitt explained, early contracts did not assert the manufacturer's control of the retailer. Prior to the 1920s, the contracts did not require the dealer to use the manufacturer's accounting system.[50] Further, during the first fifteen years, demand grew so rapidly that automakers did not impose sales quotas on their dealers. Automakers, however, did add a clause that allowed them to cancel the contracts quickly.[51] But at the same time, the contracts actively sought to cultivate long-term ties with dealers by granting each dealer an exclusive territory.[52] The exclusive territory clause held the promise of large profits, especially in a new market with booming sales, and the courts backed this promise. In 1905, for example, A. F. Schiffman, a Los Angeles dealer, signed a contract to sell Peerless cars in seven counties in southern California. When he discovered that Peerless sold cars to customers in his territory through a dealership in Toledo, Ohio, he sued. The court found that the plaintiff had maintained his agency in L.A., "paying the expenses thereof out of his own pocket." Judge Taggart concluded: "The evidence abundantly justified the finding that defendant violated its agreement not to sell Peerless machines within the territory allotted to plaintiff."[53]

But the relationship between dealers and manufacturers had an important downside. As long as manufacturers could deny the relational dimension of

---

[49] Agreement between the Wayne Automobile Company and Walter C. Masters & Company, January 16, 1905, Exhibit A, 10–12, Records and Briefs for *Masters*; Memorandum of Agreement between E. A. Jenkins Motor Co. and James Cofield, December 10, 1906, Exhibit A, *Cofield v. E. A. Jenkins Motor Co.*, 89 S.C. 419 (1911), Records of Richland County Court of Common Pleas, Judgment Rolls, Case No. 9609 (L40010), South Carolina Department of Archives and History, Columbia, SC; and Agreement between Reliable Dayton Motor Car Company and F. E. Sparks, May 28, 1907, Copy of Exhibit A, 27–30, *Sparks v. Reliable Dayton Motor Car Company*, 85 Kan. 29 (1911), Records of the Mitchell district court appealed to the Supreme Court of Kansas, Kansas State Historical Society, Topeka, Kans.

[50] Hewitt, *Automobile Franchise Agreements*, 55–56, 65–66.   [51] Ibid., 24–26, 43.

[52] Kessler, "Automobile Dealer Franchises," 1141–42, 1147–48; and Hewitt, *Automobile Franchise Agreements*, 24, 31–32, 39. Macaulay, *Law and the Balance of Power*; Macneil, "Economic Analysis of Contractual Relations," 1018–63; and Gordon, "Macaulay, Macneil, and the Discovery of Solidarity and Power in Contract Law," 569, 572.

[53] See for example, *Garfield v. Peerless Motor Car Co.*, 75 N.E. 695 (Mass. 1905); and *Schiffman v. Peerless Motor Car Company*, 110 Cal. App. 460 (1910), quote 461–62.

their dealer contracts in court – by claiming a sales contract as a close approximation to a "discrete transaction" – they exercised power by shifting liability from themselves to their dealers. Thus, through the franchise sales contract, automobile manufacturers severed the contractual relations between themselves and car buyers; via provisions to avoid liability for defective parts or delays, they limited their obligations to dealers. Kessler wrote that the sales contract let manufacturers achieve "considerable control over the process of distribution" but "without exposure to the burdens and responsibilities of an agency relationship."[54]

Following the path charted by Ronald Coase, economic and business scholars have investigated the structure of the modern firm, trying to discover why some activities were integrated within a firm and others transacted through the market. Their answers vary, but have almost always been couched in economic terms – transaction costs, path dependency, sunk costs, or specialized (tacit) knowledge.[55] Yet, these scholars have not followed through on Coase's study of social costs and asked how costs incurred by the buyers of a firm's product, consumers and dealers, might have affected the firm's structure.[56] The privity doctrine offers an explanation. Among important influences in their decision to rely on a franchise method of distribution, managers sought to shift liability for defects in a new market where the technology was imperfect and relationships uncertain.

TOWARD A COMMERCIAL MARKET: 1908–1916

In its trial against MacPherson, Buick officials were asked whether they had inspected the car's wheels. They answered that they had not inspected the wheels, implying that it was not possible to inspect them, and that in

---

[54] Macneil, "Economic Analysis of Contractual Relations," 1018–63; and Kessler, "Automobile Dealer Franchises," 1136. See also Gordon's discussion of discrete transactions in "Macaulay, Macneil, and the Discovery of Solidarity and Power in Contract Law," 569–72.

[55] On autos, see Richard N. Langlois and Paul L. Robertson, "Explaining Vertical Integration: Lessons from the American Automobile Industry," *Journal of Economic History* 49 (June 1989): 361–75; Michael Schwartz, "Markets, Networks, and the Rise of Chrysler in Old Detroit, 1920–1940," *Enterprise & Society* 1 (March 2000): 63–99; and Benjamin Klein, "Vertical Integration as Organizational Ownership: The Fisher Body – General Motors Relationships Revisited," *Journal of Law, Economics & Organization* 4 (Spring 1988): 213–26. See also Chandler, *Scale and Scope*; Oliver E. Williamson, "Transaction-Cost Economics: The Governance of Contractual Relations," *Journal of Law and Economics* 22 (October 1979): 233–61; and idem, "The Modern Corporation: Origins, Evolution, Attributes," *Journal of Economic Literature* 19 (December 1981): 1537–68.

[56] R. H. Coase, "The Problem of Social Cost," *Journal of Law & Economics* 3 (October 1960): 1–44. One of the few calls for a legal perspective in the study of the firm is found in Scott E. Masten, "A Legal Basis for the Firm," in *The Nature of the Firm: Origins, Evolution, and Development*, ed. Oliver E. Williamson and Sidney G. Winter (Oxford: Oxford University Press, 1993), 196–212. See also Gillam, *Products Liability in the Automobile Industry*, 196–210; and Arthur F. McEvoy, *The Fisherman's Problem: Ecology and Law in the California Fisheries, 1850-1980* (New York: Cambridge University Press, 1986).

the early 1900s no automaker inspected its wheels. G. W. Durham testified: "Prior to the year 1909 there was nothing done, that I know of, by
automobile manufacturers before they put the wheels under the body to
determine whether the spokes of the wheels were rotten or not." Durham
cited Packard, Pierce, Thomas, Ford, and Cadillac as firms where he "[did]
not know of any" testing.[57] In contrast to Buick's lack of inspections prior to
1909, companies undertook several steps to improve their products' quality
by the time Cardozo decided the case in 1916. Perhaps the most noteworthy vehicle was the Model T, because it offered consumers a reliable and
durable vehicle at reduced prices. Mass production was not the only source
of improvement, however. Hudson Motor Company illustrated the benefits
available from fostering constructive relations with dealers. Ford initiated
inspections of suppliers' parts. By 1910, one private organization and one
public entity had organized formal research activities intended to improve
quality throughout the industry. At this time, some firms such as General
Motors also began to support their own research efforts.

The single most noteworthy development was the advent of mass production. Historian David Hounshell described mass production not only as
the work of a group of brilliant mechanics, but as the effort to translate
the "principles of power, accuracy, economy, system, continuity, and speed"
in the production process.[58] Between 1910, when Highland Park opened,
and 1913, when the first assembly line began moving, mechanics took several steps to obtain dramatic gains in productivity. Gravity slides, conveyors, and assembly lines saved time and money by reducing the movement
of workers. The feed systems also brought continuity of process by setting
the pace of work. As Hounshell wrote, the "engineers found a method to
speed up the slow men and slow down the fast men."[59] Machine tools were
sequenced so that each operation followed directly from the previous one.
Because Henry Ford now had just one product, the T, he "provided his engineers the perfect opportunity to install single-purpose machine tools."[60] The
machines economized on space, but also offered gains in productivity in the
making of standardized parts. The parts themselves also brought savings
of time and money. Henry Ford's dictum that with mass production there
are "no fitters" rang true on his assembly lines. Without fitters, automated
machine tools produced parts with a high level of accuracy that could be
matched easily with the mating part for their assembly.[61] Interchangeability
thus improved quality, because it reduced defects borne out of deviations
from a set standard (Fig. 2.4).[62]

[57] G. W. Durham, testimony, 189–90, Records and Briefs for *MacPherson*. See also, Peck,
   Decision at Law, 47–52.
[58] David A. Hounshell, *From the American System to Mass Production, 1800-1932: The
   Development of Manufacturing Technology in the United States* (Baltimore: Johns Hopkins
   University Press, 1984), 217–61, on principles see ibid., 228–29.
[59] Ibid., 237.   [60] Ibid., 233.   [61] Ibid., 234.   [62] Ibid., 230, 250.

FIGURE 2.4. Ford Motor Company Assembly Line, circa 1914, Highland Park. This photograph shows Ford's assembly line soon after it began operation in 1913. The assembly line was based on several factors, such as the accuracy of interchangeable parts, the sequential organization of machines, the widespread use of conveyors, and the reliance on unskilled or semiskilled labor. From the Collections of the Henry Ford. Negative number P.O. 3342.

The Model T's improved quality followed as well from its service and repairs. Historian Steven McIntyre, in his study of automobile service, attributed the difficulty of servicing vehicles to two conditions. First, in the years prior to the coming of mass production, he wrote, cars "lacked easily accessible, interchangeable, standardized parts, forcing mechanics to disassemble much of a vehicle or modify parts to complete their repairs." Second, he observed, "Well-trained, experienced mechanics were in short supply in the early days of the industry, yet repair shops proliferated because of the limited capital needed to enter the field."[63] One approach was to systematize dealer service. By 1916, as McIntyre reported, Ford "began to develop standardized tools and equipment for its dealers." The intent, he concluded, was to make repairs simpler and quicker, but also to "reduce the need for skilled mechanics."[64]

---

[63] McIntyre, "The Failure of Fordism," 274–75.   [64] Ibid., 280–81.

Managers at the Hudson Motor Company also paid close attention to service. Their records indicate the sort of beneficial relationship Stewart Macaulay had argued was possible with franchises. Roy Chapin started Hudson in 1909.[65] A year later, the proud company president (who had yet to celebrate his thirtieth birthday) reported sales of $2.9 million.[66] Chapin ran a tight operation. Records from 1910 indicate that Hudson's Technical Department regularly tabulated all individual complaints in minute detail, and calculated the "Proportion of Complaints to Output" on a monthly basis.[67] For March 1910, the table summarizing reported complaints as a percent of output showed that 6.6 percent of Hudson cars received bad marks for the transmission's gear shifting and 1.3 percent experienced problems with the clutch.[68] In compiling the figures, managers also benefited from their dealers' efforts to monitor their product. In 1910, thirteen roadmen traveled to dealerships providing advice, and other managers solicited dealer complaints and suggestions.[69] Boston dealers, for example, reported "lack of power" due to "poor carburetion" (among other problems), whereas New York dealers had located a solution. By putting a "small bushing into the carburetor," they obtained "considerable more power out of the motor," and the report proposed making their idea standard.[70] Dealers listed other problems. Some objected to the vehicles' shabby appearance: cushions being too loose, finishes marred by dust covering wet paint, stained running boards, and soiled floor boards. Others cited defective radiators, "poorly made" piston rings, wheels being "loose on rear axle," "sagging" springs, and leaks in the crankcase and the transmission. Greater care in assembling and inspecting vehicles, the manager promised, would put an end to many complaints.[71]

In addition to the final inspection of cars by dealers, automakers also stepped up their inspection of suppliers' parts. In Ford's defense for another case involving a defective wheel, the manufacturer showed how much things had changed since Buick had purchased the defective wheel put on MacPherson's car. Although GM had conducted no tests in 1909, Ford had

---

[65] Hudson "Minutes" Binder, Box 1, Hudson Papers, BHL, UM.

[66] "Every Model for the Past Ten Years Has Added Lustre to the Hudson Fame," *Hudson Triangle* (June 21, 1919): 4, Folder "Hudson – Miscellaneous," Hudson Papers, BHL, UM.

[67] "Cars in Service. Proportion of Complaints to Output – 1910. Technical Department," Binder "Minutes," Box 1, Hudson Papers, BHL, UM.

[68] "Complaints," March 14, 1910, 1–2, "Cars in Service. Proportion of Complaints to Output – 1910. Technical Department," Binder "Minutes," Box 1, Hudson Papers, BHL, UM.

[69] "Weekly Conference between Manager Technical Division and General Manager," June 24, 1910, Binder "Minutes," Box 1, Hudson Papers, BHL, UM.

[70] "Complaints," March 14, 1910, 2, "Cars in Service. Proportion of Complaints to Output – 1910. Technical Department," Binder "Minutes," Box 1, Hudson Papers, BHL, UM.

[71] "Complaints," March 14, 1910, 1–3, "Cars in Service. Proportion of Complaints to Output – 1910. Technical Department," Binder "Minutes," Box 1, Hudson Papers, BHL, UM.

its tests underway by 1913, before Cardozo's ruling and the 1914 Appellate Division's ruling. Ford's brief in the Livesay case contended that its inspections of wooden wheels "were the same universally made by reputable manufacturers of automobiles."[72] Ford officials explained that they first examined all wheels upon receipt from the supplier, the W. K. Prudden Company, and eight more times in the assembly process. They also put one in ten wheels "in a special warper or press machine." If ten percent of a given lot failed this test, then the entire lot was "rejected." Ford's brief reported that should inspectors identify "any visible sign of a defect," then the "frame is scrapped," a process that led to some "one to three percent of the wheels" being "rejected" owing to such common defects as having "split spokes, split felloes, worm holes, knot holes, loose joints, open joints, short spokes, defective fit of the hubs, etc."[73] Brakes offered a second example. In 1914, Ford's lawyer responded to a case involving defective brakes, saying to his New York attorney that the brake band lining "is very carefully inspected at the time of its receipt and also when it is placed in the brake band, and that it would be almost impossible for a piece of lining such as that claimed to get into the car."[74]

Research represented yet another source for improvement in vehicles' design and manufacture. *Horseless Age* noted in 1906 and 1907 both the need for and lack of adequate research facilities.[75] In 1910, two noteworthy organizations began sustained research activities. First, the Society of Automobile Engineers (SAE), organized in 1905, established standardization committees to investigate components and materials, and recommend codes for uniform practice.[76] At the SAE, many topics of investigation were listed in 1910: "[t]he specification and heat treatment of automobile materials; the indexing and digesting of automobile engineering literature; the compilation and publishing of an automobile engineer's hand book or pocket books; seamless steel tubing; sheet metal; lock washers; limits for screws and taps; . . . automobile nomenclature; frame sections, etc."[77] A second major

---

[72] "Copy of Brief – Livesay Case," no date, "Statement of the Issues," 5–6, quote 9, Folder 75-37-30, Box 37, Acc. 75, HF; and "Points," 2, Folder 75-37-30, Box 37, Acc. 75, HF. *Ford Motor Co. v. Livesay*, 160 P. 901 (Okla. 1916).

[73] "Copy of Brief – Livesay Case," no date, "Statement of the Issues," 5–6, Folder 75-37-30, Box 37, Acc. 75, HF.

[74] FMC to Thorne, June 18, 1915, File L-2008, Box 3, Acc. 297, HF.

[75] See "Need of Testing Laboratories," *Horseless Age* 17 (May 9, 1906): 657–58; and Harry E. Dey, "Experimental Departments," *Horseless Age* 20 (October 2, 1907): 455–56.

[76] Misa provided an excellent example of the SAE's standardization work for steels used in automobiles. He noted that in 1917 the association changed its name to the Society of Automotive Engineers. Thomas J. Misa, *A Nation of Steel: The Making of Modern America, 1865–1925* (Baltimore: Johns Hopkins University Press, 1995), 213, 215–23, 229; and Rae, *American Automobile Manufacturers*, 79–80.

[77] "Standardization Committee of Society of Automobile Engineers," *Horseless Age* 26 (September 7, 1910): 326.

change in automotive research came in 1910, when the U.S. Department
of Agriculture (USDA) established the Forest Products Laboratory (FPL)
and assigned it the task of undertaking research projects to conserve wood
and reduce waste.[78] The FPL categorized several species of trees according
to their strength, resiliency, and other mechanical properties.[79] The laboratory also sought to assess the effects of moisture on trees, to develop more
effective processes for artificially seasoning wood, to identify substitutes for
more scarce and expensive species, and, as Charles Nelson found, "to determine the influence of defects upon the strength of wood so as to make possible
the revision of grading rules."[80] The FPL mattered to automakers because
several components in early autos were fabricated out of wood – the car's
body, the dash, running boards, floor boards, and seats.

Just as the FPL and the SAE initiated many research projects, individual
automakers began their own systematic research efforts. In 1911, General
Motors, for example, hired Arthur D. Little, Inc., a consulting company that
performed research projects for many companies.[81] Claude E. Cox, an automobile designer with ten years of experience, ran the consulting laboratory
for GM in Detroit. The staff included technically trained researchers in chemistry, metallurgy, electrical and mechanical engineering, paints, and materials. The researchers tested components (wheels, tires, magnetos, carburetors, brake linings, valves, piston rings, batteries) as well as materials (oils,
steels, paints).[82] Their projects included "endurance tests" of magnetos, the

---

[78] The Forest Service undertook many research projects for the wood-using industries prior to
the creation of the FPL. Charles A. Nelson, "A History of the Forest Products Laboratory"
(Ph.D. diss., University of Wisconsin, 1964), especially 24–27, 42–51, 57.

[79] Charles A. Nelson recounted, as well, that trade associations, such as the National Association of Carriage Builders and the Western Wheel Manufacturers, lent their support for
the creation of the FPL. Ibid., especially 24–27, 42–51, 57. See also Chester H. Jones, "The
Forest Products Laboratory," *Chemical and Metallurgical Engineering* 21 (December 24–31,
1919): 757–64; and "Where the Forest Meets the Laboratory," *Scientific American* 139 (July
1928): 36–37.

[80] Nelson, "A History of the Forest Products Laboratory," 46–47, 114–16, 133–38, 143–44,
quote 58–59.

[81] David Mowery reviewed Arthur D. Little, Inc. in "The Emergence and Growth of Industrial
Research in American Manufacturing, 1899-1945" (Ph.D. diss., Stanford University, 1981),
262–94. See also David Mowery and Nathan Rosenberg, *Technology and the Pursuit of
Economic Growth* (New York: Cambridge University Press, 1989), 84–90.

[82] The staff was listed at the start of each progress report. See, for example, General Motors
Company-Research Dept., Arthur D. Little, Inc. – Directors, "Progress Report of the
Research Department for the Month of November, 1911," in "GM Before 1923," GM
Files, DPL. The research staff was described in the long letter from Vice-President, Arthur D.
Little, Inc., to Thomas Neal, Esq., President, General Motors Company, June 1, 1911, Box
228, ADL, LC. The records for Arthur D. Little, Inc. are extensive. See, for example, General
Motors Company – Engineering Dept., "Progress Report of the Engineering Department for
the Month of June, 1911," July 1, 1911, 8, Box 228; General Motors Company – Engineering
Dept., "Progress Report of the Engineering Department for the Month of September, 1911,"

development of equipment to test ball bearings more effectively, the setting of "standard specifications for steels and heat treatments," the assessment of patents, and the identification and evaluation of substitutes, such as alternatives for turpentine.[83] Their reports sought to identify cheaper and more effective production methods as well as stronger and more reliable materials. Their watchword was standardization, because they wanted improved practices adopted throughout the GM divisions.[84]

By 1916, automakers had established several institutions associated with the modern firm, and in doing so, improved their products' quality. The coming of mass production had represented the most noticeable change during these years, but there were other significant developments. Hudson, for example, had established by 1910 a method for carefully monitoring the nature of repairs and the quality of its vehicles. But the relationship was also reciprocal: its dealers identified problems and shared solutions. Inspections of suppliers' parts had also begun, and, equally important, three different types of research (the SAE, the FPL, and corporate research) had been initiated to improve the quality of parts. By 1916, the market's key players were also in place. Ford had dominated the market since 1906, but two other

September 30, 1911, Box 228; and J. G. Callan, Engineer, Arthur D. Little, Inc., to C. E. Cox, General Motors Company, May 15, 1912, 36–67, Miscellaneous Technical Reports, Volume 21, Box 67, all in ADL, LC.

[83] General Motors Company-Research Dept., Arthur D. Little, Inc. – Directors, "Progress Report of the Research Department for the Month of October, 1911," 9, 16–17, 19, "GM Before 1923," GM Files, DPL; General Motors Company-Research Dept., Arthur D. Little, Inc. – Directors, "Progress Report of the Research Department for the Month of November, 1911," 7, 11, "GM Before 1923," GM Files, DPL; Engineering Department, Directors, General Motors Company to Thomas Neal, President, GMC, "Progress Report of the Engineering Department for the Month of June, 1911," 15, Box 228, ADL, LC; and Engineering Department, General Motors Company, Directors to Thomas Neal, President, GMC, "Progress Report of the Engineering Department for the Month of July, 1911," 4–5, Box 228, ADL, LC. For examples of projects undertaken by the consultants, see J. G. Callan, Engineer, Arthur D. Little, Inc., to General Motors Company, August 2, 1912, 711–40, Miscellaneous Technical Reports, Volume 21, Box 67; and Engineering Department, General Motors Company, to Thomas Neal, President, General Motors Company, Miscellaneous Technical Reports, Volume 18, Box 64, both in ADL, LC. See also General Motors Company, Research Department, Arthur D. Little, Inc., Directors, "Report of Research Department for July, August, and September," No. 196, October 15, 1912, "GM Before 1923," GM Files, DPL.

[84] For example, its report of November 1911 explained: "Mr. Zimmerschied's work has been confined entirely to investigations of troubles at the various plants and to a systematic plan of listing various steel parts which are used and the heat treatments now used, with the idea of standardizing the material specifications and heat treating specifications for all the plants." General Motors Company-Research Dept., Arthur D. Little, Inc. – Directors, "Progress Report of the Research Department for the Month of November, 1911," quote 11, "GM Before 1923," GM Files, DPL. For other examples, see Engineering Department, General Motors Company, Directors to Thomas Neal, President, GMC, "Progress Report of the Engineering Department for the Month of July, 1911," 4–5, Box 228, ADL, LC.

brands now joined the Model T. The Dodge brothers, having started a new firm in 1914, enjoyed seeing their brand reach the top five sales leaders in 1915; Chevrolet (organized in 1913) joined this elite tier in 1917.[85]

PERSISTENT DEFECTS: 1911–1914

MacPherson's complaint against Buick concerned allegedly defective hickory spokes in the car's wooden wheel. Manufacturers favored hickory because of "[t]he severe thrust, strain, twist, and compression which automobile wheels must sustain." Still, defects in hickory and other species of trees took many forms, often called "brashness." Decay initiated by fungi, a USDA researcher explained, was "a well-known cause of brashness" adding that "brash wood breaks suddenly and completely across the grain with brittleness in fracture and with a comparatively small deflection." "Shock resistance," he concluded, was "the first mechanical property affected by the progressive disintegration of wood by fungi. Wood may show a reduction in this property even before the decay has advanced far enough to be readily recognized by inspection or before the type of fracture is affected by it."[86] Wooden wheels represented one example of the persistent problem of defects. Although manufacturers, as I have just argued, took steps to establish business institutions that would improve their products' quality, vehicles still housed serious defects. Striving to design better vehicles, the research consultants at Arthur D. Little, as well as SAE engineers and the FPL, called attention to existing problems between 1911 and 1914. Ford's legal counsel also acknowledged defects as a serious problem in causing accidents and, by extension, called attention to the role of the legal requirement of privity of contract played in blocking lawsuits.

One of Arthur D. Little's first reports for GM had concerned the strength of wooden wheels. The test was conducted "in connection with an action for damages brought against the Olds Company alleging improper design of a front wheel of an Oldsmobile." In March, at the Imperial Wheel Company (where Buick purchased its wheels), the consultants tested a 36- by 5-inch wheel. "A total stress of one ton caused a cracking sound, and was evidently above the safe limit." "It would seem," the authors continued, "that the hub design could be strengthened with advantage at very small additional expense." They added in their conclusion, "We think careful tests of a

---

[85] For production figures, see Editors of Automobile Quarterly, *The American Car since 1775*, 138–39. For Chevrolet's start date, see ibid., n.p.

[86] Charles F. Hatch, "Manufacture and Utilization of Hickory, 1911," U.S. Department of Agriculture *Forest Service – Circular* 187 (1911): 1–16, quote 4; and Arthur Koehler, "Causes of Brashness in Wood," U.S. Department of Agriculture *Technical Bulletin* 342 (1933): 1–39, quotes 2, 36, 38.

number of wheels of various types should be made with a view to developing a wheel of substantially equal strength at all points."[87]

Even if components were properly manufactured, they still could put so much stress on another part to cause it to weaken and break. In 1911, Cox complained about the clutch's "violent action." If poorly designed, the clutch's sudden engagement exerted pressure on other parts of the vehicle, such as the rear axle. Repeated jarring initiated by the clutch could cause the axle to harden, or become brittle and break.[88] As cars became heavier and faster, their added weight and speed also put parts at risk of breaking, and wheels again were a fine example. In 1909, *Horseless Age* reported an increase in accidents from broken wheels. The diameter of wheels had increased, but there was no increase in the diameter of the hub or the width of the spokes. The relative changes made the wheels weaker and less resistant to lateral strains.[89] Poorly designed parts also posed fire hazards. In 1911, Cox reported that for the Oldsmobile roughly "12% of all cars shipped caught fire from back-firing through the carburetor."[90]

Cox's researchers further complained about the improper use of materials. In June 1911, they reported "a defective shaft" made with "very low carbon steel instead of 3-1/2% nickel steel as specified." In November 1911, they traced "brittle nickel steel" to the "poor practice at the rolling mills." That December, Cox further complained that "steering arms have broken, due to a low factor of safety and low grade material not properly heat treated." His staff, in turn, called for the "systematic and thorough inspection of such incoming material before acceptance."[91]

At GM, Claude Cox grew frustrated with the firm's research standards. He claimed in 1911 that other firms devoted more money to experimental research than "the entire amount spent so far on the Research Department," and that some GM divisions were not "equipped for experiment work or research work of any kind." In 1912, Cox fumed about the lack of

[87] Engineering Department, General Motors Company, to Thomas Neal, Esq., President, General Motors Company, June 6, 1911, and "Test of Wheel 36″ × 5″ Oldsmobile Made by Imperial Wheel Company, March 15, 1911, At Flint Axle Works, Flint Michigan," Miscellaneous Technical Reports, Arthur D. Little, Inc., Directors, Volume 18, 230–37, quote 230, 232, 237, Box 64, ADL, LC.

[88] Claude E. Cox to Gleason Murphy, December 27, 1911, 2, Box 6, Cox, DPL.

[89] "Increase in Number of Front Wheel Failures," *Horseless Age* 23 (March 24, 1909): 398.

[90] Claude E. Cox to Gleason Murphy, December 27, 1911, 2, Box 6, Cox, DPL.

[91] Engineering Department, Directors, General Motors Company to Thomas Neal, President, General Motors Company, "Progress Report of the Engineering Department for the Month of June 1911," July 1, 1911, 2, Box 228, ADL, LC; General Motors Company-Research Dept., Arthur D. Little, Inc. – Directors, "Progress Report of the Research Department for the Month of November, 1911," 11, 13, "GM Before 1923," GM Files, DPL; and Claude E. Cox to Gleason Murphy, December 27, 1911, 2, Box 6, Cox, DPL.

coordination between his lab and specific companies.[92] In early 1913, GM cut back its work with Arthur D. Little, and the records suggest the relationship ended that year. In their three-year association, the consultants had assisted the automaker in many regards, such as in their efforts to introduce uniform policies. Yet, the affiliation also exasperated Cox, as GM appeared to be too strapped for cash or too disorganized to fund the research on the scale that he expected.[93]

Much like the research consultants of Arthur D. Little, engineers at work for the SAE and the FPL also voiced their frustrations with defects. For SAE engineers, a common complaint was that there was so much to do simply to begin to get some control over the sources of defects. In 1913, for example, the SAE's report on motors pointed to the lack of a systematic means for comparing motors across companies. Another report, although applauding laboratory research, complained that testing devices were "crude" and in many cases "the engineer must design his own." Reviewing the inspection of springs, one engineer complained that tests existed for the overall strength and flexibility of springs, but that these tests could readily miss defects in specific details.[94] Like the SAE, the Forest Service and the FPL initially promoted laboratory research without being fully confident in their results. The scientists who wrote the 1908 circular evaluating the strength of different wooden wheels, for instance, confessed in their conclusion that some findings were "only suggestive, because of the small number of samples tested."[95]

It is rare to find detailed records of corporate lawyers' correspondence, but in the case of the Ford Motor Company an unusually large collection of letters survives for the mid-1910s. The company's chief attorney, Leslie B. Robertson, acknowledged the problem of defects while articulating what he saw as the value of the franchise sales contract in letters from 1913 and 1914. To one plaintiff's attorney, Roberts wrote, "Mr. Ruggles [a Ford dealer] is in

[92] Claude E. Cox to Gleason Murphy, December 27, 1911, quote 1; Research Department, Arthur D. Little, Inc., [CEC] to Thomas Neal, President, General Motors Co., February 15, 1912; President, Arthur D. Little, Inc., to Tracy Lyon, Director of Production, March 28, 1912; Director of Research [Cox] to Arthur D. Little, Inc., August 9, 1912; and Director of Research to Arthur D. Little, Inc., attention Mr. John G. Callan, January 15, 1913, all in Folder 6:3, Box 6, Cox, DPL.

[93] Claude E. Cox to John G. Callan, January 15, 1913, Box 6, Cox, DPL. Sloan noted that two years after its formation in 1908, General Motors absorbed twenty-five new firms. Alfred P. Sloan, Jr., *My Years with General Motors*, ed. John McDonald with Catherine Stevens (Garden City, NY: Doubleday & Company, Inc., 1964), 5, 7–9.

[94] "S.A.E. Winter Meeting a Successful Affair," *Horseless Age* 31 (January 22, 1913): 195–203, quote 198. See also "S.A.E. Summer Meeting Active and Enjoyable," *Horseless Age* 31 (June 11, 1913): 1076–85; "S.A.E. Midsummer Convention in Dayton, Ohio," *Horseless Age* 27 (June 21, 1911): 1062–66; and "New S.A.E. Standards," *Horseless Age* 33 (February 25, 1914): 342–44.

[95] H. B. Holroyd and H. S. Betts, "Tests of Vehicle and Implement Woods," *Forest Service – Circular* 142 (1908): 23.

no sense an 'Agent' of this company, nor has he any authority whatever to bind it or to receive or accept service of any papers for it." Robertson added that the branch office would furnish a copy of the dealer's "agreement" to make clear "there is no basis upon which this suit can be maintained as against this company."[96] That year he also faced a damage lawsuit from South Carolina. Robertson wanted the dealer to sign an affidavit stating that he was not Ford's agent, but the dealer asked Ford to "hold him harmless from all suits brought against him for machines sold under the terms of the contract." The Ford legal department refused to do this. Putting the firm's risk in broad terms, officials declared that it would "render us liable for unauthorized statements or agreements made by him to customers." Eventually Ford prevailed over the dealer.[97]

Ford also tried to shift liability to its wheel suppliers. In 1914, Robertson noted that he had pending "several defective wheel cases." In a letter to Ford's Arkansas attorney, he declared: "We do not manufacture wheels, nor have we ever done so, but purchase them from reliable concerns and after doing so make every inspection possible."[98] Unlike consumers who lacked a contractual relation with manufacturers, manufacturers' contracts with their wheel suppliers presumably offered them some leverage. Ford's attorney, for instance, leaned on wheel suppliers to cover half the cost of litigation.[99] The contract also mattered to the question of defects. In the case of *Olds Motor Works v. Shaffer* (Ky. Ct. App. 1911), Olds lost the lawsuit, according to Robertson, because the defect was so "apparent...that the Olds Company must have had knowledge of it."[100] But defects were also latent. Robertson wrote in regard to the Livesay lawsuit in 1914: "There is no possible means

[96] Gen'l Attorney, Ford Motor Company, to William H. Atwell, August 27, 1913, Folder 75-29-24, Box 29, Acc. 75, HF.

[97] General Attorney, Ford Motor Company, to Mordecai & Gadsden & Rutledge, September 19, 1913; Mordecai & Gadsden & Rutledge to L. B. Robertson, telegram, September 26, 1913; Ford Motor Company to Mordecai & Gadsden & Rutledge, telegram, September 27, 1913; C. F. Rizer to Ford Motor Company, telegram, September 28, 1913; and Simeon Hyde to L. R. [sic] Robertson, November 26, 1913, all in File L-2020 Johnson, Daniel 1912-1914 (damage-personal), Box 3, Acc. 297, HF.

[98] Gen'l Attorney, Ford Motor Company, to W. K. Prudden Company, October 19, 1914, Folder 75-26-16, Box 26; and Gen'l Attorney, Ford Motor Company, to Jo Johnson, Att'y, April 20, 1916; Jo Johnson to L. R. [sic] Robertson, April 17, 1916, Folder 75-40-4, Box 40, all in Acc. 75, HF.

[99] Ford wrote to its supplier, expecting the company would "reimburse us for at least fifty percent of the expense incurred in defense of this action." Gen'l Attorney, Ford Motor Company, to W. K. Prudden Company, May 23, 1916, Folder 75-39-30, Box 39, Acc. 75, HF.

[100] Lucy Shaffer was seated in a rumble seat bolted to a box on the rear of the car, and as the car climbed a hill the box cracked, causing the seat to give way. She was injured in the fall. *Olds Motor Works v. Shaffer*, 140 S.W. 1047 (Ky. Ct. App. 1911); and Gen'l Attorney to Henry W. Thorne, March 1, 1915, File L-2008, Box 3, Acc. 297, HF.

by which we could find a hidden defect, nor is there any known method of making a test which would disclose same."[101]

If Robertson expected the courts to hold wheel suppliers liable under these conditions, he also registered the impact of *MacPherson v. Buick*. In 1914, after the Appellate Division had ruled for MacPherson, Ford's local attorney urged officials to "note carefully" what Justice Kellogg had said regarding the "inspection and testing of parts . . . purchased from maker of good reputation etc. If your test is not sufficient to detect latent defects, under the holding in the last case mentioned, you would be liable to a third person for personal injuries arising from such defect covered by paint or anything else."[102] That year Robertson told his Oklahoma attorney, "If the manufacturer can be held liable for hidden defects in goods which are not made by him, it would result in a great many damage suits and put most manufacturers out of business."[103]

MACPHERSON V. BUICK: DEMONSTRATING LIABILITY IN COURT

Testifying in MacPherson's trial, Alanson P. Brush, a GM engineer, was asked how he determined a part's durability. "The most satisfactory information that we can have, in fact the only means to the designer," he stated, "is to use the customers, that is to go over the complaint correspondence. That is the most satisfactory information a designer can have."[104] The work of Arthur D. Little flatly contradicted Brush, but GM officials did not try to explain the evolution of wheel inspections from 1909 to 1913. Perhaps that exercise would only have begged the question: if Arthur D. Little could test wheels scientifically in 1912, why hadn't GM conducted such tests in 1909? Instead, GM did not mention its relationship with the consultants in the trial, and as a result, MacPherson was left to find his own method to establish the wheel's defect. The plaintiff was fortunate, nevertheless. First, the defective part was made from wood, a material that local carriage makers could assess. Second, the wheel had been manufactured in 1909 but the case was not decided until 1916. The long time interval allowed the contrast to become more obvious between GM's lack of tests in 1909 and the growing number of ways that

---

[101] General Attorney, Ford Motor Company, to Douglas B. Crane, Esq., June 6, 1914, Folder 75-26-16, Box 26, Acc. 75, HF.

[102] Henry W. Thorne to Ford Motor Company, October 8, 1914, Folder L-2008, Box 3, Acc. 297, HF.

[103] General Attorney, Ford Motor Company, to Douglas B. Crane, Esq., June 6, 1914, Folder 75-26-16, Box 26, Acc. 75, HF.

[104] Alanson P. Brush, testimony, 350–51, quote 351, Records and Briefs for *MacPherson*. Brush appears to have been the man who entered the field with a Brush runabout in 1907. See Richard S. Tedlow, *New and Improved: The Story of Mass Marketing in America* (New York: Basic Books, 1990), 119; and James J. Flink, *The Automobile Age* (Cambridge, MA: MIT Press, 1988), 35–36.

businesses sought to inspect their products. If so, this reflected the political landscape of the Progressive era. In other words, why safety mattered to Americans was a question that took on importance beyond the immediate issues at stake in MacPherson's lawsuit. Luckily for him, the specific details of his case intersected with national concerns about corporate power and liability.

Donald MacPherson held that his accident and injuries had been prompted by the car's defect: a wheel made of rotten wood. As he drove along a road at a moderate speed, the wheel's spokes collapsed, causing the car to roll over and damage his arm, wrist, and eyes.[105] As one defense unrelated to the question of defects, Buick claimed MacPherson drove too fast and his recklessness contributed to his accident and injuries. As recounted in the 1914 ruling, Buick contended that MacPherson drove at thirty miles per hour; MacPherson claimed to have traveled at less than half that speed. The question of MacPherson's driving did not deter Cardozo, however, who simply wrote that the car "was designed to go fifty miles per hour."[106]

Buick's two remaining defenses rested on its relational ties with dealers and suppliers. One, of course, was that it was not liable because it had sold the car to the Close Brothers. Cardozo dismissed this excuse, finding that even though the dealer was the immediate buyer to whom the manufacturer was responsible through the sales contract, the dealer was the one party likely not to use the car. As its second line of defense, Buick tried to shift the firm's liability back to the wheel maker, claiming it had purchased its wheels from a reputable supplier. But the defendant's own witnesses made this claim hard to stick. G. W. Durham, an engineer who had worked with many automakers since 1900, testified that the managers of car manufacturers "finally determine as to the kind of wheels they will put under the body."[107] Charles Johnson, a wheel maker for some thirty-nine years, declared: "After the wheels left the wheel maker and went to the automobile maker, the manufacturer could put on them a car of such weight as he pleases."[108] In other words, the car maker determined the balance between the car body's weight and the strength of its wheels. The court concluded that it was "too remote" to hold the maker of "component parts" negligent when Buick had a duty to inspect.[109]

Having failed to shift liability forward to the dealer or backward to the supplier, Buick's internal practices were open for legal review: had it tested or inspected its wheels? Buick's witnesses stated that they had not tested the

---

[105] MacPherson's accident is described in *MacPherson* (1912); Complaint, 4–6, Records and Briefs for *MacPherson*. See also Peck, *Decision at Law*, 41–42.

[106] *MacPherson* (1914), 462; and *MacPherson* (1916), quote 1053.

[107] G. W. Durham, testimony, 178, quote, 185, Records and Briefs for *MacPherson*.

[108] Charles Johnson, testimony, 231, quote 254, Records and Briefs for *MacPherson*.

[109] On dealers and suppliers, see *MacPherson* (1916), 1053.

wheels. E. D. Cook, who worked with a wheel manufacturer, said that his firm primed the wheels before delivery. He knew of no means for testing a wheel's "strength or any mechanical test to find out the strength of the spokes, or the quality of the hickory."[110]

The plaintiff, by contrast, relied on three local carriage makers' testimony and each carriage maker claimed twenty or more years of experience in judging hickory, the hard wood used to make the wheel's spokes.[111] George Palmer examined MacPherson's wheel soon after the accident and found "the wood was brittle, coarse grained, such as you find in old trees." He stated, "sound hickory, when it breaks, it brooms up, slivers up.... The fact that they were brittle and of poor quality indicates very little strength, not half the strength of sound wood."[112] Adelbert Payne judged hickory by its heft and its grain, finding that "different angles of the spoke expose different portions of the grain."[113] James P. Tittemore testified that whereas sound wood splinters or brooms, dead or dozy wood lacks this elasticity, and side strains cause it to break easily.[114] Their remarks were familiar ones in the industry. In a case about a defective wheel, Ford's brief recalled witnesses who described the wood as "dozy and brashy, meaning timber that would break square off and not splinter, and further showing that wood in that condition would break much more easily and upon less strain than perfectly sound timber."[115]

Buick objected to the carriage makers' testimony, arguing that such tests were not feasible because suppliers painted the wheels. Yet, to assess hickory's grain, one needed to see it, as Payne explained: "The test with the paint on is to scrape off sufficient paint to see the grain and fiber of the wood. It certainly is a perfectly feasible and easy test to determine the character of a spoke that way, and sure." Alternatively, the wood could have been inspected before it was put into the wheels. The plaintiff's witness, Otto Kleinfelder, had worked nine years as a tester and stated that the Thomas Motor Car Company had wheels shipped "in their natural wood." He also described a hydraulic pressure test where pressure was put on the hub to ascertain its

---

[110] E. D. Cook, testimony, 208, Records and Briefs for *MacPherson*.

[111] Each carriage maker began his testimony by giving his age, his years in the business, and his local residency. George A. Palmer, testimony, 50–57, Aldebert Payne, testimony, 57–72, and James P. Tittemore, testimony, 72–92, Records and Briefs for *MacPherson*.

[112] George A. Palmer, testimony, 50–51, quote 51, Records and Briefs for *MacPherson*. See also Peck, *Decision at Law*, 47–48.

[113] Payne declared: "I never let a wheel come painted; come oiled so I can see the quality of hickory used. I have invariably examined the wheels used in these various connections, with a view of determining the grades, and knots and defects." Adelbert Payne, testimony, 56–59, quote 58–59, Records and Briefs for *MacPherson*. See also Peck, *Decision at Law*, 48.

[114] James P. Tittemore, testimony, 72–74, Records and Briefs for *MacPherson*.

[115] "Copy of Brief – Livesay Case," no date, "Statement of the Issues," 7, Folder 75-37-30, Box 37, Acc. 75, HF.

strength. Buick's witness, E. D. Cook, stated he did not know of Thomas's hydraulic pressure test and thought it unusual, given common practices in the industry.[116] Buick, in a sense, pleaded for sympathy by saying that it was no different from other firms engaged in a process of innovation and in 1909 lacked methods to test products.[117]

It would be a misunderstanding to picture Cardozo's ruling as a grand turning point in prompting firms to test products.[118] Prior to *MacPherson*, automakers tested vehicles as part of their general effort to develop a viable product. By 1910, the SAE and the Forest Service had initiated tests of materials and products, and by 1911, GM had hired Arthur D. Little to evaluate inputs. Also, several court cases had weakened the privity requirement.[119] Lawyers may have tried to bolster the defense of manufacturers with evidence of inspections. Ford Motor Company's attorney thus distinguished Ford from Buick: "You will note in the Buick case no inspection or examination of the wheels was made and this seemed to be the strong point of the court in sustaining the verdict, while, in our case, we show at least nine separate and distinct inspections."[120]

The issue at stake was not simply a question of testing; MacPherson drew attention to the "bright" and "dark" sides of relational contracting.[121] In

---

[116] Respondent's Brief, 59–67, Records and Briefs for *MacPherson*; and Adelbert Payne, testimony, 62, Otto Kleinfelder, testimony, 92–94, quote 93, E. D. Cook, testimony, 208–209, Records and Briefs for *MacPherson*.

[117] In his review of the testimony, Peck emphasized that Buick relied on the testimony of a civil engineer, W. K. Hatt, who had supervised the Forest Service's tests of woods used for vehicles. According to Peck, Hatt discounted the carriage makers' knowledge of wood, finding that the critical variable in assessing the quality of wood was a tree's rate of growth as measured by the number of rings per inch. Growth of "five to twenty-five rings per inch" was considered, Peck noted, "good hickory." Still, Peck omitted a key part of Hatt's testimony. The engineer had agreed with the carriage makers in finding that weight, not just a tree's rate of growth, was an important indicator of strength. His remarks echoed the Forest Service's bulletin: "The best criterion of the value of the wood is its weight." Moreover, although Hatt asserted the value of laboratory research, he sidestepped the question of MacPherson's defective wheel. The 1908 study (circular 142, which Hatt cited) indicated that defects took many forms. In his 1933 study, Koehler cautioned against using a tree's rate of growth as a criterion for assessing its strength. Peck, *Decision at Law*, 48, 50–51; W. K. Hatt, testimony, 101–35, especially 101–8, Records and Briefs for *MacPherson*; Anton T. Boisen and J. A. Newlin, "The Commercial Hickories," *Forest Service – Bulletin* 80 (1910): 64; and Koehler, "Causes of Brashness in Wood," 11–13, 18.

[118] Nelson, *The Legalist Reformation*, 105–107, 187–88.

[119] *Huset v. J. I. Case Threshing Mach. Co.*, 120 F. 865 (8th Cir. 1903); *Kuelling v. Roderick*, 75 N.E. 1098 (N.Y. 1905); and *Statler v. Ray Manufacturing Company*, 88 N.E. 1063 (N.Y. 1909).

[120] *Johnson v. Cadillac*; and Gen'l Attorney, Ford Motor Company, to Douglas B, Crane, Att'y, May 13, 1916, Folder 75-27-3, Box 27, Acc. 75, HF.

[121] According to Gordon, Macaulay and Macneil recognized the importance of "mutual trust and solidarity" for economic development, but worried too that "power imbalances" could result in patterns of "persistent domination on one side and dependence on the other."

the market's early years, automakers had counted on ties with dealers as well as relations with suppliers who made many components that firms like GM and Ford assembled.[122] Yet both GM and Ford exercised power through their relational contracts as they tried to shift liability for defective vehicles backward to their suppliers or forward to their dealers. Although some firms, such as GM, benefited from their extended ties to research consultants like Arthur D. Little, in court the supplier or automaker needed to demonstrate tests such as Ford's wheel inspections conducted in 1913 (and perhaps earlier). Yet, Ford's managers still complained that for "latent or hidden defects" the firm would have been required to "apply extraordinary tests, which would mean to take the wheel apart, remove the spokes, scrape off the paint and apply tests to the wood, this being practically a complete destruction and rebuilding of the wheel." Like Buick, Ford counted on its relations with dealers in order to call into play the privity requirement. In its case against Livesay, aside from its contention to have demonstrated "ordinary care" thanks to its many inspections, Ford's focus on the privity requirement won the Oklahoma judge's support.[123] Not having inspected its wheels, Buick provided the technical grounds for Cardozo to restrict the privity doctrine: "If to the element of danger there is added knowledge that the thing will be used by persons other than the purchaser, and used without new tests, then, irrespective of the contract, the manufacturer of this thing of danger is under a duty to make it carefully."[124]

Cardozo's ruling came at a time when Americans' daily activities were fraught with danger. The nation's workers suffered unprecedented injuries. In the year 1890, death claimed the lives of 314 railroad employees, 214 bituminous coal miners, and 300 anthracite coal miners for each 100,000 workers employed. Historian John Witt further recalled that certain jobs were especially dangerous. The men who coupled railroad cars and those that operated a train's brakes, for instance, "died in work-related accidents at rates of 900 and 1,141 deaths per 100,000 workers per year, respectively."[125]

Gordon, "Macaulay, Macneil, and the Discovery of Solidarity and Power in Contract Law," 570.

[122] Helper, "Strategy and Irreversibility in Supplier Relations," 792–99. See also Nevins with Hill, *Ford: The Times, the Man, the Company,* 220–51.

[123] "Copy of Brief – Livesay Case," no date, "Statement of the Issues," 6–8, quote 8, Folder 75-37-30, Box 37, Acc. 75, HF; and *Ford Motor Co. v. Livesay,* 901–903.

[124] *MacPherson* (1916), 1053. William L. Prosser, *Handbook of the Law of Torts* (St. Paul, MN: West Publishing Co., 1941), 677; and Croley and Hanson, "Rescuing the Revolution," 697–98. See also Goldberg and Zipursky's critique of Prosser in "The Moral of *MacPherson,*" 1756–69.

[125] Arthur F. McEvoy, "The Triangle Shirtwaist Factory Fire of 1911: Social Change, Industrial Accidents, and the Evolution of Common-Sense Causality," *Law and Social Inquiry* 20 (Spring 1995): 621–51; and John Fabian Witt, *The Accidental Republic: Crippled Workmen, Destitute Widows, and the Remaking of American Law* (Cambridge, MA: Harvard University Press, 2004), 27.

Put another way, as historian Barbara Welke recounted, accidents resulted in the death of one worker for "every 420 employed and one injured for every 27 employed" on the railroads.[126] Pedestrians and passengers also faced serious dangers at the turn of the century. The 1911 report of the Interstate Commerce Commission (ICC) found that 129 passengers had been killed and 2,678 had been injured in accidents. In addition, 2,260 trespassers suffered injuries and 909 were killed.[127] That year a single accident in New York drew special attention to the dangerous conditions. A fire broke out at the Triangle Shirtwaist Company's ten-story building and it burned so quickly that 146 workers were trapped and killed. Some sixty-two people "jumped to their deaths." Another "40 to 50 bodies were piled up against the ninth-floor doorways." And, "[f]irefighters found 30 corpses in the elevator shafts." Arthur McEvoy explained that the accident had been a shocking event. Whereas many industrial accidents were hidden from view, the public deaths of so many garment workers, mostly young women, had stunned Americans.[128]

Accidents took on such significance for Americans that one might be tempted to conclude that the sheer numbers prompted legislatures to pass safety laws or the courts to render verdicts like *MacPherson*. Yet, legal scholarship cautions against this conclusion as a complete answer. Although the number of injuries and deaths no doubt focused Americans' attention on the problem of accidents, legal scholars have identified three cultural threads that helped make accidents a topic of vital concern to Progressives. One concerned risk-taking, and especially the gendered notions of risks men and women should bear; a second focused on causality, or how responsibility for an accident was assigned; and a third concerned the responsibility managers assumed in running giant corporations for their efficient and smooth operation, but also for their safe operation. The three ideas intertwined to bring about a new focus on corporate responsibility for accidents among workers and passengers, but also in the case of consumers and automobiles.

Between the mid-nineteenth century and the start of the twentieth century, Americans reconsidered the risks that they expected men and women to take in their lives. In her study of railroad accidents, Welke traced this shift. During the mid-1800s, railroad companies and the courts maintained that male passengers could take risks not taken by women and, as "free men," were expected to use their judgment in assessing the dangers. Thus women could expect the railroads' employees to assist them, and assume safer conditions

---

[126] Barbara Young Welke, *Recasting American Liberty: Gender, Race, Law, and the Railroad Revolution, 1865-1920* (New York: Cambridge University Press, 2001), 18.

[127] Ibid., 21.

[128] McEvoy, "The Triangle Shirtwaist Factory Fire of 1911," 621–51, especially 627, 629, 631, quote 629.

for entering and exiting railroad cars. Although these differences reflected gendered perceptions of risk-taking, by the century's close the courts faced up to the implied comparison. How would they sustain uniform treatment of the law? Indeed, if a man and a woman were injured in the same accident, would the courts be able to assign the same remedies in their cases?[129] The courts "repeatedly and sternly" instructed railroad companies not to assume that the only passengers were strong, young men. As railroads were asked to build suitable platforms for women, "the duty created was bound to benefit traveling men as well." As time passed and the vast number of cases accumulated, Welke found that the standard for women "replaced the image of 'free men.'"[130] A similar, parallel shift was seen among state regulatory agencies. Thus, she wrote that by the early 1900s "gone was the assumption that every man should be his own judge of the safety of his actions, the respect for individual ingenuity, the celebration of risk-taking, the belief that injuries were the product of unexpected events."[131]

A second shift took place in the intellectual terrain of how Americans explained accidents. McEvoy located the shift in the dramatic events of the Triangle Shirtwaist fire. Prior to the fire, indeed, throughout the nineteenth century, as McEvoy and Christopher Tomlins have explained, the labor contract denied men and women compensation for workplace injuries, and thus, hid the business activities that had produced the accidents. McEvoy wrote: "The causes as well as the costs of accidents remained hidden because systematic relationships between injuries and the organization of work remained obscure." The Triangle fire dramatically showed the system at work, as McEvoy wrote: "Like the infernal apparatus in Franz Kafka's penal colony, the Triangle fire inscribed the law of turn-of-the-century labor relations on its victims' bodies so that its meaning at last became clear."[132] Under these extraordinary circumstances, ideas championed by reformers gained currency. Whereas in the past employees were commonly blamed for accidents, the fire helped make possible a shift in "common sense" ways of understanding their causes. Rather than focus on workers' mistakes, investigators relied on a social scientific approach, accounting for events "as the manifestations of large-scale, impersonal forces instead of describing them as caused either by laws of nature or acts of individual will." With her "mountains of data," Crystal Eastman, the secretary of New York's Employer's Liability Commission, focused on the structure of the workplace. She "showed that many injuries formerly attributed to worker carelessness

---

[129] Welke, *Recasting American Liberty*, 3–136.
[130] Ibid., 99–105, quote 104.   [131] Ibid., quote 36.
[132] McEvoy, "The Triangle Shirtwaist Factory Fire of 1911," 627, 629, 631; and Christopher L. Tomlins, "A Mysterious Power: Industrial Accidents and the Legal Construction of Employment Relations in Massachusetts, 1800–1850," *Law and History Review* 6 (Fall 1988): 375–437.

were really the result of employer's control over the organization of work. Inattention, even recklessness, were not the fault of injured workers so much as they were the result of the pace of work, inadequate safety, or other structural aspects of the job that were beyond the control of individual employees." Eastman's social scientific approach thus accounted for industrial injuries "in a new way that made new laws... both conceivable and politically feasible."[133]

A third shift in attitudes about accidents built on Eastman's approach. During the early 1900s, engineers promoted a set of ideas known as scientific management. Scientific management typically was associated with workplace efficiency. Rather than leave the workplace in the hands of skilled labor, engineers argued that management was best able to put in place an efficient and smooth-running organization. But there was a corollary. Witt explained: "It was but a short step from these ideas to the theory that enterprises themselves were properly responsible for the costs of injuries incident to their operations more generally." He added: "The proposition holds that with respect to managing risk, well managed enterprises are in a superior structural and informational position than individuals such as workers and consumers. ... The claim that enterprises and managers are in the better position to prevent such accidents, however, allows the pragmatic conclusion that the enterprise (rather than the worker) can usefully be identified as the cause of the accident."[134] Witt pointed out that it was engineers who first used the term "enterprise liability" and it was in areas beyond workplace injuries where their ideas found support. Thus, he returned to *MacPherson*. "Beginning with Cardozo's 1916 opinion... the courts extended the liability of manufacturers for manufacturing defects beyond those to whom the manufacturer sold the defective product. In doing so the famous Cardozo opinion implied a new and broader view of the capacity of management to guard against manufacturing defects, and thus the obligations of management in the manufacturing process."[135]

Progressives' concern about safety took many different forms. In the case of railroad and streetcar accidents, Welke found that during the years from 1900 to 1920 "the first mass campaigns directed at changing human behaviors" focused on individuals "not because they were immoral or dangerous to others but because they were self-endangering."[136] In cities and towns, and indeed almost every railroad crossing throughout the nation, "Americans – all Americans – must be 'educated' in the right way and place to cross a street, cross the railroad tracks, get onto or off a streetcar. The clarion call as Americans entered the twentieth century was 'safety first.'"[137] In

---

[133] McEvoy, "The Triangle Shirtwaist Factory Fire of 1911," 622–26, 643–48, quotes 643, 645.
[134] Witt, "Speedy Fred Taylor," quote 40–41; and idem, *The Accidental Republic*, 103–25.
[135] Witt, "Speedy Fred Taylor," quote 45.
[136] Welke, *Recasting American Liberty*, 35–42, quote 35.   [137] Ibid., quote 36.

the case of worker injuries, Witt reported that after a period of experimentation, workmen's compensation laws were enacted in several states. "By 1917, 68 percent of the nation's wage-earning workforce – some 13 million wage earners – was covered by the still newly enacted statutes."[138]

The automobile market had emerged at a critical point in U.S. history. *MacPherson* signaled a new standard for corporate responsibility. In subsequent years, automakers would find that they could not so easily impose social costs on the buying public. It was not only the impact of Cardozo's ruling. The political climate of the Progressive era meant that several responses to the question of safety were possible. Indeed, in the next decade, a web of oversight entities would shape managers' approach to product quality. By implication, the Progressive era left a legacy for other new markets. In contrast to the case of automobiles, managers of young firms in new markets would not be able to impose the social costs of innovation on consumers. This by no means meant that risks could be regulated out of the market, but it did serve as a reminder that the allocation of social costs was a political as much as an economic phenomenon. State legislatures and the courts set standards for safety by which firms might or might not impose costs on consumers as they fostered markets for their novel products.

CONCLUSION

In the new market, automakers quickly learned about their liability to dealers and consumers that followed from making defective vehicles. Yet, firms like Buick were unable to perfect the technology quickly or thoroughly; and instead, they followed a two-pronged strategy associated with the "bright" and "dark" sides of relational contracting.[139] One strategy had been to limit a firm's liability thanks to the legal requirement of privity of contract. Although many firms initially wrote short dealer contracts, by 1908 or 1909 managers had settled on a system of franchise dealerships and made clear that the dealer was not the firm's legal representative. The second course of action focused on the relational contract's bright side: automakers invested in business relations with dealers and suppliers as well as research consultants to improve their vehicles' quality. Because innovation took place in a market context – which is to say, because automakers sold imperfect machines – as they worked to better their products they counted on both the bright and dark sides of relational contracts to transform a new market into a viable commercial market.

One conclusion from this analysis concerns the impact of liability in terms of a firm's structure and its market power. It is conventional among economic

---

[138] Witt, *The Accidental Republic*, 11.
[139] Gordon, "Macaulay, Macneil, and the Discovery of Solidarity and Power in Contract Law."

historians to equate corporate power with a firm's size or market share.[140] Yet, despite being small firms in a young market, automakers exerted considerable power through the privity doctrine when they shifted many start-up costs to dealers and consumers. Furthermore, examination of the problem of social costs has shown that liability for defects represented one important factor in managers' decision to structure mass distribution in terms of a network of franchised retailers rather than sales agents. Stewart Macaulay emphasized that manufacturers added formal provisions to contracts and initiated informal policies to foster on-going relations with their dealers. Yet, manufacturers also counted on the sales contract to deny these on-going relations in court for the sake of avoiding liability for defects. Managers had good reason to worry, as the records of Arthur D. Little revealed, because they sold such crude cars, and it was in this context that they opted to rely on franchised retailers, or what Friedrich Kessler called "vertical integration by contract."[141]

In another important sense, the privity requirement did not afford managers a complete defense against defects when seen in terms of a commercial market. As long as manufacturers wanted to enlarge the market, they faced the task of making vehicles more reliable to attract new buyers and earn their trust. The question was: how quickly would they improve their products and how soon would new car buyers discover the defects? Between 1909, the year MacPherson's runabout was built, and 1916, the year Cardozo ruled on the case, manufacturers invested in institutions to improve their products' quality. The coming of mass production in 1914 was one important piece of the puzzle. Dealers' cooperation in detecting problems and sharing solutions was a second, as Hudson's records from 1910 indicated. Manufacturers also began to inspect wooden wheels and other components, as well as to invest in research labs along with trade associations and government research organizations. In other words, several activities collectively determined a vehicle's quality, and during the 1910s, automakers had begun to invest in these activities and foster relations with dealers and suppliers to build more reliable and durable products.

For Donald MacPherson, managers' efforts had not occurred quickly enough. When he sued Buick, he asked: who should bear the social costs of innovation? His question was as much political as economic. It recognized that risks extended beyond the firm, and that the courts and state legislatures set parameters for how those risks would be allocated. MacPherson's case was also timely. Although automakers at first deflected many start-up costs,

---

[140] See for instance, Naomi R. Lamoreaux, *The Great Merger Movement in American Business* (New York: Cambridge University Press, 1987); and Thomas K. McCraw, *Prophets of Regulation: Charles Francis Adams, Louis D. Brandeis, James M. Landis, Alfred E. Kahn* (Cambridge, MA: Harvard University Press, 1984).
[141] Kessler, "Automobile Dealer Franchises," 1135.

the political and legal platform shifted under their feet during the Progressive era. It was not only Cardozo's decision, but the broad shift that took place among Americans in terms of their attitudes about the sort of risks men and women should face in travel and work, and conversely, the responsibility corporations owed to passengers, workers, and consumers. The point is significant because it meant that automakers were not only put on notice to conduct inspections, but that perceptions of safety and corporate responsibility could be found in state regulation, private oversight agencies, and public research organizations, as we will see in Chapter 4.

Recognizing the social costs of innovation brings us back, finally, to the topic of entrepreneurship. Economic scholars have substantially revised Schumpeter's concept of innovation, as seen in terms of the role of the entrepreneur. Although unusually creative individuals remain vital to an economy's development, the "entrepreneur" lives on not simply as a theoretical concept but also as an ideological construct. True to his conservative disposition, Schumpeter claimed that these risk-loving individuals deserved to be richly rewarded for boosting the economy's level of productivity and society's standard of living.[142] Popular culture continues to celebrate this view of entrepreneurs along with other risk-takers – the wildcatter, the derrick man, the futures trader. In praising the entrepreneur for assuming huge risks, the image has had another effect: it has obscured or effaced a different picture of the risks of innovation – risks that were widely distributed and absorbed by various members of society.

---

[142] Richard Swedberg recalled Schumpeter's political conservatism and his anti-Semitism with respect to the possible appointment of Paul Samuelson in the Economics Department at Harvard. He was, Swedberg wrote, "intensely hostile to the Roosevelt administration." Richard Swedberg, "Introduction to the Transaction Edition," in *Essays: On Entrepreneurs, Innovations, Business Cycles, and the Evolution of Capitalism*, ed. Richard V. Clemence (New Brunswick, NJ: Transaction Publishers, 1989), vii–xxxix, quote xi. See also Michael A. Bernstein, *A Perilous Progress: Economists and Public Purpose in Twentieth-Century America* (Princeton, NJ: Princeton University Press, 2001), 224 n. 1.

PART II

A MASS MARKET, 1916–1941

A mass market for automobiles flourished during the 1920s and, once established, held steady during the depressed 1930s. Whereas manufacturers sold 1.6 million vehicles in 1916 and 2.2 million in 1920, by 1929 sales topped five million before skidding into the Great Depression and bottoming out at 1.4 million units in 1932. Within five years, though, production recovered to 4.8 million vehicles, and firms prospered in 1940 and 1941 before production was halted in World War II. Looking at household ownership, there was a large jump from one percent of households owning cars in 1910 to twenty-six percent owning them in 1920. That figure more than doubled to sixty percent by 1930 before slipping to fifty-five percent during the 1930s.[1] In a 1929 survey, Henry Weaver, who conducted market research for the General Motors Corporation, considered the relation between a firm's market share and its many car owners. When the auto market was small, he suggested, a manufacturer might ignore some "disgruntled owners." If a firm held just two or six percent of the market, obtaining new buyers might not be difficult. But this market condition did not apply to GM. "One out of every three repeat buyers this year owns a General Motors Product." GM's future sales and profits thus depended on existing owners coming back and buying another GM vehicle.[2] GM, and by Weaver's reasoning, any large automaker, depended on customers' loyalty, which is to say, their repeat business, for the firm's long-term prosperity.[3]

---

[1] U.S. Federal Trade Commission, *Report of the Motor Vehicle Industry*, 76th Cong., 1st sess., House Document No. 468 (Washington, D.C.: U.S. Government Printing Office, 1939), 22; and Stanley Lebergott, *Pursuing Happiness: American Consumers in the Twentieth Century* (Princeton, NJ: Princeton University Press, 1993), 130.

[2] Sales Section, General Motors, "Service as Affecting Sales," May 1929, 9, File 87-11.4-3, Box 110, CFK, KU. Weaver had already recognized the trend to repeat sales. See for example, B. G. Koether to C. F. Kettering, June 17, 1927, with H. G. W., "The Manufacturer, the Dealer, and the Used Car," April 1927, File 87-11.4-1, Box 110, CFK, KU; and H. G. Weaver to Division Sales Managers, April 13, 1929, with report by General Motors Sales Section and New York Office Statistical Staff, "The Domestic Automobile Market, Its Past and Future," and Sales Section, "Price Class Analysis," November 1928, File 87-11.4-1, Box 110, CFK, KU.

[3] On managers' efforts to win car buyers' repeat business as a mass market took shape during the 1920s, see also Stephen L. McIntyre, "The Failure of Fordism: Reform of the Automobile

In his 1964 autobiography, *My Years with General Motors*, Alfred P. Sloan, Jr., traced his efforts to engineer GM's dominance of the nation's largest consumer market. To this day, his book remains a very readable account "of the logic of management in relation to the events of the automotive industry" and "a clear view of the business as a business."[4] Sloan's accomplishments were numerous and important, serving as models not only for business strategies executed by other automakers but by corporations in a range of industries. Though hardly the first corporation to advertise on a mass scale, GM married mass advertising with other marketing tools, namely wholesale and retail financing, market research, public relations, the annual model change, and the price ladder (or pyramid) of automobile brands within the GM family. Sloan cultivated something of a symbiotic relationship between marketing and the firm's internal sources of efficiency. Again, though not the first, GM invested extensively in the modern research laboratory under Sloan's leadership. He established an in-house styling department, known as the Art and Colour Section. The firm advanced a system of flexible mass production (in contrast to Henry Ford's mass production) in order to take advantage of the annual model change. Finally, Sloan developed the bureaucratic tools needed to coordinate factory production with GM's network of franchised dealers.[5]

Repair Industry, 1913-1940," *Technology and Culture* 41 (April 2000): 269-99; and Pamela Walker Laird, "'The Car without a Single Weakness': Early Automobile Advertising," *Technology and Culture* 37 (October 1996): 796–812.

4 Alfred P. Sloan, Jr., *My Years with General Motors*, ed. John McDonald with Catherine Stevens (Garden City, NY: Doubleday & Company, Inc., 1964), xxiii. My account of Sloan in the following chapters is not meant as a biography; my focus remains on particular questions about market relationships between consumers and corporations. Readers interested in Sloan's life will want to consult David R. Farber's biography, *Sloan Rules: Alfred P. Sloan and the Triumph of General Motors* (Chicago: University of Chicago Press, 2002); and Alfred D. Chandler, Jr.'s early study, *Strategy and Structure: Chapters in the History of the American Industrial Enterprise* (Cambridge, MA: MIT Press, 1962).

5 For GM's history, consult Chandler, *Strategy and Structure*, 114–62; Alfred D. Chandler, Jr. and Stephen Salsbury, *Pierre S. Du Pont and the Making of the Modern Corporation* (New York: Harper & Row, 1971), 433–604; and Alfred D. Chandler, Jr., ed., *Giant Enterprise: Ford, General Motors, and the Automobile Industry Sources and Readings* (New York: Harcourt, Brace & World, Inc., 1964). On GM's system of mass production, see David A. Hounshell, *From the American System to Mass Production, 1800-1932: The Development of Manufacturing Technology in the United States* (Baltimore: Johns Hopkins University Press, 1984); and Daniel M. G. Raff, "Making Cars and Making Money in the Interwar Automobile Industry: Economies of Scale and Scope and the Manufacturing behind the Marketing," *Business History Review* 65 (Winter 1991): 721–53. For GM's early promotion of industrial research, see Stuart W. Leslie, *Boss Kettering: Wizard of General Motors* (New York: Columbia University Press, 1983). On GM's marketing in its competitive battle with Ford, see Richard S. Tedlow, *New and Improved: The Story of Mass Marketing in America* (New York: Basic Books, 1990), 112–181. And, for GM's competitive prowess, consult Arthur J. Kuhn, *GM Passes Ford, 1918-1939: Designing the General Motors Performance-Control System* (University Park, PA: Pennsylvania State University Press, 1986). GM is singled out in specific

Sloan's strategy coincided with the firm's amazing financial performance: GM's sales surged from $567 million in 1920 to $1.5 billion in 1929, net income after taxes from $38 million to $248 million, and dividends on common stock from $17 million to $157 million. As the Great Depression gripped the nation, sales of high- and low-priced automobiles collapsed, but even so, GM never reported a loss (although it came close to doing so in 1932). Sales recovered during the mid-1930s, so much that from 1935 to 1939 sales averaged $1.3 billion, net income after taxes $178 million, and dividends on common stock $133 million. In 1940 and 1941, as GM and other automakers began converting production to the war effort, sales, net income, and dividends all exceeded their 1935–39 averages.[6] Sloan thus had every reason to point to GM's sales and profit data for confirmation of his managerial strategy.

Thirty-eight years after Sloan published his autobiography, John McDonald, who had worked for *Fortune* and had "edited" (actually, ghostwritten) Sloan's book, published his own memoir. McDonald surprised readers by telling them that, despite Sloan's standing as having directed the firm's rise to prominence, lawyers inside GM nearly blocked publication of the retired CEO's manuscript. Indeed, Sloan's autobiography would not have been published had McDonald not sued GM. McDonald remained puzzled as to what GM lawyers objected to in the manuscript. Then, late in the game, a retired lawyer hinted, as McDonald recalled, that "GM would not have objected . . . had it been my book alone," but being Sloan's publication and recognizing that Sloan was a corporate officer, the firm worried that "anything in the book could be put directly into evidence in a government suit against General Motors."[7]

Sloan in all likelihood did not need this warning. McDonald reported that problems in the text were inadvertent – the sort of thing that an overly anxious lawyer might construe as an example of monopoly power.[8] In other words, the retired CEO recalled his years as someone intent on putting

studies of advertising, styling, and public relations. Consider Roland Marchand, *Advertising the American Dream: Making Way for Modernity, 1920-1940* (Berkeley, CA: University of California Press, 1985); idem, *Creating the Corporate Soul: The Rise of Public Relations and Corporate Imagery in American Big Business* (Berkeley, CA: University of California Press, 1998); C. Edson Armi, *The Art of American Car Design: The Profession and Personalities* (University Park, PA: Pennsylvania State University Press, 1988); David Gartmann, *Auto Opium: A Social History of American Automobile Design* (London: Routledge, 1994); and Lendol Calder, *Financing the American Dream: A Cultural History of Consumer Credit* (Princeton, NJ: Princeton University Press, 1999).

[6] Sloan, *My Years with General Motors*, 214–15.

[7] John A. McDonald, *A Ghost's Memoir: The Making of Alfred P. Sloan's My Years with General Motors* (Cambridge, MA: MIT Press, 2002), 178–82, quote 181.

[8] McDonald guessed that a memo from 1921 with its specific reference to monopoly had been the source of trouble, but even then, he felt this did not qualify as a reason for "suppression by GM." McDonald, *A Ghost's Memoir*, 75–76, 151–55, 161–64, 181, quote 161.

management on a "scientific basis."[9] Still, Sloan's narrative, although accurate in many specific details or topics, was still incomplete. Naomi Lamoreaux cautioned business historians to "avoid the trap of the rational narrative," by which she meant the narratives managers have given in hindsight as logical explanations for their decisions and their firms' subsequent performance.[10] McDonald's experience offered one reason to heed this advice: GM's lawyers had good reason to exclude accounts that could be used in a lawsuit against the firm, which implied fudging questions about corporate power. In his discussion of many topics, such as corporate research and dealer relations, Sloan passed over the sort of conflicts that invited questions about corporate power, and thus offered no reason to doubt management's authority.[11]

Ronald Coase and his school of followers (Lamoreaux included) suggest another reason to consider alternative explanations for the development of a mass market and GM's development as a modern corporation. The fundamental premise underlying a growing body of scholarship in the field of information economics is the recognition that information is imperfect. This seemingly simple but critical premise is important to automakers' market relationships, including those with consumers. Although the goal of securing consumers' repeat business in a mass market seemed clear-cut, how managers accomplished this goal was anything but that.

The next four chapters address the development of a mass automobile market and the structure of the modern corporation. Chapter 3 reviews the epic struggle between Henry Ford's and Alfred Sloan's companies in the years from 1916 through the 1920s. Because Sloan came out on top, claiming healthy profits and a substantial market share, whereas Henry Ford threw in the towel and gave up on his beloved Model T, it is easy to pick a winner and a loser. But that is not my intent. Following the premise laid out by Coase, in a world of uncertain information it is not possible to obtain a single standard of efficiency.[12] Instead, firms may follow sufficiently different paths of

---

[9] Sloan liked to use the word "scientific" to describe his approach to management. See Sloan, *My Years with General Motors*, 132.

[10] Naomi R. Lamoreaux, "Reframing the Past: Thoughts about Business Leadership and Decision Making under Uncertainty," *Enterprise & Society* 2 (December 2001): 632–59.

[11] Compare my discussion in Chapters 3 and 6 to Sloan's autobiography. Sloan, *My Years with General Motors*, 279–312. On dealers, compare Sloan's narrative to Stewart Macaulay's assessment in *Law and the Balance of Power: The Automobile Manufacturers and Their Dealers* (New York: Russell Sage Foundation, 1966), 28–29, 53–54, 77–78.

[12] As Naomi Lamoreaux, Daniel Raff, and Peter Temin observe: "Under conventional assumptions, the neoclassical 'theory of the firm' yields one global optimum – that is, one equilibrium level of prices and output toward which firms' incremental trial-and-error decision making processes will inevitably push them. . . . On the other hand, the more action- and knowledge-oriented approach associated with evolutionary economics leaves open the possibility that firms' myopic decision-making processes may leave them in positions that are local, rather than global, optima. . . . Competitive pressures still operate to keep firms on their toes, but

development such that one firm could not effectively mimic another's strategy. I argue that what has become known as "path dependency" applied to the histories of Ford and GM.[13] Although GM trumped Ford, its task proved more difficult than may at first be apparent from reading Sloan's autobiography. Not only did Sloan's managers face the task of deciphering their consumers, but information problems about consumers pointed to disputes that management at GM, as well as at Ford and other automakers, confronted when trying to win consumers' loyalty and sustain their firms' profitability.

In a mass market, Sloan tackled questions of price and quality that were rooted in a conflict between consumers' welfare and evolving desires, on one hand, and management's goals of efficiency, innovation, and profitability, on the other. That is, the three cases presented what I call consumer dilemmas for management. The dilemma in Chapter 4 centers on the modern research laboratory. Though a more durable and reliable product offered a straightforward means of winning consumers' loyalty, management juggled other goals as well, such as reducing production costs and rushing innovations to market – goals that potentially reduced a product's safety. The dilemma in Chapter 5 concerns the styling department in the modern firm. Though management readily understood that the annual model change was important to winning consumers' repeat purchases, they faced internal clashes between the costs involved in styling innovations and other business goals, such as reducing the cost of retooling and changing a car's engineering. The dilemma in Chapter 6 revolves around the franchised car dealer's role in negotiating prices in each and every market transaction. Rather than simply administer a fixed price, the practice of trading in used cars to bargain down prices meant that the market transaction placed the three parties – consumers, dealers, and management – at odds since one party's gain came at the expense of the other two.

The three dilemmas materialized with the transformation of the mass market: they appeared during the early to mid-1920s, and in succeeding years, management developed different responses to these dilemmas, which by their very nature could never be fully resolved. In the case of engineering a safe product, although managers invested in corporate research, a web of oversight entities directly shaped management's approach to engineering quality. At the same time, management tried to use its public relations arm to deflect responsibility for safety to the users of automobiles. In the case

---

successful firms, even within the same industry, can differ strikingly in ways that are remarkably persistent over time." Naomi R. Lamoreaux, Daniel M. G. Raff, and Peter Temin, eds., *Learning by Doing in Markets, Firms, and Countries*, National Bureau of Economic Research (Chicago: University of Chicago Press, 1999), quote 8.

[13] Paul A. David, "Clio and the Economics of QWERTY," *American Economic Review* 75 (May 1985): 332–37.

of styling, management promoted a streamline aesthetic without ever being certain which ideas would prove popular with consumers. Instead, GM's managers invested in annual style changes as a competitive weapon, being able to afford the variations while making financially strapped competitors unable to rapidly alter their vehicles' looks appear outdated. In the case of the franchised dealer, during the 1920s and 1930s, management attempted to shift costs to dealers, but management and dealers also tried to impose costs on car buyers. During the 1930s, federal regulators tried to moderate the market's operation to make the process of setting prices fairer to consumers.

My study, I want to emphasize, does not alter certain basic ingredients in our understanding of the modern firm, as Sloan explained. His price ladder for automobile brands and use of installment credit, as well as his support of a system of flexible mass production, were important innovations. Yet, the conflicts his managers faced on a daily basis with consumers tell us that Sloan's task was more difficult than his narrative implies. For one thing, in many cases, conflicts between buyers and sellers drew attention to the state's role in the development of a mass market. Federal agencies, notably the Federal Trade Commission and the Justice Department, but also state entities and even some private organizations, became involved in different contests and thus influenced both corporate policies and the market itself. Sloan remains a distinctive manager of the twentieth century though not for his claim to scientific management, but rather for his methods for coping with the uncertainty and conflicts associated with the demand side of the market. The very uncertainty and clashes meant too that consumers' welfare was represented imperfectly by consumers themselves, interest groups, and state regulatory agencies.

3

Corporate Strategies and Consumers' Loyalty

On May 26, 1927, Edsel Ford and his father drove the fifteen millionth Model T off the assembly line at the Highland Park factory. Although Henry Ford was said to be happy on the occasion, a photograph of the event better reminds us of a funeral procession.[1] Nine months earlier, Ford had announced the end of his Model T. From the vantage point of 1921 or even 1925, the events of 1927 seemed almost unimaginable. Who would have thought that the automaker with fifty-five percent of the market in 1921 and forty-two percent in 1925 would have been brought to its knees in 1927 by General Motors, a company that had nearly gone bankrupt in 1920 (Fig. 3.1)?[2]

So dramatic was the switch from Ford to GM as setting the corporate model in the nation's largest consumer market that the key lesson was obvious: prices alone did not dictate the market's evolution. There certainly was no disputing Ford's drive to reduce costs. He had made the automobile a mass market through his marriage of the Model T and the assembly line, passing along cost savings by cutting the T's price from $950 in 1909 to $295 in 1925.[3] The entrepreneur, however, had neglected or simply opposed other aspects of the business. Ford was known for (and later joked about) his opposition to installment credit, advertising, and styling. At General Motors, executives capitalized on these shortcomings. GM created its own credit division, styling department, and industrial research laboratory.[4] Adding insult

---

[1] Allan Nevins and Frank Ernest Hill, *Ford: Expansion and Challenge, 1915-1933* (New York: Charles Scribner's Sons, 1954), 430; and David A. Hounshell, *From the American System to Mass Production, 1800-1932: The Development of Manufacturing Technology in the United States* (Baltimore: Johns Hopkins University Press, 1984), 279–80.

[2] Hounshell, *From the American System to Mass Production*, 263–80. For data on Ford's market share in 1924, see U.S. Federal Trade Commission, *Report on Motor Vehicle Industry*, 76th Cong., 1st sess., House Document No. 468 (Washington, D.C.: U.S. Government Printing Office, 1939) 27. On GM's near bankruptcy, see Alfred P. Sloan, Jr.'s account in *My Years with General Motors*, ed. John McDonald with Catherine Stevens (Garden City, NY: Doubleday & Company, Inc., 1964), 17–39.

[3] Richard S. Tedlow, *New and Improved: The Story of Mass Marketing in America* (New York: Basic Books, 1990), 155.

[4] Hounshell reviewed these developments carefully in *From the American System to Mass Production*, 263–301. The literature about this episode has flourished. Among the many studies, consult Tedlow, *New and Improved*, 112–81; Daniel M. G. Raff, "Making Cars and

FIGURE 3.1. The Fifteenth Millionth Model T (the last one) with Henry and Edsel Ford, 1927. Henry Ford was forced to shut down production because the Model T's market share had slumped. The experience served as a painful lesson that the low price of the Model T did not sustain the brand's sales. From the Collections of the Henry Ford. Negative number P.833.49148.

to injury, GM executed its marketing strategy thanks to a new method of production. Whereas Ford earned his reputation by building a system of mass production, GM's William Knudsen trumpeted the shift to flexible mass production. As historian David Hounshell recounted, Knudsen relied on "standard or general-purpose, not single-purpose, machine tools. For this reason, Chevrolet could accommodate change far more easily than could the Ford Motor Company."[5] The contrast mattered, as Hounshell recalled the six months it took before the Model A went into production; he summed up the "seeming chaos" of Ford's "unprecedented changeover" with "Charles Sorensen's invective to 'get rid of all the Model T sons-of-bitches.'"[6]

In his 1964 memoir, Alfred Sloan placed his contest with Henry Ford in the context of the market's evolution: "Now it so happened – luckily

Making Money in the Interwar Automobile Industry: Economies of Scale and Scope and the Manufacturing behind the Marketing," *Business History Review* 65 (Winter 1991): 721–53; and Arthur J. Kuhn, *GM Passes Ford, 1918-1939: Designing the General Motors Performance-Control System* (University Park, PA: Pennsylvania State University Press, 1986).

[5] Hounshell, *From the American System to Mass Production*, 264–66.

[6] Hounshell later returned to Sorensen's efforts to clean out production managers, commenting: "The great irony, which completely evaded Sorensen, was that he was the biggest of all the Model T sons-of-bitches." Ibid., 266, 292.

FIGURE 3.2. Alfred P. Sloan, Jr., stands in the first row, third from the left, 1928. Sloan established a price ladder of brands to bring order to the various companies that were held by General Motors. Courtesy of the Hagley Museum and Library.

for us – that during the first part of the 1920s, and especially in the years 1924 to 1926, certain changes took place in the nature of the automobile market which transformed it into something different from what it had been all the years up to that time." Not since the Model T's debut in 1908, he continued, "has the industry changed so radically as it did through the middle twenties." Whereas the Model T had defined the years from 1908 through the early 1920s, Sloan identified four "new elements" that redefined the market: installment credit, the pattern of buyers trading-in used cars when purchasing new vehicles, "the closed body," and the annual model change. "I say luckily for us," Sloan observed, "because as a challenger to the then established position of Ford, we were favored by change" (Fig. 3.2).[7]

Sloan's comments about the market were important in two regards. First, he called attention to the two critical elements in a product's sale – price and quality. Second, he recognized features specific to automobiles that redefined both price and quality during the 1920s. In the case of price, installment credit and the used car trade-in redefined the manner in which dealers negotiated sales with customers. For quality, a car's engineering and its

---

[7] Sloan, *My Years with General Motors*, quote 149–50.

aesthetics, both exemplified in the closed body, were redefined through corporate research and styling. It was curious that Sloan used the word "lucky" to describe GM's place in the market. Being the challenger, GM managers recognized, but also initiated the market's new characteristics and, in doing so, established business institutions to take advantage of the changes. That was a considerable undertaking.

Even so, managers at GM and the Chrysler Corporation accomplished these tasks, and as a result, changed the competitive terrain of the auto market in the closing years of the 1930s compared to the early 1910s. The most noticeable change, of course, was the rise and decline of Ford's Model T. In 1911, just three years after its introduction, Ford sold nineteen percent of all vehicles; his share nearly doubled to thirty-seven percent in 1915 and then peaked at fifty-five percent in 1919, before slipping to thirty-two percent in 1929 and holding between twenty and twenty-eight percent of sales during the Great Depression. Sales for Walter P. Chrysler's company climbed from three percent in 1925 (when the firm was organized) to eight percent in 1929 and then to roughly twenty percent through the 1930s. The big winner was GM: its market share rebounded from twelve percent in 1919 to thirty-four percent in 1929, and stayed close to forty percent through the 1930s. At the close of the Depression, four surviving players – Hudson, Nash, Packard, and Studebaker – together claimed less than ten percent of the market. Sales held by manufacturers other than the seven just mentioned came to nearly half the market in 1911, slipped to twenty-six percent in 1921, dropped to sixteen percent in 1929, and then slumped to seven percent in 1937 (Table 3.1). In the aftermath of the market's great transformation, just three major producers dominated the market.

This chapter revisits the transformation in the automobile market from the era of the Model T to the mass market as Sloan outlined. The first part reviews changes in the market as seen in the experience of Ford and its challenger, General Motors. That Henry Ford so adamantly objected to key marketing devices during the 1920s, notably installment credit and advertising, did not mean that he or his managers were oblivious to the question of consumer loyalty. In a curious twist of fortunes, Ford's policies during the teens helped make possible the very changes that favored GM during the 1920s. Just as Ford's history had conditioned its problems in the 1920s, GM's founder Billy Durant conditioned GM's opportunities in the 1920s, although Durant himself resigned in 1920. Two legacies proved important. One was the incoherent array of companies Durant had assembled. Sloan's 1921 "Product Policy" provided managers with a strategy to give order to the divisions and a blueprint for GM's competition during the 1920s. Because the 1921 policy enabled Sloan to so soundly defeat Ford, his victory argues for GM's model as the "optimal" approach to the auto market. But the case of Walter Chrysler cautions against this conclusion given his firm's amazing rise. GM's own experience merits caution as well. Its victory over Ford

Table 3.1. *The Number and Percent Share of Motor Vehicles (Trucks and Cars) Sold by Automobile Manufacturers, Selected Years, 1911 to 1937*

| Year | Total Sales (000s) | Percentage of Total Motor Vehicle Sales Made by | | | | |
		GM	Ford	Chrysler	Hudson, Nash, Packard, Studebaker	All Other Automakers
1911	210	17%	19%	–	15%	49%
1921	1,684	12	55	–	7	26
1925	4,266	19	42	3%	12	25
1929	5,358	34	32	8	10	16
1931	2,390	42	26	11	7	14
1933	1,020	41	21	23	6	11
1935	3,947	38	29	21	6	6
1937	4,809	40	22	23	8	7

Note: Figures may differ due to rounding.
Source: U.S. Federal Trade Commission, *Report on Motor Vehicle Industry*, 76th Cong., 1st sess., House Document No. 468 (Washington, D.C.: U.S. Government Printing Office, 1939), 27.

obscured a problem that GM managers faced in their drive for consumers' loyalty. Here Durant's impact on the firm prompted a second innovation by Sloan. Because the firm lacked any systematic controls, Sloan pioneered a set of statistical measures for guiding the modern, bureaucratic firm. Although those statistical controls appeared to provide clarity through the process of quantification, they could not easily grasp the demand side of the market as seen in questions about consumers' attitudes and their behavior. Moreover, statistical gauges could not resolve the conflicts management faced with the very consumers whose loyalty they sought.

THE DEMISE OF THE MODEL T

Ford Motor Company and GM entered the 1920s as very different firms. Without disputing the obvious – that Sloan's strategy prevailed over Ford's – distinctions between the firms followed not only from differences between Henry Ford and Alfred Sloan, but also from their firms' histories, which is to say, from their distinctive paths of evolution.[8] Both Ford and GM set policies important to the ways in which price and quality (both engineering and aesthetics) sold vehicles. It is worth recalling that Ford built a remarkable brand in the Model T and the cursive and italicized name "Ford Motor Company."

---

[8] On evolutionary theory, see Richard R. Nelson and Sidney G. Winter, *An Evolutionary Theory of Economic Change* (Cambridge, MA: Harvard University Press, 1982). For path dependency, consult Paul A. David, "Clio and the Economics of QWERTY," *American Economic Review* 75 (May 1985): 332–37.

Yet, as the T's very success contributed to the market's evolution, Henry Ford missed the opportunities as they emerged during the 1920s.

The italicized "Ford Motor Company" name represented the second most popular brand name next to Coca-Cola well into the late twentieth century.[9] That signature dated to the company's organization in 1903, but the brand developed around the Model T, introduced in 1908, and the assembly line, begun in 1913. Between 1910 and 1914 the car and the consequences of mass production brought Ford tremendous publicity. With mass production, hundreds of thousands of visitors flocked to the Highland Park plant, which acquired the status of a "national landmark" on the order of Niagara Falls. Mass production brought other forms of publicity. As historian David Lewis explained, the car's price cuts, including a price "rebate" in 1914 "should sales exceed 300,000 units," was announced "in virtually every newspaper in the nation." So was Ford's announcement of the five-dollar day. As the press spread the news about the wage rate and car prices, Ford managers further cultivated public relations through their own local Ford auto clubs and their aptly named journal, the *Fordowner*. Another boost came when the company created its "motion-picture department" in 1914. "Ford films," Lewis recalled, "broke the monotony in the lives of many rural folk, who jounced into villages in their Model T's by the tens of thousands on the night of the week the 'flickers' were to be shown." Thus a dealer from Silsbee, Texas, reported that Ford movies "are creating good will by the bushel."[10]

Dealer service and the Model T's repair record also played an important role in cultivating loyal consumers. "Between 1915 and 1920," historian Stephen McIntyre reported, Ford managers "introduced modern laborsaving repair tools and machine equipment to the industry, recommended extensive specialization and division of labor among dealers' mechanics, and championed progressive layout of repair shop departments." By 1925, he wrote, "Ford had completed its standardization of repair procedures and endorsed the use of piece-rate wages for mechanics."[11] The system of flat rates for repairs was meant to provide car owners a reasonable sense of the expected cost of repairs.[12] Some dealers, however, objected to flat rates, and mechanics in large and small shops undercut management's efforts to implement piece rates and control the time of repair jobs.[13] By the end of the roaring twenties, McIntyre found that "the piecework systems had fallen out of favor."[14] The

---

[9] David L. Lewis, *The Public Image of Henry Ford: An American Folk Hero and His Company* (Detroit, MI: Wayne State University Press, 1976), 489.

[10] Ibid., 51, 55, 114–17, quotes 54, 113, 117.

[11] Stephen L. McIntyre, "The Failure of Fordism: Reform of the Automobile Repair Industry, 1913-1940," *Technology and Culture* 41 (April 2000): 269–99, quote 270.

[12] Ibid., 279.   [13] Ibid., 288–90.

[14] McIntyre reflected on the events, saying: "So strong was the grip of the Fordist manufacturing paradigm on Ford executives that they never seriously considered the alternative of creating

attention given to repairs and replacement parts, though, had given Ford's car a favorable reputation. Among its competitors, Charles Kettering, the director of research at GM, praised Ford's operations in 1924: "The great thing today that is facilitating his sales is his wonderful service organization and the extreme low cost of his service parts, which can be obtained at every crossroads in the country."[15]

The one eyesore in Ford's marketing campaign was the most traditional – advertising. From 1908 through the middle of 1912, Ford advertised regularly, but spending dropped from 1913 to 1916 and stopped altogether in 1917.[16] Henry Ford claimed to cut back advertising first because he had so many orders, and second because he believed that advertising helped introduce a product, but had little benefit for established brands. His comments, however, belied another side to the company's policy. From 1917 to 1923, Ford's dealers pooled their advertising funds as required in their dealer contracts, and spent roughly $3 million annually to promote the Model T.[17] Then, once FMC began advertising between 1923 and 1926 (spending $15 million), dealers protested that Ford's techniques had failed to include local dealer's names and their distribution was unfair.[18]

Through the 1910s and early 1920s, the themes established with the initial introduction of the Model T continued. Ford managers still promoted the car's basic qualities to sustain demand – its low price, ease of use, and reliability. Yet, the very policies Ford executives had pursued during the 1910s set the stage for new opportunities as the market evolved during the 1920s. Consider the key elements that Alfred Sloan had identified with the mass market of the 1920s: credit, the closed body, annual model changes, and the used car trade-in. Ford's commitment to the Model T stood at odds with these opportunities. In the 1920s, Ford pursued the seemingly bizarre marketing strategy of portraying the Model T as unchanging. Prior to the mid-1920s, Ford had made valuable updates. Hounshell called the 1917 Model T's look "snappy," and in 1920 engineers had altered vehicles with "lowered and 'streamlined' bodies."[19] It is not completely clear what happened soon thereafter, but Hounshell observed that by 1920 the Model T "was expected to be constant." Henry Ford "feared" discussing new features as witnessed by "the hush-hush atmosphere that surrounded the

a cadre of highly skilled, factory-trained and supported mechanics capable of exercising sound judgment in the repair of customers' vehicles." Ibid., 294–98.

[15] C. F. Kettering to A. P. Sloan, Jr., President, General Motors Corporation, January 4, 1924, Box 121, CFK, KU. See also Thomas S. Dicke, *Franchising in America: The Development of a Business Method, 1840-1980* (Chapel Hill, NC: University of North Carolina Press, 1992), 62–75.

[16] Lewis, *The Public Image of Henry Ford*, 57–58. See also Tedlow, *New and Improved*, 138–39.

[17] Lewis, *The Public Image of Henry Ford*, 57, 126–27.   [18] Ibid., 190–91.

[19] Hounshell, *From the American System to Mass Production*, 274.

changes made in 1923 and 1926." He added that with the exception of the
Model A's introduction, the firm's "position on change . . . was to deny it –
to fear it – for reasons of the anticipated effects of announcements on sales
of present models." One outcome was clear: By the "mid-1920s the Model
T was outmoded. The ignition, carburetion, transmission, brake, and suspension systems, as well as the styling and appointments, made the T appear
antique."[20]

In his autobiography, Sloan offered two comments on Ford's problems.
First, he argued that the closed body quickened the Model T's demise. "The
rise of the closed body made it impossible for Mr. Ford to maintain his leading position in the low-price field, for he had frozen his policy in the Model
T, and the Model T was pre-eminently an open-car design. With its light
chassis, it was unsuited to the heavier closed body, and so in less than two
years the closed body made the already obsolescing design of the Model
T noncompetitive as an engineering design." Although Ford constructed
the T's with closed bodies, Sloan emphasized that Chevrolet sold a much
larger percentage of closed cars than did Ford.[21] Second, Sloan took issue
with Henry Ford's "static" concept of his product line. Selling just the
Model T, and selling it as a "utility" product based on its low price in a
"big-volume market" meant Ford had put all of his eggs in one basket.
"Mr. Ford, who had had so many brilliant insights in earlier years, seemed
never to understand how completely the market had changed from the one
in which he made his name and to which he was accustomed." Here Sloan
turned to the new-car, used-car development. As second-time car buyers
began to trade in their current vehicle for a new one, Sloan reported that
"they were selling basic transportation and demanding something more than
that in the new car." Although Sloan belied the role of GM in promoting
the change, he nevertheless singled out the shift that took place: "Middle-
income buyers, assisted by the trade-in and installment financing, created
the demand, not for basic transportation, but for progress in new cars, for
comfort, convenience, power, and style."[22]

Behind the trend in used cars had been a development Henry Ford had
pushed: the improved reliability and durability of vehicles. That was the
Model T's strong suit. Whereas most cars wore out in six years, the T was
estimated to last eight years.[23] Durability, though, pointed to the widespread
use of installment credit. Manufacturers were reluctant to sell a car (or any
product) on credit until they could be confident that the vehicle would not
depreciate faster than the amount owed on the loan. Not until 1912 did a
few firms begin to offer loans, and not until the late teens did they become

[20] Ibid., 275–76.   [21] Sloan, *My Years with General Motors*, 162.
[22] Ibid., 58, 162–63.
[23] Lewis, *The Public Image of Henry Ford*, 195. Tedlow made a similar point in *New and Improved*, 155.

common. Sloan reported that installment sales increased from "some very low level in 1915 to around 65 per cent for new cars in 1925."[24] The Model T was ideally suited to sales on installments. Yet, Ford resisted the creation of a credit division until 1928 when the Model A was introduced. In Hounshell's words, "Ford steadfastly refused to consider credit as a legitimate instrument of consumption."[25] Instead, the improvements Ford had pioneered both in the product and the production methods that made the T durable and made possible installment sales as a new marketing tactic were left to the firm's rivals to realize.

The improved reliability and durability of vehicles further contributed to the upending of Ford's whole product concept. Because the supply of used Model T's continued to grow rapidly as well as that for other brands, new Model T's faced a double source of competition. As Sloan observed, why would a middle-class shopper trade in "basic transportation" for another Model T? At a certain point, Ford's low prices no longer had the pull that they once did. Indeed, in 1926, Ford tried two prices cuts, but neither one stimulated sales.[26] Second, the growing supply of used cars and the T's concentration at the market's low end posed problems for Ford dealers. How were they to handle the swelling volume of used cars? Ford's initial reaction was to let dealers cope with the problem through spirited competition. He assumed, as Thomas Dicke wrote, "that more dealers automatically meant more sales."[27] But competition among dealers had its downside: inventories readily accumulated at weak dealerships. The weak dealers undercut what once had been healthy dealers. Between 1921 and 1924, historian Richard Tedlow observed that Ford dealerships increased more than "50 percent to 9,800." He concluded that the Ford franchisees had become "a disconsolate dealer organization" by 1927 with some experienced dealers reputed to have left for greener pastures with Dodge or Chevrolet.[28]

Ford's moment of truth came in 1927. Sloan summed up the consequences of an out-of-date product: "not many observers expected so catastrophic and almost whimsical a fall as Mr. Ford chose to take in May 1927 when he shut down his great River Rouge plant completely and kept it shut down for

[24] "Studebaker to Sell Automobiles on Time," *Cycle and Automobile Trade Journal* 16 (January 1, 1912): 201. See also Sloan, *My Years with General Motors*, 151.

[25] Hounshell, *From the American System to Mass Production*, 277, 293. On installment credit, see also Nevins and Hill, *Ford: Expansion and Challenge*, 465–66; and Dicke, *Franchising in America*, 75.

[26] Lewis, *The Public Image of Henry Ford*, 189–90. See also Tedlow's discussion in *New and Improved*, 169–70. The auto press recognized Ford's price strategy was reaching its limits. See Norman G. Shidle, "Has Ford Lost His Big 'Sales Punch' in the Low-Priced Field?" *Automotive Industries* 53 (October 29, 1925): 727–29.

[27] Dicke, *Franchising in America*, 76.

[28] Ibid., 75–76; "General Motors III: How to Sell Automobiles," *Fortune* 19 (February 1939): 105; and Tedlow, *New and Improved*, 163–64.

nearly a year to retool, leaving the field to Chevrolet unopposed and opening it up for Mr. Chrysler's Plymouth. Mr. Ford regained sales leadership again in 1929, 1930, and 1935, but, speaking in terms of generalities, he had lost the lead to General Motors."[29]

GM'S 1921 PRODUCT POLICY

General Motors, in marked contrast to Ford, had entered the 1920s in a state of crisis. Its founder Billy Durant resigned as president in November 1920. At that date, GM teetered on the edge of bankruptcy. Pierre S. du Pont, who held a substantial amount of GM stock, helped arrange the firm's refinancing and took over as GM's president. He held this post until the spring of 1923 when Sloan took the helm. "Manager" is not a word easily applied to Durant. He left behind a company with few if any managerial controls, and yet Durant had an important legacy at GM. The famous 1921 product policy followed directly from managers' efforts to come to grips with the disorderly collection of brands that Durant had brought together. In order to implement that marketing strategy, GM managers developed new production methods and invested in four business institutions.

In distinct contrast to Ford's one brand (plus the Lincoln), Durant had acquired motor companies and accessory firms higgledy-piggledy. Although Cadillac had staked out the market's high end, many other divisions had priced their products in competition with one another. Sloan called GM's lineup of products "irrational." For one thing, GM lacked a line of cars in "the low-price field – where the big volume and substantial future growth lay." For another, in the middle of the market, GM's divisions duplicated one another. Chevrolet's FB model, Oakland, and Olds exercised "almost identical duplication in price." Finally, Sloan objected to two more brands – Sheridan and Scripps-Booth. His frustration with Durant became apparent and justified, as Sloan wrote: "The presence of the Sheridan is a mystery to me. Mr. Durant caused General Motors to acquire it in 1920, doubtless with something special in mind. I am uncertain what. It did not have a strong organization or demand or recognizable purpose in our line."[30] Finally, Sloan took seriously the problem of GM vehicles' "poor quality and unreliability." With the exception of Buick and Cadillac, he charged all the GM lines needed serious improvement in their overall quality.[31]

In June 1921, Sloan – along with Charles Stewart Mott, who came to GM as an axle supplier; Charles Kettering, the director of GM's research efforts; Norval Hawkins, the marketing genius who left Ford; H. H. Bassett, the general manager of Buick; and K. W. Zimmerschield, the head of Chevrolet – completed their study of GM's product policy and outlined a new

---

[29] Sloan, *My Years with General Motors*, quote 162–63.
[30] Ibid., 58–60.   [31] Ibid., 61–62.

concept for the firm. Sloan proudly recalled that their proposal was "the one for which General Motors has now long been known." They first advised GM to create a complete lineup of motor car divisions to correspond to the distribution of prices in the market. There should be a low-priced motor vehicle (to compete with Ford's Model T), and other brands to move up the price (or car buyers' income) ladder. Next, they maintained, there should not be any "wide gaps" moving the car brands up the price ladder. As their third request, brands were not to duplicate one another. The committee outlined six steps on its ladder, with a price range linked to each category (the lowest bracket carried a price of $450 to $600). Within each bracket, GM brands were to engage in "quality competition." Sloan explained: "We proposed in general that General Motors should place its cars at the top of each price range and make them of such a quality that they would attract sales from below that price, selling to those customers who might be willing to pay a little more for the additional quality, and attract sales also from above that price, selling to those customers who would see the price advantage in a car of close to the quality of higher-priced competition." Sloan summed up the strategy: "This amounted to quality competition against cars below a given price tag, and price competition against cars above that price tag."[32]

The approach specifically applied to Chevrolet. Because Ford had "practically monopolized" the low-price segment of the market, as Sloan outlined, GM would not try to compete "head on." Instead, GM would "produce a car that would be superior to the Ford, yet so near the Ford price that demand would be drawn from the Ford grade and lifted to the slightly higher price in preference to Ford's then utility design."[33] This strategy did not take effect overnight. Sloan recalled that the Chevy's design as late as 1924 hardly lived up to the 1921 plan.[34] In 1926 Chevy moved closer to this goal, and in 1927 it forced the Model T's shutdown.

Sloan recognized that the product policy as advanced in 1921 had important ramifications for GM's product lineup and its production of vehicles. First, the strategy required the elimination of duplication. Although some duplication was unavoidable, GM needed to keep to one brand for one price bracket. In 1921, writing at the time the Product Policy was crafted, Norval Hawkins observed that in order to win "the cooperation of different Divisions in selling the various products" it was important that the lines not conflict.[35] Second, the policy called for different divisions to share components as a means for reducing the cost of production. Whereas Ford had relied on a "uniform product" as a way to achieve volume and cut costs, General Motors hoped to achieve volume and lower costs through the sharing of critical components across brands. The new Pontiac division,

---

[32] Ibid., 65–67.   [33] Ibid., 68.   [34] Ibid., 153.
[35] N. A. Hawkins to Operations Committee, August 2, 1921, quote 4, File 87-11.2-207, Box 123, CFK, KU.

as Sloan explained, first demonstrated the possibilities: "at that time it was widely supposed, from the example of the Model T, that mass production on a grand scale required a uniform product. The Pontiac, coordinated in part with a car in another price class, was to demonstrate that mass production of automobiles could be reconciled with variety in product."[36]

A second dimension to the cost of production was the coming of flexible mass production.[37] Like so many managers who became disgruntled with Henry Ford, William Knudsen had left Ford in late 1921 and come to GM in February 1922. Rather than follow the example set at Ford and rely on specialized, single-purpose machinery that hampered changes from model year to model year, Knudsen remade the assembly process around the widespread use of general-purpose machinery. In addition, Knudsen decentralized production at Chevrolet. During the very years when Ford's market share slipped, 1922 to 1927, Knudsen saw the introduction of three assembly plants in different locations in the U.S. to augment four existing assembly plants. He also won an agreement from superiors to have Fisher Body, the division responsible for building car bodies, locate a body plant next to each of the assembly plants, as Hounshell wrote, "so that body production could be coordinated precisely with the daily output of each assembly plant."[38] With his decentralized operations, Knudsen was able to execute distinctive changes in the car's design at a remarkably smooth pace. For the switch from a four- to a six-cylinder engine, he planned first to extend the car's wheel-base in 1928, and then to introduce the larger engine in 1929. Moreover, Knudsen planned ahead as well for the engine's assembly: He set up a "pilot line" with the new machinery to determine that the line would run smoothly, "before moving the finished machinery, jigs, fixtures, and gauges to the Flint plant."[39] So successful was Knudsen, Hounshell recalled, that upon a simple three-week shutdown to make the machine tool changes in 1929, he accomplished the switch and earned a "lavish banquet" from his appreciative colleagues.[40]

In *My Years*, Sloan devoted considerable attention to the business institutions that corresponded to the 1921 product policy and thus enabled Chevrolet to unseat the Model T. The business institutions corresponded to the four changes Sloan had identified in the automobile market. Two of those changes had been the annual model change and the closed body. In giving middle-income buyers reasons to buy something other than "basic transportation," the trade-in could be used for a down payment and the rest could be paid on installments. At just what date the annual model change became officially

---

[36] Sloan, *My Years with General Motors*, 64–66, 158. See also Raff, "Making Cars and Making Money," 721–53.
[37] Hounshell, *From the American System to Mass Production*, 263–67.
[38] Ibid., 265–66, quote 266.   [39] Ibid., 266.   [40] Ibid., 264, 266.

part of GM's marketing plan is open to question. Sloan offered: "General Motors in fact had annual models in the twenties, every year after 1923, and has had them ever since, but . . . we had not in 1925 formulated the concept in the way it is known today."[41] If not by 1925, then soon thereafter, its strategy was well underway.

Placing such importance on the annual model change, Sloan wanted to sustain each brand's quality, both its engineering and aesthetic quality. This goal was seen in terms of two institutions. In 1919, Sloan hired Charles Kettering to run GM's industrial research laboratory.[42] GM backed Kettering's lab with a generous annual budget of $375,000 in the early 1920s and roughly $2 million at the onset of World War II.[43] Sloan also paid attention to styling. In 1927 he hired Harley Earl, who designed custom automobile bodies for Hollywood stars. The Art & Colour Section, renamed the Styling Section in 1937, took charge of designing the brands.[44] Two other changes in the market, as Sloan saw them, had been the used car trade-in and the use of installment credit to sell cars. In 1919, GM managers acted on the trend toward installment sales when they created the General Motors Acceptance Corporation. It enjoyed a spectacular growth during the next decade with its net income climbing from roughly $50,000 in 1919 to $12 million in 1938.[45] The second business institution critical to these two changes was GM's network of franchised dealers. The dealer networks had dated to the initial organization of individual divisions, such as Buick and Cadillac, but they took on added importance during the 1920s. The sale of cars on time, plus the trade-in, made automotive dealers the crucial mediators in negotiating the price for the sale of each vehicle. The four changes in the automobile market were closely tied to GM's development of four institutions: the research lab, the styling department, GMAC, and the network of dealer franchises.

In addition to these institutions, GM invested heavily in advertising and public relations. By 1926 and 1927, GM had expressed its price hierarchy of brands through its mass advertising. Chevrolet was the "true value in the low price field."[46] In 1929, Chevrolet introduced its six-cylinder engine with

[41] Sloan, *My Years with General Motors*, 167.
[42] On Kettering, see Stuart W. Leslie, *Boss Kettering: Wizard of General Motors* (New York: Columbia University Press, 1983), especially 91–97, 183.
[43] Ibid., 183–84.
[44] C. Edson Armi, *The Art of American Car Design: The Profession and Personalities* (University Park, PA: Pennsylvania State University Press, 1988); David Gartman, *Auto Opium: A Social History of American Automobile Design* (London: Routledge, 1994); and Gerald Silk, ed., *Automobile and Culture* (New York: Harry N. Abrams, Inc., 1984).
[45] *United States v. General Motors Corporation et al.*, 121 F.2d 376 (7th Cir. 1941), 386.
[46] "Volume Production *makes possible Greatly* Improved Quality *Amazingly* Reduced Prices!" *Saturday Evening Post* 199 (April 2, 1927): 44.

much fanfare. As described in its advertisement, bathed in brilliant orange tones, "this impressive combination of beauty, quality and six-cylinder performance is *actually available in the price range of the four.*"[47] Pontiac was launched as a step up the price ladder, and until 1929, its main distinction from Chevrolet was its six-cylinder engine. Its advertisement announced: "With its body designed and built by Fisher, the Sport Cabriolet is the lowest-priced six-cylinder car of its type on the market." It sold for $835 and the sedan for $775.[48] Climbing another rung on the price ladder, the Oldsmobile marketed its sedan for $950. Asserting a more established lifestyle, the ad pictured two business executives conversing, and the copy claimed Oldsmobile had the benefit of many "months and miles" to prove its quality.[49] Buick typically did not advertise its price. Still higher on the price ladder, it played on the lifestyle theme of shareholders in its headline: "Dividends declared by Buick Leadership."[50] A 1929 Buick advertisement featured an erstwhile factory worker, as historian Roland Marchand observed, now a "modern Apollo," towering above the abstract city with a "luminous vehicle for popular worship" held in one outstretched hand and a document in the other. The message: "As Long As Mankind Uses Motor Cars There Will Always Be A Buick."[51] As to price, the ad reflected the status of Buick, saying: "twice as many people purchase Buicks as any other car priced above $1200 literally inspires Buick to keep everlasting faith with owners."[52] LaSalle, introduced in 1927, and Cadillac were among the elite tier of brands. LaSalle was pictured as the sporty car for the French countryside in an advertisement that announced its price ranged from $2,495 to $2,685.[53] In 1927, Cadillac's price began at $2,995. The copy explained that Cadillac was not expensive for its remarkable quality: "it is almost inevitable that the public should award to Cadillac a volume that amounts to more than half the nation's demand for fine cars.... The economies effected by the huge Cadillac production actually reverse the usual economic order and make this finest of all fine cars at the same time substantially lower in price."[54] Finally, among its institutional advertisements, GM played on different themes. One was to show the GM

---

[47] "Outstanding Beauty and Remarkable Six Cylinder Performance – at prices within the reach of all," *Saturday Evening Post* 201 (May 18, 1929): 107.

[48] "The New and Finer Pontiac Six – at New Low Prices," *Saturday Evening Post* 199 (March 26, 1927): 51.

[49] "No Doubt About It," *Saturday Evening Post* 199 (April 16, 1927): 91.

[50] "Dividends declared by Buick Leadership," *Saturday Evening Post* 199 (March 19, 1927): 43.

[51] Roland Marchand, *Advertising the American Dream: Making Way for Modernity, 1920-1940* (Berkeley, CA: University of California Press, 1985), 236–37, quote 237. The advertisement appeared in the *Saturday Evening Post* 201 (May 4, 1929): 51.

[52] "As Long As Mankind Uses Motor Cars There Will Always Be A Buick," *Saturday Evening Post* 201 (May 4, 1929): 51.

[53] "Ah, Madame!" *Saturday Evening Post* 199 (April 30, 1927): 35.

[54] "Cadillac," *Saturday Evening Post* 199 (March 26, 1927): 44.

family of brands and call attention to the pattern of families buying two cars, and doing so with the help of GMAC credit plans.[55]

Overall, GM contributed handsomely to money spent on auto advertising, which increased from $3.5 million in 1921 to $6.2 million in 1923, and then to $9.3 million in 1927.[56] In the case of other media, records survived for GM's sponsorship of radio programs at the National Broadcasting Company (NBC). GM spent $654,995 to sponsor programs between November 1927 and December 1929. From 1930 through early 1933, GM and its divisions spent another $1.8 million.[57]

GM's market power in 1940 offered one measure of how effective Sloan's strategy had been since its implementation in the early 1920s. When in 1921 the responsibility devolved on Sloan and his fellow managers to create a product policy, the firm's history – Durant's disorderly collection of companies – had a decisive impact on the strategy they chose. Sloan observed that there were other options they could have elected. Few firms at the time would dare to challenge Henry Ford in the low-price field. Yet, having inherited a particular set of divisions, GM managers charted a course in 1921 that meant initiating the distinctive strategy of creating a price ladder of GM brands combined with the strategy of "quality competition" and "price competition." Having set out on this course, GM managers also found themselves favoring the sort of production methods pioneered by William Knudsen as well as investing in business institutions, especially research, styling, the dealer networks, and GMAC, needed to effect the annual model change.

WALTER P. CHRYSLER'S COMPANY

Although Ford's poor showing seemed to confirm Alfred Sloan's strategy, the experience of the Chrysler Corporation during the interwar years serves as a healthy reminder that there was no single best competitive strategy. Walter Chrysler played the part of the underdog up against the two big automakers so well that his firm's sales skyrocketed. After leaving Buick in 1918, thanks to a dispute with Billy Durant, and then holding a few other positions, he took charge of the Maxwell Company, reviving the firm and then renaming it the Chrysler Corporation in 1925.[58] The firm sold just his namesake in the mid-price range where it ranked second in sales in 1927. Plymouth was

[55] "This is a two-car country," *Saturday Evening Post* 199 (April 9, 1927): 88–89.

[56] James J. Flink, *The Automobile Age* (Cambridge, MA: MIT Press, 1988), 191.

[57] "General Motors Corporation and Subsidiary Companies," no date, Folder 30, Box 16, NBC, WHS.

[58] Michael Schwartz, "Markets, Networks, and the Rise of Chrysler in Old Detroit, 1920–1940," *Enterprise & Society* 1 (March 2000): 79–82; and Flink, *The Automobile Age*, 70. For a general history of the Chrysler Corporation, see Charles K. Hyde, *Riding the Roller Coaster: A History of the Chrysler Corporation* (Detroit, MI: Wayne State University Press, 2003).

FIGURE 3.3. Walter P. Chrysler, 1924. Chrysler had mimicked GM's marketing strategy, but he also counted on close ties to suppliers to break into the low-price, high-volume segment of the market. Courtesy of the Detroit Public Library, National Automotive History Collection.

introduced in 1928.[59] From 1929 to 1930, its sales dropped (although not as much as did the industry average), and then sales jumped an amazing fifty percent from 1930 to 1931. "In 1933," sociologist Michael Schwartz reported, "Plymouth sold 253,000 cars, almost three times its 1931 figure, and raised its market share from 10 to 17 percent." 1936 was Chrysler's banner year. It sold "more than 450,000 vehicles," more vehicles than Ford, "to become the second largest American manufacturer" (Fig. 3.3).[60]

In many respects, Walter Chrysler succeeded because he followed the example of General Motors. First, his managers took advantage of the opportunities afforded from advertising. In the late 1920s, as Marchand related, Chrysler's advertisers had played on the modern art form of futurism with a 1927 ad of a winged car blasting out of a city under the slogan "Chrysler – triumphant." In "Chrysler Beauty *is no chance creation*," the 1929 advertisement reverted to classical motifs to impress readers with the car's styling.[61] Then, during the 1930s, the firm turned to what Marchand called

---

[59] Schwartz, "Markets, Networks, and the Rise of Chrysler in Old Detroit, 1920-1940," 83.
[60] Ibid., 87–88.   [61] Marchand, *Advertising the American Dream*, 128–29, 140–41.

"competitive copy" and "personalized copy." Nosing its way into the low-price car market, Chrysler ran ads in the early 1930s challenging car buyers to "Look at All Three." Walter Chrysler next played the part of the hard-boiled car salesman, telling readers "about his company's engineering triumphs in defiance of the depression."[62] Second, Chrysler sought to mimic GM's strategy of quality competition. Concluding that a firm was doomed unless it entered the low-price, high-volume segment of the market, he tried to replicate Sloan's strategy of "quality competition" with his Plymouth brand, as Schwartz stated: "he would create a superior car at a higher price than Ford and Chevrolet, and then introduce production efficiencies that would 'drop' the Plymouth squarely into the low-priced range."[63] Whereas Sloan had counted on William Knudsen's system of flexible mass production to execute his marketing strategy, Walter Chrysler placed his faith in outside contractors.

Suppliers proved critical to both innovation and cost reductions at Chrysler. Through his ties to suppliers, Chrysler was able to adopt new features while keeping the price of his cars low. His 1924 Chrysler car, for example, claimed to have the features of rivals priced over $5,000 when his was priced between $1,335 and $1,895. Chrysler's managers worked with Fisher Body (at the time, sixty percent of it was owned by GM) to create, according to Schwartz, "huge new stamping machines that permitted the production of the curved fenders and hoods that would later become standard on all automobiles." In addition, the car was backed with four-wheel hydraulic brakes, which Schwartz called "a luxury in 1924." It featured a special engine with aluminum cylinders, a completely new lubrication system, and other changes to reduce vibrations. All of these improvements had come about with the help of outside suppliers. As an added bonus, because the manufacturer worked with suppliers, changes in the design of specific components could be effected quickly.[64] Schwartz recalled that when GM introduced independent front suspension in 1934, "Chrysler copied it so quickly that both makers introduced the feature" in the same year.[65]

Whereas Knudsen had developed a system of flexible mass production to allow for annual change, Chrysler relied on suppliers and his newly acquired Dodge facilities. In 1932, Chrysler made good on the first part of his strategy, according to Schwartz, putting in the Plymouth new features such as "hydraulic brakes, an all-steel body, and the more rigid x-frame chassis." Further, the car impressed customers and competitors with its "Floating Power," a system for supporting the engine on rubber mountings to reduce vibration and noise.[66] In realizing the second part – cost reductions – Chrysler did not internalize the manufacture of parts, but instead "used its newly acquired facilities to house new configurations that combined previously separated

[62] Ibid., 304–309, quotes 307–308.
[63] Schwartz, "Markets, Networks, and the Rise of Chrysler in Old Detroit, 1920-1940," 84–85.
[64] Ibid., 81–83.   [65] Ibid., 92.   [66] Ibid., 87–88.

production processes." As one example, the Dodge facilities were used to construct new "larger and softer front springs" made of Mola steel – an alloy created for the task at hand. Yet, to include the new springs, Chrysler engineers redesigned the car's front end. Schwartz explained, "a torsional spring was used to connect the two front axle ends, the torque rod was primarily attached to the axle and not to the frame, and it was connected to the frame by specially designed extenders." Because "this set of changes involved the marriage of several previously separate operations, Chrysler could not effectively manage them without a consolidated manufacturing location."[67]

Walter Chrysler directed a remarkably effective campaign in which he matched the firm's marketing with its internal drive for production efficiency and product innovation. His approach followed certain aspects of GM's strategy, notably quality competition, but did not mimic GM exactly because Chrysler did not inherit Durant's collection of car divisions. Instead, he built from one mid-sized brand and daringly entered the low-priced market category. His approach also echoed the young Henry Ford in a few respects. Just as Henry Ford as an upstart took on the Selden patent group, Chrysler challenged the two big auto giants when he charged: "Look at all Three." Finally, in contrast to GM, where Sloan crafted a bureaucracy to coordinate operations and share parts among divisions, Chrysler's managers counted on their ties to suppliers to redesign their brands. As new features necessitated changes in production, suppliers helped cut costs during the 1930s. That Chrysler became the number-two automaker in 1936 Schwartz considered a "tribute" to the pervasive number and creativity of suppliers in the Detroit industrial area.[68]

PUTTING MANAGEMENT ON A "SCIENTIFIC" BASIS: STATISTICAL CONTROLS

Where Chrysler's experience had demonstrated that Sloan's model was not the "single best" approach to managing the modern firm in a mass consumer market, GM's own experience revealed another dimension to the problem of management: controlling the giant bureaucracy. In 1921, the same year that managers implemented their product policy, they also undertook a series of reforms to better control their operating divisions. Like the product policy, the new "statistical controls" followed from Durant's legacy. His complete lack of administrative controls had set the stage for the inventory crisis of 1920. In response, the new management team introduced a set of policies between 1921 and 1925 to put, as Sloan liked to say, management on a

---

[67] Ibid., 89.

[68] Ibid., 76–77. For an overview of the "hand-to-mouth" system in Detroit during the interwar years, see Michael Schwartz and Andrew W. Fish, "Just-in-Time Inventories in Old Detroit," *Business History* 40 (July 1998): 48–71.

"scientific basis."[69] Two years prior to the publication of Sloan's autobiography, the business historian Alfred Chandler detailed the new management team's efforts in his path-breaking book, *Strategy and Structure*. Chandler focused on two broad problems of administration: first, the systematic comparison of divisions through uniform accounting policies; and second, the effort to synchronize the purchase of raw materials with the production of vehicles and the size of demand for particular products.[70]

As Sloan recounted, the impetus for this reform project came from Durant's lack of controls. In 1919, for instance, Sloan had told Durant "we should have an independent audit by a certified public accountant." None had been done in the firm's eleven years, and Durant (apparently unaware of this basic task, as Sloan said he "did not have a sound concept of accounting") gave Sloan the go-ahead. Other problems were just as serious. Sloan recalled that through 1920 there were no effective mechanisms to manage cash flows between divisions. Calling the situation "almost unbelievable," he noted that there was "no effective procedure for getting cash from the points where we happened to have some to the points where we happened to need some." Buick typically held an excess, and GM's treasurer, Meyer Prentis, would have to visit Buick in Flint, Michigan. He would discuss various matters "and at last casually bring up the subject of cash. Buick's financial people would invariably express surprise at the size of Mr. Prentis' request and occasionally would try to resist the transfer of such a large amount. Naturally, this cat-and-mouse game did not result in the most efficient utilization of funds."[71]

Problems such as Mr. Prentis's cash needs came to a head in the inventory crisis of 1920, which Sloan attributed to three interconnected problems: "overruns on appropriations, inventory runaway, and the resulting cash shortage."[72] Because Durant resigned in November, in the midst of the crisis, a new team of managers took up the task of ending it and taking steps to prevent its recurrence. Aside from Sloan, Chandler identified F. Donaldson Brown as critical to the new policies, saying he "probably was as well versed as anyone in the United States in the development and use of these new administrative tools" because he had designed many of the "financial and statistical controls" put in place at the Du Pont Company.[73] Pierre S. du Pont and John Lee Pratt, both from the Du Pont Company, made it a foursome. The group, Chandler wrote, "revealed a continuing dispassionate, rational, calculating, and essentially pragmatic approach to the problems of

[69] Sloan, *My Years with General Motors*, 132.
[70] Alfred D. Chandler, Jr., carefully reviewed both developments in *Strategy and Structure: Chapters in the History of the American Industrial Enterprise* (Cambridge, MA: MIT Press, 1962), 127–53.
[71] Sloan, *My Years with General Motors*, 25, 122.
[72] Ibid., 118.   [73] Chandler, *Strategy and Structure*, 145.

management."[74] Pratt was placed in charge of an inventories committee that tried "[t]o restore order" quickly.[75] Rather than accept the status quo policy of giving operations managers an open bank account for their various requests for appropriations, Pratt proposed to restrict production managers' requests for the purchase of raw materials and parts. Starting on May 21, 1921, each division would place a "four-month forecast of expected business."[76] Every forecast was to include statistics about "plant investment, working capital, and outstanding inventory commitments as well as estimated sales, production, and earnings." It was Sloan's job to approve or alter each division's production schedule in relation to the forecasts.[77]

In 1921 and 1922, other measures were added. The Cost Accounting Section, as Chandler recounted, established a uniform accounting policy for all GM divisions. "Data from these procedures gave the division managers as well as the general office a relatively realistic picture of just what were costs and therefore profits." The firm's top officers "for the first time" could compare costs and market prices. Each division's return on investment could be calculated, and managers could then compare the division with a common financial yardstick.[78] As the new team of managers implemented these accounting and financial measures, managers of many divisions, including the Olds and Chevrolet brands, left GM. Just as the Du Pont Company's transition to "an impersonal industrial enterprise" had benefited from the family-oriented members leaving the firm, Chandler thought that the loss of these older GM managers aided "the metamorphosis of General Motors from a combination or federation of firms into a single integrated enterprise."[79]

In 1924 a second inventory crisis prompted the new managers to look more closely at the demand side of the market. In the late spring of 1924, Sloan suspected that production was running ahead of demand. But at the time, sales reports were based on data collected from the division managers, not at the retail level from the dealers. Upon a visit to dealers in St. Louis, Kansas City, and Los Angeles, Sloan concluded that production managers had been too optimistic. Sloan initiated a new policy. His report to the Finance Committee in July 1924 stated, "a procedure was developed, which it is believed, places production schedules on an entirely scientific basis."[80] This procedure required a ten-day report from each dealer, as economist Albert Bradley stated, which covered "the actual number of cars delivered to consumers, the number of new orders taken, the total orders on hand, and the number of new and used cars on hand. Each ten-day period the actual results are compared with the month's forecast, and each month, as these

---

[74] Ibid., 142.   [75] Ibid., 145.
[76] Sloan, *My Years with General Motors*, 126–27.
[77] Ibid., 127. See also Chandler, *Strategy and Structure*, 145–46.
[78] Chandler, *Strategy and Structure*, 147.   [79] Ibid., 141–42.
[80] Sloan, *My Years with General Motors*, 132.

figures are received, the entire situation is carefully analyzed to see whether the original estimate was too high or too low."[81] The reports, as Sloan emphasized, could not eliminate the problem of fluctuations in demand, but they could allow GM to keep closer watch on changes in demand and to quicken the reaction time.[82]

Sloan's enthusiasm for statistical controls in the field of business administration was timely. During the Progressive era, Americans from several different professions embraced pragmatic approaches to social problems. Sloan had earned a degree in electrical engineering from M.I.T., and statistical analysis provided a common form of communication between engineers and business administrators.[83] Sloan displayed his genuine belief in the "objectivity" of statistics in his account of the 1924 crisis. He wrote: "In a certain very important sense, this [the 1924 crisis] involved the reconciliation of the work of two kinds of persons in General Motors – essential, I should think, in any corporation with a nationally distributed consumer product. One kind is the sales manager with his natural enthusiasm, optimism, and belief that he can, by his efforts, influence total sales. The other is the statistical person who makes his analyses objectively on broad general evidence of demand."[84]

CONSUMERS AS ABSTRACTIONS: A MANAGERIAL DILEMMA

In his account of bureaucratic controls, Sloan wrote that, in the effort to synchronize production and distribution, the difficult part was estimating consumer demand. "The key element in the forecast, of course, was expected sales, from which the number of cars and trucks to be produced was determined."[85] He made a similar point in his comments about the 1921 product policy. Holding that "more than any other single factor" the policy "enabled us to move into the rapidly changing market of the twenties with confidence," he prefaced this remark by calling attention to the uncertainty managers at the time faced in seeing the elements he so clearly described with the benefit of hindsight. "We saw them [the changes] then as uncertainties, unknowns and trends, in the form of figures to study at a desk."[86] One sign of this effort to cope with uncertainty was market research. Consumer studies were premised on the idea that the market had become so large that consumers could be represented by statistics. Yet, market research, by definition, was ambiguous since the subjects of investigation defied quantification. After all, how could statistics identify and quantify car buyers' attitudes? Managers used market data as a close approximation of car buyers. But their measures

---

[81] Quoted in Chandler, *Strategy and Structure*, 150.
[82] Sloan, *My Years with General Motors*, 138.   [83] Chandler, *Strategy and Structure*, 130.
[84] Sloan, *My Years with General Motors*, 133–34.   [85] Ibid., 128.   [86] Ibid., 152.

of efficiency or effectiveness for the production, distribution, and marketing of goods remained contingent on their assumptions about consumers.

Aside from a few remarks, Sloan offered no sustained analysis of GM's consumer research division in *My Years*.[87] This was not due to the insignificance of market research. In a 1938 article, *Time* reported that GM's research staff was perhaps the largest corporate research organization in the United States. At that date, its budget was estimated to be $300,000 to $500,000.[88] Like many other companies, by the 1920s GM began tabulating statistical portraits of consumers and expanded its data gathering during the 1930s. Henry Brady Weaver led GM's in-house research staff. Weaver had come to Hyatt Roller Bearing Company in 1918, moved to GM in 1921, and at latest by 1923 served in the Advisory Staff, the staff that provided advice to GM's senior executives.[89] In 1924 he was listed as assistant secretary to the General Sales Committee, directed by Donaldson Brown.[90] By 1926, he had become the "Assistant to the Director of the Sales Section," the unit in the Advisory Staff that studied general issues about sales, service, and advertising.[91] By 1933, he was named director of GM's Customer Research Staff.[92] In 1939, when Public Relations paid part of his budget, his unit came not under Public Relations but under the Distribution division of the Operating Staff.[93]

Weaver recognized that market research at GM, like other corporations, entailed a host of problems. He readily admitted that consumers could never predict their own "likes and dislikes."[94] In another report, he opined that aesthetic design could not be termed a "scientific analysis." He also worried in private correspondence and published articles about how to sample the

[87] Ibid., 134, 136–37, 180, 240–41, 284–85.

[88] "Thought-starter," *Time* (November 14, 1938): 66, 68–70.

[89] "The General Motors Service Managers' Association Bulletin #2 – January 27, 1923," File 87-11.7-132; and "Meeting of General Motors House Organ Editors," February 8, 1923, File 87-11.7-121, both in Box 121, CFK, KU.

[90] Alfred D. Chandler, Jr., and Stephen Salsbury, *Pierre S. Du Pont and the Making of the Modern Corporation* (New York: Harper & Row, 1971), 564–65.

[91] C. S. Mott, "Organizing a Great Industrial: Tuning-up General Motors-V," *Management and Administration* 7 (May 1924): 523–27, reprinted in Alfred D. Chandler, Jr., ed., *Managerial Innovation at General Motors* (New York: Arno Press, 1979). On the Advisory Staff, see also Chandler, *Strategy and Structure*, 138–39, 153–57.

[92] I outline GM's investigations of consumers in "Consumers, Information, and Marketing Efficiency at GM, 1921-1940," *Business and Economic History* 25 (Fall 1996): 186–95.

[93] "General Motors IV: A Unit in Society," *Fortune* 19 (March 1939): 45–52, 136, 138, 141–42, 145–46, 148, 150, 152; and Sloan, *My Years with General Motors*, 189–90.

[94] Henry G. Weaver, "The Use of Statistics in the Study of the Consumer," *Journal of the American Statistical Association* 30 (1935): 183–84; idem, "Proving Ground of Public Opinion," *Journal of Consulting Psychology* 5 (July-August 1941): 149–53, especially 150; idem, "General Motors 'Purchasing Power' Index," *Manufacturing Industries* 11 (April 1926): 291–92; and idem, "The Customer Questionnaire Technique," *American Marketing Journal* 1 (July 1934): 115–18.

car-buying public and how to pose questions to it.[95] Without disputing the flawed nature of the surveys, Weaver's statistical portraits nevertheless acted as a mechanism or language by which cultural ideas about consumers were presented for management. Just as Sloan repeatedly recounted his efforts to put the firm's finances and its operations on a "scientific basis," Weaver's surveys tried to translate complex social and cultural questions about consumers into "objective" terms. Data about consumers' attitudes and behavior were tabulated and presented through different statistical measures. As such, the data illustrated ideas or assumptions about consumers that had under-pinned many of their core business activities in the distribution, marketing, and production of vehicles.

The distribution of vehicles offered one example of the relationship between statistical studies of consumers and management's goal of efficient operations. In contrast to mass production, mass distribution meant sell-ing a homogeneous product in hundreds of diverse local markets that varied according to their population, industrial base, income distribution, and other factors. Car registrations by themselves provided incomplete information, because a dealer might have poor sales for failing to promote the GM brand, or alternatively, because the market potential was limited in that particular geographic area. GM's marketers thus needed to track the very heterogeneity of local markets.

In 1926, Weaver's efforts to measure the market's potential were rewarded when he received a $2,000 prize from the Harvard Business School. Weaver's prize came for his so-called "Purchasing Power Index." For each county in the U.S., he collected four types of data: the value of farm goods and manufactured products, the number of retail outlets, population size, and income tax returns. No variable alone could provide an accurate estimate of consumers' "purchasing power." For example, a county's population offered a rough guide to the market's size. But by itself, Weaver wrote, it gave "too high an estimate for territories where there are a lot of people receiving low incomes, and too low an estimate for territories in which the people receive high incomes."[96] To determine the weights to assign each variable, Weaver compared states, because he had obtained estimates for each state's per capita income from the National Bureau of Economic Research. Based on these comparisons, he created a few categories, such as urban and southern areas. He then assigned different weights to the variables and calculated each

---

[95] "The Proving Ground of Public Opinion," no date [prepared after the 1932 National Auto-mobile Show], 6; Henry G. Weaver, "Consumer Reactions to Advertising," June 23, 1932, and attached Sales Section, "Typical Comments Provoked by the Question: 'What Is the Most Recent Automobile Advertisement that Has Attracted Your Attention?'" June 23, 1932, both in File 87-11.4-5, Box 110, CFK, KU.

[96] Henry G. Weaver, "The Development of a Basic Purchasing Power Index by Counties," *Harvard Business Review* 4 (April 1926): 275–89, quote 282.

county's "per capita purchasing power." For Alabama, this index ranged from $156 to $618. For counties with large cities, it varied from $601 to $1,107.[97] Once in place, the index helped managers properly determine the size of markets for allocating dealers in each geographic zone.[98] As Weaver wrote in 1926, the index could be "used as a foundation upon which to build sales quotas" for autos and other goods, rather than relying on "arbitrary opinion."[99]

Weaver's purchasing power index was just one of many examples of his effort to put the study of consumers on a scientific basis. In the case of advertising, he created an "advertising efficiency index." Wanting to determine where GM's advertising dollars had their greatest impact, he collected data about journals' circulation rates. But he also pursued the more difficult question of asking owners of new Chevrolets, Buicks, and Cadillacs to grade forty-four journals, saying whether they read each magazine "thoroughly" and "read the advertisements." The *Saturday Evening Post*, for example, was the most widely read magazine. Its circulation rate was 2.7 million Americans, and among GM consumers in the low-, medium-, and high-price groups, more than half received the *Post*. With the exception of *American*, *Literary Digest*, and *Good Housekeeping*, subscriptions for the rest of the journals were far below that of the *Post*. Just as circulation rates varied, so did the price of running advertisements. For a full-page "black and white" ad, the *Post* cost $8,000 per page, *American* $5,000, *Good Housekeeping* $4,000, and *Literary Digest* $4,000. GM researchers created an index based on the cost of running an advertisement in each journal.[100] For each dollar spent on advertising, for example, the *Post* reached 0.0081 percent of customers in the medium-price class, giving it an index rating of 109, or nine percent above the group's average.[101] For readers who owned low-price cars, the *Post*'s circulation index was 104; its "reading economy" index (meaning customers who read their journals through and through) came to 268; and its "advertising economy" index (meaning customers who paid careful attention to the advertisements) topped 500.[102]

Closely related to the task of measuring efficiency, statistics were used to assess the performance of GM operations, ranging from public relations to dealer service. In 1938, for instance, GM asked the Psychological

[97] Ibid., 287–88.
[98] Lyndon Brown, *Market Research and Analysis* (New York: The Ronald Press Company, 1937), 411–12.
[99] Weaver, "The Development of a Basic Purchasing Power Index by Counties," 275–76.
[100] Sales Section, General Motors, "An Analysis of Advertising Media with Particular Reference to National Magazines," June 1928, 10, 13–16, 28, File 87-11.4-1, Box 110, CFK, KU.
[101] Sales Section, General Motors, "An Analysis of Advertising Media with Particular Reference to National Magazines," June 1928, 17–18, File 87-11.4-1, Box 110, CFK, KU.
[102] Sales Section, General Motors, "An Analysis of Advertising Media with Particular Reference to National Magazines," June 1928, 19, 21, File 87-11.4-1, Box 110, CFK, KU.

Corporation to assess the impact of one of GM's PR shows, the "Parade of Progress" (a touring science show), which appeared in different cities. The GM report concluded: "The Psychological Corporation, a concern of national reputation, makes an extensive scientific survey every November and May to appraise public opinion." In Memphis the consultants found that Americans' general favorable rating of GM had improved from fifty-seven percent before the show to seventy-six percent after it.[103] Statistics (in this case, the percent change) were used to determine whether or not Americans had significantly altered their attitudes toward GM as a result of the PR show.

Another statistical gauge focused on deviations from a given average or mean. Consider, for example, dealer service. Beginning in the 1930s, a GM department tabulated "good and bad comments" from consumers about dealer service and each month identified dealers who had accumulated an "abnormal" number of complaints. A Philadelphia dealer was singled out for being responsible for seventy-five percent of complaints in his area.[104] Thus, he had been defined as abnormal based on the statistical representation of his position vis-à-vis other dealers.

Consumer studies applied as well to questions about production. Weaver's 1934 study of independent front suspension, for example, was meant to determine whether consumers expressed enough enthusiasm as to justify its production. In hindsight historian of technology William Abernathy called independent front suspension "probably the most important product innovation of the 1930s." It enhanced "handling, riding comfort, and safety."[105] Yet, at the time, managers had to consider its potential appeal. In 1936, at a GM conference, Alfred Sloan was asked about independent front suspension and an eight-cylinder engine for Chevrolet. Weaver's market research bolstered his answers. For the new suspension, he reported: "Consumer research statistics demonstrate clearly a definite appreciation on the part of the users of knee action wheels, as measured by the very large percentage of those users who will demand that feature in their next motor car purchase." By contrast, he replied that GM would not develop an eight-cylinder engine for Chevrolet in its competition with Ford. Pointing to consumer research surveys, he reported that Ford's V-8 was "losing consumer prestige."[106]

Closely related to the question of whether to produce a new mechanical feature was the question of whether consumers would pay a price high

---

[103] C. A. Lewis, "Eighth Operating Report of the Parade of Progress (January 1 to July 13)," August 16, 1938, quote 7, File 87-11.2-271c, Box 93, CFK, KU.

[104] Zone Manager to Dennis & Tull, Inc., April 10, 1936, File Man 5 Gen 5 Pat 5 Part 8, Box 3156, RG 122, NA.

[105] William J. Abernathy, *The Productivity Dilemma: Roadblock to Innovation in the Automobile Industry* (Baltimore: Johns Hopkins University Press, 1978), 191.

[106] Alfred P. Sloan, Jr., "The Question box," no. 39 and no. 40 (White Sulphur Springs, 1936), File 83-12.16, Wilkerson Collection, KU.

enough to cover production costs. Automatic transmission offered one example. By 1940, engineers had developed and tested a prototype version of
automatic transmission, or what they called "Hydra-Matic drive." At that
point, Weaver surveyed 10,000 car drivers. More excited than he had been in
some time, Weaver reported that an estimated ninety-one percent of respon-
dents were said to be favorably impressed.[107] But Weaver wanted more specific information about potential buyers' sensitivity to Hydra-Matic's price.
He asked not only whether they wanted it, but "How much would you
be willing to pay?"[108] Car buyers were given specific prices, ranging in
$10 increments from a low price of $50 up to $150.[109] Some 17.5 per-
cent of the "new car buyers" stated that they would pay "$90 extra" for
automatic transmission, for which a jubilant Weaver wrote to the director
of GM's industrial research lab, Charles Kettering: "This means an annual
market for about 500,000 Hydra-Matic jobs. Or, putting it a different way,
there is enough potential to keep the Olds factory running exclusively on
Hydra-Matic."[110]

Recognizing that consumers' sensitivity to Hydra-Matic's price was conditioned by their attitudes toward the technology, the market researchers
tried to categorize the reactions of potential buyers. Some complaints were
to be expected. Drivers asked about the transmission's dependability and its
effect on the car's pickup and ride. But one finding surprised the researchers:
because GM had played up automatic transmission's "simplicity of operation," many car buyers had received the "impression that the clutch as well
as the clutch pedal has [sic] been eliminated," and that there was no transmission. Drivers thus wondered why they had to pay more for less, as one
car driver was quoted as saying: "As I understand it the principle is very
simple, so why should it cost more?" Although just two percent of those
surveyed owned a Hydra-Matic, roughly one-third of those surveyed said
they had driven or ridden in a car with automatic transmission. The report
sketched a picture in which consumers articulated shortcomings – notably,
their reaction to its price – and it reinforced the familiar theme that automatic
transmission was a striking exception to the general public view of stalled
innovation. "Over and over again" drivers had rated the Hydra-Matic as

---

[107] Customer Research Staff, General Motors, "How 10,000 Prospective Buyers Feel About
Hydra-Matic," December 1940, 2–3, File 87-11.4-17, Box 110, CFK, KU.
[108] H. G. Weaver to Charles F. Kettering, January 15, 1941, with Customer Research Staff,
General Motors, "How 10,000 Prospective Buyers Feel About Hydra-Matic," December
1940, 13, File 87-11.4-17, Box 110, CFK, KU.
[109] H. G. Weaver to Charles F. Kettering, January 15, 1941, with Customer Research Staff,
General Motors, "How 10,000 Prospective Buyers Feel About Hydra-Matic," December
1940, 13–16, File 87-11.4-17, Box 110, CFK, KU.
[110] H. G. Weaver to Charles F. Kettering, January 15, 1941, with Customer Research Staff,
General Motors, "How 10,000 Prospective Buyers Feel About Hydra-Matic," December
1940, 2, File 87-11.4-17, Box 110, CFK, KU.

the best thing since the self-starter.[111] Weaver recommended that, based on the survey's findings, GM's Public Relations Department produce a brochure about the Hydra-Matic, much as it had done a few years earlier with the new, so-called "knee action" suspension system.[112] Weaver's study thus formed part of a marketing campaign intended to manipulate the very context in which car drivers debated the innovation. He had tried to identify the process by which drivers arrived at their sensitivity to the new feature's price and counter negative impressions through marketing.

Consumer research studies were meant to provide clarity and precision to questions about consumers that impinged on managers' efforts to achieve efficiency and profitability in their core operations: marketing, distribution, and production. The advertising index represented an attempt to efficiently allocate dollars for advertising. For distribution, Weaver's purchasing power index was meant to allocate dealers efficiently through the vast number of local markets. So too, statistics were employed to spot dealers who slipped too far below the average or mean of what GM considered acceptable performance. For production, consumer research assisted managers in deciding on whether or not to pursue certain features as illustrated with the cases of independent front suspension and the V-8 engine. Research also ventured into the difficult realm of providing a frequency distribution of car buyers' sensitivity to prices as a way to gauge whether projected revenues could justify the production of a new feature (in this case, automatic transmission).

Even as Weaver conducted these studies, he acknowledged their shortcomings: he could never be certain how to pose questions so as to obtain accurate answers.[113] Although the numbers themselves projected clarity, they could not get around the inherent murkiness of the exercise. One response elicited from managers was pragmatic: no matter how imprecise the questions upon which the data was gathered, the data still could be helpful for

---

[111] H. G. Weaver to Charles F. Kettering, January 15, 1941, with Customer Research Staff, General Motors, "How 10,000 Prospective Buyers Feel About Hydra-Matic," December 1940, 3, 5, 8, 18, File 87-11.4-17, Box 110, CFK, KU, with "Reactions of Hydra-Matic Owners," 31, File 87-11.4-17, Box 110, CFK, KU.

[112] H. G. Weaver to Charles F. Kettering, January 15, 1941, with Customer Research Staff, General Motors, "How 10,000 Prospective Buyers Feel About Hydra-Matic," December 1940, 5, 24, File 87-11.4-17, Box 110, CFK, KU. On knee action, see H. G. Weaver to C. F. Kettering, "What Keeps More Buyers from Buying G.M. Cars?" March 26, 1934, File 87-11.4-8, Box 110, CFK, KU. Internal reports substantiate Weaver's survey being used for the knee action brochure, as I note in "Consumers, Information and Marketing Efficiency at GM," 192.

[113] Weaver, "Consumer Questionnaire Technique," 115–18; idem, "The Use of Statistics in the Study of Consumer Demand," 183–84; idem, "Proving Ground on Public Opinion," 149–53; and idem, "Consumer Research and Consumer Education," *The Annals of the American Academy of Political and Social Science* 182 (November 1935): 93–100. See also my discussion in "Consumers, Information, and Marketing Efficiency at GM, 1921-1940," 187–89.

making their decisions. In the example of the advertising index, market researchers repeatedly tried to gauge the value of advertising in different journals as well as other media. Although I cannot say that GM ran advertisements in the *Post* because of the advertising index's findings, the *Post* was popular for GM and other automakers. Ten years later the Curtis Publishing Company singled out the *Post*, stating: "Automotive advertisers in 1938 invested more money in the *Post* than in the next five weeklies combined."[114] Even if imperfect, the consumer studies could help management make decisions to allocate funds, assess marketing campaigns, or provide support for whether or not to proceed with new mechanical features.

Through their presumed objectivity, the statistical studies implied a neutral perspective. Yet the types of questions posed to consumers restricted the types of information collected. For example, Weaver's researchers might ask consumers about the advantages or disadvantages of independent front suspension, but they did not provide a systematic review of the vehicles' safe design. Even so, Weaver noted in his correspondence that consumers pointed to the question of safety. In a 1934 release, for example, GM's Customer Research Staff reported that "the younger generation" was not preoccupied with a car's speed, adding that "the general subject of safety was stressed more frequently by youth than by the grown-ups."[115] As with safety, statistical portraits of consumers proved insufficient in grasping the question of fairness in prices. It was not simply that GM researchers could estimate consumers' price elasticity for major new features like automatic transmission. As the Federal Trade Commission and the Justice Department discovered during the 1930s, consumers and dealers, respectively, complained about dealers' and manufacturers' fairness in pricing vehicles.

Although Sloan identified the importance of deciphering consumer demand for the firm's efficient operation, *My Years* did not pursue the matter of consumer demand beyond statistical studies, whether the Polk figures on car registrations, the dealers' ten-day reports, or market survey data on consumers' incomes. But, in fact, consumers impinged on the firm's operations in other ways. In the case of corporate research, several interest groups expressed their concerns about safety and imposed their standards on the firm (as we will see in Chapter 4). In the case of styling, designers themselves mediated between consumers and management (the subject of Chapter 5).[116] In the case of market transactions and the pricing of vehicles, consumers

114 Commercial Research Division, Curtis Publishing Company, *Who Buys Automobiles and Automotive Products?* (Philadelphia: Curtis Publishing Company, 1939), 24.

115 Customer Research Staff, General Motors Corporation, "Release," Sept. 16, 1934, Folder 28, Box 27, NBC, WHS.

116 On the role of designers as mediators, see Jeffrey L. Meikle, *Twentieth Century Limited: Industrial Design in America, 1925-1939* (Philadelphia, PA: Temple University Press, 1979); and Regina Lee Blaszczyk, *Imagining Consumers: Design and Innovation from Wedgwood to Corning* (Baltimore: Johns Hopkins Press University, 2000).

acted on their own behalf when they negotiated with car dealers the trade-in of their old car and the price of their new vehicle (the topic of Chapter 6). Thus, the four elements of the automobile market's transformation became points for tension between consumers and the firm. Consumers appeared in different forms – sometimes representing themselves, sometimes represented by mediators, and at times represented by interest groups and regulators. Their negotiations more than statistical portraits defined the contours of this mass market.

CONCLUSION

The closed body car, installment credit, the trade-in, and the annual model change were critical elements to the automobile's mass market. Ford Motor Company, General Motors, and Chrysler Corporation each dealt with the market's transformation according to their particular histories. Henry Ford had fashioned his firm's spectacular rise around a single, reliable, plain-Jane product and his system of mass production. Though Ford initially reaped dramatic cost savings and tremendous publicity, as Sloan recounted, he failed to see and to adjust to all four of the market's changes. GM in 1920 hardly inspired confidence as a firm that could seize the initiative. Having inherited a hodge-podge of companies from Billy Durant, Sloan and the Du Pont team of managers set about to create a workable system. As it turned out, that workable system began by reorganizing the divisions into a price ladder of brands, but it included the use of flexible mass production plus the sharing of parts to make possible the marketing strategy. Sloan's plan included as well a credit agency to encourage middle class consumers to use their old car as the down payment for a new car, preferably a closed body, plus plenty of advertising to encourage sales. Although Sloan's plan put an end to the Model T, Walter Chrysler fashioned a successful alternative. Although he mimicked Sloan's marketing plan, he had developed in his career good working ties with suppliers and he relied on these connections to obtain the cost savings and introduce the innovations that made his firm competitive. There was no one best way to organize the modern firm in a mass consumer market, but Ford had clearly failed to grasp the consequences of the changes taking place during the early 1920s.

The experience of General Motors presents a second perspective to the modern firm. Much of Sloan's biography was concerned with two objectives: first, to describe the institutions that proved so important to the modern firm; and second, to explain how the management team that took over from Billy Durant was able to establish financial and operating controls and a marketing plan to not only get the firm through the crisis of 1920 but to sustain the firm's long-term growth. Like Sloan's financial controls, the consumer studies were premised on their pragmatic faith that statistics could be used to describe consumers much as they were used to track inventories. The data provided a close approximation of various aspects about consumers – what magazines they read, their income levels, their reactions to new mechanical features, their price sensitivity – that managers could use to make decisions about the marketplace: journals in which to advertise GM brands, the market potential of local markets, whether or not to produce new engineering devices, and whether those new products' prices could justify their production.

Statistical characterizations of consumers, nevertheless, offered just one particular view of the American car buyer. The data aggregated consumers in the form of abstractions. They were categorized in general groups (low-, medium-, and high-price car buyers); they mattered to GM often in terms of their average behavior or the frequency with which a sample of shoppers mentioned a particular item. In all of these cases, the data appeared objective and neutral in the way it framed consumers' answers. Still, as long as researchers asked questions premised on a congenial relationship between consumers and the firm, the answers confirmed this perspective. Although not addressed in *My Years*, consumers interacted with managers in other ways that mattered to the price and quality of vehicles as determined in a mass market. They are the subjects of the next three chapters.

4

Engineering a Mass Product

When Henry Ford introduced the Model A in 1928, the new car earned an historian's praise "as a well-designed, well-made, well-priced, and 'thoroughly up-to-date' automobile."[1] One of the Model A's improvements was safety glass (two pieces of glass bonded by a plastic sheet).[2] Henry Ford decided to adopt safety glass on the Model A not as a sales gimmick, but in response to an accident in which broken glass had injured an employee.[3] Furthermore, his decision suited consumer demands. In 1931, for example, a sales manager for Pittsburgh Plate Glass Company (PPG) sent the firm's purchasing manager a survey indicating that twenty-two percent of Ford owners or family members had been in accidents and that glass had injured nearly half of those involved. Of the 3,955 Ford owners surveyed, ninety-seven percent answered "yes" when asked whether they thought "the protective value of safety glass justifies the use as standard equipment in all automobiles," and ninety-one percent stated that they would pay $35 extra (or $3 each month in installments) to buy a car with safety glass as compared to an identical vehicle without safety glass.[4] Ford's decision to install safety glass on the Model A, however, had its downside. A 1932 memo revealed that "improper lamination" had caused "separation of the glass, strain cracks, discoloration, bubbles, etc." From 1928 to the end of May 1930, twenty percent of windshields were rejected as defective and nearly four million were replaced.[5] This was not the only headache for Ford's managers. In 1930, the company had advertised all its cars coming equipped with a "shatter-proof glass windshield" – "so made that it will not fly or shatter under the hardest

[1] David A. Hounshell, *From the American System to Mass Production, 1800-1932: The Development of Manufacturing Technology in the United States* (Baltimore: Johns Hopkins University Press, 1984), 292.
[2] For a list of cars using safety glass, see A. M. Wibel to Edsel B. Ford, October 31, 1930, Folder, "Triplex Glass Data Working Papers," MM-42-G, Box 96, Acc. 390, HF.
[3] Joel W. Eastman, *Styling vs. Safety: The American Automobile Industry and the Development of Automotive Safety, 1900-1966* (New York: University Press of America, 1984), 178-79.
[4] Frank W. Judson to A. M. Wibel, November 12, 1931, with "Total Replies Received from Ford Owners – 3955," Folder "Pittsburgh Plate Glass," Box 59, Acc. 390, HF.
[5] "Notes on the Adoption and Use of Laminated Glass by the FMC," April 12, 1932, Folder, "Data held for Pittsburgh Pate [sic] vs. Triplex," Box 96, Acc. 390, HF.

impact." Sam Baxter's accident proved otherwise. When broken glass splinters caused him to lose sight in his left eye, he sued the automaker. In a 1932 letter to PPG, the Ford Secretary's Office observed that the plaintiff did not claim that the product was "defective," rather that "he was induced to purchase his Ford car by reason of representations and warranties regarding the windshield glass." In other words, he claimed that Ford advertisements had gulled him into believing the glass was "shatterproof."[6]

This episode was more than an unfortunate example of good intentions gone sour. A product's sound engineering represented one important dimension to its quality, and managers wanted to improve their products' quality to secure consumers' loyalty for repeat purchases. Yet, managers faced a dilemma: safety innovations promised to win consumers' loyalty, but conflicted with other objectives that determined a firm's profits including the drive to lower production costs and rush new devices into production. Putting the company's experience in historical perspective, how may we account for managers' approach to product quality?

One major influence on managers was the market. Going back to the early years of the automobile industry, manufacturers had worked to improve their vehicles' reliability, durability, and safety. During the 1920s, managers sustained these goals through large investments in research and development. Even so, had market pressures alone insured a safe product, there would have been no need for other sources of discipline. One new source of oversight was *MacPherson v. Buick* (N.Y. 1916). Manufacturers reduced their chances of being sued and improved their chances of defending themselves successfully by making good on Cardozo's demand that they undertake careful inspections and tests of their products.[7] Yet, *MacPherson*'s impact, by itself, was

---

[6] Secretary's Office, Ford Motor Company, to Pittsburgh Plate Glass Company, November 21, 1932, Folder, "Pittsburgh Plate Glass," Box 59, Acc. 390, HF. *Baxter v. Ford Motor Company et al.*, 12 P.2d 409 (Wash. 1932), 411. See also Cornelius W. Gillam, *Products Liability in the Automobile Industry: A Study in Strict Liability and Social Control* (Minneapolis, MN: University of Minnesota Press, 1960), 86–87; and Lester Feezer, "Manufacturer's Liability for Injuries Caused by His Products: Defective Automobiles," *Michigan Law Review* 37 (November 1938): 1–27.

[7] As legal scholars have indicated, *MacPherson* represented a break with the past, but how sharp a break it would be and in what direction depended in part on subsequent cases. They have compared it to the many cases that led up to Cardozo's ruling, as well as to those that followed. Steven P. Croley and Jon D. Hanson, for instance, identified *MacPherson* as the first of four landmark products liability cases in the twentieth century. The other three cases were *Escola v. Coca Cola Bottling Co.*, 150 P.2d 436 (Cal. 1944); *Henningsen v. Bloomfield Motors*, 161 A.2d 69 (N.J. 1960); and *Greenman v. Yuba Power Products, Inc.*, 377 P.2d 897 (Cal. 1963). Faulting recent legal writings, Croley and Hanson singled out "market failures" as seen in terms of imperfect information, manufacturers' power over consumers, and the question of the distribution of risks. See Steven P. Croley and Jon D. Hanson, "Rescuing the Revolution: the Revived Case for Enterprise Liability," *Michigan Law Review* 91 (February 1993): 683–797, especially 695–706. In addition, Hanson and Douglas Kysar argue that firms manipulate consumers' perceived risks of defects (often through mass media), which I discuss later in this chapter. See Jon D. Hanson and Douglas A. Kysar, "Taking Behavioralism

limited; it encouraged firms to test and inspect components, but offered no further specifications. Instead, several public and private oversight agencies gave specific content to *MacPherson*.[8] The Society of Automotive Engineers (SAE), the USDA's Forest Products Laboratory, the Electrical Testing Laboratories (ETL), insurance underwriters, the Massachusetts motor vehicle administration, the Eastern Conference of Motor Vehicle Administrations, and state legislatures targeted components critical to a car's safety – bumpers, brakes, carburetors, headlights, electrical equipment, and glass windshields.

Despite this web of regulatory oversight, automakers never completely eliminated defects. Faced with a tighter regulatory environment, firms responded in two ways. First, they began to demand a new type of insurance – products liability insurance. Second, their advertisements tried to shape consumers' attitudes about automotive technology and obscure the straightforward goal of safety.

CORPORATE RESEARCH AND CONSUMERS' RISKS IN A MASS MARKET

As the automobile market expanded, leading manufacturers began to invest more heavily in research and development. No sudden event brought about this change. At least as early as 1913, the Ford Motor Company had begun to conduct inspections and test its components. As firms grew in size during the 1920s, they drew on a much larger reserve of profits to invest in research facilities. There was a payoff: the improved parts and new devices helped make cars safer.

During the 1920s, GM, Ford, and Chrysler joined the ranks of a handful of corporations funding large research laboratories. Before the 1920s, some companies (such as GM) had contracted with consulting firms (such as Arthur D. Little, Inc.), but most labs were small and tested materials and parts. The National Research Council (NRC) found that just fifteen firms employed at least fifty researchers in 1921. Firms in competitive industries like textiles and lumber could not afford large labs. By contrast, in markets dominated by a small number of large corporations, such as chemicals and electrical machinery, management invested in research.[9] Autos fit this pattern. GM, for instance, had earned $8.6 million in profits on $49 million in

Seriously: Some Evidence of Market Manipulation," *Harvard Law Review* 112 (May 1999): 1420–1572.

[8] Scott Knowles investigated products liability in terms of specific safety institutions, especially the Underwriters' Laboratories, the Consumers Union, and Consumers Research, Inc., which published *Consumer Reports*. Scott Gabriel Knowles, "Inventing Safety: Fire, Technology, and Trust in Modern America" (Ph.D. diss., Johns Hopkins University, 2003), especially 184–290.

[9] On the number of firms with large labs, see George Perazich and Philip Field, *Industrial Research and Changing Technology*, Works Progress Administration Report M-4 (Philadelphia, 1940), 66. These topics are discussed in David Mowery and Nathan Rosenberg, *Technology and the Pursuit of Economic Growth* (New York: Cambridge University Press, 1989), especially 61–79.

sales in 1910; the Ford Motor Company earned $4.2 million in net income. By 1927, GM pocketed $262 million in profits after taxes on $1.3 billion in sales. That year the firm reported a research staff of 260 personnel for the NRC's survey. Ford Motor Company earned $33 million in after-tax profits in 1927 (the year it stopped producing the Model T) and $88.4 million in 1929. Although Ford volunteered no data, Chrysler listed 143 researchers in 1927, a year in which its net income came to $22 million. Eleven years later, in 1938, Chrysler reported a research staff of 500 employees; Ford reported 100 "technical or scientific staff" and a total workforce of 250 in its laboratories. GM listed 504 employees under Charles Kettering's direction plus research staffs in specific automotive divisions, such as twenty-seven personnel at Cadillac's research lab and forty-five employees at A. C. Spark Plug Division's research facility. The automakers' labs were among the largest corporate research facilities. In 1938, only 120 out of 1,722 firms supported labs with fifty or more employees (and just fifty-four maintained labs with 100 or more employees).[10]

GM's commitment to research provided the institutional foundation for safer products. In 1919, Charles Kettering, an inventor best known for the electric self-starter, took charge of GM's research laboratory.[11] Within two years, Pierre S. du Pont, as GM's president, asked him to focus on the question of reliability. Kettering was to assess how a new car would operate after 20,000 to 30,000 miles on the road "with a definite record of troubles." That fall Kettering had tests underway.[12] Over the next three years, GM established its Proving Grounds, which Stuart W. Leslie noted "substituted scientifically designed banks, gradients, and measuring instruments for the drama of open road trials."[13] Engineers amassed annual data for the specifications and performance of new models and calculated a car's "durability

---

[10] On Chrysler's, Ford's, and GM's sales and earnings, see U.S. Federal Trade Commission, *Report on Motor Vehicle Industry*, 76th Cong., 1st sess., House Document No. 468 (Washington, D.C.: U.S. Government Printing Office, 1939), 22, 431, 557, 645. The net income for the Ford Motor Company between 1903 and 1921 is reported in Allan Nevins with Frank Ernest Hill, *Ford: The Times, the Man, the Company* (New York: Charles Scribner's Sons, 1954), Appendix 6, 647. Ford listed 100 researchers in 1933. On the size of research staffs, see National Research Council, "Industrial Research Laboratories of the United States including Consulting Laboratories," *Bulletin* 60 (July 1927): 23, 28, 48; National Research Council, "Industrial Research Laboratories of the United States including Consulting Laboratories," *Bulletin* 91 (August 1933): 74; National Research Council, "Industrial Research Laboratories of the United States including Consulting Laboratories," *Bulletin* 102 (December 1938): 52, 84, 92–93. For 1938 industry data, see Perazich and Field, *Industrial Research and Changing Technology*, 66, 68. Although Ford engineers improved their product, investments in modern research were criticized in Allan Nevins and Frank Ernest Hill, *Ford: Expansion and Challenge, 1915-1933* (New York: Charles Scribner's Sons, 1957), 249–52.

[11] On Kettering, see Stuart W. Leslie, *Boss Kettering: Wizard of General Motors* (New York: Columbia University Press, 1983), especially 91–97, 183.

[12] P. S. du Pont, President, to C. F. Kettering, July 19, 1921, File 87-11.7-61, Box 120; and P. S. du Pont to C. F. Kettering, October 4, 1921, File 87-11.7-61, Box 120, both in CFK, KU.

[13] Leslie, *Boss Kettering*, 183–84.

FIGURE 4.1. Charles F. Kettering with his Electric Self-Starter, no date. Not only was Kettering a successful independent inventor, but also effective in promoting techno-logical innovation within General Motors, where he directed the firm's industrial research laboratory. Corporate research, however, was conditioned by a network of oversight agencies including the Society of Automotive Engineers, the Bureau of Standards, insurance underwriters, and state regulatory agencies. Courtesy of the Detroit Public Library, National Automotive History Collection.

costs" at 25,000 miles figuring in the effects of repairs, gas, oil, and tires.[14] Whether GM's products were more dependable or cheaper to operate than their competitors' brands is hard to say, but the data reflected the company officials' commitment to determining the competitiveness of GM products on the basis of dependability and durability.[15] Thus, Kettering was able to design components systematically, test their properties (strength, dura-bility, flexibility), and review vehicles under controlled driving conditions (Fig. 4.1).[16]

[14] "General Motors Pricing Policy *Better Value at the Same Price or Equal Value at Reduced Price* Chevrolet History 1925–1939," File 87-4.18-56, Box 20, GMC/Proving Ground Collection, KU.

[15] The Proving Ground is described in a GM brochure. Department of Public Relations, General Motors Corporation, "Putting Progress Through Its Paces: The Story of General Motors Proving Ground," May 1937, Box 3170, RG 122, NA.

[16] Leslie, *Boss Kettering*, 183–84.

Kettering's lab conducted a wide variety of research projects, some of which both improved safety and made cars more reliable. Crankcase ventilation offered one illustration. With crankcase dilution, as Leslie observed, consumers found that "their timing chains and other engine parts were broken or badly pitted." Engineers traced the problem to water, which caused particularly sulfurous fuels "under the right conditions of dilution" to "produce a sulfuric acid that ate tappets, piston rings, and other engine parts." Ventilators to dissipate the gas were introduced on Cadillac in 1925, and soon thereafter on other makes.[17] Kettering also had his way with four-wheel brakes. As Leslie recounted, by 1927 his research had "led to the universal adoption of the system by all the General Motors divisions." Further, "[a]s an inducement to customers," Leslie recalled, Kettering "suggested that General Motors offer four-wheel brakes as a free option the first year, and write off the expense to advertising. The divisions followed this advice and the demand for the brakes subsequently soared."[18]

During the 1920s, corporate research labs developed new devices as well as improved many existing components, including four-wheel brakes, crankcase ventilation, a longer-lasting fanbelt, a crankshaft balancer, a mechanical fuel pump, and "synchromesh" transmission. More features were developed in the 1930s, such as hydraulic brakes, the all-steel body, and independent front wheel suspension.[19] As they increased a car's durability, many features reduced repairs. For example, Sloan noted that crankcase ventilation eliminated repair bills and saved operating costs: oil was changed roughly every 2,000 (not 500) miles for a four-to-one savings. In the case of the fanbelt, Sloan recalled that the old belt was at risk for unpredictable breaks, and even then it lasted just a few thousand miles. After GM's technical staff lengthened the fanbelt's life, it became a negligible part of automobile repairs.[20] Overall, these improvements corresponded with lower operating costs: between 1926 and 1939, the automobile trade association reported a fifty-percent drop in the cost per mile of operating a passenger car.[21] Related

[17] Ibid., 197–99.   [18] Ibid., 188–89.

[19] Leslie, *Boss Kettering*. See also for an internal GM report noting durability, "The Manufacturer, the Dealer, and the Used Car," April 1927, 8, File 87-11.4-1, Box 110, CFK, KU; and the list of successive engineering changes with dates and remarks in G. M. Engineering Staff, "General Motors Developments," December 10, 1956, File 87-4.19-16, Box 21, GMC/Proving Ground, KU; "Progress in Design in comparison with customer tastes and desires," File 87-4.19-4, Box 20, GMC/Proving Ground, KU; G. M. Engineering Staff, "General Motors Developments," August 4, 1955, File 83-1.8-4, Wilkerson Collection, KU; and Alfred P. Sloan, Jr., *Adventures of a White-Collar Man* (New York: Doubleday, Doran & Company, 1941), 160–63, 185–88. See also the U.S. Federal Trade Commission, *Report of the Motor Vehicle Industry*, 909–19.

[20] Sloan, *Adventures of a White-Collar Man*, 160–63.

[21] According to the Bureau of Labor Statistics, the cost of living for thirty-two large cities was reported as falling twenty percent during the same years. Automobile Manufacturers

data indicate that vehicles also became safer. The standardization of safety glass in vehicles during the 1930s, after Ford's period of experimentation, reduced the number of accidents and injuries from glass cuts.[22] Compared to the average of 30.7 deaths caused by auto accidents per 10,000 cars in 1913 (the first year in which data was collected), the figure dropped to an all-time low of 10.6 deaths in 1926. During the 1930s, the number of deaths remained well below the rate for 1913, but rose above the 1926 level, ranging from 11.1 to 14.4 per 10,000 vehicles.[23]

MacPHERSON V. BUICK AND THE AMBIGUOUS NATURE OF INSPECTIONS

Corporate initiatives could not alone take credit for this decline in accidents. Cardozo's landmark ruling built on earlier cases and was reinforced by subsequent rulings. For instance, the U.S. Appeals Court reiterated Cardozo's message in *Johnson v. Cadillac Motor Car Co.* (2nd Cir. 1919), holding manufacturers responsible for inspecting their products.[24] The *New York Times*

Association, *Automobile Facts and Figures*, 22nd ed. (Detroit: Automobile Manufacturers Association, 1940), 72.

[22] Eastman, *Styling v. Safety*, 178–79.

[23] The Automobile Chamber of Commerce reported data collected by the National Safety Council. National Safety Council, *Accident Facts*, Public Safety Series No. 17 (Chicago: National Safety Council, Inc., 1928), 19; idem, *Accident Facts*, 1933 ed. (Chicago: National Safety Council, Inc., 1933), 34; and Automobile Manufacturers Association, *Automobile Facts and Figures*, 22nd ed., 84. By contrast, total accidents during the 1920s soared, and were the subject of investigation by legal realists in Committee to Study Compensation for Automobile Accidents, *Report to the Columbia University Council for Research in the Social Sciences* (Philadelphia: Press International Printing, 1932). John Henry Schlegel examined these realists and social scientists in *American Legal Realism and Empirical Social Science* (Chapel Hill, NC: University of North Carolina Press, 1995), 105–14.

[24] *Johnson v. Cadillac Motor Car Co.*, 261 F. 878 (2nd Cir. 1919). Jain concluded that *MacPherson* sustained a limited view of the automobile as "a mass-produced consumable and therefore did not press the issue of technical innovation." In her reading, "the establishment of the National Highway Transportation Safety Administration (NHTSA) signaled a new common sense about the extent to which manufacturers should ensure that their products are crashworthy." Although important safety measures dated to the 1960s and 1970s, I argue that a web of oversight agencies (public and private) did "press the issue of technical innovation" prior to 1960. The regulation did not focus on the vehicles' overall crashworthiness, but on critical components, such as brakes, bumpers, and safety glass. This is the topic of this chapter. I also argue that regulatory oversight was imperfect and managers made tradeoffs between safety and other concerns, such as the cost of production. Thus, autos housed some old defects and contained new ones as well. Sarah S. Lochlann Jain, "'Dangerous Instrumentalities': The Bystander as Subject in Automobility," *Cultural Anthropology* 19, no. 1 (2004): 61–62, 75–77, quotes 62–63, 76. See also Eastman, *Styling v. Safety*; and Gillam, *Products Liability in the Automobile Industry*, 174–93. For a discussion of regulation in the years since 1960, see Jerry L. Mashaw and David L. Harfst, *The Struggle for Auto Safety* (Cambridge, MA: Harvard University Press, 1990).

noted that the decision meant that an automaker or other manufacturer would be "held liable for defects in an article causing injury to a purchaser, even though the purchase is made through an intermediary."[25] In his survey of nearly all products liability cases involving automobiles at the appellate level from the early 1900s through the 1950s, Cornelius Gillam reported that in response to *MacPherson* a firm's "most obvious defense" was evidence "that reasonable care was in fact used in the manufacturing process."[26] That standard, he continued, stiffened over time, but the message that corporations could defend themselves by demonstrating proper care in inspections was not lost on the leading manufacturers.

By the late 1920s, Gillam recounted, automakers had created "their own inspection systems in wheel manufacturing plants," and, as time passed, they "continued to refine their inspection systems."[27] Ford's record is perhaps most detailed. By the date of Cardozo's ruling in 1916, Ford's legal department had already included inspections and tests in its defense.[28] Eleven years later, in 1927, when Ford faced another damage suit for a defective wheel, the wheel supplier provided thorough tests for the year the wheel was made, and described a testing lab, a chemical lab, and a lab for heat treatment tests among other tests.[29] Brakes offered a second example. In a 1929 case involving defective brakes, Buick offered in its defense several inspections: two men on the conveyor line inspected all brake parts; brake inspectors studied "every cotter key or pin" to ascertain its strength; and once the Flint factory shipped the car to its local market, two factory men inspected

---

[25] "Holds Makers Liable. Court of Appeals Establishes New Rule in Automobile Case," *New York Times* (March 15, 1916): 4. See also "Maker Liable for Car's Defects," *Eastern Underwriter* 17 (April 7, 1916): 1, 16; "Maker Loses New 'Wheel Case,'" *Horseless Age* 37 (April 1, 1916): 289; Elton J. Buckley, "Manufacturer Legally Responsible for Damage," *Metal Worker* 85 (June 23, 1916): 863; and A. L. H. Street, "Liability of Machinery Manufacturers," *Iron Age* 95 (January 21, 1915): 222–23.

[26] Gillam described the standard warranty, but observed that, in all the cases he reviewed, automakers had never based their defense on the standard warranty's disclaimer. Instead, they operated within the framework set out by *MacPherson*. Gillam, *Products Liability in the Automobile Industry*, 174–76, 189–93, quotes 162, 191. As noted in Chapter 2, many manufacturers had included these warranties since the early 1900s.

[27] Ibid., 188.

[28] Gillam cited the case of wheels to illustrate his point, noting that Ford had emphasized nine tests in its 1916 lawsuit. Ibid.

[29] E. R. Jacobi, Kelsey-Hayes Wheel Corporation to Nicoll, Anabel & Nicoll, November 16, 1927; Hayes Wheel Company, "Testing Laboratory Some of the Standard Tests" (no date, pamphlet); [illegible] Cahill "Manufacture and Inspection," November 16, 1927; Edward J. Foley, Wood Wheel Division, Kelsey Wheel Company, "Timber – Source of Supply, Method of Assembling Ford Automobiles," November 15, 1927; "Torque Tests on Ford Wheels," (no date [1929]); "A Comparison of Black Primers for Wood Wheels," Hayes Wheel Company, Laboratory Report No. 3677, April 15, 1924; Laboratory Report No. 3945-6-7, May 14, 1924; and Laboratory Report No. 3954 & 3955, June 5, 1924, all in Folder 75-78-5, Box 78, Acc. 75, HF. Gillam makes a similar point in *Products Liability in the Automobile Industry*, 188.

FIGURE 4.2. Final Inspection of 1939 Chevrolets, Flint, Michigan. In *Macpherson v. Buick* (N.Y. 1916), Judge Benjamin Cardozo sent the message to automakers that their best defense in lawsuits was evidence of tests and inspections of their cars. Courtesy of the Detroit Public Library, National Automotive History Collection.

the brakes, including brake connections, and the steering system. When the dealer sold the car, the brakes (and other parts) were inspected yet again.[30]

In spite of the many inspections and the money invested in corporate research, management's goal of improving product quality competed with other seemingly desirable business strategies, such as reducing production costs and marketing new features. Many defects followed from the process of manufacturing vehicles, and records for the Ford Motor Company provide valuable documentation. From the 1920s through the 1930s, Ford tabulated dealers' complaints. By the mid-1930s, the Service Department listed specific defects, the branches filing complaints, the number of complaints, and a description of the problem and action taken (Fig. 4.2).

A sample of the reports illustrates both the persistence of defects and also Ford's efforts to address problems quickly and systematically. In 1926, road-men summarized dealers' complaints as including "frozen brakes," "poor material in emergency brake bands," "glass breaking," "defective floor

---

[30] *Rotche v. Buick Motor Company*, 193 N.E. 529 (Ill. 1934), 531; and Gillam, *Products Liability in the Automobile Industry*, 188 n. 8.

boards," and "lamp brackets breaking at welds."[31] Although the details for Ford's 1926 reports were sparse (frozen brakes simply received the notation "Install drain in the dust plate" and "Follow up Double Acting Cam"), reports from the 1930s were more detailed. In its bulletin of April 4, 1933, the Service Department reported that dealers in Okalahoma City complained that the ignition coil for the Model 40 was "defective," causing the coil to short. Eight more complaints were filed from Chicago and others from Denver.[32] In its report of October 2, 1933, the Service Department noted some twenty complaints coming from Dallas in one month regarding "rear shock absorber arms breaking." Penned on top of the complaint was the remark: "Got a bad heat of steel in from Great Lakes [sic] a few forgings got thru [sic] before cracks were detected. All ok now."[33] In its bulletin of May 21, 1936, the Service Department listed fourteen branches that had filed a total of 3,042 complaints. Under remarks, the rear brake drums were said to have been replaced with a new design and officials were "installing new experimental wedges."[34] For its report of April 2, 1937, the Service Department cited eighteen branches with over 1,200 complaints about brakes grabbing or locking "at slight pedal pressure, throwing passengers out of seats." The report noted the use of new brake wedges and new springs. In addition, Dearborn asked Atlanta to test new brake assemblies that came with "special linings." Five branches sent sixty-eight complaints about mud slipping past the "brake and drum" and coating the "entire brake [m]echanism." Furthermore, "mud & gravel packs up around brake cross shaft making same inoperative." Samples had been sent to officials at Dearborn (P. E. Martin and L. S. Sheldrick) and "[s]pecial drums to prevent mud & silt entering between brake plate and drum" had been shipped to five branches "for test purposes." In addition, "Cross shaft & cross members [were] redesigned" and "dust shields designed for holes in cross members." Production was set to go in six weeks.[35]

---

[31] "Department communication to Mr. Klann," February 11, 1926; and K. O. Kanzler, "Notes on Complaints," February 19, 1926, Folder, "Complaints – General – 1926," Box 168, Acc. 94, HF. The many complaints often called attention to dealers' service. On this topic, see Stephen L. McIntyre, "The Failure of Fordism: Reform of the Automobile Repair Industry, 1913–1940," *Technology and Culture* 41 (April 2000): 269–99.

[32] K. O. Kanzler, "Notes on Complaints," February 19, 1926, Folder, "Complaints – General – 1926," Box 168, Acc. 94, HF; and Service Department, "Departmental Communication," April 4, 1933, Folder "M22a – Complaints on cars from Service Department," Box 64, Acc. 390, HF.

[33] Service Department, "Departmental Communication," October 2, 1933, Folder "M22a – Complaints on cars from Service Department," Box 64, Acc. 390, HF.

[34] Service Department, "Departmental Communication," May 21, 1936, Folder "M22a – Complaints on cars from Service Department," Box 64, Acc. 390, HF.

[35] The problem of brakes grabbing was reported by numerous branches again in the Service Department's report of August 12, 1937. Service Department, "Departmental Communication," April 2, 1937; and "Departmental Communication," August 12, 1937, both in Folder "M22a – Complaints on cars from Service Department," Box 64, Acc. 390, HF.

Internal correspondence among GM managers, though not as plentiful in the archives as notices for Ford, illustrated similar production problems, especially the tradeoff between safety and the cost of components and the defects born out of sloppy assembly or inspections. At a GM executive meeting in 1934, Henry Crane asked his fellow managers if any had heard of "clutch chatter"? Calling it a "most unpleasant characteristic," he declared: "The real trouble is that the clutches are designed with practically no factor of safety, solely to save a small amount of cost." He also cited brakes, charging that although GM had initially led the field, it now "skimped on carrying out the details, leaving too small a factor of safety."[36] At a 1941 product meeting, GM's leading executives discussed the quality of its 1942 vehicles. They cited several factors affecting quality, including the shift of assembly men to war production, and "the problem of labor slowdowns." They further noted that the "bodies and sheet metal were also more difficult to build than usual and the dies not quite up to standard." Managers took special note of certain products and plants. They complained about "Pontiac spring squawks and grabbing brakes," and traced problems with Buick engines to "a combination of carburetor trouble, manifold leaks, spark plug troubles and excessive oil consumption." As further "evidence" of Buick's "lowered quality," they cited "the number of broken steering gears experienced on the 1941 models as a result of steering gear misalignment." Top officials debated whether the Central Office's inspectors should "shut down the assembly lines" if a "desired standard" was not reached. They also proposed setting up "another million dollars and give Buick dealers a liberal allowance to correct all difficulties."[37]

Aside from problems in the design of parts and the production of vehicles, serious risks of injury followed from marketing innovations, notably the major innovation of the early 1920s – enclosed cars.[38] Because they kept out bad weather, "closed bodies" became enormously popular, but the new design created three major problems. The first concerned the quality of lumber. Through most of the 1920s, body builders stretched steel skins over wooden frames. Enclosed vehicles demanded much stronger wood than open cars so as to prevent their beams from warping or breaking. Body builders, for instance, prized ash for beams, but complained that "brashy ash"

---

[36] Henry M. Crane, "More and Better Friends of General Motors," Third General Motors Executive Conference, White Sulphur Springs, West Virginia, October 19–21, 1934, 8–11, File 77-7.4-1.13-1, Mott Papers, KU.

[37] "Product Meeting Held in Styling Auditorium on Thursday, October 16, 1941," 2–3, File 87-11.4-19, Box 110, CFK, KU.

[38] In the case of railroads, Welke wrote: "Technological advances or even simple operating changes could dramatically increase danger or introduce new hazards." Barbara Young Welke, *Recasting American Liberty: Gender, Race, Law, and the Railroad Revolution, 1865-1920* (New York: Cambridge University Press, 2001), 28. Knowles traced the efforts of the Underwriters' Laboratories and the Consumers' Union to reduce new products' risks. Knowles, "Inventing Safety," 260–86.

(a light, weak wood) was difficult to distinguish from sound ash, and "a certain amount often gets by and into the finished body, where it occasionally fails in service under conditions which would not ordinarily cause breakage."[39] In addition, water seeped into the roofs of many cars, as Alfred Sloan recalled in his autobiography: "The center portion of the roof was covered with a synthetic rubber material joined to the steel side panels. But water, dirt, and so forth collected in this juncture, causing a gradual deterioration of the roof. In a salt atmosphere the process was accelerated. Fisher Body was hard pressed to keep up with warranty replacements."[40] The second problem was carbon monoxide poisoning. Because glass windows sealed a vehicle, Travelers Insurance found that "over 60 per cent. of all cars of all kinds ... contain measurable concentrations of carbon monoxide, and that 7 per cent. of them contain quantities that may cause collapse." The report blamed poor maintenance and defects. Where leaks in manifolds and mufflers or "a defective car heater" let carbon monoxide escape, gaps in floor boards directed the gas into the passenger compartment.[41] Third, glass often broke and cut passengers. By 1930, GM's two premier lines (Cadillac and LaSalle) had adopted safety glass, but the volume brands had not.[42] As late as 1932, Alfred Sloan declared that he could not justify the expense to shareholders; as he explained to Lammot du Pont, "I am trying to protect the interests of the stockholders of General Motors and the Corporation's operating position – it is not my responsibility to sell safety glass."[43] GM and Ford illustrated different problems: Sloan framed his response to safety glass in terms of unwanted increases in the cost of production; Ford experienced

---

[39] Arthur T. Upson and Leyden N. Ericksen, "Wood Requirements of the Body Industry," *Automotive Manufacturer* 65 (September 1923): 21–24, 29, quote 23.

[40] Alfred P. Sloan, Jr., *My Years with General Motors*, ed. John McDonald with Catherine Stevens (Garden City, NY: Doubleday & Company, Inc., 1964), 275.

[41] The test was conducted in 1933. "Hand-Cranking and Carbon Monoxide," *Travelers Standard* 24 (January 1936): quote 3–5. See also "Carbon Monoxide in Automobiles," *Travelers Standard* 22 (March 1934): 41–52; and Eastman, *Styling vs. Safety*, 68–69, 177–78.

[42] Alfred P. Sloan, Jr., to Lammot du Pont, April 15, 1932, Defendants' Exhibit No. 353, Deposition, Deft's Exs. #18.3, volume 18, *United States of America v. E. I. Du Pont de Nemours and Company, General Motors Corporation, United States Rubber Company, Christiana Securities Company, Delaware Realty and Investment Corporation, Pierre S. du Pont, Lammot du Pont, Irene du Pont, defendants*, Civil Action No. 49-C-1017-1, Imprints Department, Hagley. Eastman, *Styling vs. Safety*, 179–80.

[43] For a list of cars using safety glass, see A. M. Wibel to Edsel B. Ford, October 31, 1930, Folder, "Triplex Glass Data Working Papers," MM-42-G, Box 96, Acc. 390, HF. Alfred P. Sloan, Jr. to Lammot du Pont, April 15, 1932, Defendants' Exhibit No. 353, Deposition, Deft's Exs. #18.3, volume 18, *United States of America v. E. I. Du Pont de Nemours and Company, General Motors Corporation, United States Rubber Company, Christiana Securities Company, Delaware Realty and Investment Corporation, Pierre S. du Pont, Lammot du Pont, Irene du Pont, defendants*, Civil Action No. 49-C-1017-1, Imprints Department, Hagley.

a high rate of defects born out of his decision to include the feature before it was perfected.

Compared to the early years of the auto industry, corporate research efforts accelerated during the 1920s and 1930s and were associated with a marked decline in the number of automobile accidents as measured per car. The records of automobile companies, however, remind us that defects were not eliminated. Indeed, although some problems diminished or even disappeared, others often took their place, notably those associated with the major marketing innovation, closed bodies, and the many glitches in the production of cars. *MacPherson* had resulted in managers inspecting their incoming materials and parts more carefully. Yet, a number of problems apparently slipped past the inspectors. When consumers were asked in surveys, as one GM study noted: "The necessity for greater safety is frequently mentioned."[44]

PUBLIC AND PRIVATE OVERSIGHT

Consumers were represented by several public and private organizations that conditioned managers' approach to product quality. Just as Ford had inspections underway at least by 1913 for its wooden wheels, one industry professional society, the SAE, and one public organization, the USDA's FPL, had initiated research intended to improve the quality of automobile materials and components beginning in 1910. During the 1920s, the SAE and the FPL stepped up their efforts to raise quality standards and were assisted by the Bureau of Standards. In addition, insurance underwriters toughened their codes for evaluating a vehicle's safety. And, while these measures could not compel automakers to set minimum quality standards, state regulators could and did impose codes for lighting systems, brake systems, and safety glass.

Throughout the 1920s, the SAE established tougher norms. In the case of bumpers, SAE engineers warned that they offered little protection if improperly secured to the vehicle, and in 1921 set standards for brackets used to hold bumpers.[45] In 1924 the SAE added new codes, requesting that bumpers be set at a uniform height, such that when two cars met, one bumper would hit the other car's bumper, not its body.[46] Lacking its

---

[44] H. G. Weaver, "Tremendous Trifles," October 12, 1932, 1–2, File 87-11.4-5; and Customer Research Staff, General Motors, "Final Report of 1933 Surveys," November, 1933, 29, File 87-11.4-7, both in Box 110, CFK, KU.

[45] "Insurance Features Topic at Dayton," *S.A. E. Journal* 15 (December 1924): 486–88. See also L. P. Halladay, "Bumper-Fitting Standardization," *S.A.E. Journal* 1 (September 1917): 222; "Motor-Car Bumpers," *S.A.E. Journal* 15 (October 1924): 359–62; and Eastman, *Styling vs. Safety*, 12–13.

[46] "Current Standardization Work," *S.A.E. Journal* 9 (September 1921): 209–10; and "Standards Committee Division Reports," *S.A.E. Journal* 14 (June 1924): 628. See also Eastman, *Styling vs. Safety*, 12–13, 70–71.

own research facilities, the SAE worked with other organizations. Among government agencies, the USDA's FPL graded maple, elm, birch, hickory, red gum, and many other types of trees according to their "strength as a beam stiffness or post, shock resisting ability, and hardness."[47] As the price for ash increased, the FPL undertook a study in cooperation with the SAE's Body Division to identify substitutes according to the particular mechanical properties of the species of trees and the particular body parts. Red gum, although lighter and weaker than other woods, was used in open cars, "except lock pillars where it has not given satisfactory service." Oak, being strong and shock-resistant, was "used in large quantities for floor-boards and seat frames."[48] The FPL also examined seasoning methods in an effort to prevent defects, and investigated the causes of brashness and the nature of decay in woods.[49] The SAE worked with a second federal agency, the Bureau of Standards, to design equipment and test components.[50] As late as 1924, the method for testing brakes was that a tester "drives to a line marked on the road and applies his brakes. The distance from the line to the point where he comes to a full stop" was taken as "supposedly a measure of his brake efficiency." The method was open to errors in a driver's own actions and the vehicle's speedometer. The Bureau's W. S. James developed the decelerometer to measure the ability of brakes to stop vehicles free from these distortions.[51]

In addition to these organizations, automobiles received considerable attention from insurance underwriters and offered one example of the many products subject to the inspections of the Underwriters' Laboratories (UL).

[47] "Substitutes for Ash in Automobile Bodies," *S.A.E. Journal* 9 (September 1921): 181; and J. A. Newlin and Thomas R. C. Wilson, "Mechanical Properties of Woods Grown in the United States," U.S. Department of Agriculture *Bulletin* 556 (1917): 1–47.

[48] Arthur T. Upson and Leyden N. Ericksen, "Wood for Automobile Bodies," *S.A.E. Journal* 14 (February 1924): 165–70, quote 170; idem, "Wood Requirements of the Body Industry," 21–24, 29, quote 24.

[49] H. J. Rosenthal, "The Effects of Kiln-Drying On Commercial White Ash," *Automotive Industries* 41 (October 16, 1919): 774–79; J. S. Boyce, "Decays and Discolorations in Airplane Woods," U.S. Department of Agriculture *Bulletin* 1128 (1923): 1–51; Ernest E. Hubert, "The Diagnosis of Decay in Wood," *Journal of Agricultural Research* 29 (1924): 523–67; and Arthur Koehler, "Causes of Brashness in Wood," U.S. Department of Agriculture *Technical Bulletin* 342 (1933): 1–39.

[50] The Bureau of Standards was created in 1901 as a government agency and employed a staff of approximately 600 by 1917. Its work was described in "The National Bureau of Standards," *S.A.E. Journal* 1 (August 1917): 132–39.

[51] The American Instrument Company began marketing the decelerometer at least by 1926. See American Instrument Company, "The James Brake Inspection Decelerometer" (Washington, D.C.: American Instrument Company, no date), in Folder "Brakes – 1926, Ford, 4 Wheel, Misc.," Box 166, Acc. 94, HF. On the Bureau of Standard's role in developing equipment and helping to set brake standards, see "Brake-Performance Studies," *S.A.E. Journal* 14 (February 1924): 236–38; "Brake Performance Improved: Washington Section and Bureau of Standards Give Demonstration of Better Braking," *S.A.E. Journal* 14 (April 1924): 369–70; and "Braking and Safety," *S.A.E. Journal* 16 (January 1925): 19–21.

The UL was created in 1901 as a non-profit research organization under the supervision of the National Board of Fire Underwriters. Historian Scott Knowles argued that the UL acquired considerable scope during the 1920s and became a "national laboratory." Its authority, he concluded, turned on "its ability to anticipate risks presented by new technologies, manage risks presented by existing technologies, and publicize fire risk not as a mysterious force of nature but as a calculable and tractable scientific problem."[52] In 1918, the UL established an automobile council and underwriters worked with the SAE to establish categories for evaluating fire and collision hazards. Eighty-five items figured in the evaluation of fire hazards. Vehicles could receive up to 8,000 points for their overall score and were graded in ten categories. For collision hazards, underwriters studied several components, such as the brake, the clutch, the steering system, and the headlamps. For fire hazards, underwriters investigated the location and construction of the fuel tank, the fuel lines, carburetors, electrical equipment, exhaust pipes, and mufflers.[53]

In 1921, the new system surprised Ford when its dealers protested that insurance rates on Model T's had skyrocketed fifty percent. One dealer quoted from an insurance company's letter: "Fire rates for Ford Automobiles have been materially advanced on 1921 models because of serious mechanical and structural defects, mainly in wiring systems." The letter continued: "These defects would be conducive to fire from short circuits, and in fact, underwriters have already experienced frequent and serious losses because of this." Whereas competitors' makes had not experienced such rate increases, the dealer wrote in a huff that a Ford owner would need to pay $120 in insurance and that the high rates hurt his sales.[54]

While the UL established penalties for failure to improve a vehicle's safety, the lab's engineers and inspectors also assisted manufacturers, as Knowles

---

[52] Knowles, "Inventing Safety," 195–211, quote 197, 219–59; and idem, "Lessons in the Rubble: The World Trade Center and the History of Disaster Investigations in the United States," *History and Technology* 19 (2003): 23–24. A brief description of the UL's activities is found in "The Organization, Purpose and Methods of Underwriters' Laboratories," (Underwriters' Laboratories, 1921).

[53] "Underwriters' Laboratories Form Automobile Council," *S.A.E. Journal* 3 (September 1918): 240–41; A. R. Small, "Automobile Locking-Device, Classification and Theft Insurance," *S.A.E. Journal* 9 (August 1921): 97–99; "Insurance Features Topic at Dayton," *S.A.E. Journal* 15 (December 1924): 486–87; and "Fire Hazards of Automobiles," *S.A.E. Journal* 13 (September 1922): 247.

[54] Sidney K. Bennett to Ford Motor Company, Attention Mr. Gaston Plantiff, July 11, 1921; W. T. Fishleigh, Experimental Engineer, to Underwriters' Laboratories, Attention – Mr. C. R. Alling, May 3, 1922; and W. P. Young to W. T. Fishleigh, May 8, 1922, all in Folder "Underwriters Lab. 1926," Box 180, Acc. 94, HF. In 2005 dollars, the insurance would have amounted to $1,309. Calculations were made with the consumer price index at the Federal Reserve Bank of Minneapolis: http://minneapolisfed.org/Research/data/us/calc/index.cfm, August 24, 2006.

recounted, by testing products and tracking their performance over time.[55] Bumpers offered one valuable example. The UL set two basic standards for their design: first, "[t]he bumper shall be so easy of installation that an average mechanic can effect it with an ordinary kit of tools"; and second, the bumper "shall be so designed that it can be maintained in a reliable condition by the ordinary automobile owner." The UL translated its demands into specific requirements for the manner in which bumpers were secured to the vehicle's frame. The insurance engineers further instructed automakers "to insure a reasonable degree of uniformity of parts and assembled device." Once tests had been satisfactorily met, UL inspectors made "regular and frequent" follow-up visits to check on the quality of the bumpers.[56] Like bumpers, the underwriters' nonprofit testing laboratory conveyed the stricter standards through their inspections of many other components.[57] The UL published lists of its approved automotive devices, naming the manufacturer and specific components. Bumpers, carburetors, fire extinguishers, locking devices, lamps, and windshield wipers were all listed by the UL.[58]

This oversight process worked to corporations' benefit in many cases. Compared to Ford's insurance problems due to fire risks in 1921, by 1923 GM's in-house study of the Model T reported: "The insulation has been made heavier and all wires are enclosed in heavy looms where it is required that they pass points where chaffing is likely to take place. The installation of this new style wiring has also reduced [Ford's] insurance rates."[59] In 1924, insurance rates again influenced Ford executives. Contemplating the sale of Fordson tractors for use in commercial buildings, the experimental engineer, W. T. Fishleigh, saw the need for the UL's approval since "the question

[55] Knowles, "Inventing Safety," 195–211.
[56] Engineer, Casualty Department, Underwriters' Laboratories, to Manufacturers of Bumpers for Passenger Automobiles, January 16, 1924, Revised May 16, 1924, Folder "Underwriters Lab. 1926," Box 180, Acc. 94, HF.
[57] "Fire Hazards of Automobiles," *S.A.E. Journal* 13 (September 1923): 247. The procedures for bumpers were described in Engineer, Casualty Department, to Manufacturers of Bumpers for Passenger Automobiles, May 16, 1924, Folder "Underwriters Lab. 1926," Box 180, Acc. 94, HF; and M. M. Brandon to Ford Motor Company, Attn: T. J. Little, Jr., November 28, 1925, and "Procedure for Inspections at Factories," both in Folder "Underwriter's Laboratories," Box 159, Acc. 94, HF.
[58] Underwriters' Laboratories, "List of Inspected Automotive Appliances," (Underwriters' Laboratories, April 1922), Box 180, Acc. 94, HF; Underwriters' Laboratories, "List of Inspected Automotive Appliances" (Underwriters' Laboratories, April 1921); and *Automobile Insurance Manual Showing Models, List Prices and Symbols for Passenger and Commercial Automobiles Also Rules, Rates and Premiums for Theft, Collision, Property Damage, Tornado, Cyclone, Windstorm, Hail, Earthquake, Explosion, Water Damage, Riot, Insurrection and Civil Commotion Insurance for the State of Louisiana* (Chicago, IL, 1923).
[59] "Improvements made on Ford Cars During the Last Three Years," March 10, 1923, File 87-11.7-27, Box 119, CFK, KU.

of general fire insurance risk always comes up when use of such tractor equipment is proposed." The UL's George Becker asked Fishleigh to alter the tractor's design, including moving the layout of the fuel line such that gasoline leaks would "not impinge on electrical equipment or exhaust lines." Once modified, the Fordson was approved for use in "warehouses, factories and the like, without [an] increase in standard fire insurance rates."[60]

A network of oversight entities thus encouraged higher standards, but did not compel compliance. The SAE requested that manufacturers adopt its voluntary codes to benefit all members of the industry. The FPL freely disseminated information throughout all wood-using industries, but claimed no authority over private manufacturers.[61] It could not compel automakers to buy wood of a given grade. Underwriters' standards were important, but not foolproof. The UL rated components and established an arbitration process for disgruntled clients. But appliances could pass UL tests yet still earn poor marks from the UL and present serious risks. In the mid-1920s, flimsy headlamps and defective brakes fit this category.[62]

For critical components, state regulators directly shaped corporate research. Lighting systems offered one example. By 1921, fourteen states had passed laws for electric lights, and by 1925, the number of states had tripled to forty-five. That year motor vehicle commissioners from ten eastern states formed a conference to assess lighting devices. The conference followed standards established by the Illuminating Engineering Society (IES). The conference also worked with a second organization, the Electrical Testing Laboratories (ETL). Although small in size with a staff of nine individuals in 1921 and roughly fifteen in 1927, the ETL earned its bread and butter from "commercial testing and inspecting."[63] Based on the IES's standards

---

[60] W. T. Fishleigh to Mr. Liebold, May 2, 1925; Geo. D. Becker to Ford Motor Car Company, Attention of Mr. W. T. Fishleigh, September 9, 1925; W. T. Fishleigh, departmental communication, December 29, 1925; Geo. D. Becker to Ford Motor Car Company, Attention of Mr. W. T. Fishleigh, September 26, 1925; and Geo. D. Becker to Ford Motor Company, Attention of Mr. W. T. Fishleigh, November 17, 1925, all in Folder "Underwriters Lab.," Box 180, Acc. 94, HF. For other examples, see Knowles, "Inventing Safety," ch. 6.

[61] Charles August Nelson, "A History of the Forest Products Laboratory" (Ph.D. diss., University of Wisconsin, 1964), 159, 190–92, 205, 217–18.

[62] Knowles found that the UL established the arbitration process in its effort to secure its authority in relation to clients. Disgruntled customers who had their goods rejected by UL engineers could appeal to the Bureau of Standards. Knowles, "Inventing Safety," 241–46. On the SAE, see "Standards Committee Division Reports," 625–28.

[63] The IES was founded in 1906, and in 1927, when it submitted its brief description to the National Research Council, it simply stated its mission was to promote "the theory and practice of illuminating engineering" as well as to spread "knowledge relating thereto." It listed fourteen sections or chapters around the nation. James J. Shanley, "Automobile Head-Lamp Regulation," *S.A.E. Journal* 13 (September 1923): 249; and "Motor Vehicle Electric Lighting Laws," Folder "Laws & Legislation 1926," Box 172, Acc. 94, HF. Information

and ETL's tests, the conference approved twenty-two lighting systems. In response to the growing number of state laws, as early as 1921 Ford had the ETL test its headlamps subject to the requirements for states that had endorsed the IES's standards.[64] GM's 1923 report complimented Ford's "'H' headlight lens" for providing "[e]xcellent road lights without glare."[65] But events took a turn for the worse in 1925. The registrar for motor vehicles in Massachusetts, Frank Goodwin, warned Ford and other firms that the "construction [of their lights] is so flimsy as to render the headlamp unsuitable for practical use." He added: "we are going to insist upon rigid enforcement of the lighting laws" and, if need be, the state would "compel owners of automobiles to replace defective headlamp equipment if it is not... in compliance with our law."[66] That fall Goodwin's engineer in charge of electrical equipment, A. W. Devine, distributed a copy of his article published in the *S.A.E. Journal* along with a four-page bulletin about proper construction.[67]

In 1925, regulators also rejected GM's headlamps. When the ETL tested the headlamps, the engineer J. H. Hunt reported the deflected beam proved too difficult for GM's officials to adjust and, as Hunt admitted, the adjustment was "too technical a matter for the average owner to carry out successfully." Having failed to obtain New Jersey's regulatory approval, GM failed to obtain the Eastern Conference's approval. The company, Hunt suggested, could threaten "legal action," but doing so meant "having to contend with persistent opposition in the future." He instead proposed that

about IES is reported in National Research Council, "Handbook of Scientific and Technical Societies and Institutions of the United States and Canada," *Bulletin* 58 (May 1927): 147. ETL submitted its description to National Research Council, "Industrial Research Laboratories of the United States including Consulting Laboratories," *Bulletin* 16 (December 1921): 31–32; and idem, "Industrial Research Laboratories," *Bulletin* 60 (July 1927): 41.

[64] W. T. Fishleigh to Attention – Service Manager, June 3, 1922; Electrical Testing Laboratories, "Report No. 37168 Test of Ford Type H Automobile Headlight Lens Rendered to the Ford Motor Company," December 15, 1921; and Bureau of Standards, Department of Commerce, Report No. Tel-33025, "Test of 8–1/8 inch Type 'H' Ford Automobile Headlamps Submitted by State of New York, Tax Department, Albany, NY," [stamped] January 21, 1922, all in Folder "Lights – Lens Ford Approvals," Box 192, Acc. 94, HF.

[65] "Improvements made on Ford Cars During the Last Three Years," March 10, 1923, File 87-11.7-27, Box 119, CFK, KU. Eastman found that the problem of glare from headlamps for causing accidents had dated back to the 1910s. Eastman, *Styling vs. Safety*, 9–11, 13.

[66] Manager, Washington Branch, to Attention Mr. Fishleigh, June 5, 1924; E. Austin Baughman, Secretary, Eastern Conference of Motor Vehicle Administrators, to Ford Motor Company, May 9, 1925; and Frank A. Goodwin to the Automobile Headlamp Manufacturer, May 28, 1925, all in Folder "Lights – Lens Ford Approvals," Box 192, Acc. 94, HF.

[67] A. W. Devine, Engineer in Charge, Equipment Section, Commonwealth of Massachusetts, Department of Public Works, to the President of Each Automobile Company, September 10, 1926, and Frank A. Goodwin, by A. W. Devine, "Bulletin Electric Headlamp Design and Construction," November 18, 1925, all in Folder "Lights – Lens Ford Approvals," Box 192, Acc. 94, HF.

GM replicate the ETL testing devices so officials could be confident of the results when ETL tested its equipment. Hunt also wanted the company to improve its lighting devices, because better headlamps would be "very easily demonstrated" to consumers and thus "should be of real sales advantage." In December, he further suggested that GM produce its own headlamps. Although he anticipated no cost savings from doing so, Hunt wanted the ability to control the quality of headlights as a step toward assuring regulatory approval.[68]

Regulatory oversight also covered brakes. Massachusetts's registrar reported to truck makers in 1925 "that 75% of the trucks in use had defective brakes and many of them could not be repaired so as to stop the vehicle within the required distance." The decelerometer, an apparatus developed by the Bureau of Standards, had enabled regulators to identify defective brakes and enforce the state's law. Goodwin's letter instructed managers that they could "avoid difficulty with their customers" simply by making their brakes "sufficiently strong and durable to stand up in service." He offered some "leeway" to allow firms time to redesign and resubmit their brakes, but warned that his twenty-two state inspectors were checking trucks and prepared to identify defective equipment.[69]

Broken glass posed another serious hazard. When invited to express their feelings about safety glass for the 1931 study, consumers voiced comments such as, "'Law Should Require it' and 'Safety glass should be compulsory.'"[70] Ford had faced the difficult problem of overcoming defects in manufacturing safety glass, whereas other manufacturers, notably GM, had refused to install safety glass at all. By 1934, as safety historian Joel Eastman recounted, states began passing laws requiring safety glass be used in cars. The campaign of safety glass proponents resulted in a compromise: safer glass for the front windshield, but a cheaper, somewhat inferior glass for side windows.[71]

In his review of product defects, information economist Michael Spence pictured three options for state intervention: the state could undertake a campaign "to inform consumers"; it could impose liability on producers

---

[68] Although I do not know the outcome of Hunt's request, what I found important was the way he evaluated GM's options. J. H. Hunt to C. F. Kettering, June 4, 1925; and J. H. Hunt to J. E. McEvoy, December 11, 1925, both in File 87-11.7-136, Box 121, CFK, KU.

[69] Frank A. Goodwin to Ford Motor Co., November 18, 1922; and Frank A. Goodwin to The Manufacturers of Trucks, no date [stamped September 9, 1925 and September 18, 1925], both in Folder "Brakes – 1926, Ford, 4 Wheel, Misc.," Box 166, Acc. 94, HF. Eastman discussed safety problems for brakes, including the limitations of hydraulic brakes, in *Styling v. Safety*, 2–3, 12, especially 59–61.

[70] Automobile Accident Prevention Bureau, Detroit, "Summary of Replies to Safety Glass Questionnaire to Automobile Owners," 6, Report from Ernst & Ernst, October 15, 1931, Folder "Pittsburgh Plate Glass," Box 59, Acc. 390, HF.

[71] Eastman, *Styling v. Safety*, 178–80.

"above the levels that are voluntarily undertaken"; or it could regulate a product's design.[72] My account puts the second two options in historical perspective for the case of automobiles. Large firms such as GM voluntarily invested in research and development, wanting to sell more reliable and safer vehicles as part of their goal of securing consumers' loyalty in a mass market. But this overall goal obscured conflicts companies faced between a vehicle's safe design and the drive to lower production costs and market new devices. That *MacPherson* altered managers' calculus is clear from their inspections and tests. Managers also absorbed regulators' lessons to varying degrees. As a response to underwriters, Ford improved the Model T's wiring system and thus lowered its insurance rates. Responding to state regulators, GM's Hunt thought it prudent not to challenge authorities but to improve and further market GM's headlamps. Yet, the safety glass requirement reiterated the message that GM and Ford struck deals between safety and other goals; regulation of this distinctly dangerous material further indicated the state's role in imposing minimum standards. Finally, regulatory oversight remained imperfect. As consumers sued automakers, Gillam found that the outcome of their cases depended in part on the technology in question. Some components, such as wheels or glass, were much easier to determine as defective than other components, such as transmissions.[73]

Because defects persisted and liability rules stiffened, automakers pursued two courses of action simultaneously. One response was premised on the cold, hard realities of defective products. Beginning in the teens, automakers and other manufacturers began to demand products liability insurance. With time, underwriters were able to develop this market to enable manufacturers to spread product risks and manage the cost of defective products. Automakers also pursued a second course of action. They tried to cultivate Americans' good will so that car buyers associated positive attributes with automobiles, and they downplayed a car's dangers. At GM, the public relations department operated on the premise that Americans' attitudes were amenable to change, and, thus, worked to manipulate Americans' perception of a car's positive and negative features.[74]

---

[72] Spence, "Consumer Misperceptions, Product Failure and Producer Liability," 561. Welke offered an example of the first option in the public safety campaign for traveling on street cars and railroads during the Progressive era. Welke, *Recasting American Liberty*, 35–42. For an assessment of market failures by legal scholars, see for example, Croley and Hanson, "Rescuing the Revolution," 683–797; and Hanson and Kysar, "Taking Behavioralism Seriously: Some Evidence of Market Manipulation."

[73] Gillam, *Products Liability in the Automobile Industry*, 117–22, 126–28, 134–35.

[74] I have benefited from a pair of essays by Jon Hanson and Douglas Kysar. See Jon D. Hanson and Douglas A. Kysar, "Taking Behavioralism Seriously: The Problem of Market Manipulation," *New York University Law Review* 74 (June 1999): 630–749; and idem, "Taking Behavioralism Seriously: Some Evidence of Market Manipulation."

PUBLIC RELATIONS AND SHAPING RISKS

Paul Garrett, GM's director of public relations, joined the problem of safety and the role of PR when, at a conference of GM executives in 1934, he called for better testing of GM vehicles. "We need to impose on ourselves and on the industry" an understanding of "the mounting toll of motor fatalities that threaten to strangle our business if we continue like an ostrich to keep our head in the sand, in the happy thought that not our cars but our careless drivers are to blame." Garrett warned that public hostility to vehicles "is growing," and he pictured a time when, "without seeming to know it," the industry could be "nearly enclosed by the threat of one piece of legislation after another."[75] Garrett may have been focused on the pressing topic of safety glass legislation, but his public relations activities were intended to make sure this sort of outcome did not come to pass. His activities were guided in part by the legal context: because the courts typically did not link corporate advertising to the misrepresentation of products to consumers, Garrett and other PR executives were able to construct their views of safety through a wide range of advertising and public relations campaigns.

In 1932, one of the few exceptions to the legal view that advertising was not tied to product defects was a case about a defective car that came before the Supreme Court of Washington. At issue was the question of whether a plaintiff could sue an automaker under an "express-warranty theory."[76] Gillam wrote, "liability for breach of warranty usually is limited, in the automobile cases, to those with whom the defendant is in privity of contract," but in *Baxter v. Ford Motor Co.*, the judge's ruling had "emphasize[d] misrepresentations of fact in the defendant's advertising and sales literature, and treat[ed] mercantile exhortations as express warranties." The technology in question was safety glass. Ford Motor Company had advertised all its cars coming equipped in 1930 with a "shatter-proof glass windshield."[77] Glass splinters, however, caused Sam Baxter to lose sight in his left eye. The Washington court linked his injuries to the messages conveyed through Ford's marketing, and drew the broad conclusion: "Radio, bill boards and the products of the printing press have become the means of creating a large part of the demand that causes goods to depart from factories to the ultimate consumer." The court returned to the privity requirement: "It would

---

[75] Paul Willard Garrett, "The Importance of the Public," Third General Motors Executive Conference, White Sulphur Springs, West Virginia, October 20, 1934, 7, quote 10, File 77-7.4-1.13-2, Mott Papers, KU.

[76] Gillam, *Products Liability in the Automobile Industry*, 83–99, 126–28, quote 84.

[77] Ibid., 84–85. Ford's claim was reprinted in *Baxter v. Ford Motor Company et al.*, 12 P.2d 409, 411 (Wash. 1932). Lester Feezer surveyed automobile products liability suits in 1938. See his essay, "Manufacturer's Liability for Injuries Caused by His Products: Defective Automobiles," 1–27.

be unjust to recognize a rule that would permit manufacturers of goods to create a demand for their products by representing that they possess qualities which they, in fact, do not possess; and then, because there is no privity of contract existing between the consumer and the manufacturer, deny the consumer the right to recover if damages from the absence of those qualities, when such absence is not readily noticeable." Ford's marketing had claimed qualities that its goods lacked – shatterproof glass. Picturing Ford's advertising as an express warranty, the court permitted the consumer to seek damages.[78]

Compared to most cases, *Baxter* was rare because most lawsuits did not turn on an express warranty but instead focused on corporate negligence resulting from defective parts.[79] As Gillam recounted, plaintiffs were often frustrated by the task of establishing a manufacturer's negligence in the making of defective parts.[80] Cases like *Baxter* were also limited, because firms quickly responded to the court's ruling. Ford, for instance, backed off its exaggerated claims and, by 1938, advertised "safety" (not shatter-proof) glass. Its literature, Gillam offered, "tended to stress its clarity and freedom from distortion rather than its resistance to mechanical damage."[81] In a similar lawsuit about broken glass, an injured passenger sued the glass maker. The court, however, dismissed the lawsuit based under a warranty theory. Rather than advertise its glass as "bulletproof," the Second Circuit held in *Rachlin v. Libby-Owens-Ford Glass Co.* that "bullet-proof glass was not practically 'available' for a car of ordinary model of body," and the manufacturer had only said that the glass gave "greater protection than ordinary glass."[82] Thus, short of exact factual misrepresentations, the automaker typically was not held liable to the consumer unless the plaintiff established the manufacturer's negligence for defects.

Writing in 1960, Gillam had claimed that manufacturers had had the capacity to manipulate the market through advertising: "The manufacturer controls his product and dominates its marketing; he makes direct representations to the consumer through the media of mass communication and is for all practical purposes solely able to ascertain the truth of what he says." He added: "The social costs of defects in manufacture are costs properly chargeable to the automobile industry and by it to automobile consumers in

---

[78] *Baxter v. Ford* (1932). After a second trial in which the verdict was for the plaintiff, Ford appealed but the court affirmed the lower court's judgment. *Baxter v. Ford Motor Company*, 35 P.2d 1090 (Wash. 1934). Gillam, *Products Liability in the Automobile Industry*, 126–28. Feezer, "Manufacturer's Liability for Injuries Caused by His Products: Defective Automobiles," 1–27.

[79] In 1939, a Michigan court reached the same conclusion in a similar case about a safety roof. See *Bahlman v. Hudson Motor Car Co.*, 288 N.W. 309 (Mich. 1939).

[80] Gillam, *Products Liability in the Automobile Industry*, 104–76, 192.

[81] Ibid., 84–96, quote 93.

[82] Ibid., 93–94. *Rachlin v. Libby-Owens-Ford Glass Co.*, 96 F.2d 597 (2nd. Cir. 1938), 600.

general; the manufacturer is the nexus of the risk-shifting function and the law properly imposes it upon him."[83]

Gillam wrote as part of the first generation of legal scholars who held manufacturers accountable for manipulating the marketplace. As legal scholars Jon Hanson and Douglas Kysar explained, these older legal scholars "seemed to have relied on their own intuitive understanding of human psychology and consumer products markets" when they "called for expansion toward enterprise liability."[84] According to Hanson and Kysar, since the 1960s studies in the field of cognitive psychology brought to light the importance of "cognitive illusions" or "cognitive biases."[85] For instance, people tend to favor programs phrased in positive terms (number of lives saved) not negative terms (number of lives lost) even though the outcome would be the same in the two cases.[86] Because the "illusions" vary systematically and are to a degree predictable, Hanson and Kysar wrote that individuals may be manipulated by other actors in the market, including (though not limited to) corporations. Manipulation, they wrote, was "the utilization of cognitive biases to influence peoples' perceptions and, in turn, behavior."[87] In the case of product risks, they singled out the importance of "affect heuristics." Affect referred to intuitive or emotional reactions, and heuristics to "mental rules of thumb." They explained: "Reliance on experiential thinking has important consequences for individual perceptions of risk. In contrast to the

---

[83] Gillam, *Products Liability in the Automobile Industry*, 89.

[84] Hanson and Kysar, "Taking Behavioralism Seriously: Some Evidence of Market Manipulation," 1568.

[85] Hanson and Kysar, "Taking Behavioralism Seriously: The Problem of Market Manipulation," 633–34. See also Jon D. Hanson and David Yosifon, "The Situation: An Introduction to the Situational Character, Critical Realism, Power Economics, and Deep Capture," *University of Pennsylvania Law Review* 152 (November 2003): 129–346; and Croley and Hanson, "Rescuing the Revolution."

[86] The experiment was conducted by Amos Tversky and Daniel Kahnemann. It represented an example of what they called "framing effects." Hanson and Kysar explained: "People prefer program A because it is framed in terms of guaranteed lives saved; people reject Program C because it is framed in terms of guaranteed lives lost." The authors cite many other examples. In one case, a group of Yale undergraduates were given false reassurance about their abilities to predict coin tosses correctly or incorrectly. Believing that they had not been "lucky or unlucky," the students instead thought they were more skilled or less skilled as predictors. "Indeed, a significant portion of the subjects reported that their performance would be hampered by distraction and that they would improve with practice!" This experiment illustrated what was called the "illusion of control." As another type of cognitive bias, the authors write that "individuals rely on heuristics, or mental rules of thumb to 'reduce the complex tasks of assessing probabilities and predicting values to simpler judgmental operations.'" In a test, people were asked to identify whether there were more women's names read than men's names. Some of the names included "famous" people, and in response, the answers turned out to follow the balance between famous men and women, not all men and women. This sort of problem was called an "availability heuristic." Hanson and Kysar, "Taking Behavioralism Seriously: The Problem of Market Manipulation," 644–45, 659, 663.

[87] Ibid., 637.

expected utility maximizer of the economist's model – who would assess all risks based solely on a probabilistic analysis of costs and benefits – the experiential thinker can be expected to view risks as multidimensional concepts entailing a range of beliefs, prejudices, and predispositions."[88] Furthermore, they reported, recent studies had found "the costs and benefits posed by risks are inversely related." When people associate positive attributes with a technology, they tend to assume low risks, and conversely, when they associate negative ideas with a technology, they tend to assume it carries high risks.[89]

Automakers, particularly General Motors, illustrated this sort of corporate manipulation during the 1920s and 1930s. One approach was to embellish a corporation's general or specific claims to providing safety. An Oldsmobile advertisement from 1930 advised: "Virtually every bit of material is subjected to rigid chemical or physical tests before it is specified for use in these cars, and again during the manufacturing process."[90] It was not the advertisement's obligation nor its purpose to review the discrepancies from this standard. Recall, for instance, the many cases in Ford Motor Company's files of defects that had slipped past inspectors. The advertisement was intended to invite Americans' confidence in corporate research, not to give a careful accounting of the proportion of cars made with a "bad heat of steel" or other flaws. Automakers also exaggerated the safety of specific features. GM, for instance, launched a public relations campaign claiming, as historian David Farber explained, that the supposedly independent "Better Transportation Ventilation Committee, whose membership [included] dozens of prominent architects, engineers, and designers," was pleased with the health benefits of GM products, and in the process, earned GM some "free advertising" in the *New York Times*.[91] Some ads showed the danger of serious accidents while trying to promote a product's safety benefits. In one advertising campaign, Jim Ellis wanted to show the safety of GM's independent front suspension. "To prove that front-tire blowouts did not throw cars equipped with Knee Action out of control, the men at the Proving Ground exploded a dynamite cap in the front tire of a car going 70 miles an hour, and it came to a straight line stop." Although some people objected to an advertisement of this sort, claiming it was "bad psychology to suggest that a tire might blow out," Ellis got to tell his story.[92]

Chrysler tried a similar ploy in 1935. It photographed its Plymouth rolling over to emphasize the car's safety – its ability to withstand such harsh accidents. In December of that year, David Murphy purchased a Deluxe model

---

[88] Ibid., 669.   [89] Ibid., 671.

[90] "The Scientist, too, Adds His Skill in Building These Fine Cars," *Saturday Evening Post* 202 (March 29, 1930): 106.

[91] David R. Farber, *Sloan Rules: Alfred P. Sloan and the Triumph of General Motors* (Chicago: University of Chicago Press, 2002), 162.

[92] Jim Ellis, *Billboards to Buicks* (London: Abelard-Schuman, 1968), 106.

Plymouth and, a month later, in January 1936, his car skidded on the road's surface that was "oiled" and "wet and slippery" and it rolled over completely.[93] Murphy sued Plymouth, arguing that the firm had created the impression through its advertising that its cars were capable of protecting him from this sort of accident. Had the company misled Murphy? The court ruled it had not. The photographs did not, according to the court, amount to a misrepresentation of a fact concerning the car's qualities. As with *Rachlin*, *Murphy* thus reaffirmed a broad leeway in which advertisements might well exaggerate a vehicle's safety features.[94]

As a second approach to safety, corporations manipulated the general cultural context in which firms or consumers took responsibility for the possible causes of accidents. Without acknowledging product defects, GM as a good corporate citizen sponsored radio programs that included short lessons to educate consumers with safety tips about driving cars. Episodes for a 1935 program run on National Broadcasting Company's radio networks proposed that the issue be framed in terms of friendly conversations. Examples included having "[a]n average driver interviewed... on hand signals, stressing the necessity for hand signals and clarifying the three generally used signals for left turn, right turn and stop." Another segment called for a representative of a fire department "telling brief simple rules of what the driver should do when he heard the fire siren approaching."[95] GM ran its safety tips on NBC radio at the same time that it helped organize the Automobile Safety Foundation (ASF). The foundation was formed in response to the publicity surrounding Joseph Furnas's essay on automobile accidents. As Farber explained in his biography of Alfred Sloan, the ASF was spearheaded by Sloan with the support of other members of the auto industry. The foundation did not focus on "the safety of the auto itself." In other words, it did not call attention to the product's dangers, but instead defined its mission as "'encouraging safe and efficient use of streets and highways.'"[96] From 1935 through the mid-1960s, the ASF provided grants to colleges and state agencies to improve roads, "study and reform traffic courts," create courses for high school students, develop street signs, study traffic engineering, and establish police officers' traffic control duties.[97] Thus, the foundation undertook several helpful programs while focusing on accidents in terms of drivers or bystanders and not the flawed product.[98]

---

[93] *Murphy v. Plymouth Motor Corporation et al.*, 100 P.2d 30 (Wash. 1940), 31. Gillam, *Products Liability in the Automobile Industry*, 95–96.

[94] *Murphy v. Plymouth*; and Gillam, *Products Liability in the Automobile Industry*, 95–96.

[95] Stuart Hawkins, Commercial Program Department, to M. A. Hollinshead, Campbell Ewald Company, November 6, 1935, Folder 7, Box 37, NBC, WHS.

[96] Farber, *Sloan Rules*, 181–82.   [97] Ibid., 181–82 n. 86.

[98] On the subject of injuries sustained by bystanders, see Jain, "'Dangerous Instrumentalities,'" 61–94.

In a third approach, automakers engaged in a series of promotional activities that today would likely fall under the rubric of "lifestyle" campaigns. As Hanson and Kysar explained, marketers fostered a "positive affective response toward an item or activity to underestimate concomitantly the risks that the item or activity poses."[99] In GM's case, the different PR campaigns linked automobile technology to themes such as racing, entertainment, and scientific progress, rather than to the responsibility for safety in the design and operation of vehicles. The campaigns were aimed at teenagers, especially boys, and sought to create good will for GM as an institution while associating "positive" attributes with automotive technology.

One campaign was known as the Fisher Body Craftsman's Guild. Started in 1930, its first honorary president was Daniel Carter Beard, the "great Boy Scout leader."[100] GM introduced the guild to male students in high schools, through the YMCA or the Boy Scouts; members entered an annual model-building competition for college scholarships.[101] Indeed, as historian Ruth Oldenziel discussed, competition was restricted to boys. More to the point, the guild "helped socialize Fisher boys as technophiles and sought to groom them as technical men ready to take their places as managers or engineers in GM's corporate world."[102] From 1930 to 1945, students created a model of the original Fisher Body carriage (often seen at the bottom of Fisher advertisements); and, starting in 1937, they were allowed to create model automobiles. According to Oldenziel, "by 1960 over eight million male teenagers between the ages of 12 and 20 had participated in the guild through national, state, and local contests and clubs."[103] The program yielded future employees. Ted Mandel applied his scholarship from a 1937

[99] Hanson and Kysar, "Taking Behavioralism Seriously: Some Evidence of Market Manipulation," 1506.

[100] "General Motors and the Fisher Body Craftsman's Guild," no date [1957], no page, File 86-1.5-1b, GMC/History Collection, KU. Ruth Oldenziel writes: "By 1933, the guild's organization had covered over 600 major cities and many more other communities." Ruth Oldenziel, "Boys and Their Toys: The Fisher Body Craftsman's Guild, 1930–1968, and the Making of a Male Technical Domain," *Technology & Culture* 38 (January 1997): 60–96, especially 78.

[101] Oldenziel, "Boys and Their Toys," 60–96, especially 66 and 81.

[102] Ibid., 62, quote 65.

[103] Fisher Body Division, "*Fisher Body Craftsman's Guild*," no date, 4, File 86-1.5-1b, GMC/History Collection, KU. Oldenziel provides somewhat different dates, finding that from 1937 to 1945 students could make either the coach or their own models. Starting in 1947, students no longer could build coaches. See Oldenziel, "Boys and Their Toys," 66, 83, 88–90, quote 66, 70. Oldenziel cautioned that she could not verify independently the numbers, but concluded that large numbers of boys took part and, further, they acquired important skills to undertake the projects. "Contest rules demanded that all parts be handmade, which necessitated the ability to build a miniature Napoleonic Coach...from scratch, to read complicated patterns, to draft accurately, carve wood painstakingly, work metal, paint, and make upholstery with utmost care." In addition, for older boys, they "had to construct functioning mechanical parts: windows could slide, steps could be folded away,

competition to a mechanical engineering degree at Wayne University and then came to GM to work in the Development Section of Fisher Body. In 1937, Masaji B. Sugano won first prize in the state of Wyoming and later became a "senior designer" in GM's Styling Section. Oldenziel offered 1968 as an example: in that year, "55 percent of the creative design staff at GM had been involved in the Fisher Body Craftsman's guild, while many other former contestants occupied key positions in other large corporations."[104] Perhaps of equal value for public relations, the contests received free publicity. By the 1950s, one study reported that there were several "local [radio] shows throughout the country devoted almost entirely to interviews with the boys and officials of the Guild."[105]

During the 1930s, an even more popular event for GM was the All-American Soap Box Derby, sponsored by the Chevrolet Motor Division along with selected newspapers. In 1937, the Derby attracted some 100,000 contestants, and its final competition held in Akron, Ohio, alone drew 100,000 spectators. GM put the total number of watching "prospects" at more than 3.5 million, making a good return for the program's $150,000 annual expense.[106] Paul Garrett, director of public relations, claimed that "for the cost of one page in the Saturday Evening Post," Chevrolet's Soap Box Derby "rolled up" tremendous attention in the "popularly read sections of newspapers" (meaning, I take it, the sports page), which he said "could not have been bought for any money." Garrett was not afraid to state the obvious: Chevrolet's favorable press had been "potent" in focusing buyers' attention on GM products.[107] Thus, the Soap Box Derby entertained boys and their parents in associating automobiles with racing and speed, but did not simultaneously educate the teenagers about the dangers of speeding.

GM's most spectacular activity during the 1930s was the "Parade of Progress."[108] The Parade consisted of a caravan of buses that put on exhibits

---

spoked wheels and cambered axles that could turn, and a working leaf-spring suspension." Ibid., 70.

[104] "General Motors and the Fisher Body Craftsman's Guild," no date [1957], no page, File 86-1.5-1b, GMC/History Collection, KU. In general, see Oldenziel, "Boys and Their Toys," 75–76, quote 75.

[105] Fisher Body Division, "*Fisher Body Craftsman's Guild*," no date, 3, File 86-1.5-1b, GMC/History Collection, KU. Oldenziel makes a similar point in "Boys and Their Toys," 70–71.

[106] J. P. Gormley to C. F. Kettering, April 15, 1938, and C. P. Fisken to C. F. Kettering, July 22, 1937, Unprocessed File, General Motors Divisions: Chevrolet Motor Company, CFK, KU. See also "G. M. III: How to Sell Automobiles," *Fortune* 19 (February 1939): 109.

[107] Paul Willard Garrett, "The Importance of the Public," October 20, 1934, 8, File 77-7.4-1.13-2, Mott Papers, KU.

[108] Roland Marchand discussed the Parade of Progress as a critical part of GM's public relations campaign of the 1930s in *Creating the Corporate Soul: The Rise of Public Relations and Corporate Imagery in American Big Business* (Berkeley, CA: University of California Press, 1998), 283–291.

about science and technology.[109] Most stops were small cities, like Bakersfield, Calif., Tuscaloosa, Ala., Buffalo, N.Y., Manchester, N.H., and Peoria, Ill.[110] Before each show, a GM official scouted the town. Posters were distributed and newspapers and associations contacted.[111] The advance work evidently paid off. Attendance rates from the Parade's inception to July 1938 came to thirty-three percent of the average population in cities visited; in 1939, this figure rose to forty-three percent; and in 1941, it topped fifty percent.[112] From 1936 to the end of 1939, 8.7 million Americans had visited the shows; and by the end of 1941, the figure exceeded ten if not twelve million.[113] The Parade made scientific research fun. At each stop, the caravan's crew unpacked and for a few days, under a big tent, they called on Americans to "Bend a Railroad Rail by Hand!," "See the Law of Gravity Defied," "See the 'Magic Eye' Transmit Music," or "See your Voice Turned into Light!," among many other attractions.[114] General Motors made no obvious sales pitch: "The stress," one internal report stated, "is definitely on

[109] The original Caravan consisted of twenty-five trucks, eight Streamliners, and nineteen cars. C. A. Lewis, "Thirteenth Operating Report of the Parade of Progress, February 26 – September 30, 1941," October 27, 1941, File 87-11.5-26, Box 115, CFK, KU.

[110] This represents only a fraction of the total number of towns and cities visited. For the first half of 1938, the Parade visited some twenty-six cities, including Mexico City (where 447,306 visitors attended the shows), and took time off for the New York World's Fair. C. A. Lewis, "Eighth Operating Report of the Parade of Progress (January 1 to July 13)," August 16, 1938, 2, File 87-11.2-271c, Box 93, CFK, KU; "General Motors Parade of Progress (Supplement to Yearly Itinerary)," December 31, 1936, File 87-11.2-271, Box 93, CFK, KU; C. A. Lewis, "Eleventh Operating Report of the Parade of Progress, June 1 – December 31, 1939," March 8, 1940, 2–3, File 87-11.2-271f, Box 93, CFK, KU; and C. A. Lewis, "Thirteenth Operating Report of the Parade of Progress, February 26 – September 30, 1941," October 27, 1941, 7, File 87-11.5-26, Box 115, CFK, KU. See also Marchand, *Creating the Corporate Soul*, 286–87.

[111] C. A. Lewis, "Eighth Operating Report of the Parade of Progress (January 1 to July 13)," August 16, 1938, 8, File 87-11.2-271c, Box 93, CFK, KU.

[112] C. A. Lewis, "Eighth Operating Report of the Parade of Progress (January 1 to July 13)," August 16, 1938, 2, File 87-11.2-271c, Box 93, CFK, KU; C. A. Lewis, "Eleventh Operating Report of the Parade of Progress, June 1 – December 31, 1939," March 8, 1940, 3, File 87-11.2-271f, Box 93, CFK, KU; and C. A. Lewis, "Thirteenth Operating Report of the Parade of Progress, February 26 – September 30, 1941," October 27, 1941, 1, File 87-11.5-26, Box 115, CFK, KU.

[113] I do not have figures for 1940, but for 1941, attendance as of the end of September came to nearly 2.5 million, bringing the total to 11.2 million. Attendance for 1940 in all likelihood came to at least 2 million, and total attendance from 1936 through 1941 to 13 million. C. A. Lewis, "Thirteenth Operating Report of the Parade of Progress, February 26 – September 30, 1941," October 27, 1941, 1, File 87-11.5-26, Box 115, CFK, KU; and C. A. Lewis, "Eleventh Operating Report of the Parade of Progress, June 1 - December 31, 1939," March 8, 1940, 3, File 87-11.2-271f, Box 93, CFK, KU.

[114] "Here Today! The General Motors Parade of Progress!" advertisement, no date [Newspapers, 1936]; and "General Motors Parade of Progress, Souvenir Edition" [February 27, 1936], File 87-11.5-15, Box 115, CFK, KU. Marchand, *Creating the Corporate Soul*, 288.

the institutional story of progress, better values, increased comforts."[115] GM targeted school children. Some tours included lectures to children at their own schools.[116] In other cases, the Caravan put on "special shows" for high school as well as college students.[117] After the show had left town, the Caravan ran the advertisement: "We hope we set a boy to dreaming."[118] By 1941, GM introduced a new advertisement: "Tomorrow it will be His World."[119]

In internal correspondence, GM officials labeled the programs "propaganda."[120] They were not in any sense simply educational, but served to ingratiate General Motors into the lives of Americans. One report noted that the Parade fostered "in the minds of the youths a favorable impression of General Motors as an institution – and they will be an important group in the not too distant future."[121] Although the Parade of Progress was the most dazzling program, it had a short-term impact on communities, whereas the Craftsman's Guild and the Soap Box Derby became annual events in local communities and their schools. In a narrow sense, the programs were intended, in the language of management, to have children "pre-sell" their parents on GM cars.[122] By reading GM literature, a student presented "one of the quickest and most effective ways" of conveying the ideas "into the consciousness of his father, his mother and his older brothers."[123] But the institutions also represented ways in which GM entertained children as it instructed them about mechanical technology. Even if only a fraction became GM employees, many acquired lessons about mechanical knowledge and a majority, GM officials hoped, had acquired a lasting appreciation of this particular auto manufacturer. Thus, the public relations campaigns offered a way to cultivate attitudes about automotive technology focused on the

[115] "Ninth Operating Report," 12, File 87-11.2-271d, Box 93, CFK, KU.

[116] "Ninth Operating Report," 8–9, File 87-11.2-271d, Box 93, CFK, KU.

[117] C. A. Lewis, "Eighth Operating Report of the Parade of Progress (January 1 to July 13)," August 16, 1938, 8, File 87-11.2-271c, Box 93, CFK, KU.

[118] C. A. Lewis, "Eighth Operating Report of the Parade of Progress (January 1 to July 13)," August 16, 1938, 5, File 87-11.2-271c, Box 93, CFK, KU. The advertisement also won a national award in 1938. "Ninth Operating Report," 7, File 87-11.2-271d, Box 93, CFK, KU. Marchand, *Creating the Corporate Soul*, 288–91.

[119] C. A. Lewis, "Thirteenth Operating Report of the Parade of Progress, February 26 – September 30, 1941," October 27, 1941, 10, File 87-11.5-26, Box 115, CFK, KU.

[120] H. G. Weaver to Charles F. Kettering, August 27, 1935, and attached report, Customer Research Staff, no title, July 1935, 37–39, File 87-11.4-9, Box 110, CFK, KU.

[121] C. A. Lewis, "Second Operating Report of the General Motors Previews of Progress (July 20th to December 31st 1937)," January 28, 1938, File 87-11.2-282, Box 95, CFK, KU.

[122] C. A. Lewis, "Second Operating Report of the General Motors Previews of Progress (July 20th to December 31st 1937)," January 28, 1938, 1, 24–28, File 87-11.2-282, Box 95, CFK, KU.

[123] C. A. Lewis, "Second Operating Report of the General Motors Previews of Progress (July 20th to December 31st 1937)," January 28, 1938, 26, File 87-11.2-282, Box 95, CFK, KU.

technology's fun – its speed, the design of car bodies, the entertainment of science "tricks" – rather than on the technology's dangers or even its mere utility.

The Parade of Progress, the Soap Box Derby, advertisements for knee action brakes, the sponsorship of radio programs on NBC all offered General Motors techniques for using mass media to reach Americans, including school-age children. Some programs, such as the ASF and the NBC safety tips, provided useful information. Yet, by omitting the potential for accidents born out of the product's defects or design flaws, the ASF implicitly encouraged Americans to think of accidents in terms of drivers' actions rather than the car's faults.[124] Efforts to have car buyers underestimate vehicles' risks were apparent in the range of advertisements. Chrysler could picture unsafe activities (rollovers) and intentionally or unintentionally encouraged readers to believe the vehicle protected them from these sorts of accidents. Yet, the courts, as indicated in *Murphy*, held that this case lacked any factual inaccuracies, and therefore, the firm had not misrepresented its product. The public relations campaigns went still further, encouraging Americans to associate ideas of youth, speed, and technological progress with automobiles. Repeated for several years, the campaigns helped cultivate favorable attitudes toward GM and automotive technology, which is to say, they encouraged Americans to focus not on the product's hazards but on what Hanson and Kysar called positive "affect heuristics."[125]

PRODUCTS LIABILITY INSURANCE

Although managers tried to downplay automobile defects through public relations, they also tried to cope with the persistence of defects through a second strategy: they began to demand products liability insurance. This new insurance had the potential to provide manufacturers with one means of making losses due to liability for defects manageable and predictable, and automakers were among the first purchasers of this coverage.[126] Their reliance on products liability insurance, however, depended on other firms also seeking coverage, but at first, insurance underwriters faced the problem of adverse selection with only firms most at risk of lawsuits applying for coverage. This problem resulted in large losses relative to their premiums and threatened to stall the market's growth. The situation

---

[124] On the subject of a car's design and dangers, see for example, Jain, "'Dangerous Instrumentalities,'" 61–94.

[125] Hanson and Kysar, "Taking Behavioralism Seriously: Some Evidence of Market Manipulation," 1506.

[126] Gillam noted manufacturers' reliance on products liability insurance in *Products Liability in the Automobile Industry*, 193–95.

changed, however, as stricter legal standards plus an increased public awareness and willingness to sue companies broadened the mix of firms seeking coverage.

By the time of Cardozo's ruling in 1916, automakers had begun to obtain insurance for product defects. Again, Ford's experience offers a valuable example, and as had been the case with product testing, its desire for insurance predated *MacPherson*. In a lawsuit concerning a defective wheel, Ford's attorney wrote in 1916 that the Royal Indemnity Company now "carr[ies] our insurance risks against suits for alleged defective parts. Our insurance covers all cars manufactured and sold for the past three years and all claims of this nature should be promptly reported to the Royal Indemnity Company."[127] Apparently, Ford's legal department initially had misunderstood the nature of its coverage. In an earlier case, dating to 1914, Robertson had expressed the view that its public liability insurance covered defective repairs, but the underwriter quickly corrected him, emphasizing that it covered injuries to non-employees on Ford's premises, not injuries caused by defective repairs or products.[128] But by 1916, Ford had obtained public and products liability insurance, and in succeeding years its lawyers worked with insurance companies in handling lawsuits.[129] In a case involving a broken wheel on a Model T purchased in 1915, Robertson requested and the Royal Indemnity Company agreed to settle this case (along with two others) and have Ford reimburse the underwriter. The claim examiner wrote: "We believe that a settlement of $70.00 in these three cases is cheaper than defending the suits."[130] Again, in a case begun in 1924 over a defective wheel, Ford worked with its underwriter. The plaintiff demanded $50,000; Ford now had coverage from the General Accident Insurance Company for up to $10,000. The attorneys involved in Ford's litigation proposed "that an adjustment out of court might be the wisest and most expedient course to pursue." They accomplished this goal in late 1927 for $2,500.[131]

---

[127] L. B. Robertson, Gen'l Attorney In re: Julius Prezenik, Evelyn Prezenick, July 29, 1916, Folder 75-46-5, Box 46, Acc. 75, HF.

[128] Gen'l Attorney, Ford Motor Company, to New England Casualty Company, January 20, 1915; and J. H. H. Liability Claim Department, New England Casualty Company, to L. B. Robertson, General Attorney, Ford Motor Company, January 23, 1915, both in Folder 75-30-6, Box 30, Acc. 75, HF.

[129] See for example, Gen'l Attorney, Ford Motor Company, to New England Equitable Ins. Co., September 20, 1915, Folder 75-38-27, Box 38, Acc. 75, HF.

[130] Claim Examiner to L. B. Robertson, Ford Motor Co., December 18, 1916, Folder 75-38-26, Box 38, Acc. 75, HF.

[131] E. E. Juntunen, Legal Department, Ford Motor Company, to DeLancey Nicoll, Jr., December 12, 1924; John Vernon Bouvier, Jr., to De Lancey Nicoll, Jr., December 31, 1924; John Vernon Bouvier, Jr., to De Lancey Nicoll, Jr., November 19, 1927; and B. H. McNamara, General Accident Fire and Life Assurance Corporation, to Nicoll, Anable & Nicoll, December 22, 1927, all in Folder 75-78-4, Box 78, Acc. 75, HF.

Ford had been among the first U.S. companies to obtain this type of coverage. In his 1953 dissertation, John McTeer Briggs stated that the field "originated in England sometime between 1890 and 1900 as a result of a series of poisoning cases." But the field remained small. Although Ford obtained insurance in the 1910s, underwriters first officially recorded premiums for products liability as a distinct subfield of insurance in the amount of $115,000 in 1924.[132] Premiums jumped to $1 million by 1933. Further, despite the Great Depression, premiums tripled to $3.6 million in 1937 and then rose to $6.5 million in 1944.[133] Lacking records for manufacturers or underwriters, I cannot offer a detailed chronology of which firms sought coverage. Some firms became self-insurers – as the press noted, by 1937 Ford relied mostly on self-insurance.[134] Although more removed than corporate records, the trade press suggested how underwriters addressed the problem of adverse selection in order to foster the new market.

In 1934 James M. Cahill of Travelers Insurance surveyed the new field, complaining of large, indeed unacceptable, loss ratios (the ratio of losses to premiums). Because of the high loss ratios, agents had not tried to sell this type of insurance; instead, a narrow range of companies, notably makers of "foods, cosmetics," and goods for which retailers required insurance, wanted coverage. The upshot was "a very adverse selection of business against the insurance companies." Cahill nevertheless thought the demand for insurance would broaden thanks to an altered legal context. Recent court decisions had further chipped away at the privity requirement. *Baxter v. Ford Motor Co.*, he noted, did not involve negligence, but instead focused on a factual statement conveyed through mass advertising.[135] Legal oversight entailed other measures. "Violation of pure food and drug acts," he wrote, was now taken as "sufficient to show negligence and permit a recovery, since these statutes are enacted for the public's protection from the very harm suffered." According to the Uniform Sales Act, now effective in thirty states, "[w]ritten guarantees, labels, etc., are express warranties." Cahill also recognized that much uncertainty remained in assessing liability, as he hedged his bets in writing: "even today, injured persons face the possibility of a test case, since

[132] John McTeer Briggs, "Products Liability Insurance" (Ph.D. diss., University of Wisconsin, 1953), quote ch. 1, 2; and M. A. Gesner, "Products Liability Insurance is Constantly Growing Field; Prospects for this Cover Numerous," *Weekly Underwriter* 132 (June 22, 1935): 1239.

[133] James M. Cahill, "Product Public Liability Insurance," *Proceedings of the Casualty Actuarial Society* 21 (New York: Casualty Actuarial Society, 1934–1935), 26; John M. Parker, "What About Product Liability?" *Eastern Underwriter* 40 (May 5, 1939): 27; and J. Harry Bibby, "How to Protect Yourself Against Lawsuits When Products Fail," *Sales Management* 56 (June 1, 1946): 93.

[134] "Big Auto Negligence Suit Against Ford Co.," *Eastern Underwriter* 38 (January 8, 1937): 38.

[135] Cahill, "Product Public Liability Insurance," 26–29. *Baxter v. Ford* (1932).

the more stringent rules imposing liability are not yet decided law in most jurisdictions."[136]

Manufacturers and underwriters also reported a growing public awareness of the meaning of liability.[137] In 1931, according to Procter & Gamble's insurance manager, makers of food products were especially vulnerable to damage suits.[138] Public awareness widened beyond food products during the 1930s, and was matched by new tensions between retailers and manufacturers. Kimball & Price, a New York retailer, reported that products liability claims averaged $133 per case in 1936.[139] As one response, large retailers and chain stores began demanding that any manufacturer that sold them products agree to a "hold harmless" clause in their contracts.[140] In addition, Woolworth's, Sears, and Kresge's began "insisting on product liability insurance" for manufacturers who wanted their business. The insurance broker A. P. Connor noted in 1937 that mass retailers demanded that manufacturers provide "them with certificates of products liability insurance, thereby extending the coverage to the store in the event of a claim being made against the latter."[141]

Given these market conditions, underwriters had two options. First, they could conduct their own tests of products. In 1928, Travelers set up a Chemical Engineering Laboratory in its Engineering and Inspection Division, and one of its principal activities was to test products for defects and to study

[136] Cahill, "Product Public Liability Insurance," 28–30; and "Demand for Products Liability Constantly Increasing with Many Potential Risks Uncovered," *Weekly Underwriter* 140 (June 24, 1939): 1325–26. On the Uniform Sales Act, see also "Products Liability Needs Vigilant Treatment," *National Underwriter* 41 (June 17, 1937): 26.

[137] This public awareness in all likelihood reflected changes in Americans' attitudes toward corporations and safety that dated to the Progressive era, yet the trade press did not delve into the political or medical context surrounding consumers' lawsuits. For public attitudes about safety, see Knowles, "Inventing Safety"; idem, "Lessons in the Rubble," 9–28; Arthur F. McEvoy, "The Triangle Shirtwaist Factory Fire of 1911: Social Change, Industrial Accidents, and the Evolution of Common-Sense Causality," *Law and Social Inquiry* 20 (1995): 621–51; Welke, *Recasting American Liberty*; John Fabian Witt, *The Accidental Republic: Crippled Workmen, Destitute Widows, and the Remaking of American Law* (Cambridge, MA: Harvard University Press, 2004); and idem, "Speedy Fred Taylor and the Ironies of Enterprise Liability," *Columbia Law Review* 103 (January 2003): 1–49.

[138] L. H. Wiggers, "Products Liability Insurance," *Insurance Series* Ins. 3 (New York: American Management Association, 1931), 3.

[139] "Products Liability becoming Big Problem for Retailer," *National Underwriter* 40 (June 25, 1936): 30.

[140] "Need Hold Harmless Cover," *National Underwriter* 40 (May 28, 1936): 32; and Cahill, "Product Public Liability Insurance," 27. Briggs recalled that hold-harmless clauses reflected the "bargaining strength" of retailers, and that underwriters were "not friendly" toward the agreements. Briggs, "Products Liability Insurance," ch. 6, 34–35.

[141] "Products Liability Sales is Stimulated by Chain Stores," *National Underwriter* 39 (February 21, 1935): 35. On Connor, see "Products Liability Needs Vigilant Treatment," 26; and E. S. Banks, "A. P. Connor of Phila. Is Nationally Known Products Liability Expert," *Eastern Underwriter* 37 (January 10, 1936): 34.

manufacturers' production methods.[142] Second, underwriters could forgo the business. In 1937, one of the most senior agents, A. P. Connor, declared that he was "quite selective" and took roughly one in ten risks. Writing in 1953, Briggs noted that two underwriters prohibited certain products, including "cosmetics," "fertilizers," and "tires."[143]

Products liability insurance pointed to the circuitous route by which corporations registered a stricter legal climate. Whereas initially a small range of firms demanded insurance, gradually more producers sought coverage. That mass retailers forced manufacturers to get insurance indicated a stricter business and legal climate. Underwriters, by testing products, identified and reduced risks. Yet, because agents like Connor claimed to turn away so much potential business, they indicated their inability to control defects. Insurance underwriters, then, set parameters by which technological defects could be lowered to the point of being insurable, and in this way, they facilitated the growth of many, but not all markets.

CONCLUSION

With the development of a mass market, managers invested in corporate research and reduced an automobile's dangers as seen in terms of the overall decline in the number of accidents per car. That did not mean corporate managers had vanquished the problem of defects. In his study of products liability, Gillam held that manufacturers should bear the "social costs of defects" since they were at "the nexus of the risk-shifting function."[144] As the mass market took shape between 1914 and 1941, manufacturers assumed more responsibility for the quality of their vehicles, but they also took steps to deflect responsibility and to protect themselves from the consequences of their inability to fix defects.

One conclusion concerned the impact of the market. In the industry's early years, firms were small in size, and though the market was competitive, companies initially sold highly imperfect machines. As the number of competitors shrank and a few large firms dominated the market, they invested large sums in corporate research. Charles Kettering illustrated the benefits to be had from a giant corporation funding the systematic research

---

[142] John Parker listed among goods subject to chemical tests at Travelers "lipsticks, beer cans, flash bulbs, pop bottles, tear gas, face powders, flavoring extracts, fire extinguishers, liquors, soft drinks, false eyelashes, aspirin, canned foods, tooth pastes, rouge, kitchen utensils, electrical fixtures and candy." Parker, "What About Product Liability?" 27. E. R. Granniss, "Chemistry and Safety," *The Travelers Standard* 21 (August 1933): 146–53. Briggs considered underwriters' research studies standard in "Products Liability Insurance," ch. 6, 2–25.

[143] "Big Field Opened but It Needs Care," *National Underwriter* 41 (April 1, 1937): 33, quote 48; and Briggs, "Products Liability Insurance," ch. 6, 26–27.

[144] Gillam, *Products Liability in the Automobile Industry*, 89.

in automotive technology. Overall, the Big Three automakers ranked among the 120 leading research firms in the U.S. Their research projects resulted in important improvements, such as crankcase ventilation, four-wheel brakes, and independent front suspension. Those innovations certainly contributed to the drop in the number of accidents as measured on a per-car basis.

A second conclusion concerned the persistence of defects. As the mass market emerged, managers found they were forced to make tradeoffs among competing goals. Thus, while the objective of winning consumers' loyalty seemed obvious, it was not clear whether to elect to improve a car's safety or reduce production costs.[145] It was still uncertain how to balance safety with the day-to-day problems of manufacturing cars, as Ford's service reports revealed. One is left wondering, as well, how often management shipped new parts to dealers, asking them to test their quality. Also, as Ford's experience with safety glass indicated, firms ran into conflicts over the goal of marketing new innovations quickly or bringing them to market slowly to better judge their safety. Product quality posed an intractable problem for management. Unable to find their own balance to these tradeoffs, a variety of public and private organizations emerged to represent consumers and they actively shaped corporate research.

New to corporate managers were stricter legal standards. In response to *MacPherson*, managers established inspection systems and improved testing procedures. But *MacPherson* by itself was limited in its impact. Put differently, its influence came in conjunction with several other forces. Government-sponsored research organizations such as the FPL and the Bureau of Standards helped rate materials and design testing devices. The industry's engineering organization, the SAE, formed several divisions to promote uniform standards for many components, including seemingly simple devices such as bumpers. Within private markets, automakers also felt the effects of underwriters' actions. Through their rating system and laboratory, insurance agents encouraged managers to take a constructive approach to the numerous details in a vehicle's design. Moreover, state regulators mandated new standards and checked equipment through their motor vehicle administrations. Managers, in turn, absorbed this oversight to varying degrees. GM offered one example in the case of headlights, and Ford another for its wiring system.

Although regulatory oversight tightened in succeeding years, managers also sought to deflect responsibility for safety through efforts to persuade

---

[145] This is not to say that the tradeoff applied to all innovations. In some cases, technology both reduced costs and improved safety. One example was the all-steel, one-piece turret tops that GM introduced on its brands during the 1930s. A second example was the widespread use of electric welding that became popular during the 1920s. I discuss these examples in Chapter 5.

Americans of their responsibility in making safe products and taking appropriate actions to promote automotive safety.[146] GM cultivated good will through PR campaigns such as the Parade of Progress and the sponsorship of radio programs on NBC. These media campaigns, especially those aimed at school-age boys, were meant to foster attitudes toward the technology not associated with its dangers, but focused on ideas about speed, creative design, and the excitement of scientific discovery. Sloan had recognized the problem of safety when he helped found the ASF. Yet, the ASF worked within a framework that defined safety in terms of drivers' or other individuals' actions, not the cars' flaws. GM marketers intuitively understood cognitive psychologists' "affect heuristic," and tried to shape consumers' attitudes.[147]

Unable to eliminate defects, firms simultaneously pursued a second course of action: they demanded products liability insurance. In seeking coverage, managers opened themselves to underwriters' requests that they reduce defects. Yet, underwriters did not – indeed could not – compel management to eliminate the tension between safety and other business goals. Put another way, products liability insurance freed managers from having to resolve the tradeoff between safety and the defects that were byproducts of efforts to lower production costs or market new features. Technological defects were brought under stricter oversight. But there was no perfect resolution in terms of the courts, public regulation, or private insurance.

---

[146] See for example, Stan Luger, *Corporate Power, American Democracy, and the Automobile Industry* (New York: Cambridge University Press, 2000).

[147] Hanson and Kysar, "Taking Behavioralism Seriously: The Problem of Market Manipulation," 637; and idem, "Taking Behavioralism Seriously: Some Evidence of Market Manipulation," 1506.

5

A Machine Age Aesthetic

Automotive insiders dated the coming of streamlining in automobiles to the early 1910s. The meaning of the term was elastic initially, signaling simply a shift away from the carriage trade and to the integration of the body with the chassis. From Paris, one American wrote to Roy Chapin, the president of Hudson, in 1913: "Stream line bodies are just as much the rage in France as in Germany. Nobody will look at a car with a box-like bonnet and an abrupt break at the dash. They all have to have a clean run from radiator cap to stern." The writer was confident enough to predict: "In my opinion there will be further developments in this direction and the fashionable touring car in the near future will be one with no external fittings: no straps for the top, lamps let into the scuttle dash, nothing on the running boards, spare tires hidden in a special locker."[1] That transformation had begun a few years earlier. As one writer observed, "somebody conceived the brilliant idea of putting a pair of front doors on a four-passenger, long, open body, and making all panel surfaces flush."[2] At the close of World War I, designers raised and widened the hood so that it matched the car's body and appeared as an integrated whole. A GM public relations book about design thus drew the conclusion, as visualized in the 1922 Jordan "Playboy," that "the touring car and sports car began to achieve the low-slung, racy look."[3]

Promoted as a sports car, the Jordan Playboy ran unique advertisements, the most famous being that of June 23, 1923 (Fig. 5.1).[4] "Somewhere West of Laramie" explained: "There's a savor of links about the car – of laughter and lilt and light – a hint of old loves – and saddle and quirt. It's a brawny thing – yet a graceful thing for the sweep o' the Avenue."[5] Nothing could have been more different from Jordan's Playboy than the closed body sedan

---

[1] W. F. Bradley [illegible] to Roy D. Chapin, January 21, 1913, Box 1, Chapin Papers, BHL, UM.

[2] William H. Emond, "A Brief History of Auto-Coachwork Design," *Motor Vehicle Monthly* 58 (December 1922): 11.

[3] Public Relations Staff, General Motors, *Styling – The Look of Things* (Detroit, MI: General Motors Corporation, 1955), 33.

[4] "Somewhere West of Laramie," *Saturday Evening Post* 195 (June 23, 1923): 129.

[5] Frank Rowsome, Jr., *They Laughed When I Sat Down: An Informal History of Advertising in Words and Pictures* (New York: McGraw-Hill Book Company, Inc., 1959), 118.

Somewhere West of Laramie

SOMEWHERE west of Laramie there's a broncho-busting, steer-roping girl who knows what I'm talking about.

She can tell what a sassy pony, that's a cross between greased lightning and the place where it hits, can do with eleven hundred pounds of steel and action when he's going high, wide and handsome.

The truth is—the Playboy was built for her.

Built for the lass whose face is brown with the sun when the day is done of revel and romp and race.

She loves the cross of the wild and the tame.

There's a savor of links about that car—of laughter and lilt and light—a hint of old loves—and saddle and quirt. It's a brawny thing—yet a graceful thing for the sweep o' the Avenue.

Step into the Playboy when the hour grows dull with things gone dead and stale.

Then start for the land of real living with the spirit of the lass who rides, lean and rangy, into the red horizon of a Wyoming twilight.

FIGURE 5.1. "Somewhere West of Laramie," *Saturday Evening Post* 195 (June 23, 1923): 129. This advertisement became one of the most famous of the 1920s thanks to its emotional and romantic overtones. The car itself stood out as a low-slung convertible in contrast to the tall and boxy closed cars of the 1920s. Alfred Sloan called the closed car an "ungainly contraption." Courtesy of the University of Texas Libraries, The University of Texas at Austin.

of the 1920s. Until 1919, most cars had been open models, but during the 1920s the closed body car became more affordable, extremely popular, and by 1926, as Alfred Sloan reported in *My Years with General Motors*, the closed body became "dominant."[6] The closed body's aesthetics, however, were no match for the Jordan Playboy. Sloan explained: "The new closed car was a high, ungainly contraption, with narrow doors and a belt line... high above the already high hoods. General Motors' closed cars of 1926 were 70 to 75 inches or more high, as compared with 51 to 57 inches in 1963."[7] Sloan worried about the impact of styling on car sales, saying in a 1926 letter, "I am sure we all realize... how much appearance has to do with sales; with all cars fairly good mechanically it is a dominating proposition and in a product such as ours where the individual appeal is so great, it means a tremendous influence on our future prosperity." Sloan continued: "Are we as advanced from the standpoint of beauty of design, harmony of lines, attractiveness of color schemes and general contour of the whole piece of apparatus as we are in the soundness of workmanship and other elements of a more mechanical nature?"[8]

In an effort to tackle this styling problem, in 1927 GM established its design department, called the Art and Colour Section (renamed the Styling Section in 1937). As director of this department, Harley Earl dedicated the next fifteen years to streamlining GM's five major brands. His visual images – a longer and lower car – required changes in a vehicle's engineering and its production technology.[9] The process of translating aesthetic ideas into new shapes could be expensive and risky. When GM halted car production as the U.S. entered World War II, Earl looked back and quipped: "I have watched them spend upwards to $50 million since I have been here to drop cars 3 inches."[10] How did a manager justify $50 million for three inches?

---

[6] Alfred P. Sloan, Jr., *My Years with General Motors*, ed. John McDonald with Catherine Stevens (Garden City, NY: Doubleday & Company, Inc., 1964), 266. For development of the closed body during the 1920s, see Robert Paul Thomas, "Style Change and the Automobile Industry During the Roaring Twenties," in *Business Enterprise and Economic Change: Essays in Honor of Harold F. Williamson*, ed. Louis P. Cain and Paul U. Uselding (Kent, OH: Kent State University Press, 1973), 118–38; and idem, "An Analysis of the Pattern of Growth of the Automobile Industry: 1895-1929" (Ph.D. diss., Northwestern University, 1965).

[7] Sloan, *My Years with General Motors*, 267.   [8] Ibid., 268.

[9] Although Earl is closely associated with making cars look lower and longer, the image of cars looking lower and longer was already noted by industry observers. See for instance, W. L. Carver, "Aesthetic Appeal Has Been Motif in Body Design," *Automotive Industries* 52 (June 25, 1925): 1116–18.

[10] "Minutes of Meeting," May 21, 1941, File 87-11.4-18, Box 110, CFK, KU. Earl's work is described in the following accounts: Stephen Bayley, *Harley Earl and the Dream Machine* (New York: Knopf, 1983); C. Edson Armi, *The Art of American Car Design: The Profession and Personalities* (University Park, PA: Pennsylvania State University Press, 1988); and David Gartman, *Auto Opium: A Social History of American Automobile Design* (London: Routledge, 1994). See also Gerald Silk, ed., *Automobile and Culture* (New York: Harry N.

This was the dilemma of aesthetic design. Managers knew that styling sold cars, but they could not predict consumers' tastes – that is, they could not be confident which styles would sell. By portraying the Model T as the unchanging auto, Henry Ford made it easy for Chevrolet to demonstrate the value of styling for sales. Indeed, so obvious was the contrast that it obscured GM's problem: without the ability to predict consumers' tastes, how would the firm manage aesthetic design? Inside GM, designers complicated this task. Managers relied on these creative individuals, but their work could not be judged easily by the standards of rational management. The consequences of their aesthetic choices for a firm's profitability increased, moreover, as shapes and colors affected other business activities – the cost of assembly, the ease of service, and the simplicity of engineering.

In this chapter, I examine management's approach to styling as exemplified in the experience of General Motors. Styling was part of GM's marketing strategy, and in 1921 GM managers, led by Sloan, had formulated the company's strategy as a price hierarchy of brands. Cadillac was at the top, Chevrolet at the bottom, and the other brands – Buick, Oldsmobile, Oakland (later dropped), and Pontiac – were in between. Although it was not apparent in 1921, within a few years managers recognized that the closed body was critical to their main challenge of the decade: Chevrolet's attack on the Model T. So important had the closed body become by 1926 that the problem of styling influenced the structure of the firm: management decided to integrate backward and acquire the Fisher Body Corporation, the exclusive manufacturer of GM's closed bodies.[11] The purchase of Fisher Body and the demise of the Model T brought to a close one phase of the marketing strategy. A second phase opened as GM managers sought to make the closed body's style variations part of the annual model change, which had become critical to GM by the mid-1920s. It required carefully coordinated alterations in styling along with improvements in a car's engineering. To this end, GM managers undertook a second institutional change: they established a new styling staff. Earl's job was to take control of the design for the five car divisions. That he succeeded did not necessarily mean that he produced the most novel designs. The most modern American auto mass-produced in the era was arguably the Cord 810. The Cord's styling, however, required choices in production and engineering that GM managers could not tolerate. Large and powerful by the late 1930s, GM was able to pursue a different

Abrams, Inc., 1984); and Michael Lamm and Dave Holls, *A Century of Automotive Style: 100 Years of American Car Design* (Stockton, CA: Lamm-Morada Publishing Co., 1996).

[11] Benjamin Klein, Robert Crawford, and Armen A. Alchian, "Vertical Integration, Appropriable Rents, and the Competitive Contracting Process," *Journal of Law and Economics* 21 (October 1978): 308–10; and Benjamin Klein, "Vertical Integration as Organizational Ownership: The Fisher Body-General Motors Relationship Revisited," *Journal of Law, Economics & Organization* 4 (Spring 1988): 199–213.

course: its managers restricted designers' aesthetic ideas in order to create bodies in shapes suited to the routines of the business of making, selling, and servicing automobiles.

AN INSTITUTIONAL BASIS FOR STYLING AT GM

Although in 1921 managers did not necessarily anticipate the importance of the closed body to GM's marketing strategy, it would go on to be critical to Chevrolet sales as well as the industry as a whole. The trend toward the closed body was initiated by Hudson's sale of the new Essex brand. In 1921 Hudson sold a closed body priced at just $300 above the touring model. As early as February 1922, GM's Charles Kettering concluded that "the development and marketing of the Essex Coach has entirely changed the public's mind relative to closed cars." The Essex continued to narrow the gap in prices between open and closed models such that the gap had been eliminated by 1925.[12] As the price of closed bodies fell, Sloan found that Chevrolet's "percentage of closed-body production rose from about 40 per cent in 1924 to 73 per cent in 1926 and on to 82 per cent in 1927."[13] For the industry, the figures were almost identical, as "the closed body developed rapidly from 43 per cent of the industry in 1924 to 72 per cent in 1926 and 85 per cent in 1927."[14] Moreover, the car's body represented a large part of the cost of each vehicle's production. Historian of technology William Abernathy estimated that for 1913, the open body on a Model T accounted for twenty-eight percent of production costs, whereas the closed body exceeded the cost of the chassis, accounting for sixty-one percent of all production costs.[15] The cost of the closed body argued for better coordination of the design and production of vehicles, and as one step, in 1919 GM acquired sixty percent of the Fisher Body Corporation's stock and signed a long-term, ten-year contract with Fisher Body. The contract specified that GM would purchase all of its closed bodies from Fisher Body, although Fisher Body would be able to sell closed bodies to other car manufacturers.[16]

GM did not absorb Fisher Body in 1919. H. H. Rice, general manager of Cadillac, offered an explanation for not acquiring Fisher in a long memo he submitted in April 1922. At that date, Fisher Body wanted to make all of Cadillac's bodies (open and closed), but Rice objected to giving Cadillac's

[12] Sloan, *My Years with General Motors*, 158–59. [Charles Kettering] to Mr. du Pont, February 20, 1922, File 87-11.7-62, Box 120, CFK, KU.

[13] Sloan, *My Years with General Motors*, 161–62.   [14] Ibid.

[15] William J. Abernathy, *The Productivity Dilemma: Roadblock to Innovation in the Automobile Industry* (Baltimore: Johns Hopkins University Press, 1978), 25.

[16] Klein, Crawford, and Alchian, "Vertical Integration, Appropriable Rents, and the Competitive Contracting Process," 308–10; and Klein, "Vertical Integration as Organizational Ownership," 199–213, especially 201.

open bodies to Fisher. Fisher's reputation was for its quality. The memo noted "to say that a car was equipped with a Fisher body was an indication that no expense had been spared rather than a proof of low manufacturing cost."[17] Aside from claiming that Fisher Body held no cost advantage in making open bodies relative to Cadillac's own operations, Rice's managers wanted to maintain their own production facilities as a check to see that Fisher's costs were kept in line. They also worried about sudden stops in the manufacturing process. "Production at Fisher Body Corporation's plant," the memo recalled, had been halted by a strike that ran for two and a half months. Of the $10 million of goods in production, all would have been lost had it not been for the fact that production of open bodies was underway at Cadillac and thus $3.5 million of goods were produced. The consequences of fires also worried Rice. "Danger of interruption to our production from *fire* is great because Fisher's do all of their milling in one plant and should this plant burn, all of Cadillac's production would stop."[18]

Rice saw problems as well from the merchandising of car bodies. In the case of the open body, Cadillac marketed "an exclusive design." But he fretted, "this can hardly be said of our closed bodies." Fisher Body could fail to undertake the investment in machine tools necessary to sufficiently distinguish Cadillac's closed body from other brands. To make this point, he quoted from one GM sales person who had seen a Studebaker at a recent auto show. Mr. Harfst's memo said in part: "Frankly, the body work, including hardware, upholstery and windshield operating devices are so like Cadillac closed bodies, a casual buyer would say there is no difference. As a matter of fact, I noticed that one of Becker's salesmen was having quite a hard time trying to convince a prospect that the Cadillac closed body was better than the Studebaker body." Cadillac also appeared to be similar to the much cheaper Buick sedan: "Buick closed bodies are unquestionably good and their Victoria looks so much like a Cadillac job that two people lately have mentioned to us that they have walked up to Buick cars on the sidewalk in mistake for their own Cadillac Victorias."[19]

Rice's complaint was important because similarities in appearance undercut the price hierarchy of brands. The need to distinguish designs so as to create the price ladder was related to the question of coordination: "We have

---

[17] H. H. Rice, General Manager, to C. S. Mott, April 14, 1922, with Memorandum to H. H. Rice "Manufacture or Purchase of Open Bodies," April 14, 1922, 2, File 87-11.7-186a, Box 123, CFK, KU.

[18] H. H. Rice, General Manager, to C. S. Mott, April 14, 1922, with Memorandum to H. H. Rice "Manufacture or Purchase of Open Bodies," April 14, 1922, 4–5, File 87-11.7-186a, Box 123, CFK, KU.

[19] H. H. Rice, General Manager, to C. S. Mott, April 14, 1922, with Memorandum to H. H. Rice "Manufacture or Purchase of Open Bodies," April 14, 1922, 6, File 87-11.7-186a, Box 123, CFK, KU.

had to spend a great deal of time and attention on the problems of design and manufacture of our closed bodies now and we shall continue to have to do this for open bodies should Fisher take this over." Rice further complained: "Under the proposed arrangement with Fisher, it would be necessary for us to release commitments several months ahead of what we need to do on open bodies in order to secure the production we need. Once these commitments were released, we would not have the same close control that we now have in the case of our open bodies."[20] Cadillac's managers thus concluded that they should not give the production of open bodies to Fisher Body. Indeed, they proposed shifting some of the production of closed bodies to Cadillac from Fisher Body.[21]

In contrast to Rice's 1922 memo, by 1926 Fisher Body's fortunes had improved. For one thing, the manufacturer obtained tremendous gains in productivity. Whereas it took fifty-six days to complete a car body in 1922, it took sixteen in 1926. Part of the gain followed from the division of labor. Recalling the lessons of Adam Smith's pin factory, the Fisher Body works doubled the number of men working on the assembly line from 1,200 to 2,400. The *General Motors Distributor* reported the gains: "This increase in the workers on each body not only means that the manufacturing processes have been broken up into twice as many operations and that each man is more highly specialized on a certain piece of work, but it has also resulted in a proportionately greater speed throughout the manufacture."[22] In the plant section for metal parts, Fisher Body had adopted the use of electric welding. "The machines not only do the work many times faster than is possible by the old hand method, but they do it more efficiently as the parts are as definitely joined together as though they were one piece of metal."[23] Echoing the savings found on Ford's assembly line, at Fisher, "traveling belts, conveyor lines or trucks carry the finished product to the place on the assembly line where it will be put on the frame." As workers were positioned along the assembly line, each person was equipped with the tools and brought the materials for his or her attention. "There is no walking from place to place to find a tool or a part, every move has a definite purpose, and all lost

---

[20] H. H. Rice, General Manager, to C. S. Mott, April 14, 1922, with Memorandum to H. H. Rice "Manufacture or Purchase of Open Bodies," April 14, 1922, 3, 7, File 87-11.7-186a, Box 123, CFK, KU.

[21] H. H. Rice, General Manager, to C. S. Mott, April 14, 1922, with Memorandum to H. H. Rice "Manufacture or Purchase of Open Bodies," April 14, 1922, 7, File 87-11.7-186a, Box 123, CFK, KU.

[22] "Building the Famous Fisher Bodies," *General Motors Distributor* (Second Quarter, 1926): 13, 24, File 83-1.8-7a, CFK, KU.

[23] "Building the Famous Fisher Bodies," *General Motors Distributor* (Second Quarter, 1926): 24, File 83-1.8-7a, CFK, KU. On closed bodies, see also Abernathy, *The Productivity Dilemma*, 24–26, 183–85.

motion is eliminated."[24] Another savings came from the adoption of DUCO paint. Abernathy explained that older methods of painting shades other than black had required 106 days, much of the time "spent drying." But DUCO "reduced painting time to three days. Steel bodies made baking feasible, and this further reduced production time." Overall, using the example of the Model T, Abernathy reported large reductions in the cost of producing closed bodies. Whereas closed bodies cost $247 as compared to $63 for an open body on a touring car in 1913, the cost had dropped in succeeding years so that "by 1928 a closed steel body cost only five percent more than an open body."[25]

Fisher Body Corporation's improved fortunes came as well from its efforts to build its own brand identity through advertising. In contrast to the usual equation that lower prices signaled lower quality, Fisher Body asserted that its high quality had been preserved through production in quantity. The claim was made through the advertised image of a female figure, known as the Fisher Body Girl (FBG). In ad after ad, Fisher followed a set format with the headline "Fisher Bodies." Picturing the FBG in some fun or sophisticated activity (unrelated to autos), the copy conveyed a brief message (unrelated to FBG). In 1923, one advertisement showed FBG going to a masquerade party with the comment that "the symbol – Body by Fisher – is accepted now as an indication that the car conforms throughout to the highest standards of value."[26] In June of that year, FBG appeared as a bride with the message: "Only as great an institution, with the same artists, the same manufacturing abilities, and the same thousands of skilled workers, could fabricate the wide variety of motor car bodies produced by Fisher."[27] In January 1924, FBG went sledding, graced in a bright winter white outfit. The message attributed the increased demand for closed cars "to the production by Fisher of closed bodies of such beauty, convenience and durability that they have changed the conception of motoring comfort. Fisher products are distinguished by the emblem – Body by Fisher."[28] In April the following year, she appeared gently handling two high-strung dogs. The message addressed the variety of cars: "The emblem – Body by Fisher – is everywhere acclaimed as conclusive evidence of the fine craftsmanship, notable style and valuable improvements which are exclusive to Fisher products. Only the immense facilities of Fisher are capable of producing such high closed-car values in all price divisions."[29] The advertising historian Roland Marchand observed that as the "heroine

---

[24] "Building the Famous Fisher Bodies," *General Motors Distributor* (Second Quarter, 1926): 24, File 83-1.8-7a, CFK, KU.

[25] Abernathy, *The Productivity Dilemma*, 25–26.

[26] "Fisher Bodies," *Saturday Evening Post* 195 (February 3, 1923): 33.

[27] "Fisher Bodies," *Saturday Evening Post* 195 (June 23, 1923): 43.

[28] "Fisher Bodies," *Saturday Evening Post* 196 (January 19, 1924): 35.

[29] "Fisher Bodies," *Saturday Evening Post* 197 (April 25, 1925): 57.

of the Fisher Body ads," FBG "was slender, youthful, and sophisticated. Her finely etched facial features formed a slightly aloof smile, suggesting demure self-confidence in her obvious social prestige and her understated sexual allure." Designed by the advertiser McClelland Barclay, FBG according to Marchand "gained credit for attracting the attention of women as much as men."[30] She became one of the most recognizable advertising images during the 1920s, and as such, she had succeeded early on in creating a brand image of the company and its product – the closed car.

Just as Fisher Body raised its productivity and its brand value, the closed body became critical for GM's most important division, Chevrolet. The 1921 Product Policy had called on Chevrolet to compete against the Model T by focusing on quality competition. The Chevrolet would be priced above the Model T and it would offer more features than the T. In 1922, the strategy was underway. In a March advertisement, the "most economical motor car" was offered for $525. The ad listed several features of the Chevrolet, such as "National Headlight Lenses," "a slanting windshield," "an oil gauge on the dash," "pockets in all four doors," and "a standard gear shift lever." So pleasing was the Chevrolet, the ad challenged, "there is no lower priced automobile in the world that has the qualities of Chevrolet."[31] In 1925, Chevrolet replaced its "delicate rear axle" and "miserable cone clutch." New features included "a dry plate disc clutch, stronger universal joints and a semi-floating rear axle that was far more durable than the previous design."[32]

In developing its brand image, Chevrolet focused on themes of its "utility" or its "economical transportation" as applied to several activities. In 1923, Chevrolet announced it was "The Car for the Girl in Business." Since "[t]he modern business woman needs her own personal transportation," she was advised to buy Chevrolet's Utility Coupé for $680. The ad explained that the body was by Fisher, and its "artistic fittings, stream lines and riding comfort" would serve "her quality requirements." Playing to the theme of utility, the advertisement claimed its little car to have the "lowest per mile cost."[33] As Sloan had explained in *My Years*, critical to Chevrolet's assault on the Model T's market share was its sale of closed bodies when the Model T did not offer a good sedan because its chassis was too light.[34] Like the "Girl in Business," many other Chevy ads focused on its closed bodies. In 1923, Chevy asked: "Is Your Wife Marooned During the Day?" The

[30] Roland Marchand, *Advertising the American Dream: Making Way for Modernity, 1920-1940* (Berkeley, CA: University of California Press, 1985), 179, 181.

[31] "Chevrolet Announces a Complete Standard Motor Car for $525," *Saturday Evening Post* 194 (March 4, 1922): 43.

[32] Arch Brown, "The Car that Toppled the Model T," *Special-Interest Autos* 55 (February 1980): 11–17, quote 13.

[33] "The Car for the Girl in Business," *Saturday Evening Post* 195 (February 17, 1923): 39.

[34] Sloan, *My Years with General Motors*, 162.

answer the ad offered was a Utility Coupé.[35] The small car was again the answer to the question: "Do You Believe in Attractive Packages?" Here the car would provide for good presentations to the small businessman.[36] In 1924, a Chevy sedan was pictured for the advertisement, "The Economical Quality Car." The Utility Coupé appeared yet again "For the Small Family." The ad did not skirt finances. "Finally, and most important," the copy read, "its low price and low maintenance costs make it feasible for the family of modest income."[37] Promoting its sedan in "Quality Cars at Quantity Prices," Chevrolet told readers that it was "operating mammoth manufacturing and assembly plants throughout the United States in which thousands of skilled workmen are turning out 2500 Chevrolets per day." To wit, "Our New low prices have been made possible through doubling our productive capacity."[38]

The same criticisms that Rice had raised in 1922, objecting to Fisher Body's manufacturing all of Cadillac's car bodies, could now be answered in a new way. In contrast to 1922, by 1926 Fisher had obtained substantial productivity gains associated with the volume of cars made on its assembly line. Also, Fisher had concentrated on making closed bodies, and the market had tended toward closed cars by 1926. In their advertising, Fisher Body and Chevrolet acknowledged the cost savings associated with quantity production. If, as economist Benjamin Klein reasoned, Fisher Body Corporation wanted to acquire extra profits from GM, Fisher could use its cost savings (gained from its large output of Chevrolets) to subsidize other GM divisions but also other GM competitors.[39]

In 1922, Rice complained of the lack of audits to keep track of Fisher Body's costs.[40] The cost savings that followed from quantity production were tied to the problem of the similarity among brands. In contrast to

---

[35] "Is Your Wife Marooned During the Day?" *Saturday Evening Post* 195 (January 20, 1923): 37.

[36] "Do You Believe in Attractive Packages?" *Saturday Evening Post* 195 (February 3, 1923): 35.

[37] "The Economical Quality Car," *Saturday Evening Post* 196 (January 5, 1924): 41; and "For the Small Family," *Saturday Evening Post* 196 (February 2, 1924): 43.

[38] "Quality Cars at Quantity Prices," *Saturday Evening Post* 196 (January 19, 1924): 43.

[39] Klein, "Vertical Integration as Organizational Ownership," 199–213. In a brief note, Richard Brooks and Susan Helper discounted Fisher's opportunism. They emphasized GM managers' desire to better coordinate operations, a conclusion that I also reach. Brooks and Helper also claimed that GM managers wanted to block the ability of competitors to get bodies from Fisher, but I argue that GM managers worried about the ability to distinguish their brands. As a third factor, Brooks and Helper also stated that GM wanted to take advantage of Fisher management. See Richard Brooks and Susan Helper, "GM and Fisher Body," *Journal of Economic Perspectives* 14 (Spring 2000): 233–34.

[40] H. H. Rice, General Manager, to C. S. Mott, April 14, 1922, with Memorandum to H. H. Rice "Manufacture or Purchase of Open Bodies," April 14, 1922, 4, File 87-11.7-186a, Box 123, CFK, KU.

1919, by 1925 changes in the production process had brought about substantial cost savings. In particular, the widespread stamping of major body parts – doors, front and side panels, rear panels – required large initial expenditures for dies. Here was a tradeoff: the dies quickened the production of body parts and reduced unit costs, but they also gave up the "individuality" of cars.[41] Considering the extent to which body builders shared dies across different brands or manufacturers, it was not surprising that Rice complained that Cadillac looked too much like Studebaker. Put differently, should Cadillac and other divisions want to distinguish the look of their bodies from other brands, they needed to establish more control over the design process.

In 1925 and 1926, GM executives recognized the value of Fisher Body. Sloan recalled Fisher Body's contribution to Chevrolet. "As early as February 3, 1925, in the Executive Committee, 'Attention was called to the fact that Chevrolet's sales are at present limited by its ability to produce new models, which is largely determined by the ability of Fisher Body Corporation to supply closed bodies.'" That year one of the Fisher brothers, Lawrence, replaced Rice as head of the Cadillac division.[42] Then, in 1926, the volume of GM car sales increased nearly fifty percent.[43] The firm's executives decided to buy out Fisher Body Corporation for the sum of "664,720 shares of common stock."[44] Their decision came in part because of the rapid growth in the demand for closed cars, but it also reflected management's concern about coordinating design and production.[45] Sloan wanted to be able to distinguish the companies' brands from competitors but also from each other. "Each line of General Motors cars produced should preserve a distinction of appearance, so that one knows on sight a Chevrolet, a Pontiac, an Oldsmobile, a Buick, or a Cadillac."[46] Management's decision came as well with the new importance of the annual model change. Sloan dated this policy to 1925 or soon thereafter.

---

[41] George J. Mercer, "Standard Bodies are Now Produced at One-Third Pre-War Cost," *Automotive Industries* 53 (September 24, 1925): 492–94; and K. W. Stillman, "All-Steel Bodies Now Possible with Moderate Productions," *Automotive Industries* 53 (November 5, 1925): 778–81. My analysis differs from that given by Robert Paul Thomas. Thomas did not consider the body builder as separate from the manufacturer. Thomas also stopped his analysis with the 1920s. Major new cost savings came during the 1930s with the stamping of car roofs. See Thomas, "Style Change and the Automobile Industry During the Roaring Twenties," 118–38.

[42] Sloan, *My Years with General Motors*, 161.   [43] Ibid., 194.   [44] Ibid., 198.

[45] On the rapid growth in the demand for closed cars, see Richard N. Langlois and Paul L. Robertson, "Explaining Vertical Integration: Lessons from the American Automobile Industry," *Journal of Economic History* 49 (June 1989): 371–74; and Klein, "Vertical Integration as Organizational Ownership," 199–213.

[46] Sloan, *My Years with General Motors*, 265.

GM'S ART AND COLOUR SECTION

The annual model change called for systematic variations in a car's styling and engineering from year to year. Sloan and his managers could have employed outside design consultants; indeed, many of the nation's largest firms had begun to do so during the 1920s and 1930s. They hired a select number of outstanding industrial designers, including Henry Dreyfuss, Norman Bel Geddes, Raymond Loewy, Walter Dorwin Teague, and Harold Van Doren.[47] On the other hand, many small firms operating in competitive industries, especially ceramics, established in-house departments, populated by anonymous designers, to fashion their products.[48] GM blended the two: it created a large in-house styling staff headed by the impressive Harley Earl. Earl was given an unprecedented opportunity. Until the mid-1920s, the design of car bodies and the manufacture of the chassis were separate endeavors. Sloan reflected on the "awkwardness" of the closed-body cars as part of what he called the "design process" in which the design of the body was distinct from that of the chassis. Sloan emphasized this point, noting that "the car divisions designed and built the chassis as a separate unit complete with cowl, fenders, running boards, and hood. Fisher Body then designed and built a body with doors, windows, seat, and roof, which also was assembled separately.... The final appearance of the cars reflected the independence of the two operations."[49] It was Earl's job to streamline GM cars. Cultural historian Jeffrey Meikle mused that the streamlined aesthetic of the Depression decade, with its smooth, integrated surfaces, conveyed ideas of perfection, efficiency and control; and yet, the process of design could be complicated, risky, and anything but perfect.[50]

One challenge Earl faced was institutional support. There was no precedent for Earl's position at GM, and, in fact, Earl's job entailed the transfer of considerable authority from Fisher Body engineers to the Art and Colour Section. Sloan admitted in *My Years* that divisional managers were slow to welcome Earl, and to assist Earl, Sloan gave him his "personal support."[51] In 1927, with a staff of ten designers and forty other personnel,

[47] Consult Jeffrey L. Meikle's path-breaking study, *Twentieth Century Limited: Industrial Design in America, 1925-1939* (Philadelphia: Temple University Press, 1979). See also Glenn Porter, *Raymond Loewy: Designs for a Consumer Culture* (Wilmington, DE: Hagley Museum & Library, 2002).

[48] Regina Lee Blaszczyk, *Imagining Consumers: Design and Innovation from Wedgwood to Corning* (Baltimore: Johns Hopkins University Press, 2000). See also Philip Scranton, "Diversity in Diversity: Flexible Production and American Industrialization, 1980-1930," *Business History Review* 65 (Spring 1991): 27–90; idem, "Manufacturing Diversity: Production Systems, Markets, and an American Consumer Society, 1870-1930," *Technology & Culture* 35 (July 1994): 476–505; and idem, *Endless Novelty: Specialty Production and American Industrialization, 1865-1925* (Princeton, NJ: Princeton University Press, 1997).

[49] Sloan, *My Years with General Motors*, 267.   [50] Meikle, *American Plastic*, 91–98.

[51] Sloan, *My Years with General Motors*, 269–70.

Earl set about establishing his styling department. One asset in his favor was his appearance: he cut a striking presence, being roughly six foot-four and happy sporting blue suits with yellow ties in contrast to the usual conservative business attire. The designer Thomas Hibbard claimed Earl "would stand out like a toucan among the grackles."[52] Earl's physical image was matched by his control over design publicity. Hibbard recalled that Earl insisted that he alone receive any publicity outside the firm.[53] By contrast, he gave credit to his staff within GM, and he gave "effective presentations" to the divisions' managers, thus getting the approval he wanted for his proposed ideas.[54] David Gartman attributed much to Earl: he had fought off narrow-minded engineers to establish a lasting institutional presence for industrial design; and he was "an uncanny commercial critic, with an extraordinary ability to anticipate the sales success of a design."[55] By 1941, he commanded a staff of 300 individuals and was fabled to have a direct phone line to Sloan (Fig. 5.2).[56]

Earl certainly cultivated his image as a great critic of auto design, but this did not necessarily mean he or GM managers could be confident of knowing which styles would capture consumers' fancies.[57] Within the Art and Colour Section, one report proclaimed: "Style setting is risky business."[58] Color illustrated this risk. In 1923, GM surprised consumers and competitors when it sold the first mass-produced automobile, the Oakland, painted not black but eggshell blue.[59] Once the joy of having any shade but black had faded, stylists worried about predicting successful colors.[60] In an effort to select shades, the Art and Colour Section worked with dealers to collect data about the popularity of colors by region and car division. One unexpected result proved to be the color black. By 1929, black had made its comeback, and was painted on twenty-four percent of GM cars. No longer was it seen as neutral, but it was in favor for different reasons. One study singled out black offset with "another color as trim" as "going very big in all cities of the

---

[52] Thomas Hibbard, "Early Days in GM Art & Colour," *Special-Interest Autos* 23 (July–August 1974): 41–43, 54, especially 42.

[53] Ibid., 43.   [54] Ibid., 42.   [55] Gartman, *Auto Opium*, 85.

[56] Bayley, *Harley Earl and the Dream Machine*, 70.

[57] Gartman relied on designers' accounts to write his book. Not surprisingly, his history promoted their perspective. Different actors inside GM articulated other views. One advertiser, who worked for Harlow Curtice, the head of the Buick division, recalled that Curtice put pressure on Earl to improve Buick's styling in the early 1930s. Jim Ellis, *Billboards to Buicks* (London: Abelard-Schuman, 1968), 110.

[58] Art and Colour Section, "Forecast with colour news and notes," May 1929, 4, File 87-11.4-3, Box 110, CFK, KU.

[59] Stuart W. Leslie, *Boss Kettering: Wizard of General Motors* (New York: Columbia University Press, 1983), 191–94.

[60] Art and Colour Section, "Forecast with colour news and notes," November 1929, 4, File 87-11.4-3, Box 110, CFK, KU.

FIGURE 5.2. Harley J. Earl is pictured driving the LaSalle, 1927. Earl was hired to run GM's new styling department. He assisted managers who faced the dilemma of knowing that styling sold cars but were uncertain about which styles proved popular. Courtesy of the Detroit Public Library, National Automotive History Collection.

FIGURE 5.3. General Motors Art and Colour Section, late 1920s. Although the Art and Colour Section went on to be a large division within GM, it began with a modest staff of ten designers. From the Collections of the Henry Ford. Negative number P.O. 18458.

first and second class."[61] Using dealers' data, then, the design department could watch and adjust colors on a short-term basis. Managers dedicated to rational management, notably Sloan, liked this sort of "scientific" data. Yet, the dealers' information clearly had its limits: it could not predict which colors might fit car buyers' tastes one or two years hence. This question was beyond scientific measurement (Fig. 5.3).

Colors were not the only problem in predicting consumers' tastes. O. E. Hunt, GM's Vice President in charge of Engineering, acknowledged the same problem applied to the car's engineering. One example turned on the choice between all-steel and composite bodies, which consisted of steel skins stretched over a wood frame. Believing that consumers had acquired the general impression that steel, being used in "ships, railway coaches and modern buildings," is more durable and less of a fire risk than composite bodies, Hunt reasoned that the car buyer "is apt to resent, as a reflection on his intelligence, the argument that steel reinforced with wood is better than steel alone." Should the buyer think steel is "superior," Hunt continued, "he is certainly likely to let his beliefs influence his buying." When this public view is "deeply rooted," Hunt thought it as much a "fact" as any "scientific finding,"

[61] Art and Colour Section, "Forecast with colour news and notes," June 1929, File 87-11.4-3, Box 110, CFK, KU. See also Art and Colour Section, "Forecast with colour news and notes," November 1929, 4, File 87-11.4-3, Box 110, CFK, KU.

and thus "harder to change than it is to satisfy." The trick, of course, was ascertaining consumers' beliefs.[62]

Acknowledging the uncertainty inherent in knowing one's car buyers, GM surveyed consumers in the 1920s and 1930s. Yet, even with market research, Sloan acknowledged its limitations: "Responses to sketches, and to survey questions, are often undependable. It is an axiom of marketing research that automobile customers never know whether they like the product well enough to buy it until they can actually see the real thing." In planning to design cars two years ahead of the date of their sale, Sloan further cautioned: "Even the two-year period usually required now imposes a severe strain on the corporation's ability to gauge the market correctly."[63]

The ambiguity associated with consumers and the matter of the car's appearance was readily illustrated in the particular case of streamlining. Inside GM, the director of industrial research, Charles Kettering, wrote in 1933 that as an engineering proposition, streamlining was not feasible. It did not reduce wind resistance, but instead resulted in a "longer vehicle with increased weight and cost." The passenger, Kettering concluded, "gained nothing."[64] Yet Kettering and others were well aware that GM consumer surveys indicated at least by 1932 that "rank and file" car owners favored an "aero-dynamic design." One report traced the popularity of aerodynamics to such purveyors of popular culture as *Popular Science* and *Popular Mechanics* magazines, Buck Rogers comic strips, and toys sold in 10-cent stores.[65] At the 1932 fall auto show in New York, Weaver found that close to eighty percent of viewers favored streamlining.[66] In early 1933, Hunt wrote that he was "pretty well satisfied" that "body styling is going to trend toward streamlining." He thought GM should follow this direction; but as in the case of color, it was difficult for Hunt and others to specify what forms streamlining would take. Once again, as Weaver acknowledged, consumers' "likes" and "dislikes" about streamlining could not be distilled into any pure, scientific findings.[67]

[62] O. E. Hunt, "Fitting the Product to the Consumer," October 19–21, 1934, 8–9, File 77-7.4-1.13-2, Mott Papers, KU.

[63] Sloan, *My Years with General Motors*, 239.

[64] C. F. Kettering to A. P. Sloan, April 27, 1933, File 87-11.5-6, Box 114, CFK, KU.

[65] "Streamlining from the Consumer Viewpoint," December 1, 1932, File 87-11.4-5, Box 110, CFK, KU.

[66] H. G. Weaver "Preliminary Report on New York Show Questionnaire," January 1, 1933, File 87-11.4-7, CFK, KU. See also "Streamlining, etc.," April 23, 1932, File 87-11.4-5, Box 110, CFK, KU.

[67] O. E. Hunt to Chief Engineers of Car Divisions, February 1, 1933, File 87-11.4-7, CFK, KU. See also H. G. Weaver to O. E. Hunt, October 8, 1932, File 87-11.4-5, Box 110, CFK, KU; and O. E. Hunt to Alfred P. Sloan, July 25, 1933, File 87-11.5-8, Box 114, all in CFK, KU. I discuss GM's surveys and the problems of tracking consumers in "Consumers, Information, and Marketing Efficiency at GM, 1921-1940," *Business and Economic History* 25 (Fall 1996): 186–95.

GM's automobiles were comparable to the many streamlined products of the Depression decade – anything from radios to pencil sharpeners – but the process of design at GM was more complicated than that for most goods. Auto designs changed more frequently than many other goods fabricated with steel. Further, changes in styling were costly and risky for the product's engineering, its production, and further down the road, its service and upkeep. Like other firms with in-house designers, styling at GM required careful analysis of materials, a car's engineering and service, and its production techniques. Yet unlike ceramics or furniture companies in competitive markets between the late 1920s and 1930s, GM acquired considerable power in its market.[68] It is within this context of GM's power that we can see the efforts of officials to manage the creative process of automotive design.

MANAGING DESIGN FOR A MACHINE AGE AESTHETIC

As a complex machine, a car's styling was tied to its engineering, production, materials, and service. Ideally, managers wanted styling to move in sync with these elements of its business, yet that was not assured. Inside the firm, Sloan relied on designers who evaded rational management. Outside the firm, competitors' novel styles could potentially force GM to engage in costly retooling.[69] One might assume that Earl captivated buyers with pleasing styles. But I suggest an alternative: because they could not know which styles would be most popular, GM managers sought the best of both worlds – styling that sold cars but fit within GM's business parameters of production, engineering, and service.[70] In creating an aesthetic suited to business constraints, there was a tradeoff. Managers restricted the aesthetic possibilities in a car's design. One measure of this tension between business and aesthetics was the contrast between Gordon Buehrig's Cord 810 and GM's own cars of the late 1930s.

When in the late 1920s GM put in place its design department, the timing was noteworthy. Between the late 1920s and the mid-1930s, a remarkable shift in the construction of car bodies boosted the tooling cost and,

---

[68] Blaszczyk, *Imagining Consumers*; Scranton, "Diversity in Diversity"; idem, "Manufacturing Diversity"; and idem, *Endless Novelty*.

[69] Chrysler's Airflow is given as a typical example, and one that failed in part because of its unattractive styling. See especially Armi, *The Art of American Car Design*, 64–66; and Meikle, *Twentieth-Century Limited*, 140–52. By contrast, I study the Cord 810 because it exemplifies how a car's aesthetics created varied business problems. Arthur J. Kuhn, *GM Passes Ford, 1918-1939: Designing the General Motors Performance-Control System* (University Park, PA: Pennsylvania State University Press, 1986), 221–22.

[70] Jean-Pierre Bardou, J. Chanaron, and Patrick Fridenson, *The Automobile Revolution: The Impact of an Industry*, trans. James M. Laux (Chapel Hill, NC: University of North Carolina Press, 1982), 153.

FIGURE 5.4. Construction of wood skeleton bodies to which wire screen mesh, textiles, and finally sheet metal were applied. Courtesy of the Auburn-Cord-Duesenberg Museum.

hence, the stakes inherent in aesthetic design. Until the late 1920s, car bodies consisted of steel skins stretched over wooden frames, but by 1937 they had become "all-steel." The shift to steel required substantial new investments in dies and stamping equipment, especially giant stamping machines for a car's roof. Gordon Buehrig, an industrial designer who worked in the 1920s and 1930s, recalled the cost of tooling for wood bodies ranged from $30,000 to $50,000. In the case of all steel bodies, however, the initial expenditure for tooling jumped to more than $10 million or even $20 million. But as more cars were produced, plants operated at a faster pace and the total cost of production for each car (including labor and materials) fell sharply so that the average cost per car with steel construction was lower than costs based on machinery for wood frames.[71] Still, with such large capital investments, Buehrig

---

[71] Buehrig put the figure at $200 million, but this seems too high. Kimes and Akerson, for instance, reported $27 million for retooling the 1937 Chevrolet. Beverly Rae Kimes and Robert C. Akerson, *Chevrolet: A History From 1911*, 2nd ed. (Kutztown, PA: Automobile Quarterly, Inc., 1986), 83. The production of wooden frames are illustrated in "Building the Famous Fisher Bodies," *General Motors Distributor* (Second Quarter, 1926): 12–13, 24, File 83-1.8-7a, Wilkerson Collection, KU.

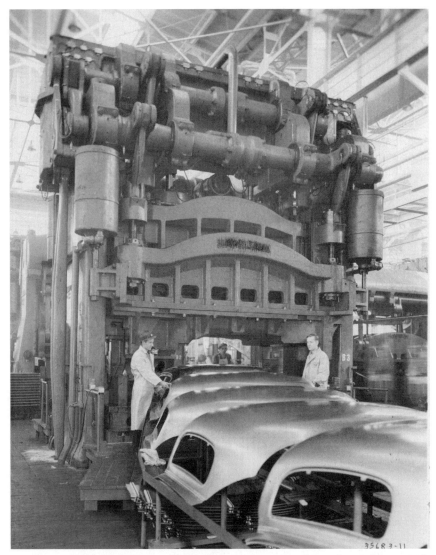

FIGURE 5.5. Turret Top Press in Fisher Body Factory, Grand Rapids, Michigan. With giant presses, the initial capital costs were much higher than the cost of tooling with wooden frames. Courtesy of the Detroit Public Library, National Automotive History Collection.

wrote, "the gamble was so much greater," and companies wanted to fashion a "prototype body because it was very important that they be right when they got their car on the market" (Fig. 5.4 and Fig. 5.5).[72]

---

[72] "Reminiscences of Gordon Buehrig," 2–5, 1984, Vol. I, Acc.1673, HF. See also "Reminiscences of Alex Tremulis," 8–9, June 1986, Acc.1673, HF.

Much depended on designers, but they proved to be an odd lot. Much like industrial research, the design of auto bodies was a creative activity. But the comparison stops there. For one thing, there were no clear-cut educational standards for industrial designers. A key feature for industrial research laboratories was their reliance on individuals who earned advanced degrees. By the 1920s, specialized fields existed for engineering, chemistry, physics, and mathematics, with their own journals and leading scholars. As these individuals applied their abstract propositions to concrete problems, they developed their theories and expanded the possible projects they could tackle effectively. In hiring engineers and scientists, GM screened applicants based on their work at major universities. No art school, by contrast, taught automotive design in the 1920s and 1930s. Earl recruited some stylists from custom body companies; he also resorted to hiring graphic designers and sculptors (valued for knowing how to work with clay). In looking for ideas, these individuals did not turn to a "scientific" body of knowledge, but rather frequented race tracks, read magazines, and studied other fast-moving vehicles like airplanes and boats.[73] For managers, it was hard to assess their results. GM's Proving Ground employed statistical measures to judge mechanical features, but aesthetic design defied quantification.

To make matters worse, designers frequently left. Their oral histories are filled with complaints about days stuck in some repetitive task. John Foster noted that his "biggest recollection" were "details – doing 1,800 tail lights and 400 hood ornaments and 300 side ornaments; hubcaps by the hundreds – there always seemed to be an indecisive area where nobody could really decide what a thing should look like."[74] Others cited the competition, the politics of the job, and Earl's prickly personality. Many were fired (including one because Earl did not like the way he walked), and others left for higher pay. Raymond Loewy, who handled Studebaker's styling, attracted Clare Hodgman and Virgil Exner, two top GM designers. Another stylist, Rhys Miller, got the best of Earl when he jumped to Chrysler before Earl had a chance to fire him.[75]

73 "Reminiscences of Strother MacMinn," May 19, 1986, Acc.1673, HF; "Reminiscences of Rhys Miller," 39–42, May 15, 1986, Acc.1673, HF; and "Reminiscences of John Najjar," 23–25, October 28, 1981, Acc.1673, HF.

74 Michael Lamm, "Harley Earl's Scrapbooks: Fabulous design studies from GM's 1935-40 styling staff," *Special-Interest Autos* (May–June 1976): 22–27, 53, especially 26; "Reminiscences of John Foster," 6, May 14, 1986, Acc.1673, HF.

75 "Reminiscences of Virgil Exner, Jr. for Virgil Exner, Sr.," 23–24, August 3, 1989, Acc.1673, HF. On turnover, Alex Tremulis notes he worked for twenty auto companies. See "Reminiscences of Alex Tremulis," 7, June 1986, Acc.1673, HF. For Earl's firings, see "Reminiscences of Clare MacKichan," 7, October 7, 1986, Acc.1673, HF; "Reminiscences of Strother MacMinn," 15, May 19, 1986, Acc.1673, HF; "Reminiscences of William L. Mitchell," 19, August, 1987, Acc.1673, HF; and "Reminiscences of John Reinhart," 1, November 3, 1984, Acc.1673, HF.

One major challenge was to design cars in a way that this turnover did not matter. In this regard, Earl could not propose new designs himself because he could not draw.[76] Instead, he implemented an organizational strategy: he created a secretive and at times harsh organization. By 1936 each division – Cadillac, Chevrolet, Buick, Oldsmobile, LaSalle – had its own closed studio, and as art historian Edson Armi argued, "Mister Earl" was the only person to have keys to each compartment.[77] As many critics noted, Earl thus kept full knowledge of the various designs while inhibiting stylists' own comparisons. As a second tactic, in the late 1930s his administrator, Howard O'Leary, paid young designers to attend a GM design school. One pupil recalled that GM took most applicants but eventually hired a handful and fired the rest.[78] A few designers who held plum jobs also stayed. William Mitchell was one example. Because he directed and took responsibility for the work completed in the Cadillac studio, stylists could come and go without affecting a model's look.[79] This system suited Earl, and designers – even the ones who left GM – unanimously cited his domination over the design process.

That Earl created a system to manage GM styles did not mean, however, that he obtained complete control of designers. Many creative individuals left GM, as did Gordon Buehrig, whom I discuss further on. Nor did Earl necessarily produce the most stylish cars or even maintain the most "efficient" method for designing automobiles. GM stayed ahead of Chrysler largely because design remained second to engineering.[80] One might have assumed the same condition applied to the Ford Motor Company, but inside this personally run firm, Henry Ford's son, Edsel, was in love with auto aesthetics.[81] He first worked with body manufacturers, and then, in 1935, brought design inside the company under the direction of Eugene Gregorie. Armi reasoned that although Gregorie lacked GM's techniques and worked with fewer designers – having a staff of perhaps fifty compared to hundreds at

[76] Armi, *The Art of American Car Design*, 24–34; "Reminiscences of Clare MacKichan," 14, October 7, 1986, Acc.1673, HF; "Reminiscences of Strother MacMinn," 28, May 19, 1986, Acc.1673, HF. See also Gartman, *Auto Opium*, 85.

[77] Armi, *The Art of American Car Design*, 30–31, 206.

[78] Ibid., 30–31; "Reminiscences of Clare MacKichan," 7, October 7, 1986, Acc.1673, HF; "Reminiscences of Joseph Oros," 8, 14, April 17, 1985, Acc.1673, HF; "Reminiscences of Frank A. Bianchi," 3, May 24, 1987, Acc.1673, HF; and "Reminiscences of Alex Tremulis," 6, June, 1986, Acc.1673, HF.

[79] When Earl retired in the late 1950s, Mitchell took control of GM design. On Mitchell, see Margo MacInnes, ed., *Power In Motion: the Automotive Design Career of Bill Mitchell* (Dearborn, MI: Henry Ford Museum & Greenfield Village, 1989).

[80] Gartman, *Auto Opium*, 121–25; "Reminiscences of Adrian Gil Spear," 49–58, February 5, 1985, Acc.1673, HF; "Reminiscences of Eugene T. Gregorie," 8, May 14, 1986, Acc.1673, HF; and "Reminiscences of Rhys Miller," 36–43, May 15, 1986, Acc.1673, HF.

[81] "Reminiscences of Eugene T. Gregorie," Acc.1673, May 14, 1986, HF; and "Reminiscences of Alex Tremulis," 5, June 1986, Acc.1673, HF.

GM – his designs were not surpassed.[82] Lincoln, for example, caught GM off guard when it introduced its Zephyr in 1936.[83] Gregorie, Armi concluded, accomplished as much as Earl with a much smaller staff and far fewer resources.

Earl succeeded, then, by a very different standard: he achieved the twin goals of creating a brand identity for each of the five divisions and achieving continuity in design as cars were streamlined during the 1930s; and he accomplished these goals while working within the business constraints of a car's engineering, production, and servicing. Michael Lamm summed up Earl's work in creating brand identities this way: "It was Earl's effort – and in some ways his genius – that gave distinctive design symbols and easy to recognize ornamentation to GM's five car lines. Silver streaks, for example, traditionally said Pontiac. Portholes meant Buick. Tailfins were Cadillac. Rockets symbolized Oldsmobile – all this being instantly recognizable from half a block away despite quite a bit of body interchangeability."[84] In Hollywood, Earl could be "flamboyant," as one designer recalled, in designing stars' custom bodies. "At GM, he, of course, had to re-orient himself and fit into the high-production world and its generally conservative approach."[85] To this end, Earl favored specific visual images. As Lamm recalled, he liked "tall hoods as reflecting big, powerful engines." He wanted bumpers to be bright chrome and low so as to "draw the eye downward and make the whole car look lower."[86] When he first came to GM, Earl styled the 1927 La Salle. The auto displayed his efforts to create visual images of movement through simple decisions, for instance, to emphasize horizontal lines and to shorten vertical lines (which implied immobility). Windows were changed as well. Rather than three side windows of the same proportion, Earl lengthened the driver's window and gradually shortened the width of the two rear windows, thus giving the sense of forward motion.[87] He also sought to round off sharp corners, again to imply movement. One designer recalled, "In contrast to its square-cornered contemporaries, La Salle's new look came via graceful tablespoon fenders, smooth hood contours, and a reproportioning [sic] of the side windows on the sedans for a fleeter look. Corners were rounded wherever possible."[88]

Perhaps Earl's most important business objective was to match his aesthetic of streamlining to the business of producing and selling cars. GM

[82] Armi, *The Art of American Car Design*, 34–37; and "Reminiscences of Eugene Bordinat, Jr.," 7–9, June 27, 1984, Acc.1673, HF.

[83] Armi, *The Art of American Car Design*, 34–37; and "Reminiscences of William L. Mitchell," 23, August 1987, Acc.1673, HF.

[84] Lamm, "Harley Earl's Scrapbooks," 26.

[85] Hibbard, "Early Days in GM Art & Colour," 42.

[86] Lamm, "Harley Earl's Scrapbooks," 26.

[87] Public Relations Staff, General Motors, *Styling – The Look of Things*, 35.

[88] Jeffrey I. Godshall, "La Salle: A Brief History of the Marque from Before the Beginning to Beyond the End," *Special-Interest Autos* 2 (May–June 1971): 38–43, 54, quote 40.

managers wanted to change the style of cars with a gradual continuity. Sloan had said as much in *My Years*: "The changes in the new model should be so novel and attractive as to create demand for the new value and, so to speak, create a certain amount of dissatisfaction with past models as compared with the new one, and yet the current and old models must still be capable of giving satisfaction to the vast used-car market."[89] Earl's response as seen in a streamlined aesthetic was to make cars lower and longer.[90] Sloan outlined the successive changes associated with this theme as they were introduced during the Depression. In 1933, the car's body was lengthened "in an attempt to cover some of the ugly projections." The "radiator was covered with a grille" and the gas tank also was hidden from view.[91] In 1935, GM adopted the all-steel, one-piece roof on its models. A development in the steel industry made possible "sheet steel in eighty-inch widths" that were now wide enough to stamp the roofs. The trunk of the car was integrated into the body and extended backwards, as shown in the 1938 Cadillac Special. Also, the cars were lowered through a drop frame that "took a dip between the axles."[92]

At the same time as Earl gradually streamlined GM's vehicles, the designs exacted a competitive force on other brands. As the cost of tooling rose during the 1930s, many manufacturers could not afford the expense and dropped out of the market. Peerless, Pierce-Arrow, Marmon, and Duesenberg went under.[93] Abernathy summed up the effects on competition with these words: "In 1928, fifteen makes of cars had annual unit sales of less than twenty-five thousand. At the beginning of World War II, there was only one: Cadillac."[94] Medium-sized firms were also hard pressed to retool.[95] Designers who left GM to work for Hudson, for instance, complained that the firm was so short of cash that it funded only minor alterations or "facelifts." Little wonder that these cars appeared out of date when compared to a new Chevy or Buick.[96]

THE CORD 810

Among medium-sized firms, the Auburn Automobile Company gambled on a dramatic alternative. Errett Lobban Cord, an entrepreneur in good times and bad, controlled the auto manufacturer. In 1929, he introduced his namesake, the Cord L-29, the first production car to employ front wheel drive. This was more than a technical matter. Front wheel drive had been popularized by Harry Miller, a famous race car driver of the 1920s. By putting the device into

[89] Sloan, *My Years with General Motors*, 265.   [90] Ibid., 274.   [91] Ibid.

[92] Ibid., 275–76.

[93] James J. Flink, *The Automobile Age* (Cambridge, MA: MIT Press, 1988), 218.

[94] Abernathy, *The Productivity Dilemma*, 184.

[95] "Reminiscences of Gordon Buehrig," 2–6, 1984, Acc.1673, HF.

[96] "Reminiscences of Holdon N. Koto," 17, June 17, 1985, Acc.1673, HF; and "Reminiscences of Betty Thatcher," 6, April 17, 1985, Acc.1673, HF.

regular production, the firm lowered the vehicle's height and created a new image equating speed with a low-slung model. Because of its appearance and the quality of its drive, the car proved to be a sensation. Moreover, thanks to Cord's talents as a salesman, this manufacturer of fancy automobiles flourished in the 1920s, rising to the rank of thirteenth in overall car sales.[97]

The 1930s, however, proved especially difficult for manufacturers that sold cars to the middle and upper end of the auto market. Still, Auburn officials tried to sustain the firm's innovative spirit in engineering and aesthetic appearance. In 1933, management lured the designer Gordon Buehrig away from GM, and Buehrig took with him a design sketch that he turned into the 1936 Cord 810 – perhaps the most aesthetically modern U.S. automobile of the Depression decade.[98] Buehrig created a clean, uninterrupted surface with a boxy, "coffin" front end sandwiched between two big, rounded fenders. More than just fitting the aesthetics of streamlining, the Museum of Modern Art wrote that the car's forward motion called to mind "the driving power of a fast fighter plane."[99] It also boasted many "firsts." For instance, it came with retractable headlights, patterned after landing lights on airplanes (a driver cranked the lights open using handles on either side of the instrument panel). To make the car "recognizable at night," Buehrig got rid of exterior lamp brackets and put the taillights to the left and right side of the car's trunk. As part of its clean look, he replaced the radio's "buggy whip" antenna with one that ran underneath the car; similarly, the gasoline cap was made flush with the sheet metal; and the Cord had no running board. The car set style trends for being low-slung, a distinction it achieved because its front wheel drive removed the need for a drive shaft and the back seat could be moved off the rear axle. Inside the car, Buehrig modeled the instrument panel after airplane panels with huge gauges and added a special Magnavox lighting mechanism to make the gauges glow (Fig. 5.6).[100]

The Cord's engineering further reinforced its streamlined image. In theory, streamlining had proposed to cut wind resistance and thus increase the car's

---

[97] Josh B. Malks, *Cord 810/812: Timeless Classic* (Iowa, WI: Krause Publications, 1995), 12–19.

[98] Malks notes that, in 1959, when *Fortune Magazine* asked 100 industrial designers to select the "best mass-produced objects ever," the Cord 810 ranked fourteenth. In 1982 *Motor Trend* polled designers to select the ten most appealing automobiles (domestic and foreign built), and their "favorite was the 810/812 Cord." It was also featured as one of eight autos in the Museum of Modern Art's 1951 exhibition, and in the Brooklyn Museum's 1986 exhibition of designs in "The Machine Age." See Malks, *Cord 810/812*, 230. See also Gordon Buehrig with William S. Jackson, *Rolling Sculpture* (Newfoundland, NJ: Haessner Publishing Company, 1975); Dan Post, *The Classic Cord* (Arcadia, CA: Dan R. Post Publications, 1952); H. Janes, "Front Wheel Drive," *Automobile Quarterly* 1 (1962-63): 373–81; and Lamm and Holls, *A Century of Automotive Style*, 240–41.

[99] Museum of Modern Art, *Eight Automobiles: An exhibition concerned with the esthetics of motor car design* (New York, 1951).

[100] Buehrig, *Rolling Sculpture*, 80–89.

FIGURE 5.6. Cord 810 with Sonja Henie, 1936. The Cord 810 was ranked as one of the most modern automobiles of the Depression decade. Courtesy of the Detroit Public Library, National Automotive History Collection.

efficiency and speed. Automobile engineers quickly rejected the theory, but what exactly made a car more "efficient" or faster on the road could be conditioned by a vehicle's engineering. The Auburn engineers essentially reversed the formula between the car's streamlined shape and its speed. Rather than the shape increasing the car's "efficiency," the Cord's Lycoming V-8 engine made it the fastest vehicle on the road in Depression America. In 1937, the Cord 810 set a speed record of 107 miles per hour in a twenty-four-hour non-stop test in Salt Lakes, Nevada. That same year it also posted the fastest time in Indianapolis to win the Stevens Challenge Trophy and held on to it for the next sixteen years. The Cord also had plenty of pickup, taking just five seconds to accelerate from zero to thirty miles per hour, eleven seconds to reach fifty miles per hour.[101]

The Cord's engineering and styling intended to excite drivers; yet the car's designers, including Buehrig, underestimated the problems the car's shape and mechanics created for its production and maintenance. Its low look

[101] Malks, *Cord 810/812*, 189–200. Acceleration times are reported in "Cord 812," *Road and Track* (June 1957): 29.

depended on its front wheel drive. This system was expensive to produce, and because it was so rare in the 1930s, an owner was hard pressed to find someone to service it. The driver certainly hoped not to break down in a spot far from a big city, but chances were better than average that he or she would. The worst problem was the transmission; the brakes also proved unreliable and the front wheels shimmied. Some minor features irked drivers as well; the ventilator, for example, typically leaked in the rain.[102] Furthermore, the Cord's styling drove up the cost of its production. The roof, for instance, was made in six or seven parts and then welded together. Anytime simple stamping was replaced with welding, labor time and production costs rose sharply.[103] For a company already strapped for funds at a time when the Depression cut short its potential customers, the Cord's special styling ultimately proved too costly. The firm filed for bankruptcy protection in August 1937.

The Cord, as a low, integrated, powerful automobile, nevertheless forecasted the direction of automotive design.[104] GM's response was significant. Without any serious competition, designers incorporated many of the Cord's stylistic innovations, provided that they suited GM's engineering and production technology. Some imitations entailed no conflict. For example, by 1938 GM cars sported horizontal (not vertical) grilles.[105] The car's height, however, was difficult to lower. The Cord's low, powerful image depended on front wheel drive and unit body construction, but GM stuck with rear wheel drive. The firm ultimately achieved a lower "look" thanks to a revised frame that "dipped between the axles" and a new, hypoid axle that lowered the floor of the car.[106] GM modified and included other Cord features. By

---

[102] Malks, *Cord 810/812*, 80, 104, 113, 115, 125–28, 235–39.

[103] Buehrig liked to recount the ways he saved money, such as buying an obsolete bumper that spared the firm any tooling costs. He failed in his memoir to mention more expensive items. Buehrig, *Rolling Sculpture*, 89; and Malks, *Cord 810/812*, 140, 212–13. When the Hupp Motor Car Company bought the Cord dies, it faced similar problems: "Auburn's presses, for which the Cord dies were designed, were relatively small. So the Cord was built of many pieces welded together with hand-applied lead covering the seams. This was problem enough in a relatively high priced car; it was a disaster when applied to a low priced vehicle." Malks, *Cord 810/812: Timeless Classic*, 212; Jeff Godshall, "Cords in Disguise, Part I, The Skylark-Hollywood Story," *Special-Interest Autos* 65 (October 1981): 20–27; and idem, "Cords in Disguise, Part II, The Skylark-Hollywood Story," *Special-Interest Autos* 66 (December 1981): 18–25.

[104] Lamm, "Harley Earl's Scrapbooks," 24, 27; and Gartman, *Auto Opium*, 129.

[105] Kimes and Akerson, *Chevrolet: A History From 1911*; Gartman, *Auto Opium*, 129, 132; and Armi, *The Art of American Car Design*, 115–21.

[106] In 1955, GM's styling staff produced a booklet about historical changes in automobile styling. It outlined ties between engineering and aesthetic design. For lowering the body, it noted that the development of hypoid gear and pinion "helped lower the propeller shaft, a limiting factor in locating the floor level." See Public Relations Staff, General Motors, *Styling – The Look of Things*, 38. See also Sloan, *My Years with General Motors*, 274–75; and Kimes and Akerson, *Chevrolet: A History From 1911*, 89.

FIGURE 5.7. Chevrolet Assembly Line, Flint, Michigan, circa 1937. Styling fit the constraints of mass production at General Motors. Courtesy of the Detroit Public Library, National Automotive History Collection.

1940, GM cars incorporated head- and taillights into the body, but the head-lights were not retractable (a difficult job) and taillights were not always in the trunk. The gas tank caps remained exposed and radio aerials remained the "buggy whips" in good part because they worked better than the Cord's hidden antenna. Finally, on the production line, GM rarely put up with the cost of welding. Bill Mitchell, head of GM's Cadillac studio, explained the constraints of dies for shaping steel: "to get the die out . . . you had to have the radius." "The dies had big round radiuses, and the fenders curved. Before, all that lean look was handmade, see."[107] This is not to say that engineers dictated styling. Mitchell took special pride in his 1938 Cadillac 60 Special. But his vehicle, unlike Buehrig's, fit within GM's parameters for flexible mass production. Armi found: "The direction of change thus became obvious from the view of production. The . . . pure torpedo fender had to give way to bulbous and segmental shapes or to straight-ended fender tails in order to speed manufacture" (Fig. 5.7).[108]

[107] Quoted in Armi, *The Art of American Car Design*, 219–20. See also ibid., 67–69.
[108] Ibid., 68.

Insisting that a car's styling satisfy its production parameters, GM officials could more readily price their car to meet the realities of the Depression. From 1928 to 1938, the price of Cadillac, GM's most expensive car, fell thirty-nine percent to $2,185. LaSalle, the next car down the price ladder, fell fifty percent in these years to $1,320. By comparison, the Cord 810 sold for $2,500 to $3,500.[109] Part of Cadillac's price advantage reflected its choices in production, part perhaps reflected subsidies from other divisions of the GM car family. In any case, the Cord's styling and engineering effectively priced it out of the market. Little wonder that the Auburn Automobile Company closed its doors in 1937.

CONCLUSION

As with china, furniture, jewelry, and many other consumer goods, the styling of automobiles figured intimately in a car's sale, and yet managers were never assured of knowing consumers' tastes.[110] Recall, for instance, the matter of streamlining. GM's market research indicated that by 1932 Americans favored a streamlined aesthetic. Their studies, however, could not specify what form this image should take any more than they could predict that the color black would return to favor in 1929 at fancy east and west coast resorts. Management faced the added risk of not being able to judge industrial designers in any way comparable to scientists or engineers in their research labs. Finally, as GM shifted from wooden frames to all-steel car bodies, the cost of tooling rose sharply, driving up the initial capital expense and the risks associated with styling.

Auto design, then, was "risky business." For a firm dedicated to rational management, GM officials might well have preferred not to sell cars predicated on styling because it was inherently difficult to predict customers' reactions. But this was not their choice to make. Sloan clearly recognized the importance of styling for General Motors. One new feature had been the closed body car, a second the annual model change. Sloan called attention to both developments in *My Years*, outlining the institutional foundation for styling. He did not, however, fully assess the implications of the annual model change or the closed body for the firm's structure or its competition with other brands.

During the 1920s, as Sloan made clear, the closed body became a critical feature of the mass market. The closed body had figured in two developments in GM's move to dominate the market. First, although it is conventional to account for Chevrolet's success vis-à-vis the Model T in terms of its

---

[109] Malks, *Cord 810/812*, 268–69. "Car Comparison for Dubrul," no date, File 87-4.18-56, Box 20, GMC/Proving Ground, KU.

[110] Blaszczyk, *Imagining Consumers*; Scranton, "Diversity in Diversity"; idem, "Manufacturing Diversity"; and idem, *Endless Novelty*.

marketing (credit and advertising) and flexible mass production, the closed body represented an additional dimension to this competitive saga. In the very years when Chevrolet made its assault on the Model T, Fisher Body obtained large cost savings through increased productivity on its assembly line. Chevrolet played up its closed body in its advertising. The theme of utility, or "economical transportation," often showcased closed body options – the coupé or the larger sedan. Second, the closed body had figured in the question of brand identity. As GM set about marketing its price ladder of five brands, it ran into the problem that the style of the make's body could look too much like another brand below its price or, just as bad, too much like a competitor's brand. It was possible, as Rice's memo suggested, that GM could have opted to produce its own closed bodies, but their ten-year contract with Fisher Body, signed in 1919, had locked GM into an exclusive reliance on this one body builder. Further, Fisher Body had established its brand image of quality through its "Fisher Body Girl" advertisements claiming to provide quality (imagined through the slender female body) to all price divisions. The particular evolution of the market had thus shaped the structure of the modern firm as the closed body's role in GM marketing had led management to integrate backward and buy out the Fisher Body Corporation in 1926.

The year before GM purchased Fisher Body, Sloan had discussed the importance of the annual model change for GM. The CEO liked to organize business affairs, and the annual model change had the effect of providing order to the constant process of updating GM products. It meant, as well, that GM managers needed to acquire closer control over the styling of vehicles. In his study of mass production, historian of technology David Hounshell identified design as a business risk when he explained the productivity dilemma firms faced in choosing production technology to either boost efficiency or accommodate changes in a product's design.[111] At General Motors, managers made styling fit within the boundaries of GM's corporate strategy. Earl's system of "anonymous" creativity, as Armi explained, supported creative individuals despite the high turnover of designers.[112] Further, GM took advantage of its size and growing market power. As the initial capital expenditure for producing all-steel bodies rose, GM's small competitors vanished and its medium-size rivals could not afford to match GM's annual alterations. Buehrig's Cord 810 provided one novel alternative, and yet it proved unacceptable by GM's own service, engineering, and production standards. Styles of course changed at the nation's largest auto manufacturer. But GM made design fit the machinery along the assembly line;

[111] David A. Hounshell, *From the American System to Mass Production, 1800-1932: The Development of Manufacturing Technology in the United States* (Baltimore: Johns Hopkins University Press, 1984).
[112] Armi, *The Art of American Car Design*, 23.

its streamlined shapes were appropriately characterized as a "machine age" aesthetic.

Nevertheless, the Cord 810 had challenged GM. On the racetrack it set speed records and, on the road, its styling won critics' praise. No matter how tempting it is to judge the success of a car's design by a firm's sales, that GM prospered while the Cord's manufacturer disappeared should not be taken as any reflection on the cars' aesthetics. The comparison suggests, instead, a sense of how GM's market power and resources allowed officials to select or shun ideas embodied in an innovative car such as the Cord 810. GM's styling proved more conservative than the Cord's. Put differently, by fitting within the competitive price constraints for engineering and producing cars, Earl's styling accommodated the many different aspects of the firm's strategy for dominating the market and thus determining the car a buyer could purchase and drive.

6

The Franchised Car Dealer and Consumers' Marketing Dilemma

As the automobile market evolved, so did the role of the franchised dealer.[1] Whereas in the early 1900s dealers had concentrated on selling new cars, during the 1920s a large proportion of car owners became repeat customers. Alfred Sloan drew the implication for dealers: "When the used car came into the picture in a big way in the 1920s as a trade-in on a new car, the merchandising of automobiles became more a trading proposition than an ordinary selling proposition."[2] The dealer's business evolved with two more changes associated with the transformation of the mass market – the annual model change and installment credit. These marketing tools had not been critical in the early market. For example, few cars were sold on installments prior to the mid-1910s and GMAC was not organized until 1919. Yet, during the 1920s a majority of new cars were sold on installments. Furthermore, by the mid-1920s, the annual model change had been established. It redefined dealers' business because at the end of each year's production run, the dealer needed to sell off the old year's models as the next year's models were introduced.[3] The year-end clearance became an annual event in the businesses of automobile dealers, just as installment credit and the used car trade-in became defining characteristics.

With this market transformation, automakers still counted on a network of loyal and stable franchised dealers.[4] Indeed, as legal scholar Friedrich Kessler noted: "The manufacturer is vitally interested in the success of his dealer organization since it is his sole outlet to the public."[5] Harlow Curtice, as GM's president, later reaffirmed this mutuality: "Legally he [the dealer] is not the agent of the manufacturer. Yet, in his community he is looked upon as the manufacturer's representative." The dealer's success "depends importantly upon the quality and value of the product with which the manufacturer has provided him." The manufacturer's success, in turn, "is determined in substantial degree by how well his 'representatives' the dealers – perform

[1] Alfred P. Sloan, Jr., *My Years with General Motors*, ed. John McDonald with Catherine Stevens (Garden City, NY: Doubleday & Company, Inc., 1964), 136–39, 279–312.
[2] Ibid., quote 282.   [3] Ibid., 285–86.   [4] Ibid., 282.
[5] Friedrich Kessler, "Automobile Dealer Franchises: Vertical Integration by Contract," *Yale Law Journal* 66 (July 1957): 1135–90, especially 1159.

their functions. An unusual mutuality of interests exists between the automobile manufacturer and the dealer."[6]

Despite this "mutuality of interests," dealer relations were so bad that in 1938 the Federal Trade Commission (FTC) launched a major investigation of automobile dealer relations.[7] In the ensuing months, hundreds of dealers were interviewed; numerous documents were collected about dealers' operations and management's practices; and a report of more than one-thousand pages was issued in 1939. The investigation, initiated by members of Congress at dealers' request, drew attention to what dealers called management pressure or "coercion." Indeed, so fierce were their complaints that the Department of Justice filed an antitrust suit against the Big Three automakers. Ford and Chrysler signed consent decrees, but GM stood trial and was convicted of antitrust violations.[8]

Why had the FTC and the Justice Department found relations between dealers and manufacturers so strained? Part of the answer stemmed from the leverage manufacturers maintained over dealers. Kessler identified this leverage as a result of dealers' sunk assets. To encourage on-going relations, dealers made large capital investments in their show rooms and service facilities. Given the manufacturer's ability to cancel a franchising contract abruptly, and given the dealer's inability to transfer assets readily, the manufacturer gained leverage over the dealer's operations.[9] In other words, once the dealer invested the capital and could not easily move it, the manufacturer could pressure the retailer with the threat of cancellation (and thus the potential loss of capital).[10] Yet, the problem of sunk assets offered only a partial answer. It identified the *potential* for management to

---

[6] Curtice is quoted in Kessler, "Automobile Dealer Franchises," 1137.

[7] In his autobiography, Sloan made only passing reference to the federal regulators. See Sloan, *My Years with General Motors*, 309. On dealers' complaints as motivation for the investigation, see U.S. Federal Trade Commission, *Report of the Motor Vehicle Industry*, 76th Cong., 1st sess., House Document No. 468 (Washington, D.C.: U.S. Government Printing Office, 1939), 147.

[8] The FTC investigation was submitted as U.S. Federal Trade Commission, *Report of the Motor Vehicle Industry*. For a summary of antitrust charges, see Charles Mason Hewitt, Jr., *Automobile Franchise Agreements* (Homewood, IL: Richard D. Irwin, Inc., 1956), 103–106. The court's opinion is found in *United States v. General Motors Corporation, et. al.*, 121 F.2d 376 (7th Cir. 1941). On dealer-manufacturer relations after World War II, see Stewart Macaulay, *Law and the Balance of Power: The Automobile Manufacturers and Their Dealers* (New York: Russell Sage Foundation, 1966); and Gillian K. Hadfield, "Problematic Relations: Franchising and the Law of Incomplete Contracts," *Stanford Law Review* 42 (April 1990): 927–92. For dealer relations prior to and immediately following the war, see Friedrich Kessler, "Automobile Dealer Franchises," 1135–90.

[9] Kessler, "Automobile Dealer Franchises," 1138, 1140, 1149, 1156.

[10] Hewitt, *Automobile Franchise Agreements*, 103–106; Kessler, "Automobile Dealer Franchises," 1135–90; Macaulay, *Law and the Balance of Power*; and Hadfield, "Problematic Relations," 927–92.

FIGURE 6.1. The Pearce Chevrolet Dealership, 1937. Dealers invested large amounts of capital in their retail and service operations. Once invested, it was difficult for a dealer to sell the facilities. As a result, management claimed leverage over dealers: GM could threaten the dealer with cancellation and thus the loss of capital. Courtesy of the Detroit Public Library, National Automotive History Collection.

pressure or coerce dealers, but not the *circumstances* under which they might do so (Fig. 6.1 and Fig. 6.2).[11]

I locate the circumstances in the market context, where dealers mediated between managers and consumers. In this middle position, dealers found that the very features of a mass market – the annual model change, installment credit, and the used car trade-in – created conflicts between themselves and managers. As styling choices for consumers proliferated, for instance, management faced a more complex job producing popular vehicles. Inaccuracies

---

[11] Like legal scholars, then, my work examines the conflict between automakers and dealers, recognizing the power management exerted in its relations with dealers. Again, like legal scholars, I recognize the importance of sunk assets as a critical component in this conflict. My work differs, though, in that as I examine the tensions between dealers and managers, I keep in mind the market's evolution – namely, consumers' marketing dilemma. Whereas both consumers and dealers turned to the state, the marketing dilemma was not resolved through interest group politics. Indeed, as I argue, none of the three parties found a solution.

FIGURE 6.2. The Spacious Showroom of the Ernest Ingold, Inc., Chevrolet Dealership of San Francisco, 1937. Dealers complained to federal investigators that management pressured them to undertake unwanted expenditures, such as enlarging their retail operations. Courtesy of the Detroit Public Library, National Automotive History Collection.

in coordinating the production of cars with dealers' orders or consumers' demands resulted in unwanted cars (and costs) that either dealers or the manufacturer shouldered. A higher allowance for a used car meant lower profits for dealers and, should dealers reduce their demand for new cars, lower profits for manufacturers. And, when car buyers financed their purchases, managers and dealers squared off regarding who wrote the loans and pocketed the profit from financing sales. Given the details in marketing automobiles, it was not simply that management addressed the question of profitability in terms of the efficient distribution of vehicles, as Sloan maintained, but that they also faced a marketing dilemma. Automakers had sought consumers' loyalty, but the three parties – consumers, dealers, and management – confronted one another uneasily in the marketplace because one party's gain came at the expense of the other two.

How did managers develop their relational ties with franchised retailers to cope with the marketing dilemma? By the mid-1920s, managers were aware of this dilemma and responded in different ways. First, they tried to shift costs to dealers; second, they worked with dealers and tried to shift costs to car buyers. Then, during the late 1930s, the FTC and the Justice Department intervened in the market and attempted to establish a fairer basis for market transactions. Sloan had pictured a process of management that made certain dealers adhere to a given standard of efficient operations. Yet, the marketing dilemma meant that managers' task was more complicated – trying to manage the conflicting interests but unable to resolve them. The modern form of mass distribution as a system of dealer franchises made evident that the goal of efficient operations could not be separated from the power that management exerted in the marketplace. Unable to resolve the marketing dilemma, the distribution system instead fostered a modern basis of distrust among the market's participants.

FRANCHISED DEALERS AND THE MARKET FOR AUTOS

General Motors, Ford, and Chrysler developed vast networks of franchised dealers. In 1941, on the eve of the United States's entry into World War II, 17,360 dealers were franchised to sell GM products, of which roughly 7,800 were Chevrolet dealers. Ford and Chrysler also maintained large networks. In 1941, there were 7,000 Ford dealers and 10,000 Chrysler dealers. Overall, there were 38,700 new car dealers.[12] The retailers' importance to the economy was based as well on the number of men and women they employed. For instance, GM dealers hired 190,000 mechanics, sales agents, bookkeepers, and other individuals.[13]

The relationship between dealers and management was defined through the franchise contract or sales agreement. Having been granted "an area of sales responsibility for cultivation," as Sloan recalled, the dealer agreed to invest capital for a sales room and service facilities; to hire sales agents and mechanics; to advertise and undertake other activities to "cultivate his area of responsibility"; and to stock the manufacturer's parts in order to provide continuous service. Failure to do so could result in the dealer's contract being cancelled. Obligations also applied to automakers. The manufacturer agreed to sell nearly all its "trademarked" product through its franchised dealers; to invest capital in styling and research to "ensure that the product is desirable"; and to provide "technical help and programs" to dealers.[14] In maintaining this vast dealer network, managers faced common problems in achieving their goal of an efficient distribution system combined with a

[12] Bedros Peter Pashigian, *The Distribution of Automobiles, An Economic Analysis of the Franchise System* (Englewood Cliffs, NJ: Prentice Hall, 1961), 77–78. For total GM figures, see Sloan, *My Years with General Motors*, 295–96 n. 1.

[13] Sloan, *My Years with General Motors*, 295–96 n. 1. [14] Ibid., 280–81.

stable dealer organization. One such problem was the allocation of dealers. How was management to know how many dealers were needed in a given geographic territory? A second problem concerned dealers' performance.[15] How would management determine whether their franchised agents fully exploited their market in selling their goods?[16] A third problem was the year-end clearance of cars. How would dealers sell the remaining cars without damaging their profits? A fourth problem simply was the need for "two-way communication," or the need to establish a basis for reaching constructive answers for questions about dealers.

Within the context of the 1920s and 1930s, GM's experience stood out as especially important in shaping dealer relations. First, although all three major manufacturers faced charges from the Justice Department, only GM stood trial and, thus, records from the appeals court apply only to GM. GM was distinctive as well because its chief executive officer, Alfred Sloan, clearly articulated management's goal in defining dealer relations. His biography offers a perspective that differs from the federal narratives. Finally, in contrast to Ford, which suffered in its organizational framework, GM exemplified the rational bureaucratic firm. Therefore, although Ford, GM, and Chrysler all confronted the marketing dilemma associated with a mass market, GM remains my primary focus because of its experiences during the 1920s and 1930s.

In the mass auto market of the 1920s, managers at GM and at other manufacturers faced the tradeoff between competitive and bureaucratic approaches to dealer relations. As a partial limitation of competition, automakers came to rely on the exclusive sales arrangement. If dealers marketed only GM vehicles, such as Chevrolet or Buick, they would devote all their energies to GM products.[17] Similarly, if Ford dealers only sold Ford vehicles, then, presumably, they would apply their full efforts to promoting the Ford brand. Yet, how would managers know that dealers had applied their full efforts to marketing their cars? Henry Ford's approach was to rely

---

[15] Ibid., 284.

[16] Economists have studied agency or control problems that shape relations between the franchisor and its franchisees. Important examples include Paul Rubin, "The Theory of the Firm and the Structure of the Franchise Contract," *Journal of Law and Economics* 21 (April 1978): 223–33; Antony W. Dnes, "The Economic Analysis of Franchise Contracts," *Journal of Institutional and Theoretical Economics* 152 (June 1996): 297–324; F. Lafontaine and M. E. Slade, "Retail contracting and costly monitoring: Theory and evidence," *European Economic Review* 40 (April 1996): 923–32; Patrick J. Kaufman and Francine Lafontaine, "Costs of Control: The Source of Economic Rents for McDonald's Franchisees," *Journal of Law and Economics* 37 (October 1994): 417–53; and G. F. Mathewson and R. A. Winter, "The Economics of Franchise Contracts," *Journal of Law & Economics* 28 (October 1985): 503–26.

[17] Hewitt, *Automobile Franchise Agreements*, 88. Other manufacturers began to monitor their dealers more closely beginning in the early 1920s. U.S. Federal Trade Commission, *Report of the Motor Vehicle Industry*, 288.

on competition among his firm's dealers. But competition among dealers had its downside: too many dealers could result in inventories accumulating at weak retailers. When Ford finally modified his approach in 1938, GM had already opted for a different method, one predicated on a reduction of competition in favor of bureaucratic control.[18]

Soon after he joined General Motors in 1918, Sloan and his team of managers set about establishing an effective dealer network for a mass market.[19] Officials worried that too much competition among dealers could hurt their profits and, by extension, cause them to neglect service and to damage GM's reputation among car owners.[20] To avoid this situation, management decided to limit the number of dealers in any given territory. GM contracts also carried a threat: the firm claimed the right to cancel a dealer's contract with little if any notice.[21] GM was not alone in this regard. Ford, Chrysler, and other automakers also included cancellation clauses in their dealer agreements.[22] Still, cancellation was a blunt instrument, and rather than threaten this course of action, GM officials chose to increase their bureaucratic oversight.

As a first step in this bureaucratic approach, management allocated dealers to regions based on the size of a given market. Wanting to "penetrate the market as effectively as possible," management thought "it was necessary to have the appropriate number of dealers, each of the appropriate size and in the appropriate location." The trick, as Sloan observed, was "to determine these locations." Because management was uninformed about local automobile markets, during the 1920s officials "began to make economic studies of the market and its potential in terms of population, income, past performance, business cycle, and the like."[23] This method of allocating dealers pleased Sloan, as he thought it offered "a rational approach to the problem of distribution."[24]

As a second step, managers developed various accounting procedures and, by 1927, GM dealers were required to follow a standardized accounting system.[25] Officials assembled data for each dealer's sales of new vehicles, used

---

[18] Hewitt, *Automobile Franchise Agreements*, 75–76. See also Richard S. Tedlow, *New and Improved: The Story of Mass Marketing in America* (New York: Basic Books, 1990).

[19] Sloan, *My Years with General Motors*, 136–39, 279–312.

[20] Manufacturers could also pack more dealers into a market, but this option ran the risk of having weak retailers undercut their healthy counterparts. See Dicke's discussion in *Franchising in America*, 67–79.

[21] Sloan, *My Years with General Motors*, 295–96 n. 1.

[22] U.S. Federal Trade Commission, *Report of the Motor Vehicle Industry*, 124–25.

[23] Sloan, *My Years with General Motors*, 284.   [24] Ibid., 285.

[25] Ibid., 136, 287. For General Motors and the industry in general, see the U.S. Federal Trade Commission, *Report of the Motor Vehicle Industry*, 110–14, 118–21, 123–25, 140–45, 254–58, 289–94. For inventories, see Alfred D. Chandler, Jr., *Strategy and Structure: Chapters in the History of the American Industrial Enterprise* (Cambridge, MA: MIT Press, 1962), 145–53; and Arthur J. Kuhn, *GM Passes Ford, 1918-1939: Designing the General*

vehicles, accessories, revenues and costs tied to service, a dealer's debts, the percent of net working capital in receivables, the used car inventory, and fixed and variable expenses. Officials as a matter of routine organized data by zones and cities to keep track of the overall percentage of profitable dealers, undercapitalized dealers, and other measures used to compare retailers and identify troubled firms. For instance, in 1930, minutes of GM's General Sales Committee cautioned that used cars that lingered on a car lot for more than ninety days signaled a dealer headed for trouble. The old vehicles tied up working capital and, as they continued to depreciate, foretold greater losses. The balance between sales and profits for new, as compared to used, cars could indicate dealers who were too cautious, or conversely, too "greedy for business."[26]

Aside from using accounting data to monitor dealers, managers found the information valuable in coordinating production and distribution. Sloan, for instance, noted that managers tabulated on a ten-day basis the level of dealers' inventories to keep production in line with retail demand. M. E. Coyle, the general manager of the Chevrolet Division, offered one example. When dealers' ten-day reports indicated a sudden increase in inventories and slowdown in sales in November 1937, management decided to cut production of new cars.[27] Another tool in coordinating production and distribution was GM's credit agency, GMAC. It assisted dealers in purchasing automobiles. Yet, as economist Martha Olney has detailed, in helping dealers, GMAC allowed factory managers to cope with the tendency for car sales to be concentrated in the spring and early summer of each year. Manufacturers wanted to keep assembly-line production relatively stable and, lacking storage space to stockpile cars for each sales season, they began the practice of selling cars to dealers who had storage space. Insofar as dealers may have lacked the cash to finance these purchases, GMAC helped by providing wholesale credit.[28] GMAC thus assisted the factory, as one senior manager explained, in "regularizing production."[29]

Motors Performance-Control System (University Park, PA: Pennsylvania State University Press, 1986), 203–209.

[26] U.S. Federal Trade Commission, *Report on Motor Vehicle Industry*, 222, 242, and in general, 173–76, 215–22, 240–45, 288–91. In 1938, for example, Pontiac reported that used car losses had to be kept to a minimum by maintaining a thirty-day turnover. R. A. Dickinson, Business Management Department, "Monthly Report on Dealer Operating Results – May 31, 1938," July 6, 1938, Box 3156; E. J. Hogan to Regional, Assistant Regional and Zone Managers, April 28, 1938, Box 3156; and H. B. Hatch to H. L. Horton, October 8, 1937, Box 3156, all in RG 122, NA.

[27] "M. E. Coyle Testimony," 1764–65, Records and Briefs for *General Motors*. Sloan, *My Years with General Motors*, 129–39.

[28] Martha Olney, *Buy Now, Pay Later: Advertising, Credit, and Consumer Durables in the 1920s* (Chapel Hill, NC: University of North Carolina Press, 1991), 119–28.

[29] "Donaldson Brown Testimony," 997–98, April 1940, Records and Briefs for *General Motors*.

In order to coordinate production and distribution, management undertook one special program regarding the year-end clearance. Sloan called the liquidation of the old model a "permanent feature of the business." He dated the problem of liquidating old models to the late 1920s, and explained that the problem arose because production runs were planned in advance "based on prospective demand." Although dealers during much of the 1920s covered the cost of liquidating the old models themselves, GM began to assist them. "In 1930 we made it a matter of policy to help the dealer dispose of his excess stock at the end of the model year." The firm did so by offering dealers "an allowance on the unsold, new vehicles in stock when new models were announced." The allowance was given to three percent of a dealer's estimated supply of cars for the following year.[30]

As one last policy, GM improved communications between its dealers and management. GM management, having visited dealers in their local markets, decided to provide a formal means of communication and created in 1934 the General Motors Dealer Council. The council's purpose, as Sloan recounted, was not to administer policy. Instead, the forty-eight dealers worked with the leading executives to formulate policy, especially in regard to the dealer's sales agreement, that is, the contract upon which dealers entered their relations with the manufacturer. Sloan chaired the council.[31] In addition, in 1938, GM established the Dealer Relations Board to review those cases in which dealers brought complaints directly to the firm's senior managers.[32]

As Sloan presented management's solution to the four problems that greeted them during the early 1920s, managers had decided not to rely simply on competition among dealers to sell cars. Instead, they opted for a rational, bureaucratic solution – collecting data to allocate dealers of the appropriate size to the appropriate geographic territories. They also began collecting data about dealers' operations on a monthly basis to compare dealers and identify any retailers who had fallen below the average norm. Recognizing the special problem of the liquidation of the year-end models, Sloan's team of managers had taken steps to make allowances for dealers. Presumably, as Sloan wrote, the bureaucratic allocation of dealers, combined with the systematic monitoring of dealers' operations, ensured "a group of sound, prosperous dealers as business associates."[33]

FRANCHISING IN THE MASS MARKET: DIVERGENT INTERESTS

In contrast to Sloan, the records of the FTC and the Justice Department indicated that the dealers' businesses were not in harmony with those of the manufacturers. In other words, a dealer's basis for turning a good profit could prove to be at odds with a manufacturer's profit strategy. Consumers'

---

[30] Sloan, *My Years with General Motors*, 284–86, quote 284.
[31] Ibid., 291.   [32] Ibid., 294.   [33] Ibid., 280.

marketing dilemma brought this conflict between dealers and management into full view by 1925. In administering policies for installment credit, the sale of new and used cars, and the year-end clearance, management was unable to avoid divergent interests between the automaker and the dealer; instead, management tried to impose costs on its franchisees.

The gap between Sloan's narrative and the FTC's report indicated that communication between dealers and management was a larger problem than Sloan acknowledged. Sloan called attention to the need for "two-way" communication, but he did not explore which specific topics were in need of communication. For the Dealer Relations Board, he stated that it "enabled the dealer who had a complaint to appeal directly to the top executives of the corporation" without explaining the conditions that might prompt dealers to do so.[34] Nor did he detail the policies reviewed by the Dealer Council. Further, the Dealer Council was not an elected body; as Sloan noted, "each year I chose a different panel of dealers." In his analysis of manufacturer–dealer relations, legal scholar Stewart Macaulay observed that because they were appointed by GM, the council's members did not necessarily express the voices of their fellow dealers but "told top management just what it wanted to hear."[35] The FTC also questioned the role of the Dealer Relations Board, stating that it had been established as a way to avoid the "arbitrary treatment of dealers by factory field representatives."[36] This remark begged the question: What was arbitrary in the treatment of dealers? What role did field representatives play?

Sloan made little mention of these field representatives, but they were a vital part of the process of administering GM's policies and monitoring dealers' performance. By 1938, Chevrolet had roughly 5,000 factory managers in place to supervise about 9,000 dealers.[37] The field men checked to make sure dealers filled out the many forms according to GM standards. They watched expenses to see that dealers put enough – but not too much – money into reconditioning used cars. They reviewed customer complaints to single out dealers who failed to provide helpful service. They tracked the rate of turnover of used cars, making certain that working capital was not "frozen" by used cars sitting on car lots. On these and many other topics, factory representatives kept a watchful eye.[38] But there was another role for

---

[34] Ibid., 294.

[35] Ibid., 209–11, 200, quote 291; and Macaulay, *Law and the Balance of Power*, 28–29, 53–54, 77–78, quote 28.

[36] U.S. Federal Trade Commission, *Report on Motor Vehicle Industry*, 176.

[37] "Government's Summation by Mr. Baldridge," 1862, April 1940, Records and Briefs for *General Motors*. U.S. Federal Trade Commission, *Report on Motor Vehicle Industry*, 112.

[38] The FTC collected various examples. W. E. Cabeen, Zone Manager, to Claude Simmons, Dallas Motors, Inc., August 25, 1937; M. I. Noll, Office Manager, to Wm. Carson, Indianapolis, Indiana, May 25, 1938; Service and Mechanical Manager to J. H. Bates, Weburn,

accounting data and for GMAC financing. They not only served to monitor dealers by presumed objective standards, but also were used to actively shape dealers' businesses.

One source of tension concerned new car sales because management wanted dealers to sell as many cars as possible. At first glance, this task seems obvious. But the question of new sales was complicated for dealers given the burden of used car sales. As dealers at GM, Ford, and Chrysler understood, depending on the old car's allowance (meaning the dollar value given when the old car was traded-in), the losses on the used car's resale could more than absorb the gross profit earned on the sale of the new car. Once the deal was "washed out" (meaning the trade-in resold), the retailer could have increased revenues but decreased profits.[39] For dealers, then, not every sale was a good one. For management, a profitable dealer was not a sure sign of one who had done the most to sell their products. (The dealer could have restricted business to the sale of those new cars whose profit exceeded the loss on the resale of the trade-in.) As one response, management closely watched new car registrations. The R. L. Polk & Company distributed figures to automakers for the sale of brands at their local site of registration.[40] The data permitted GM officials, like their counterparts at other auto manufacturers, to track dealers' sales on a ten-day basis to determine whether they were selling a given "percentage of cars in their price class." Those who fell behind, as one dealer noted, were "ripe" for receiving "special pressure."[41]

Pressure took different forms. In 1938, William Holler, the general sales manager for Chevrolet, was inspired to set up paired contests among his dealers by the upcoming Joe Louis–Max Schmeling championship boxing match. Winners of each bout – determined by who sold the most cars – received a banquet dinner on the night of the official fight.[42] Sales pressure of this sort was not peculiar to automobiles, nor did dealers find it pernicious.[43]

Massachusetts, June 10, 1937; H. J. Walsh, Zone Manager, to E. B. Hatch, Detroit, November 23, 1936; Assistant Zone Manager to E. B. Mohr, Mohr Chevrolet Company, Dallas, Texas, May 10, 1937; and H. B. Hatch to H. L. Horton, October 8, 1937, all in Box 3156, RG 122, NA. I discussed factory representatives in "Consumer Negotiations," *Business and Economic History* 26 (Fall 1997): 101–22, especially 106–108.

[39] J. J. Baney, "Field Report for C. M. Woodward," June 26 and 28, 1938, 5, Box 3108, RG 122, NA.

[40] U.S. Federal Trade Commission, *Report on Motor Vehicle Industry*, 179–80, 222, 241–44; and Sloan, *My Years with General Motors*, 136.

[41] U.S. Federal Trade Commission, *Report on Motor Vehicle Industry*, 180. GM records given to the FTC indicate that dealer sales were assessed based on a percentage of a given price class. See, for example, H. L. Horton to R. G. Schulte, November 17, 1938, Box 3156, RG 122, NA.

[42] H. L. Horton to W. E. Holler, May 14, 1938, Box 3156, RG 122, NA.

[43] J. J. Baney, "Field Report for C. M. Woodward," June 26 and 28, 1938, 5–6, Box 3108, RG 122, NA.

But dealers did complain about the pressure to take more cars than their territory justified. One dealer recounted, "if you [the factory] engage a dealer long enough," then he will "capitulate" for the extra stock. Where "factories have been guilty of loading the dealer beyond his capacity and the potentialities of his territory," he concluded that dealers "sell new cars for less than a fair return in order to satisfy the manufacturers' demands for percentage of price class." Another Chevy dealer complained, "Frequently when we order one model car, [the] manufacturer substitutes another model to complete [the] carload. Then [the factory] back-orders [the] model ordered and ships [it] at some later date."[44] A third dealer complained that strikes reverberated on their businesses: "In 1937, due to strike conditions in [the] early part of year I was very short of cars, but later on I received a few too many, resulting in forced sales at losses."[45] The FTC found that some thirty percent of Chevy dealers reported that prior to 1938 they had been "oversupplied" with cars.[46] Chevrolet was not unusual. A Buick dealer reported that the factory often would "insist" on sending cars with radios or other unordered accessories to push up their sales.[47] A Ford dealer recalled that when "many cars" were sent to him without his order in 1929, "[t]hreats came from the branch manager to the effect that if the cars were not accepted his contract would be canceled."[48] Another Ford dealer, as the FTC summarized his experience, received "unwanted colors of cars." Yet, "if the company's attention is called to this fact, the mistake will be corrected by shipping an additional [railroad] carload of cars so that the dealer may get the one car of the color he wanted."[49] So common were complaints that the FTC issued this statement: "One of the most frequent complaints of dealers is that manufacturers compel them to take more new cars than they can profitably handle with the result that in order to dispose of them they are obliged to make excessive trade-in allowances or to cut cash prices."[50]

Just as dealers and managers differed when it came to the topic of selling new cars, they diverged when it came to the problem of matching production and distribution. The goal of efficiency in coordinating mass production and mass distribution remained elusive inasmuch as efficiency implicitly depended on knowing car buyers' "tastes and preferences" when they had a

---

[44] U.S. Federal Trade Commission, *Report on Motor Vehicle Industry*, 206. John J. Baney, "Field Report for J. E. Harris," September 19, 1938, 4, Box 3107, RG 122, NA.

[45] U.S. Federal Trade Commission, *Report on Motor Vehicle Industry*, 205.

[46] John J. Baney, "Field Report for J. E. Harris," September 19, 1938, 4–5, Box 3107; "Field Report of Joseph A. Schlecht," August 2, 1938, 3–4, Box 3108, both in RG 122, NA; and U.S. Federal Trade Commission, *Report on Motor Vehicle Industry*, 204, 206, 208, and 275. More cases are reported in the FTC's report and provided in the U.S. government's antitrust suit against General Motors. Macaulay called attention to these problems in *Law and the Balance of Power*, 17–18.

[47] U.S. Federal Trade Commission, *Report on Motor Vehicle Industry*, 275.

[48] Ibid., 200.   [49] Ibid., 204.   [50] Ibid., 173.

choice of many different features. Robert E. Griffin, the distribution manager of the Olds Motor Works, stated as one example that the 1938 Olds included two engine series – a six cylinder and an eight; ten colors with three different types of trim; two rear axle gear ratios; and several accessories.[51] Based on a consumer's selections, a dealer wrote a purchase order and placed it with a factory. Presumably the factory would fill the order as specified, but this ideal was hard to achieve. Joseph M. Hendrie, the distribution manager for Chevrolet, stated that in dealing, for example, with an order for ten cars, the production may proceed as expected for five cars, but parts may be delayed for the other five. So, Hendrie offered, the factory substituted cars to fill the order.[52] The start of a new model year also posed problems. M.E. Coyle, the vice president and general auditor of Chevrolet Motor Company, recalled that at the beginning of a new year, production was estimated against the sales department's projections, so the initial distribution of cars did not necessarily match local market demands. Finally, given the scale of production, cars could only be parked in a waiting yard a few days before being shipped out.[53] Each of these details in the production process meant that factories shipped cars that dealers did not necessarily order or want.

Dealers called particular attention to the oversupply of cars at the end of the model year. The year-end clearance had been one of the four problems Sloan identified. According to the retired president, GM introduced a policy in 1930 to help dealers sell the last remaining cars of the previous model year. But the FTC indicated that Sloan had recognized the problem sooner and considered it serious. In a 1925 memo, as the FTC reported, he stated: "just before the close of the season" dealers were forced to take cars "that they couldn't possibly sell except at a loss." He continued, "This loss had been sufficient in some cases to absorb their profits for the entire year."[54] Although Sloan had hoped that the 1930 policy would alleviate the problem, apparently it had not. Chevrolet dealers, for instance, told FTC interviewers in 1938 that they had been pressured to take cars at the model's year end. One reported: "In August of 1937 we were overstocked by a shipment sent to us without our order so that when the 1938 models came out we still had about twenty 1937 models on hand."[55] The FTC report relayed similar sentiments from other car divisions. "Several Pontiac dealers," the study indicated, "complained quite bitterly as to the factory's policies in regard to forcing them to take cars in the clean-up period in 1937."[56] Ford dealers

---

[51] "Robert E. Griffin Testimony," 1175–76, March 1940, Records and Briefs for *General Motors*.

[52] "Joseph M. Hendrie Testimony," 1018–38, February 1940, Records and Briefs for *General Motors*.

[53] "M. E. Coyle Testimony," 1760–81, April 1940, Records and Briefs for *General Motors*.

[54] U.S. Federal Trade Commission, *Report on Motor Vehicle Industry*, 174.

[55] Ibid., 206.   [56] Ibid., 207.

told a similar story. One reported to the FTC examiners that except for the year of their interview, he had been forced to take cars: "Practically every year prior to 1938, at the close of the model year, I have been compelled to take more cars than I could dispose of and had to sell them at prime cost – a marked contrast from 1938." Another Ford dealer told of having an "oversupply" of cars from 1931 through 1934. "During the clean-up season, the latter part of the year, they would force dealers to take more cars than they could sell at a profit in order to clear their branches of all models, frankly stating that the dealer was not expected to make a full profit on all the cars that were sold."[57] Chrysler dealers offered similar experiences. One recalled being forced to take four vehicles, being threatened that if he refused the cars, management would not send him new cars. Another Chrysler dealer recalled, as the FTC reported, "Up to 1938 [the] factory representative would call and tell us what we had to take. I would ask him what we were going to do with them. He would laugh and say 'Run 'em in the lake.' Then we would have to go out and trade wild and loose."[58]

The potential for conflict in all of these matters was further aggravated by the topic of credit. According to the court in the antitrust case against GM, prior to 1926 GMAC earned $2.5 million on a volume of $300 million. But GMAC's business doubled between 1925 and 1926, when it earned $5 million in net income on a volume of $600 million. Its business continued to thrive during the Great Depression. Between 1935 and 1938, the volume of business averaged $1 billion annually and net income averaged $14 million each year.[59] By the late 1930s, fifty percent of GM dealers financed all vehicle purchases and another twenty-six percent financed at least half their cars with GMAC.[60] GMAC was not alone. According to the Justice Department, finance companies aligned with the three major manufacturers received large amounts of financing from dealers.[61]

The change in GMAC's fortunes and dealers' complaints dated to the mid-1920s when GM officials changed their credit policies. Whereas independent finance companies had offered non-recourse paper, GMAC decided to require the "dealer indorsement [sic] of retail paper," meaning that it was "recourse liability."[62] (With non-recourse the credit agency was responsible for the vehicle should the borrower default on the loan; with recourse liability, the dealer was responsible.) To offset this requirement, in 1925 management added a "dealer's reserve." The reserve came to twenty percent of the finance charge for an installment loan, and once the car buyer

[57] Ibid., 204.   [58] Ibid., 195, quote 200.   [59] *United States v. General Motors*, 397.
[60] U.S. Federal Trade Commission, *Report on Motor Vehicle Industry*, 286, and in general, 920–47. See as well the lengthy court opinion in the Justice Department's suit against GM. *United States v. General Motors*, 386–97.
[61] U.S. Federal Trade Commission, *Report on Motor Vehicle Industry*, quote 280.
[62] *United States v. General Motors*, 392.

had "liquidate[d] his obligation," then the amount of the reserve would be "credited to the dealer on the books of GMAC."[63] Along with this policy, between 1919 and 1925, GMAC held loans to "a reasonable period" of typically twelve months and required a down payment of "one third the selling price."[64] But the policy proved unpopular, especially in western states, and events came to a head in southern California. In 1925, three competitors' brands were outselling Chevrolet. Their advantage, as GM officials saw it, was their credit plans. Despite setting higher interest rates, the loans offered longer terms and smaller down payments; they also were non-recourse paper. In Los Angeles in a conference meeting in November 1925, top GM officials called for an "immediate solution." They decided to prohibit non-recourse paper. One top manager was quoted as saying: "the corporation would not deviate from its policy, which required the sales department to do everything in their power to convince the dealers that any plan of financing that would cost the customer more than the GMAC rates was not a sound policy."[65]

Beginning in the mid-1920s, dealers complained of being "coerced" to use GMAC financing or risk some form of retribution. Former GM officials testified that credit and sales managers swapped information so that they could identify dealers who did not use GMAC financing.[66] Robert Smith had operated one of the largest franchises in San Francisco in 1925 and ran his own financing company, which cleared $15,000 a month in profits. He testified in the antitrust case that GM officials forced him to shut down his finance business.[67] In another case in 1925, Thayer Morrow had been a Chevrolet dealer in Peoria, Illinois, and, at that time, he relied on "an independent discount company, but sometime in 1926 he turned to GMAC exclusively." Morrow based this decision on two conversations he had with GM officials. In one, a field representative for Chevrolet warned Morrow "that if we [the dealers] wanted to get cars when the new models came out we had better play ball and use GMAC." [68] These sorts of conflicts continued into the 1930s. A Pontiac dealer "desired to finance his wholesale purchases and retail sales through a discount company owned by a personal friend, but he was required to agree to use GMAC 100% as a condition precedent to securing his franchise contract." In 1936, GMAC stopped providing a Buick dealer with wholesale credit "because of his failure to give GMAC a sufficient amount of retail paper." When the Buick dealer began using a local finance company, he "experienced a great deal of trouble receiving the models he ordered." Other dealers in his area had no trouble, however. When a Chevy dealer began using a local finance company,

---

[63] Ibid., 391.   [64] Ibid., 391–92.   [65] Ibid., 392–93.
[66] See "Government's Summation by Mr. Baldridge," 1866–67, April 1940; and "Testimony of William B. McClain," 245–57, January 1940, Records and Briefs for *General Motors*.
[67] *United States v. General Motors*, 393.   [68] Ibid.

"he was shipped cars of different model[s] and design from those ordered."
Another Chevy dealer used GMAC but not for at least half his loans. In
that case, cars with "unordered accessories in great quantities were forced
on him."[69]

Whether dealers used their own choice of finance company or GMAC
represented a conflict of interest. Part of the conflict concerned a dealer's
ability to sell cars. For example, farmers might want to "pay a third down,
and wait six months and pay the other two-thirds balance in one payment."
But dealers reported that GMAC would "insist" on monthly payments.[70] In
another instance the FTC observed that some dealers offered flexible plans
for teachers, who made payments when they received their salaries during the
school year.[71] As a third example, a dealer might have many customers "who
were employees of a local discount company, and hence it was easier to sell
to them by using the facilities of their employer."[72] From GM's perspective,
however, dealers who used GMAC financing served GM in two regards: they
channeled earnings directly into the corporation's coffers, and they reduced
the cost of GMAC having to solicit new business. GMAC also served as a tool
to check on dealers. In his closing statement, the Justice Department's lawyer
recalled the experience of a Pontiac dealer who gave GMAC eighty percent of
his business. The factory had "him in their grip" and shipped him cars he had
not ordered. He did not object since his capital was "tied up in the business
and he does not want to have his franchise canceled."[73] Without independent
financing, would dealers put up less fuss about accepting unpopular models?
Would they be more agreeable to taking cars at the year-end clearance?[74]

Although not as extensively as GM, Ford and Chrysler also exerted pressure on their dealers to rely on credit agencies associated with the manufacturers. According to the FTC, forty-two percent of Ford dealers obtained at
least half their financing from Ford's credit agency, Universal Credit Company, and thirty-six percent of Chrysler dealers obtained at least half their
financing through Commercial Credit Company.[75] One Ford dealer recalled

---

69   Ibid., 395–96. See also examples from the FTC investigation, such as John J. Baney, "Field
     Report on J. E. Harris," September 19, 1938, Box 3107, RG 122, NA; and U.S. Federal
     Trade Commission, *Report on Motor Vehicle Industry*, 109.
70   See "Opening Statement by Mr. Baldridge," 89, January 1940, Records and Briefs for *General
     Motors*.
71   U.S. Federal Trade Commission, *Report on Motor Vehicle Industry*, 950.
72   *United States v. General Motors*, 397.
73   See "Government's Summation by Mr. Baldridge," 1896–97, April 1940, Records and Briefs
     for *General Motors*.
74   In his autobiography, Sloan simply noted that GMAC was investigated and that (at the time
     of the book's writing in 1964) dealers were free to choose their source of financing. Sloan, *My
     Years with General Motors*, 305–309. Hewitt, *Automobile Franchise Agreements*, 104–106.
75   U.S. Federal Trade Commission, *Report on Motor Vehicle Industry*, 281.

being instructed "on a number of occasions," as the FTC reported, that "[i]f you expect to get new cars you must use the Universal Credit Co." A Chrysler dealer who relied on an independent finance company recalled being pressured to switch to Commercial Credit Company, "not a week passing without the subject being brought up. On innumerable occasions he was unable to get his orders filled."[76] Overall, the FTC estimated that roughly a fifth of Ford dealers had been pressured to rely on Universal Credit, and a quarter of Chrysler dealers to rely on Commercial Credit.[77]

At the root of the conflicts between dealers and management was the market relationship between dealers and consumers. Managers and dealers squared off over the question of fully exploiting markets, given the practice of used car trade-ins. Also, the difficulties dealers and managers faced in coordinating a factory's production with dealers' sales proved more complex, because consumers could choose from a wide range of colors, accessories, and other items. In one sense, Sloan described the accounting policies and credit financing as key tools for creating a rational dealer network. Yet, because the firm saddled dealers with extra vehicles, the accounting reports did not simply serve as an objective measure of a dealer's ability to run the business, but represented an artifact of the particular costs managers shifted to dealers given the difficulties GM faced in coordinating production with consumers' demands. Although Ford and Chrysler signed consent decrees, the Justice Department convinced the courts that GMAC intended not simply to smooth out the production cycle but to garner added revenues. Insofar as managers could never obtain a complete grip on consumers' behavior, they could and did shift the costs of their inaccuracies to dealers.[78] Moreover, one of the many choices that consumers should have had was which financing company to use, but GM limited this choice for the sake of its profitability.

TRYING TO RESHAPE THE DEMAND SIDE OF THE MARKET

As GM developed its credit and accounting systems to shape dealer relations, managers and dealers also tried to condition market relations between dealers and car buyers when it came to the question of used car trade-ins. During

---

[76] Ibid., quotes 283, 286.   [77] Ibid., 282, 285.

[78] Other issues concerning market transactions were raised during the 1930s. Thomas Dicke, for instance, writes that anti-chain legislation in the mid-1930s prompted oil manufacturers to convert company outlets to franchises. Although he did not consider the impact of this legislation on autos in his case study of Ford, automakers had opted to rely on franchises prior to 1930; they also had written into their contracts clauses explicitly declaring that the franchisee was not the manufacturer's agent. On the question of fleet sales, GM included a clause outlining a dealer's obligations, but this issue did not prove to be a bone of contention in dealers' complaints to the FTC. Dicke, *Franchising in America*, 85–116.

the 1920s, the very growth of a mass market for automobiles contributed to a burgeoning supply of used cars. One GM report expected the number of used cars in the low-price car market to match the number of new cars by 1928.[79] By the late 1930s, GM reports found that ninety percent of new Chevrolet purchases entailed trades.[80] Trade-ins were at the heart of dealers' profitability because large allowances on used vehicles could mean reselling the old car at a loss – potentially absorbing the gross profit earned from the new car's sale. One 1927 GM report concluded that trade-ins induced "a highly destructive" competition among dealers for which their profits could be "diminished if not wiped out altogether."[81] The problem mattered to GM since dealer losses on used cars cut back "the ability of dealers to purchase new cars."[82] GM and its dealers experimented with various policies intended to restrict consumers' ability to negotiate the elements of a car's purchase: trading the used car, setting the new car's price, and working out the details of the finance plan.

As unlikely as it may sound, in the mid-1920s Chevrolet introduced a plan to permanently destroy "junkers." They wanted to reduce the supply of the oldest cars, thus curbing buyers' chances of using them to bargain down prices on new vehicles. Under the "Chevrolet Used Car Disposal Plan," Chevrolet increased each new car's price by $5 "and allowed the dealer a rebate of $25 to apply on a junk car when five new cars had been purchased." In other words, "a definite allowance of $25 was made for demolishing each junk car when the dealer had purchased five new cars."[83] By 1926, at the latest, a junking program was standard in Chevrolet's dealer contracts.[84] The junkyards were employed throughout the country. By 1929, the plan was broadened and sponsored by the National Automobile Chamber of Commerce, Inc., the forerunner to the Automobile Manufacturers Association.[85] Under Ford's junking program in 1930, 40,755 cars were demolished, and they had a "net recovery of approximately $12.50 per car."[86] Dealers

[79] Koether told Kettering that the bulletin covered different aspects of the problem of used cars and had been written for "internal distribution among our passenger car Divisions." B. G. Koether to C. F. Kettering, June 17, 1927 with H. G. W., Sales Section, "The Manufacturer, the Dealer, and the Used Car," April 1927, 39, 54, File 87-11.4-1, Box 110, CFK, KU.

[80] H. L. Horton to W. E. Holler, May 14, 1938, 3, Box 3156, RG 122, NA.

[81] B. G. Koether to C. F. Kettering, June 17, 1927 with H. G. W., Sales Section, "The Manufacturer, the Dealer, and the Used Car," April 1927, 39, 54, File 87-11.4-1, Box 110, CFK, KU. The FTC dated GM's recognition of the impact of used cars on new car sales to 1925. U.S. Federal Trade Commission, *Report on Motor Vehicle Industry*, 215.

[82] U.S. Federal Trade Commission, *Report on Motor Vehicle Industry*, 221–23.

[83] Ibid., 92–93.   [84] Hewitt, *Automobile Franchise Agreements*, 86–87.

[85] U.S. Federal Trade Commission, *Report on Motor Vehicle Industry*, 43–48, 92–94, 219. Sales Section, General Motors, "The Junker Problem," June 1928, File 87-11.4-1, Box 110, CFK, KU; and H. G. W., Sales Section, "The Manufacturer, the Dealer, and the Used Car," April 1927, 8, File 87-11.4-1, Box 110, CFK, KU.

[86] U.S. Federal Trade Commission, *Report on Motor Vehicle Industry*, 92–93.

gladly passed FTC investigators the "party line" that old cars were "unsafe" on highways and should be eliminated.[87] This was a new twist on safety, because in both cases the intent was to demolish each "junker," so that, as Grant instructed, "it cannot be repaired and resold. To accomplish this purpose, smash starting motor, generator and coil, carburetor and manifolds, cylinder head, cylinder block, and transmission.... Break the radiator, head lamp, and instrument board and drive the grease plug into the rear axle. The dealer may then sell the car for junk."[88]

The junkyards did not stop trade-ins, and company-run plans disappeared at the end of 1933 when the National Recovery Administration (NRA) went into operation. Dealers anticipated that the NRA's minimum price codes for used cars would alleviate the trade-in menace.[89] But the NRA expired in 1935, and dealers had to resort to other tactics. One, dating back to the late 1920s, was the cooperative work of so-called "appraisal" bureaus. Dealers set up local bureaus to share information about the price of used vehicles. A Los Angeles dealer told an FTC investigator that they had established their bureau in 1935 and all local Chevrolet dealers were members. When a potential customer asked about a trade-in price, the dealer could call a central phone number to learn what bids other dealers had made. Dealers acknowledged the system's obvious limitations to the extent that any member could bow out and undercut the effort to fix prices. Still, the bureaus offered some help, otherwise dealers would have had no incentive to support them. The Los Angeles dealer who discussed his bureau with the FTC interviewer noted that the local dealer association had GM approval for the plan, and that factory officials (a point the FTC sustained) and other dealer organizations asked for information to set up bureaus in other markets. The bureaus were not confined to GM dealers. In the Muskegon area of Michigan, "dealer-members" of the bureau accounted for ninety-six percent of cars sold in the area. In Los Angeles, the so-called Hollywood plan began with sixty-three dealers but, by 1937, had "101 out of 108 dealers in the area."[90] An Illinois dealer, who served as secretary of his state's dealer association,

---

[87] In 1930 under the Highway Safety Plan, dealers scrapped some 350,000 cars. "Application of the National Automobile Chamber of Commerce for Consideration by the Jury of Award of the American Trade Association Executives of the Highway Safety Plan which involves Junking Old Cars," January 10, 1931, 1, Box 3108, RG 122, NA.

[88] Grant gave his instructions in a 1929 bulletin, "Proposed Highway Safety Plan," quoted in U.S. Federal Trade Commission, *Report on Motor Vehicle Industry*, 94. Records in the FTC files are extensive on this topic. See, for instance, J. J. Baney, "Field Report of C. M. Woodard," July 26 and 28, 1938, 9, Box 3108, RG 122, NA. H. G. W., Sales Section, "The Manufacturer, the Dealer, and the Used Car," April 1927, 8, File 87-11.4-1, Box 110, CFK, KU; and H. G. Weaver to C.F. Kettering, July 21, 1928, with report, "Junker Problem," June 1928, 12–15, File 87-11.4-1, Box 110, CFK, KU.

[89] U.S. Federal Trade Commission, *Report on Motor Vehicle Industry*, 96.

[90] Ibid., 370–72.

reported that many bureaus were in use and had helped eliminate what he called "the over-allowance evil." This dealer asserted that the practice did not entail questions of price fixing. The FTC found that the practices may not have violated interstate commerce laws but were still unfair under state laws. Moreover, dealers ran bureaus in several states, including Michigan, Wisconsin, Minnesota, Pennsylvania, Illinois, Missouri, and Virginia.[91]

Dealers also tried to alter prices through "padding" car sales and "packing" car loans. They offered a large allowance on a customer's trade-in, but made up this loss by padding the price of a new vehicle. In an internal letter, Sloan observed that this action was premised on the idea that "psychologically speaking, a big allowance for a used car is more effective in selling a new car than a lower price on the new car."[92] The padding worked to the extent that GM advertised cars as the factory price plus freight and taxes, for which the sum for freight and taxes was not specified. The FTC noted the "frequent practice of either motor-vehicle manufacturers or dealers of adding to the factory price a transportation charge . . . greater than that actually incurred by the manufacturer." It called for "regulation" to provide "each retail purchaser with an itemized invoice showing in detail the components of the local taxes, the cost of accessories, and all other charges."[93] It took nearly twenty years but, in 1958, Congress passed a new law requiring manufacturers to "affix a label on the window glass of each new car shipped to a dealer" with "detailed information" about "the manufacturer's suggested retail price."[94]

At the same time, the FTC found that since 1929 roughly sixty percent of all new and used cars were sold with installment financing, and it charged dealers with "packing" interest fees on car loans.[95] Here, they worked with finance companies to raise payments, counting on the hope that a car buyer could not calculate monthly payments and so would not identify the extra fees.[96] The executive vice president of GMAC, Ira McCreery, testified in 1940

---

[91] Harry H. Carter, "Report on Chevrolet Dealer Association," no date [1938]; H. H. Carter, "Field Report: Rudolph Kysela," August 29, 1938; John J. Baney, "Field Report of C. M. Woodard," July 26 and 28, 1938, 7–8; and John J. Baney, "Field Report of C. W. Coons," August 24, 25 and 27, 1938, all in Box 3108, RG 122, NA. The L.A. example and others were reported in U.S. Federal Trade Commission, *Report on Motor Vehicle Industry*, 371–400, 1075.

[92] Alfred P. Sloan to C. S. Mott, January 26, 1938, File 77-7.4-3.6, Mott Papers, KU; Sloan, *My Years with General Motors*, 299–300; and Macaulay, *Law and the Balance of Power*, 16.

[93] U.S. Federal Trade Commission, *Report on Motor Vehicle Industry*, 111, quote 1077.

[94] Sloan, *My Years with General Motors*, 300; and Macaulay, *Law and the Balance of Power*, 71.

[95] U.S. Federal Trade Commission, *Report on Motor Vehicle Industry*, 920.

[96] Packs, for instance, might consist of money added to a dealer's loss reserve that exceeded what was needed to manage the risk of losses. Packs also came in the form of a "dealer's bonus." Ibid., 932.

that GMAC refused such loans because they would result in consumers' losing confidence in GM.[97] Still, to the extent that dealers used other financing agencies, they could and did pack prices. Sloan concluded, "dealers in a community will get together and all agree to pack certain amounts. We, of course, keep after those things ... but it does happen, no matter how aggressive we may be."[98]

In the autumn of 1935, GM introduced a new finance campaign, under the title "the 6% plan." The plan tried to put an end to dealers' packs while boosting GM's finance business. It offered consumers a lower rate of interest than competitors' plans, a point Sloan declared and the FTC verified. But the plan ran into trouble in its wording. The reference to "6%" was not a reference to a six percent rate of interest, since the rate varied depending on the length of the loan. A multiplier of half of one percent applied. A twelve-month loan carried a six percent rate, but an eighteen-month loan had finance charges of nine percent and a twenty-four-month loan came with a twelve percent rate. The FTC put an end to this advertising in 1938.[99] In the meantime, the plan prompted other complaints. GM tried to stop dealers' packs, which initially gave dealers an incentive to work with independent finance companies. GM tried to make this choice futile by educating consumers about finance plans. If consumers could spot packs, then dealers would have no reason to use them and no reason to turn to independent finance companies. Still, dealers protested that GMAC had "coerced" them to rely on the factory-controlled finance division. Further, they contended that GMAC could set lower rates to the extent that the company's cost of soliciting business was lower because dealers had been cut out of the business.[100]

In the end, dealers persisted in padding prices and packing loans. Rather than shrug off the FTC's exposure of dealers' practices, GM managers – despite their frustration with dealers – quickly came to their defense. Neil Borden, a Harvard Business School professor, wrote that by 1939 GM "started a magazine campaign which stated very plainly the policy of the corporation and its dealers on delivered prices." The firm also initiated a "plainview price tag" for which dealers hung in their showrooms signs that clearly listed a car's price, its taxes, and transportation and accessory fees. A new advertising campaign pictured a friendly dealer chatting with Mr. and Mrs. Car Buyer, in which a smaller insert carried the theme: "You can see

[97] "Testimony of Ira G. McCreery," 175–76, January 1940, Records and Briefs for *General Motors*.

[98] Alfred P. Sloan to C. S. Mott, January 26, 1938, File 77-7.4-3.6, Mott Papers, KU; and U.S. Federal Trade Commission, *Report on Motor Vehicle Industry*, 932, 940–44, 1074, 1076.

[99] U.S. Federal Trade Commission, *Report on Motor Vehicle Industry*, 934, 941, 972.

[100] Consumers also lost flexible payment plans that dealers had offered them, as noted above. Ibid., 933–44. *United States v. General Motors*.

the Value...And you can see the price." GM kept up its campaign about dealers through 1940 and 1941. For 1941, Borden noted that the GM car dealer was presented as "a fine businessman and a leader in his local community. The campaign tied the local dealer with General Motors through the theme 'Partners in Progress through Service.'" The campaign further carried the headline: "A Good Life for Any Man/General Motors? – Right Here on Main Street."[101] GM marketers thus asserted that GM dealers were models of integrity in local communities while never directly addressing the FTC's findings.

Buying a car meant haggling over specific details: the old car's trade-in value, the new car's price, and the terms of installment loans. The FTC discovered that for each activity dealers tried to tilt the negotiations to their favor. When it came to used cars, they had tried to destroy jalopies at company-run junk yards, had relied on the NRA's price codes, and had established their own appraisal bureaus. For new car prices, the ambiguity in transportation and other fees allowed retailers to inflate prices. Finally, financing terms were more complicated, but dealers could and did pack loans. If car buyers remained suspicious of dealers, the FTC also linked complaints to automakers because they had worked with dealers so their interests were aligned. In the case of used cars, for instance, dealers' losses limited their demand for new cars. The problems consumers faced were of a scale that exceeded any one buyer's ability to redress. Instead, they were represented in the market by state regulators. The FTC had halted the misleading advertising of GM's 6% plan, and federal legislation in 1958 made new car prices transparent. The problems of valuing trade-ins and finance charges were more difficult to legislate, and remained sources of contention long after the Depression.[102]

RETHINKING THE RELATIONSHIP BETWEEN DEALERS AND CONSUMERS

If dealers felt squeezed by management's pressures to sell more cars and by consumers' determination to lower the price of a new vehicle, they also linked these two concerns to a third problem: competition in their own ranks. In contrast to Ford's reliance on competition among dealers, GM allocated a given number of dealers to a geographic territory based on the estimated demand in that region. But dealers complained to FTC investigators that

[101] Although Borden detailed this marketing campaign, he conveniently obscured the FTC's investigation, obliquely noting that "in 1939, the subject of 'price packing' was in the minds of all car buyers." Neil H. Borden, *Advertising: Text and Cases* (Chicago: Richard D. Irwin, Inc., 1950), 525–28.

[102] Dealers' packs persisted into the 1950s. See Macaulay, *Law and the Balance of Power*. In 2000, two suits were filed charging racial discrimination in dealers' handling of credit. See Diana B. Henriques, "New Front Opens in Effort to Fight Race Bias in Loans," *New York Times* (October 22, 2000), A1, A26; and idem, "Extra Costs on Car Loans Draw New Legal Attacks," *New York Times* (October 27, 2000), A1, A23.

"fringe" dealers – dealers outside the assigned region – "stole" their business. Some aggrieved retailers attributed the practice of crossing into another dealer's territory to a dealer's attempt to meet unreasonably high sales quotas. Others faulted undercapitalized dealers who "traded wild" in used cars.[103] Whatever the cause, the competition demoralized dealers, and, in this context, William Holler, the General Sales Manager of the Chevrolet Division, tried an alternative approach in his focus on dealers' commitment to a specific market.

Since the 1920s, GM had allocated a given number of dealers to a specific market territory. Determining the optimal number of dealers in a region meant estimating the demand or "potential" for cars in that territory. Further, measuring dealers' performance in sales and profitability also required an objective measure of demand because a dealer's low profits could follow from mismanagement or from a region's limited potential (meaning too many dealers relative to consumers' ability to purchase cars).[104] In the early 1920s, GM officials created an index of consumer demand for each county in the nation. Still, the index left unanswered how to cope with variations in consumers' cost of living or variations in the distribution of income.[105] Because dealers suffered when demand collapsed with the onset of the Depression, Holler decided to reallocate his sales force so dealers not only prospered in flush times, but also survived depressed markets.

Testifying in 1940 for GM's antitrust case, Holler recalled that whereas in the 1920s Chevrolet had simply expanded the number of dealers as its sales rose, in the early 1930s, once markets collapsed, its dealers suffered terribly. In 1933, he decided to create a new basis for allocating his dealers. To establish the optimal number of car dealers for a particular geographic territory, Holler faced the task of estimating the level of demand in each local territory. He recounted having "two field crews of statisticians" – one

[103] J. J. Baney, "Field Report of C. M. Woodward," July 26 and 28, 1938, 5, Box 3108; Harry H. Carter, "Field Report: Rudolph Kysela," August 29, 1938, Box 3108; John J. Baney, "Field Report of J. E. Harris," September 19, 1938, 5, 8, Box 3107, all in RG 122, NA. The FTC reported more than ninety percent of GM dealers made "excessive allowances" on used cars (meaning offered a trade-in price in excess of the car's "fair market value"). U.S. Federal Trade Commission, *Report on Motor Vehicle Industry*, 240–41.

[104] Dealers and management acknowledged the problem of gauging consumer demand in a market. See, for example, John J. Baney, "Field Report for J. E. Harris," September 19, 1938, 5, Box 3107, RG 122, NA.

[105] H. G. Weaver, "The Development of a Basic Purchasing Power Index by Counties," *Harvard Business Review* 4 (1926): 275–88. For an example of this sort of data, see Sales Section, GMC, "Income Tax Returns 1922, Montgomery County, Ohio (Dayton)," no date, CFK, File 87-11.4-1, Box 110, KU. See also Weaver's address to the Sales Executives Division of the American Management Association, "To Fix Territorial Sales Quotas," *Automotive Industries* 54 (June 17, 1926), 1061–62; and Sloan, *My Years with General Motors*, 136–37, 284–85. I discussed Weaver's index in "Consumers, Information and Marketing Efficiency at GM," *Business and Economic History* 25 (Fall 1996): 186–95, especially 189–90.

for the eastern half and one for the western half of the U.S. – travel to cities and counties where they gathered "all the statistics with reference to crops and business and economic conditions." Once the figures were converted to estimates of demand for each market, Holler set new targets for the optimal number of dealers. "If we have eight dealers in the field," Holler noted as an illustration, but we estimate that only six can survive in good times and bad, "we so notify the region and zone people that they can have ample time to consolidate or to liquidate the account."[106] In other words, rather than err on the side of too small a potential, Holler chose the reverse, and effectively gave dealers a greater opportunity to turn a profit.

Holler also expected dealers to take greater responsibility for their territories. In early 1937, one memo declared that Chevrolet wanted each dealer "to capitalize on local good-will and become a figure in the community. This takes an investment of time and money on the dealer's part." Chevrolet offered its help. On the demand side, shoppers could hurt dealers to the extent they went in search of the best bid on their used cars. Whereas more dealerships translated into more places where a buyer could play dealers against each other, the sales management had reduced the number of dealers. On the supply side, officials noted that the shape of retailing was changing. Dealers located in the heart of cities were finding it difficult to sell used cars. Evidently, used car buyers tended to "avoid 'marble fronts.'" Although the dealers wanted to set up used car lots outside their cities, sales managers worried this option would spark new "brother-dealer" competition.[107] Management put some teeth into its protective efforts in the late 1930s. Dealers could now sign agreements with GM whereby any retailer who encroached on another dealer's market would be fined $25 per car. The same LA dealer who told the FTC interviewer that all the area's Chevy dealers supported a used car appraisal bureau also reported that the city's dealers supported the "protected territory program."[108]

In 1941, Chevrolet's General Manager reported that Chevy had trimmed its dealers nine percent from 1929 to 1936, and another twelve percent by 1940. Yet sales per dealer increased thirty-one percent in these same years. Each dealer sold on average ninety-four cars in 1929 and 123 in 1940.[109] With the exception of 1937, Chevy kept its sales well ahead of Ford and Plymouth. From twenty-nine percent of its price class in 1929 (an off year),

---

[106] "William E. Holler Testimony," 1639–41, April 26, 1940, Records and Briefs for *General Motors*.

[107] William Holler to all Chevrolet Dealers, August 10, 1939, and H. L. Horton to W. M. Holler, January 26, 1937, 3–7, Box 3156, RG 122, NA.

[108] The FTC reported higher fines of $35 on Chevies and $200 on Cadillacs. Harry H. Carter, "Field Report: Rudolph Kysela," August 29, 1938, 5, Box 3108, RG 122, NA; "G. M. III: How to Sell Automobiles," *Fortune* 19 (February 1939): 105; and Dicke, *Franchising in America*, 118–22.

[109] Bill Holler to C. S. Mott, August 10, 1942, File 77-7.4-3.5, Mott Papers, KU.

its market share rebounded to forty-one percent in 1936. Further, despite their protests to the FTC, Chevy dealers had earned a net profit each year since 1933, averaging $5,800 per dealer in 1936 and $6,600 per dealer in 1940. After "years of constant work," Holler credited the Chevrolet Dealer Organization as "the strongest and best organization in the field today."[110]

As a management problem, Holler's strategy never addressed the pressures dealers faced. It did not stop car buyers from negotiating their trade-ins. It did not alleviate the costs dealers faced in terms of problems in coordinating production and distribution, or the pressures to sell more cars. All of those problems remained. But Holler had given dealers more breathing room to cope with the sources of tension. He had essentially left more money on the table for dealers, and he had reduced the number of dealers that required supervision, thereby reducing managerial costs.

CONCLUSION

In his account of the modern firm, Sloan explained the development of GM's network of franchised dealerships as a set of decisions to carefully coordinate production and distribution, and to maintain a network of healthy retailers. To this end, he declared: "Uncertainty and efficiency are as far apart as the North Pole is from the South." He singled out "proper accounting" as the key to seeing that each dealer knew "the facts about his business."[111] Reports for dealers' sales, costs, earnings, balance sheets, and inventories brought clarity to their operations. Managers trusted the numbers to identify retailers' "soft spots" systematically and correct their operations.[112] The data also helped GM match production with shifts in the level of demand. Sloan outlined a similar role for GMAC. The corporation's financing division both assisted dealers in purchasing cars wholesale and smoothed the flow of automobiles from the company's factories to the dealers' showrooms. Sloan thus outlined a set of tools for assessing dealers "objectively" and achieving efficiency in the coordination of production and distribution.[113]

The FTC's and the Justice Department's records invite an alternative explanation for how managers relied on franchised retailers. The federal agencies first altered the problem to be explained. Rather than account for a healthy network of dealers and an efficient method of distribution, they pointed to what I have called consumers' marketing dilemma. Behind the tools meant to

---

[110] Profits included owners' salaries, and the earnings translated into a fifty-six percent average return on net working capital for the years from 1933 to 1941. Bill Holler to C. S. Mott, August 10, 1942, File 77-7.4-3.5, Mott Papers, KU. Bedros Pashigian finds that GM dealers reported a twenty-seven percent return on equity after taxes in 1940. Pashigian, *The Distribution of Automobiles, an Economic Analysis of the Franchise System*, 212–16. Sloan, *My Years with General Motors*, 296.

[111] Sloan, *My Years with General Motors*, 287.   [112] Ibid., 288.   [113] Ibid., 134.

entice buyers were problems for managers and dealers: Who shouldered the costs that followed from inaccuracies in matching production with dealers' orders? Who absorbed the costs of used car trade-ins relative to achieving greater new car sales? And who earned the interest from financing cars? Different implications followed the recognition of consumers' marketing dilemma and the question of how profits or costs would be distributed in market transactions.

One implication concerned the key accounting and credit policies. Faced with the task of sharing profits or costs, managers not surprisingly exerted power in trying to allocate costs to dealers: they pushed cars on their retailers, encouraged retailers to take cars at the end of a model year, shipped cars not ordered, and shipped cars loaded with accessories. Accounting policies did not offer an objective measure of dealers' performance, but the numbers represented artifacts of the power that management exerted by shifting unwanted cars from themselves to dealers. Credit also carried a different meaning. Aside from offering dealers a means to finance wholesale purchases, GMAC reallocated profits from dealers' financing agencies or local communities' finance companies to GM directly. Further, to the extent dealers relied on GMAC financing, access to credit offered management a tool for pressuring dealers to take orphaned cars. From Sloan's perspective, accounting and credit represented tools for objective management; acknowledging the marketing dilemma GM faced, accounting and credit reflected the power managers exerted in their relations with dealers.

A second implication concerned dealers' relations with consumers. FTC investigators uncovered various dealer practices that justified consumers' lack of trust. From the late 1920s through the 1930s, dealers had tried to curb consumers' ability to negotiate a car's price by destroying used cars at company-run junk yards; they had used appraisal bureaus to share information about consumers' trade-ins; and they had padded new car prices and packed car loans. Taking the franchise contract at face value, dealers purchased cars at a discount to the retail price and had no need to squeeze consumers over the new car's price. But given the marketing dilemma as seen in used cars and given management's pressures in pushing unpopular or year-end models on dealers, as well as management's pressure to set high sales quotas, dealers tried to recover their profits by squeezing dollars out of car buyers' wallets and purses. In other words, car buyers' distrust of dealers reflected a modern method of distribution and a modern system of marketing. Further, although consumers attributed their grievances to dealers, managers shared in the goal of restricting buyers' negotiating abilities, because dealers' prosperity benefited the company's fortunes.

A third implication addressed the role of the state. The conflicts in marketing automobiles had prompted dealers and consumers to call on the state to alter market relationships. Dealers were the most vocal and, as pressures intensified during the worst years of the Depression, their complaints first prompted the FTC's investigation and then the Justice Department's antitrust suit. Still, the conflicts did not end with the Depression. As Stewart Macaulay recounted, dealers continued to turn to the state to curb manufacturers' power in shaping their relationships.[114] Much like dealers, consumers also found relief in federal legislation. The 1958 law requiring window stickers was intended to make information about prices transparent for car buyers and to limit dealers' padding of prices. In each of these many details of the market's operation, the state served as a crucial, if imperfect, restraint on management's pressure on dealers or dealers' pressure on consumers.

GM responded in different ways to the political investigations. When the FTC publicized dealers' pricing tactics, managers initiated a marketing campaign to assert dealers' trustworthiness within local communities. What effect such claims had on buyers is hard to ascertain. A second response came from William Holler: he reduced the number of dealers and enlarged their markets. His approach avoided the consequences of political investigations and eased the tensions between dealers and management. He thus mitigated the conflict between GM and its retailers without ever resolving consumers' marketing dilemma.

---

[114] Regarding dealer contracts, Sloan noted that in 1955, after a study of the situation, management offered dealers the option of five-year sales agreements and allowed dealers to "nominate" a person to take over the business on the dealer's death. Sloan did not offer an accounting of the political context in which these changes took place. Macaulay noted that the five-year contract was announced at the time the Senate had called GM executives to testify in hearings. Macaulay, *Law and the Balance of Power*, 28–29, 53–54, 77–78; and Sloan, *My Years with General Motors*, 209–11, 300, quote 291.

PART III

A MATURE MARKET, 1945–1965

In 1935–1936, census takers surveyed U.S. households about their consumption expenditures. The findings made the point that the pattern of automobile ownership was skewed in keeping with the unequal distribution of income. The richest 12.5 percent of Americans purchased fifty-two percent of all new cars. The richest fifth of Americans bought two-thirds of all new cars. Used cars were more evenly distributed among households, with the thirty-seven percent of families in the middle bulge of the income ladder accounting for forty-seven percent of used car purchases.[1] Still, the census reported, among the poorest forty-two percent of families, two-thirds did not operate cars. By contrast, among the richest 12.5 percent of families, eighty percent of these families possessed automobiles.[2]

Franklin Roosevelt's New Deal experimented with different policies intended to counter the effects of the Depression and shape long-term patterns in the standard of living. One set of policies followed the strategy of establishing a floor against the economy's hardships, such as the Federal Deposit Insurance Corporation's minimum guarantee of bank deposits and the Fair Labor Standard Act's minimum wages.[3] Another approach had been to refinance American debts. The advent of twenty-five-year home mortgages requiring only small down payments let families better manage payments on a month-to-month basis.[4] A third approach to battling the Depression had

---

[1] National Resources Planning Board, *Family Expenditures in the United States: Statistical Tables and Appendixes* (Washington, D.C.: U.S. Government Printing Office, 1941), Tables 1 and 348, 1 and 113.

[2] Ibid., Tables 1 and 12, 1 and 4. For the lowest third of the population, I calculated a weighted average of families with cars based on the distribution of families by income as reported in Table 1.

[3] On the minimum wage, see for example, Gavin Wright, *Old South, New South* (New York: Basic Books, 1986), 219–25. On banking laws, an overview is given by Thomas K. McCraw in *Prophets of Regulation: Charles Francis Adams, Louis D. Brandeis, James M. Landis, Alfred E. Kahn* (Cambridge, MA: Harvard University Press, 1984), 170–71.

[4] Lizabeth Cohen, *Making a New Deal: Industrial Workers in Chicago, 1919-1939* (New York: Cambridge University Press, 1990); and Kenneth Jackson, *Crabgrass Frontier: The Suburbanization of the United States* (New York: Oxford University Press, 1985). Farm loans were also redefined with long-term, amortized mortgages during the 1930s. See Sally H. Clarke, *Regulation and the Revolution in United States Farm Productivity* (New York: Cambridge University Press, 1994).

come in the form of changes in the distribution of economic power. In the wake of the Wagner Act of 1935, organized labor tackled the core manufacturing industries of autos, steel, and rubber. Thanks to collective bargaining, unions such as the United Auto Workers (UAW) began to secure higher wages and related benefits.[5]

That the New Deal established a minimum wage floor and provided security in terms of bank deposits and unemployment benefits no doubt assisted many Americans, yet these policies did not alter the standard of living in such a way as to expand the ranks of automobile buyers. During the 1930s, lenders eased the terms of automobile loans, lengthening the maturities of installment notes from twelve to eighteen months as well as shrinking the size of down payments as a share of the new car's price (Tables 7.6 and 7.7). Yet, the overall pattern of auto ownership remained unchanged during the 1930s. Whereas sixty percent of households owned cars in 1929, the figure slipped to fifty-five percent from the start of the Depression through the war years (Table 7.1). Among city dwellers, most families relied on public transportation – streetcars and subways. Their decisions reflected the cost of auto ownership, since families spent $114 on average for autos in 1935–1936, but paid just $16 for other types of transportation.[6]

Wanting to expand the automobile market, manufacturers faced the prospect of selling cars to families further down the income ladder. Just as income represented one social hierarchy, automakers needed to expand the auto market in relation to hierarchies defined by race and gender. The Jim Crow South had blocked upward mobility for the vast numbers of African Americans living in these areas. But even in northern cities, such as Detroit, African Americans found job mobility difficult and discrimination prevalent.[7] Patterns of segregation and discrimination applied to women as well. In several manufacturing industries such as furniture and iron and steel, the factories typically hired no female workers. The differences in types of jobs were reflected in the earnings of men and women, as the vast majority of women in manufacturing earned sixty percent of their male counterparts' salaries. Similar patterns prevailed in other parts of the economy. Married women encountered special barriers in the form of marriage bars – policies in which companies or schools fired women when they got married or refused

[5] In general on the subject of the UAW during the 1930s, see Ronald Edsforth, *Class Conflict and Cultural Consensus: The Making of a Mass Consumer Society in Flint, Michigan* (New Brunswick, NJ: Rutgers University Press, 1987), 157–89. See also Cohen, *Making a New Deal*.

[6] National Resources Planning Board, *Family Expenditures in the United States*, Table 11, 4.

[7] Thomas J. Sugrue, *The Origins of the Urban Crisis: Race and Inequality in Postwar Detroit* (Princeton, NJ: Princeton University Press, 1996). For the South, see Wright, *Old South, New South*; and Robert A. Margo, *Race and Schooling in the South, 1880-1950: An Economic History* (Chicago: University of Chicago Press, 1990).

to hire married women.[8] Furthermore, many groups of Americans, including women, persons of color, and persons of retirement age were restricted in their access to credit, and thus to the financing of big-ticket durable goods like automobiles.[9]

While New Deal policies did not change income patterns to a significant degree during the 1930s, World War II brought about an abrupt and striking set of changes to the U.S. economy. First, there was the interruption of consumer markets. From February 1942 through September 1945, General Motors stopped making automobiles, and instead produced $12 billion worth of military goods – tanks, armored cars, trucks, bombers, guns, shells, engines, and related equipment. Overall, GM accounted for roughly eight percent of all military hardware purchased by the U.S. government during the war.[10] Ford and Chrysler similarly devoted their efforts to wartime production.[11] As measured by the expansion of war-related plants, GM spent $911.7 million, Ford $371.7 million, and Chrysler $313.3 million.[12] Second, the war created unprecedented demands for labor. As part of the war effort, the unions agreed to the Little Steel formula. It provided for a fifteen percent increase in wages for the duration of the war as part of a general effort to control prices.[13] In addition to new agreements with organized labor, the demand for labor also resulted in the transformation of the workforce. General Motors hired 750,000 new workers during World War II, and the share of women in GM's workforce rose steadily from ten percent at the end of 1941 to thirty percent at the end of 1943.[14] Overall, the percentage of women in the U.S. workforce climbed to thirty-seven percent in 1944, with half of all women at work at some point during the year. For married women, the statistics showed an increase from 13.9 percent in 1940 to

[8] Claudia Goldin, *Understanding the Gender Gap* (New York: Oxford University Press, 1990), Tables 3.2 and 3.3, 64, 74, and Table 6.1, 162.

[9] National Consumer Law Center, *Credit Discrimination*, 3rd ed. (Boston: National Consumer Law Center, Inc., 2002).

[10] Alfred P. Sloan, Jr., *My Years with General Motors*, ed. John McDonald with Catherine Stevens (Garden City, NY: Doubleday & Company, Inc., 1964), 376–78.

[11] In general on the role of business during World War II and efforts to manage the economy, see Hugh Rockoff, *Drastic Measures: A History of Wage and Price Controls in the United States* (New York: Cambridge University Press, 1984); and idem, "United States: ploughshares to swords," in *The Economics of World War II*, ed. Mark Hanson (New York: Cambridge University Press, 1998), 81–121. On Chrysler during the war, see Charles K. Hyde, *Riding the Roller Coaster: A History of the Chrysler Corporation* (Detroit, MI: Wayne State University Press, 2003), 127–47.

[12] Allan Nevins and Frank Ernest Hill, *Ford: Decline and Rebirth, 1933-1962* (New York: Charles Scribner's Sons, 1963), 226.

[13] Meg Jacobs, *Pocketbook Politics: Economic Citizenship in Twentieth-Century America* (Princeton, NJ: Princeton University Press, 2005), 194–95.

[14] Sloan, *My Years with General Motors*, 382.

22.5 percent in 1944.[15] Although many women left paid jobs with the war's end and the economy's reconversion, by 1950 28.6 percent of women were in the workforce.[16]

The market for automobiles had been stagnant during the 1930s and early 1940s, but after World War II it expanded rapidly. Whereas nearly half of all U.S. families did not own an automobile at the end of World War II, by the mid-1970s, eighty percent of families owned at least one vehicle, and roughly a quarter of families owned two or more cars (Table 7.1). That the auto market's expansion coincided with the postwar prosperity did not mean, however, that this prosperity had caused the market's expansion. Whether we can attribute the market's expansion to postwar prosperity depends on the role of other factors, such as trends in the price of new and used vehicles, but also changes in families' budgets, work patterns, the cost of production, credit policies, and corporations' marketing strategies.

Chapter 7 traces the auto market's maturation in relation to the overall development of the U.S. economy. Although scholars typically treat the economy in terms of the state's macroeconomic policies, the last chapter examines the market and the economy in terms of three institutions – the firm, the family, and the state. Corporations mattered to the auto market's expansion, since management determined the cost of producing cars and thus the pricing patterns for new and used vehicles. Families mattered to the pattern of auto purchases, first in how family members allocated their earnings for household expenditures – food, clothing, housing, and transportation – and second in how they allocated their labor, including the labor of women in the home or the workforce. The state had a direct impact on the automobile market in terms of the role the federal government's fiscal and monetary policies. In particular, the Board of Governors of the Federal Reserve System set credit policies as part of its assignment in watching inflation. As the Fed considered its policies for the economy as a whole, it also influenced credit terms for consumer markets dependent on credit financing, notably the automobile market.

Chapter 7 thus presents the development of the U.S. automobile market in terms of the evolution of the firm, the family, and the state. These institutional changes, whether intended or not, had important consequences for the automobile market. It was possible that the market could have broadened through the sale of a small, inexpensive vehicle to Americans on the lower rungs of the income ladder, but this did not happen. The market expanded in keeping with the marketing strategy that Alfred Sloan had developed during the 1920s, as automakers sold large, expensive vehicles defined in terms of a price hierarchy of brands. Alternatively, the expansion of the U.S. auto

---

[15] Susan M. Hartmann, *The Home Front and Beyond: American Women in the 1940s* (Boston: Twayne Publishers, 1982), 77–78.
[16] Ibid., 92.

market might have been associated with the leveling of social hierarchies associated with race and gender, but this also did not happen. The market matured with the vast majority of new car buyers being white men who were heads of families. Prior to the passage of the Equal Credit Opportunity Act in 1974 and its amended version in 1976, few women (married or single), persons of color, and retired persons could obtain the credit commonly needed to purchase automobiles.[17] Lenders such as GMAC restricted access to credit and thus placed their trust in select borrowers, while excluding many others.

The firm, the family, and the state conditioned the maturation of the automobile market, and the three institutions evolved within the political climate of the postwar years, which is to say, the Cold War. The Cold War calls to mind the great East-West diplomatic struggles of the postwar era, including the Berlin Blockade, the Korean War, and the Cuban Missile Crisis. Yet, the Cold War was also felt at home in Americans' political ideas about the economy. The federal government focused on promoting the growth of the U.S. economy in its competition with the Soviet Union. As part of the Cold War ideology, business objected to any interference with the free enterprise system. That women need not work represented one measure of success of the capitalist economy, and that they could purchase the vast variety of consumer goods represented a second measure of success according to the Cold War gender ideology.[18] Prior to the coming of the ECOA in 1974, the automobile market matured in keeping with the skewed distribution of income and with social hierarchies associated with traditional views concerning the firm and the family in the U.S. economy.

[17] In general, see National Consumer Law Center, *Credit Discrimination.*
[18] See especially, Elaine Tyler May, *Homeward Bound: American Families in the Cold War Era,* rev. ed. (New York: Basic Books, 1999). Other important works on the subject of the Cold War ideology include Lizabeth Cohen, *A Consumers' Republic: The Politics of Mass Consumption in Postwar America* (New York: Knopf, 2003); Jacobs, *Pocketbook Politics*; and Sugrue, *Origins of the Urban Crisis.*

7

Automobiles and Institutional Change

As the Volkswagen Beetle broke into the U.S. automobile market, the firm ran a number of unusual advertisements during the 1960s. One pictured two identical suburban houses side-by-side. The Joneses owned the house on the left, the Kremplers the one on the right. The first scene pictured the two homes and indicated that Mr. Jones and Mr. Krempler each had $3,000. Scene two told TV viewers that Mr. Jones spent his $3,000 on a car. In scene three, with his cash, Mr. Krempler purchased "a new refrigerator . . . a new range . . . a new washer . . . a new dryer . . . a new record player . . . two new television sets . . . and a brand new VW." Scene four pictured a VW Bug pulling into the Kremplers' driveway with this message: "Now Mr. Jones is faced with that age-old problem . . . Keeping up with the Kremplers."[1] But contrary to the VW ad, Mr. Jones could acquire the same items with his $3,000 by employing credit. According to the following scenario, Mr. Jones put $700 down on his new car and applied for a three-year auto loan with low monthly payments. Then he made down payments for his home appliances, record player, and TV, and took out new consumer loans, again with low monthly payments. Mr. Jones still had some cash left to make a down payment on another new item to be purchased on installments. Perhaps he had just seen *The Graduate* and decided to buy a new furniture set made of vinyl, the most up-to-date plastic for 1969.[2]

The story of Mr. Jones and Mr. Krempler fits into a postwar era in which the automobile market expanded to the vast majority of households. Whereas nearly half of all families (forty-six percent) did not own automobiles in 1948, most families (seventy-nine percent) owned at least one vehicle and nearly a quarter of households owned two or more vehicles in

[1] Alfredo Marcantonio, David Abbott, and John O'Driscoll, *Is the Bug Dead? The Great Beetle Ad Campaign* (New York: Stewart, Tabori & Chang, 1982), 82. Phil Patton put the Bug in historical perspective in *Bug: The Strange Mutations of the World's Most Famous Automobile* (New York: Simon & Schuster, 2002). See also Thomas Frank's discussion of the Bug in *The Conquest of Cool: Business Culture, Counterculture, and the Rise of Hip Consumerism* (Chicago: University of Chicago Press, 1997), 59–68.

[2] Conversation with Jeffrey L. Meikle, November 6, 2002. See also Jeffrey L. Meikle, *American Plastic: A Cultural History* (New Brunswick, NJ: Rutgers University Press, 1995). Meikle examined the cultural meaning of plastic as it was used in *The Graduate*.

Table 7.1. *Families Owning Automobiles, Selected Dates*

Year	Total	One Auto	Two or More Autos	Did Not Own a Car
1989	84%			
1983	86			
1970	82	54%	28%	18%
1965	79	55	24	21
1960	77	62	15	23
1955	70	60	10	30
1950	59	52	7	41
1949	56	48	3	44
1948	54			46
1935	55			45
1930	60			40
1920	26			74
1910	.1			99
1900	0			100

Note: The tally of data for 1949 is inaccurate as reported in the original source.
Sources: For 1900 through 1989, see Stanley Lebergott, *Pursuing Happiness: American Consumers in the Twentieth Century* (Princeton, NJ: Princeton University Press, 1993), 130; and for 1948 to 1970, see U.S. Bureau of the Census, *Historical Statistics of the United States: From Colonial Times to the Present* (Washington, D.C.: U.S. Government Printing Office, 1976), series Q 175, 717.

1965 (Table 7.1).[3] Although the VW became enormously popular as a sturdy, cheap automobile during the 1960s, by that time the market had matured through the sale of American-made vehicles. They were sold through a marketing strategy of a price hierarchy of brands combined with planned obsolescence. GM, Ford, and Chrysler sold new cars to wealthy consumers, and so enticed them with altered designs that in a few years they traded in their existing vehicles for updated models. The Big Three also maintained a price ladder. Tempting middle-class buyers to purchase new Chevrolets, automakers hoped to keep them coming back as their family incomes rose – trading in their old Chevy for a Pontiac and then a Buick, and, for a small elite, a Cadillac. Or, in the case of Ford, management hoped car owners would graduate from a Ford to a Mercury, and then a Lincoln.[4]

[3] For 1948, the first postwar year available, see U.S. Bureau of the Census, *Historical Statistics of the United States: From Colonial Times to the Present* (Washington, D.C.: U.S. Government Printing Office, 1976), series Q175, 717. For comparable figures on the automobile market's growth during the postwar years, see Lizabeth Cohen, *A Consumers' Republic: The Politics of Mass Consumption in Postwar America* (New York: Knopf, 2003), 123.
[4] Alfred P. Sloan, Jr., *My Years with General Motors*, ed. John McDonald with Catherine Stevens (Garden City, NY: Doubleday & Company, Inc., 1964), 58–70, 136–38, 166–68, 238–47,

How are we to account for the market's expansion given U.S. automakers' marketing strategy? Conventional wisdom holds that Americans purchased autos thanks to the postwar prosperity. Although the Big Three had stopped producing vehicles during World War II, the interruption created a pent-up demand for cars immediately after the war. Thanks to the GI bill and homebuilders, many veterans (and non-veterans) purchased new homes in the suburbs, thus finding that they needed autos for transportation. Government agencies promoted this suburban shift through their construction of new roads and highways. Furthermore, higher incomes associated with the general economic prosperity during the 1950s plus the reallocation of household expenditures enabled the majority of Americans to purchase cars.[5]

The experience of Mr. Jones, as just recounted, suggests that postwar prosperity did not by itself bring about the market's expansion. Automobiles imposed a significant financial burden on family budgets. Rather than bank on higher incomes, families purchased new and used vehicles thanks to an innovation in the market for installment credit. By reducing the size of down payments and lengthening the terms for repayment, lenders reduced

---

264–78. Historians, of course, have written about this marketing strategy. For automobiles, consult Richard S. Tedlow, *New and Improved: The Story of Mass Marketing in America* (New York: Basic Books, 1990), 3–21, 112–81. A recent study of planned obsolescence is found in Shelley Nickles, "'Preserving Women': Refrigerator Design as Social Process in the 1930s," *Technology and Culture* 43 (October 2002): 693–727. To focus on marketing is not to diminish the importance of developments on the production side. Daniel Raff has argued, perhaps most forcefully, of the importance of changes in production that had made possible GM's marketing strategy during the 1920s. See Daniel M. G. Raff, "Making Cars and Making Money in the Interwar Automobile Industry: Economies of Scale and Scope and the Manufacturing behind the Marketing," *Business History Review* 65 (Winter 1991): 721–53. Chrysler's production strategy differed from GM's. See Michael Schwartz, "Markets, Networks, and the Rise of Chrysler in Old Detroit, 1920–1940," *Enterprise & Society* 1 (March 2000): 63–99. On Ford's and GM's production methods, see also David A. Hounshell, *From the American System to Mass Production, 1800-1932: The Development of Manufacturing Technology in the United States* (Baltimore: Johns Hopkins University Press, 1984), 217–301.

5 In his account, James Flink emphasized both the "forced savings during the war" and the efforts of unions to secure wage gains for Americans further down the income ladder. As I report in Table 7.3, the distribution of income remained highly skewed. In addition, Flink pointed to the decision to focus resources on highway building and to dismantle mass transit systems. Both his points are valuable, but do not fully explain how most Americans purchased vehicles. See James J. Flink, *The Automobile Age* (Cambridge, MA: MIT Press, 1988), 358–76, quote 359. On the development of highways, see Mark H. Rose, *Interstate: Express Highway Politics, 1941-1956* (Lawrence, KS: Regents Press of Kansas, 1979). For an account of suburbanization, see Kenneth Jackson, *Crabgrass Frontier: The Suburbanization of the United States* (New York: Oxford University Press, 1985). Cohen synthesizes the politics of consumption and takes issue with the conventional focus on postwar prosperity in *A Consumers' Republic*. For the diffusion of gas and electrical systems, see Mark H. Rose, *Cities of Light and Heat: Domesticating Gas and Electricity in Urban America* (University Park, PA: Pennsylvania State University Press, 1995).

automobiles' annual financial burden.[6] The plausibility of this account depends on quantitative evidence. The first part of this chapter offers a quantitative portrait of automakers' marketing strategy in relation to families' distribution of income and the financial burden of auto ownership. This study leads to the conclusion that it was not simply rising family incomes, but also the new, liberalized credit terms that allowed the auto market to mature in keeping with Detroit's marketing strategy of a price pyramid combined with planned obsolescence. In other words, automakers marketed cars in keeping with the highly unequal distribution of income; and they counted on the new credit terms to sell vehicles to shoppers further down the income ladder.

This quantitative exercise indicates that, although executives applied a similar marketing strategy during the 1950s as they had in the 1920s, the institutional context had changed. The rest of the chapter examines the market's maturation from the perspective of three institutions – the family, the firm, and the state. The modern firm was critical in setting policies that caused auto prices to rise as fast as Americans' postwar incomes, thus calling into question the ability of prosperity by itself to account for the market's expansion. The state was critical in determining credit policy, and thus, permitting new, liberalized terms for auto loans. The family was critical in allocating labor, including women's labor, to offer a means to buy expensive consumer goods without credit. Why family incomes proved sufficient for some car buyers but not others; why auto prices rose during the 1950s in contrast to the teens and twenties; why the Board of Governors of the Federal Reserve Board (the Fed) eased credit terms during the 1950s – these are questions about the institutional context that collectively shaped, if inadvertently, the automobile's expansion in keeping with the skewed distribution of income.[7]

---

[6] U.S. Board of Governors of the Federal Reserve System, *Consumer Instalment Credit* (Washington, D.C.: U.S. Government Printing Office, 1957), Part I, Volume I "Growth and Import," 27, 135–36. Cohen emphasizes the role of credit in *A Consumers' Republic*, 123–24.

[7] Numerous scholars of consumption, including Jackson Lears, Regina Blasczyk, Roland Marchand, and Susan Strasser have noted the importance of installment credit for the sale of automobiles or other products, but have not examined the nature of credit or its impact on the shape of consumer markets. There are important exceptions. One is Lendol Calder's valuable institutional and cultural study of credit during the years prior to World War II. Economic historian Martha Olney has provided the most detailed review of installment credit for the years prior to World War II. In her work, Olney charted the growth of credit, identified its importance for smoothing production flows from manufacturers to car dealers, and examined the terms of installment loans, especially their high rates. Lizabeth Cohen has also identified the importance of credit in her study of postwar consumption. Cohen called special attention to the subsidies returning GI's received (who were often white and male) as compared to other groups of Americans, notably women. T. J. Jackson Lears, *Fables of Abundance: A Cultural History of Advertising in America* (New York: Basic Books, 1994); Regina Lee Blaszczyk,

It was also telling that the advertisement concerned Mr. Jones and not his wife. During the very years when the auto market became entrenched as a daily necessity, creditors routinely denied credit to women (married and single). Lenders like GMAC also denied credit to persons of color and persons over the age of sixty-five. Thus, they placed their trust or faith in some borrowers, while excluding large categories of other consumers. The marketing strategy not only suited a skewed distribution of income, but also one that reflected prevailing social inequalities based on race, gender, and age.

PRELUDE: THE POSTWAR MARKET

With the end of World War II, U.S. automakers quickly moved to convert their plants from wartime production to consumer goods. Auto sales climbed from 1.8 million units in 1946 to 6.3 million in 1950 and reached 8.3 million in 1967.[8] As output rose, the industry consolidated. Most independent firms failed. Studebaker closed its doors in 1966. Hudson and Nash merged to form American Motors, a company that claimed less than three percent of the industry's sales.[9] The Big Three were in their glory years. GM continued to dominate the market, claiming roughly forty-five percent of sales during the postwar expansion. The biggest turn-around was the Ford Motor Company. Henry Ford's control of the firm during the late 1930s and war years had resulted in several managerial problems: the labor force was demoralized; political infighting was rampant; the firm lacked basic financial controls; and management had yet to establish a sound organization, clearly delineating responsibilities. When Henry Ford II assumed the presidency in September of 1945, he began rehabilitating the firm, and by 1949, with the help of a former GM executive Ernie Breech, the grandson had established the company as a well-organized and viable competitor.[10] During the 1950s, Ford displaced Chrysler as the number two producer. FMC's share of the market averaged twenty-four percent in 1950 and twenty-seven percent in 1960. Chrysler experienced good and bad years as the quality and appeal of its brands varied. In 1957, the firm garnered eighteen percent of sales, but in 1959, its

---

Imagining Consumers: Design and Innovation from Wedgwood to Corning (Baltimore: Johns Hopkins University Press, 2000); Susan Strasser, *Satisfaction Guaranteed: The Making of the American Mass Market* (New York: Pantheon Books, 1989); Lendol Calder, *Financing the American Dream: A Cultural History of Consumer Credit* (Princeton, NJ: Princeton University Press, 1999); Martha Olney, *Buy Now, Pay Later: Advertising, Credit, and Consumer Durables in the 1920s* (Chapel Hill, NC: University of North Carolina Press, 1991); and Lizabeth Cohen, *A Consumers' Republic*.

[8] Lawrence J. White, *The Automobile Industry since 1945* (Cambridge, MA: Harvard University Press, 1971), 290–306.

[9] Ibid., 10–18, 290–306.

[10] Allan Nevins and Frank Ernest Hill, *Ford: Decline and Rebirth, 1933-1962* (New York: Charles Scribner's Sons, 1963), 228–72, 294–345.

share slipped to a low of eleven percent.[11] Still, overall, Chrysler along with Ford and GM faired well during the postwar expansion. From 1946 through 1967, their average rate of return on assets came to fifteen percent for GM, ten percent for Ford, and eight percent for Chrysler.[12]

Prosperity offered no answers to the dilemmas that faced the automobile industry prior to World War II. Automobile dealers remained frustrated in their relations with management. By the mid-1950s, the National Association of Automobile Dealers sought legislation in Congress to prevent automakers' coercive tactics. Members of Congress were well disposed to find fault with the Big Three automakers. The "Good Faith" act proposed to protect dealers from management's heavy-handed practices. Yet in order to satisfy the Justice Department and to forestall a veto from President Eisenhower, the bill was amended. Legal scholar Stewart Macaulay found that good faith as stated in the bill was still defined to mean that franchisors and franchisees would "act in a fair and equitable manner toward each other so as to guarantee the one party freedom from coercion, intimidation, or threat of coercion." The bill qualified this declaration with the point that "recommendation, endorsement, exposition, persuasion, urging or argument shall not be deemed to constitute a lack of good faith."[13]

Did the bill assist dealers? Macaulay found that the act provided little benefit. For one thing, it was costly for a dealer to bring a suit against a manufacturer. For another, the courts faced a question of interpretation. Did the act protect "a dealer *only* from coercion or intimidation?"[14] Alternatively, was the legislation more expansive in its coverage of unfair practices? The courts took the more cautious option, and thus, the act would only help a dealer who was able to "prove coercion."[15]

The federal government also intervened in the safe design of vehicles. One key figure in the move toward regulation was Ralph Nader. His book, *Unsafe at Any Speed*, documented the problems of poorly designed vehicles.[16] The book's publication in 1965 coincided with Senate hearings about automobile safety during which industry officials admitted to having conducted 426 separate recalls of automobiles between 1960 and 1966. They further admitted that they had contacted dealers, not consumers, and that they had no records of whether the vehicles were repaired.[17] In 1966, Congress passed the

[11] White, *The Automobile Industry since 1945*, 290–306. Chrysler's history is told in Charles K. Hyde, *Riding the Roller Coaster: A History of the Chrysler Corporation* (Detroit: Wayne State University Press, 2003), 149–86.

[12] White, *The Automobile Industry since 1945*, 249.

[13] Stewart Macaulay, *Law and the Balance of Power: The Automobile Manufacturers and Their Dealers* (New York: Russell Sage Foundation, 1966), 60–69, quote 69.

[14] Ibid., 103.   [15] Ibid., 106.

[16] Ralph Nader, *Unsafe at any Speed: the designed-in dangers of the American automobile* (New York: Grossman, 1965).

[17] Stan Luger, *Corporate Power, American Democracy, and the Automobile Industry* (New York: Cambridge University Press, 2000), 71–72.

National Traffic and Motor Vehicle Safety Act. By 1970, the National Highway Transportation Safety Administration (NHTSA) administered safety standards for the industry.[18] Legislation in 1974 further improved regulation: the NHTSA was given the authority to force manufacturers to recall cars with defects and to make them cover the cost of repairs.[19] Still, the law was far from ideal. Because defects were left open to definition, manufacturers could try to contest the charges.[20]

In the postwar years, automakers relied on institutions developed during the 1920s and 1930s. Federal regulation had modified, but had not changed the underlying dilemmas that management faced. In the case of the price of vehicles, automakers still counted on dealers to mediate between themselves and consumers. Automakers relied on the industrial research lab to fashion new features. The research lab continued to face tradeoffs between safety and other goals, such as innovation or cost reductions. The safety legislation added national oversight to the state regulations, but even national legislation did not resolve the dilemma over safety. Finally, in the case of marketing automobiles, management still faced a dilemma concerning automobile styling. (The tradeoffs between styling innovation and the cost of production are discussed later in the chapter.) Compared to the prewar years, the institutional character of the automobile market after World War II was much the same. What then had changed? Part of the answer was the market's expansion between 1945 and 1965.

MARKETING AUTOMOBILES: A QUANTITATIVE PORTRAIT, 1945–1965

The Big Three staked their profitability on the expansion of the automobile market, which meant selling cars to consumers further down the income ladder. Reiterating a point first established by the 1935–1936 census of consumption, the 1950 census found car ownership to be correlated with income. Two-thirds of the thirty-seven percent of families with incomes below $3,000 (representing the poorest families) did not own automobiles; by contrast, eight in ten of the twenty-two percent of families in the richest income bracket with incomes of $5,000 or more owned vehicles.[21] For car owners, there was a hierarchy of brands. At GM, five brands ranked from the lowest- to the highest-priced make: Chevrolet, Pontiac, Oldsmobile, Buick, and Cadillac.[22] In 1954, you could have driven home in a new Chevy, the

---

[18] Ibid., 73–74.   [19] Ibid., 81–82.   [20] Ibid., 82.

[21] Bureau of Labor Statistics, U.S. Department of Labor, *Study of Consumer Expenditures, Incomes and Savings: Statistical Tables, Urban U.S. – 1950*, volume 18 (Philadelphia: University of Pennsylvania, Wharton School of Finance and Commerce, 1957), Tables 1–1 and 1–10, 2 and 11.

[22] James M. Rubenstein, *Making and Selling Cars: Innovation and Change in the U.S. Automotive Industry* (Baltimore: Johns Hopkins University Press, 2001), 192, 206.

Table 7.2. *Families Who Purchased GM, Ford, and Chrysler Brands, 1954*

Families Who Bought a New:	Percent of New Car Families with $5,000 or More Income	Family Income		New Car Price	
		Average	Median	Average	Median
General Motors:					
Cadillac	98.8%	$30596	$23306	$5,023	$4,958
Buick	84.3	10972	8438	3,352	3,330
Oldsmobile	88.4	11793	9063	3,393	3,352
Pontiac	76.8	8505	6978	2,995	2,996
Chevrolet	69.4	8251	6308	2,301	2,286
Ford Motor Company:					
Lincoln	96.7	$23179	$17738	$4,844	$4,920
Mercury	87.6	10800	7969	3,164	3,195
Ford	73.6	8220	6538	2,466	2,429
Chrysler:					
Chrysler	88.0	$14864	$9977	$3,834	$3,866
DeSoto	85.1	11441	8442	3,380	3,368
Dodge	74.8	8043	6766	2,800	2,828
Plymouth	61.5	6936	5837	2,332	2,305

Note: Data is based on the *Survey of Consumer Finances*, conducted by the Survey Research Center of the University of Michigan, Ann Arbor, MI.
Source: Market Research Division, U.S. News & World Report and Benson & Benson, Inc., *The People Buying New Automobiles Today* (U.S. News Publishing Corporation, 1955), 17, 32.

largest selling brand, for the average price of $2,301. Putting down an extra $694, you could have climbed a step up the price ladder and for $2,995 bought a new Pontiac. Oldsmobile and Buick carried roughly the same prices, with Oldsmobile selling for $3,393 and Buick for $3,352. Cadillac, however, trumped all other brands, costing more than twice the price of Chevrolet at $5,023 on average (Table 7.2). Similar patterns were found in the case of the Ford Motor Company and Chrysler. At Ford, average prices rose from $2,466 for its namesake to $3,164 for the Mercury brand and then to $4,844 for Lincoln. Chrysler's four brands did not reach the heights of Cadillac or Lincoln, but nevertheless followed a ladder starting with Plymouth priced at $2,332, and then rising to Dodge at $2,800, DeSoto at $3,380, and then Chrysler at $3,834.[23]

[23] Cross reported that the price gap diminished from the 1930s to the 1950s: although a Cadillac sold for four times the price of a new car in 1930, it was down to 1.7 times new car prices, on average, in 1955. See Gary Cross, *An All-Consuming Century: Why Commercialism Won in Modern America* (New York: Columbia University Press, 2000), 92.

What the price hierarchy did not make clear was that most people who bought the five brands, including those who purchased Chevies, Fords, and Plymouths, were among the richest thirty or forty percent of the population. *US News & World Report*'s market research study, based on the Fed's Survey of Consumer Finances, noted that the richest thirty-eight percent of the population, with incomes in excess of $5,000 on average, accounted for three-quarters of all new car purchases in 1954.[24] The median income of new car purchasers of Chevrolet in 1954 was $6,308, and their average income was $8,251, placing most buyers of the low-priced brand in the richest third of the population.[25] Incomes for Ford buyers were almost identical to buyers of the Chevrolet brand (Table 7.2), and although families who bought Plymouths had in general lower incomes, their average income was $6,936 and median income was $5,837 (Table 7.2). Among mid-priced brands, the average income of Buick buyers was $10,972 (median income was $8,438), placing them within the richest twenty percent of the population.[26] Mercury and DeSoto again showed similar patterns (Table 7.2).

The patterns make sense because the distribution of income was so skewed. A glance at Table 7.3 indicates that the richest five percent of families earned twenty percent of all income in 1954, and the richest fifth of families claimed forty-five percent of all income. The bottom forty percent of the population made just sixteen percent of all income that year. To be sure, the distribution of income was less unequal than it had been during the 1920s, and less unequal than it would become during the 1990s, but the distribution was

---

[24] Market Research Division, *U.S. News & World Report*, and Benson & Benson, Inc., *The People Buying New Automobiles Today* (U.S. News Publishing Corporation, 1955), 6, 17. This study was based on a survey sponsored by the Fed. Beginning in 1946, the Fed paid for surveys of consumers' finances and regularly reported the surveys' findings in the *Federal Reserve Bulletin*. The databases for the annual surveys, as well as the code books, are archived at the Inter-university Consortium for Political and Social Research (ICPSR) at the University of Michigan. See, for example, the database concerning 1954 in Economic Behavior Program, Survey Research Center, University of Michigan, "Survey of Consumer Finances, 1955," [computer file and codebook], ICPSR 3600, Conducted by University of Michigan, Survey Research Center, ICPSR ed., Ann Arbor, MI: Inter-university Consortium for Political and Social Research, September 1999, http://www.icpsr.umich.edu/cocoon/ICPSR-STUDY/03600.xml, August 24, 2006. A technical account of the survey is offered in "1955 Survey of Consumer Finances: Technical Appendix," *Federal Reserve Bulletin* 41 (May 1955): 471. The Survey Research Center, under the direction of George Katona, produced several publications based on its surveys. See for example, George Katona, *The Mass Consumption Society* (New York: McGraw-Hill Book Company, 1964); and idem, *The Powerful Consumer: Psychological Studies of the American Economy* (New York: McGraw-Hill Book Company, 1960). Cohen noted other research organizations in *A Consumers' Republic*, 132–33.

[25] Market Research Division, *U.S. News & World Report*, and Benson & Benson, Inc., *The People Buying New Automobiles Today*, 17, 18.

[26] Ibid. Data for the income distribution is reported in Bureau of the Census, *Historical Statistics*, series G 319–336, 302.

FIGURE 7.1. Chevrolet Impala, 1959. Although Chevrolet represented the bottom rung of GM's price ladder of brands, the Impala was expensive and most of its new-car buyers were among the richest third of the population. Courtesy of the Detroit Public Library, National Automotive History Collection.

still highly skewed. By implication, most households did not buy new cars, but instead purchased used cars. For 1954, the Fed reported that more than twenty percent of consumers bought automobiles, but car dealers sold twice as many used as new vehicles (Fig. 7.1).[27]

The pyramid of GM car brands can be mapped against consumers' incomes (Fig. 7.2).[28] The five GM brands represented a pyramid because far more Chevrolets were sold than Buicks or Cadillacs, but GM sold the vast majority of new cars to consumers in the top thirty to forty percent of the income distribution. Ford and Chrysler likewise sold most of their new vehicles to

[27] "1955 Survey of Consumer Finances: Purchases of Durable Goods in 1954," *Federal Reserve Bulletin* 41 (May 1955): 466, 474. Gary Cross reported a similar conclusion for data from 1957 as reported in an article in *U.S. News & World Report*. In 1957, most new cars were purchased by Americans in the top income brackets, even Chevrolet; conversely, most Americans purchased used cars. See Cross, *An All-Consuming Century*, 89; and "New Cars: Who Buys Them, How They're Paid For," *U.S. News & World Report* (March 14, 1958): 84–86.

[28] Rubenstein offered one pyramid of the five GM brands for the entire population of car buyers, but did not distinguish between new and used vehicles. The Fed's Survey of Consumer Finances revises this picture. Rubenstein, *Making and Selling Cars*, 206.

Table 7.3. *Distribution of Income, 1954 (reported in 1954 dollars)*

Distribution of Families	Share of Income	Lower Income Limit	Average Income by Group
Top 5%	20.3%	$12,350	$21,761
Top 20%	45.2	7,100	12,096
Second 20%	22.5	5,120	6,019
Third 20%	16.4	3,700	4,401
Fourth 20%	11.1	2,200	2,975
Fifth 20%	4.8	not listed	1,289

Source: U.S. Bureau of the Census, *Historical Statistics of the United States: From Colonial Times to the Present* (Washington, D.C.: U.S. Government Printing Office, 1976), series G 319-336, 301-302.

families in the top third of the income distribution. The 1954 survey should not surprise us when it revealed that two-thirds of new car buyers held managerial, professional, or semiprofessional occupations; nine in ten were heads of families, male, and married.[29] Most used cars were sold to middle-income households; and few cars were bought by families in the bottom twenty percent of the income distribution (Fig. 7.3).

As national prosperity after World War II lifted the incomes of Americans, more families purchased automobiles in keeping with the income ladder. One study summarized data about car ownership for four groups of families: African Americans, white laborers, white wage earners, and white salaried households. White salaried families had the highest incomes and the highest rates of auto ownership each year. However, over time, the incomes of the other groups and their real expenditures increased, and so did their rates of auto ownership. For instance, in 1935, white salaried households' average real expenditures (in 1972–73 dollars) were $7,184, and white laborer households' average real expenditures were $3,663. By 1960, white laborer households reported average real expenditures of $7,218, or a few dollars more than the white salaried households' 1935 costs. Whereas seventy-six percent of white salaried families and thirty-three percent of white laborer families owned cars in 1935, by 1960 white laborer households had caught up with salaried families' 1935 level of ownership with seventy-eight percent owning automobiles. By 1960, with higher incomes, ninety-four percent of white salaried families owned cars.[30]

[29] Market Research Division, *U.S. News & World Report*, and Benson & Benson, Inc., *The People Buying New Automobiles Today*, 10, 22, 23, 25, 26.

[30] Clair Brown, "Consumption Norms, Work Roles, and Economic Growth, 1918–80," in *Gender in the Workplace*, ed. Clair Brown and Joseph A. Perchman (Washington, D.C.: Brookings Institution, 1987), Table 5, 28–29, Table 6, 30.

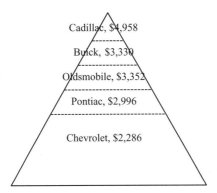

FIGURE 7.2. Market Share and Median Prices for General Motors' Five Brands, 1954
Notes: The pyramid represents the market share for new cars held by the five GM brands in 1954, beginning with Chevrolet and moving up to the top brand, Cadillac. GM's total market share was 50.7 percent, and the five brands each claimed the following shares: Chevrolet, 25.6 percent; Pontiac, 6.5 percent; Oldsmobile, 7.4 percent; Buick, 9.3 percent; and Cadillac 2.0 percent. The pyramid is stylized since the market shares do not represent an exact pyramid. My pyramid is based on a revised model of a price pyramid created by James M. Rubenstein in *Making and Selling Cars: Innovation and Change in the U.S. Automotive Industry* (Baltimore: Johns Hopkins University Press, 2001), 206.
Sources: For the market share of GM's five brands, see Ronald Henry Wolf, "General Motors: A Study of the Firm's Growth, Its External Relationships, and Internal Organization" (Ph.D. dissertation, Vanderbilt University, 1962), Appendix C, Table 2, 479-80; for the 1954 median prices of the five brands, see Table 7.2.

In general, postwar prosperity was felt among Americans: family incomes increased 129 percent from an average level of $2,335 in 1929 to $5,356 in 1954. (Incomes increased forty-six percent once adjusted for inflation.)[31] Yet, prices of automobiles rose *pari passu*. Chevrolet provides a useful example as the entry-level automobile with the largest market share. In 1929, Chevrolet's price tag ranged from $525 to $725; in 1948, its price had doubled to $1,280, according to one GM executive who testified to a congressional subcommittee; and, in 1954, the price increased eighty percent to $2,301 (Table 7.2).[32] Whereas family incomes had increased 2.2 times between 1929

---

[31] Figures are calculated from U.S. Bureau of the Census, *Historical Statistics*, series G 308–309, 301.

[32] For Chevrolet prices, see "Chevrolet Prices: 1920–31 Incl.," File 83-1.4-9, and "Profits, Prices and Products," Statement and Discussion before Subcommittee on Profits of the Joint Committee on the Economic Report by M. E. Coyle, Executive Vice President of GM, Washington, D.C. 12/20/48, File 83-1.9-51, Wilkerson Collection, KU. See also "General Motors Pricing Policy *Better Value at the Same Price or Equal Value at Reduced Price* Chevrolet History 1925–1939," and "*Chevrolet,*" both in File 87-4.18-56, Box 20, GMC/Proving Grounds, KU. Daniel Raff and Manuel Trajtenberg calculated an unweighted index of automobile prices in

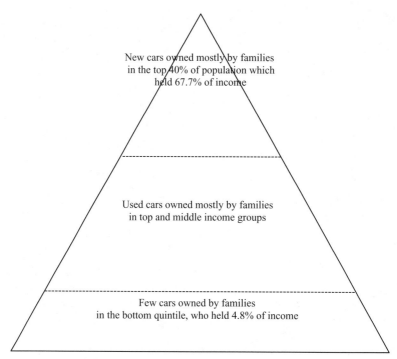

FIGURE 7.3. Distribution of Car Sales by Income Groups, 1954.
Notes: New cars were concentrated among the richest thirty-eight percent of the population; families in the top and middle income groups accounted for most used car sales; and families in the bottom twenty percent of the population bought few cars.

My pyramid is based on a revised model of a price pyramid created by James M. Rubenstein in *Making and Selling Cars: Innovation and Change in the U.S. Automotive Industry* (Baltimore: Johns Hopkins University Press, 2001), 206.
Sources: For the distribution of income in 1954, including the lower limit income for each quintile, see Table 7.3; and for purchases of cars by income groups, see "1955 Survey of Consumer Finances: Purchases of Durable Goods in 1954," *Federal Reserve Bulletin* 41 (May 1955): 475.

and 1954, the price of a Chevrolet had increased between three and four times. During the 1950s, car prices kept pace with gains in family incomes. The Fed reported a fifty percent increase in new car prices, on average, and a fifty-eight percent increase in average used car prices for the decade,

current and constant dollars, and illustrate the indices with two diagrams covering the years from 1906 to 1940. Daniel M. G. Raff and Manuel Trajtenberg, "Quality-Adjusted Prices for the American Automobile Industry: 1906-1940," in *The Economics of New Goods*, ed. Timothy F. Bresnahan and Robert J. Gordon, National Bureau of Economic Research (Chicago: University of Chicago Press, 1997), 78–79.

whereas family incomes (unadjusted for inflation) rose roughly fifty-three percent.[33]

New or used, automobiles imposed a hefty cost on household budgets. One historian observed that "transportation costs rose from 9.5 percent to 11.5 percent of personal disposable income" between 1950 and 1960. Autos did not constitute the entire share of transportation costs. In 1960, they accounted for 13.7 percent of consumption expenditures and "other travel and transportation" accounted for 1.5 percent, bringing the total cost of transportation to 15.3 percent of consumption expenditures. Because consumption expenditures were a portion of disposable income, an auto's share of disposable income was smaller than its share of consumption expenditures. In 1960, when the census covered rural and urban households, automobiles accounted for fourteen percent of expenditures on average.[34] The figures also were reported for all households, not those households that owned vehicles. For instance, adjusting figures for the seventy-six percent of families who owned automobiles in 1960, the cost of autos was eighteen percent of family expenditures on average.[35] Among families owning cars in 1950, vehicles absorbed nineteen percent of budgets on average.[36] By 1973, when most families owned cars, transportation costs were twenty percent of African American, eighteen percent of white laborer, nineteen percent of white wage earner, and eighteen percent of white salaried family expenditures.[37] The financial burden of automobile ownership may be expressed in different ways, but the important point is that cars absorbed a significant part of family outlays.[38]

---

[33] Figures are calculated from U.S. Bureau of the Census, *Historical Statistics*, series G 308–309, 301.

[34] James J. Flink, *The Automobile Age* (Cambridge, MA: MIT Press, 1988), 287; and Bureau of Labor Statistics, U.S. Department of Labor, "Consumer Expenditures and Income: Total United States, Urban and Rural, 1960–61," BLS Report No. 237-93 (February 1965): 11.

[35] In the 1960 survey, seventy-six percent of those surveyed reported owning cars. The data were reported as "average income, expenditures and savings," and automobiles accounted for 13.7 percent of total "expenditures for current consumption." Because these figures are average data for all those surveyed, I divided the figure by .76 to arrive at the share of costs for automobiles among those households that did own a car. This exercise led to the conclusion that autos accounted for eighteen percent of household budgets. My figures for 1960 are calculated from data reported in Bureau of Labor Statistics, U.S. Department of Labor, "Consumer Expenditures and Income," 11.

[36] Bureau of Labor Statistics, U.S. Department of Labor, *Study of Consumer Expenditures, Incomes and Savings*, 3, 11.

[37] Brown, "Consumption Norms, Work Roles, and Economic Growth, 1918–1980," Table 4, 24–25.

[38] Gary Cross offered a lower figure for the cost of ownership, noting "the share of household budgets for cars dropped from 6.2 percent to 4.6 percent between 1955 and 1960." Cross based his comment on an article in *U.S. News & World Report*, but he did not include the cost of "gasoline, tires, repairs." Looking at the cost of automobiles in terms of their

The expense of automobiles also varied with families' incomes. For 1950 and 1960, families who owned vehicles in the very richest income bracket expended the smallest percentage of their expenditures on autos, twelve percent. In the next income bracket, autos consumed sixteen percent of budgets in 1950 and 1960. Most families who owned cars in the middle income brackets spent roughly seventeen percent of their budgets in 1950, and eighteen percent in 1960. For the bottom two catagories of the income distribution, autos accounted for twenty-three and thirty-four percent of family budgets for those reporting cars in 1950, and nineteen and twenty-one percent of their family budgets in 1960.[39]

Although cars imposed a large burden on the annual budgets of American households, changes in the terms of credit made those burdens more manageable. As was the case during the 1920s and 1930s, during the postwar years many families relied on installment credit to finance automobiles. In 1950, fifty-seven percent of used cars and forty-one percent of new car sales involved installment financing (Table 7.4). The amount of installment debt rose dramatically. In 1929, automobile paper amounted to $1.4 billion (or $15.9 billion adjusted for inflation in 2005 dollars); it plunged in the early years of the Great Depression, but rebounded to $1.5 billion in 1939 (or $21.0 billion in real dollars). Installment debt dwindled during the war years, but with the burgeoning peacetime economy, auto paper rose to $5 billion in 1949 ($37.6 billion in real dollars), and it reached $16 billion by 1959 ($109.7 billion in real dollars). Total installment credit followed a similar pattern, jumping from $39.8 billion (real dollars) in 1929 to $262.8 billion (real dollars) in 1959 (Table 7.5). Part of this increase reflected a greater proportion of indebted households. Whereas just twenty-four percent of households held installment debts in 1935–1936, forty-seven percent were indebted by 1956.[40]

In the years when more families assumed debts, the terms for installment loans became more generous. First, during the mid-1950s, the size of down

purchase, operation, and maintenance, the data reported in *U.S. News & World Report* indicated that consumers spent 12.6 percent of their dollars on cars in 1955 and 10.9 percent in 1960. Total transportation costs came to 13.9 percent in 1955, twelve percent in 1960. The journal's article did not provide a full citation for its source of data, and so it is not possible to follow up on the nature of the data in this case. Flink, *The Automobile Age*, 287; Cross, *An All-Consuming Century*, 179; and "Big Change in Buying Habits – What It Means to Business," *U.S. News & World Report* (February 6, 1961): 73–75.

[39] To repeat, figures are adjusted in terms of the expenditure for automobiles relative to those families who owned automobiles. Bureau of Labor Statistics, U.S. Department of Labor, *Study of Consumer Expenditures, Incomes and Savings*, 3, 11; and Bureau of Labor Statistics, U.S. Department of Labor, "Consumer Expenditures and Income," 11.

[40] Geoffrey H. Moore and Philip A. Klein, *The quality of Consumer Instalment Credit*, National Bureau of Economic Research (New York: Columbia University Press, 1967), 21. Cross also notes the general trend toward longer maturities for auto loans in *An All-Consuming Century*, 92. Cohen traces the growth of indebtedness in *A Consumers' Republic*, 123–24.

Table 7.4. *Families' Method of Payment for Purchase of New and Used Automobiles, Selected Years, 1947 to 1970*

Year	Families Owning Automobiles	All Passenger Cars		New Cars		Used Cars	
		Full Cash	Installment or Other Borrowing	Full Cash	Installment or Other Borrowing	Full Cash	Installment or Other Borrowing
1970	82%	47%	53%	34%	66%	52%	48%
1965	79	48	52	40	60	53	47
1960	77	38	62	33	67	41	59
1955	70	38	60	39	60	37	60
1950	59	47	52	54	46	41	57
1949	56	50	49	56	43	47	52
1948	54	59	39	66	33	55	42
1947	n.a.	65	35	71	29	63	37

Note: Data is based on the *Survey of Consumer Finances*, conducted by the Survey Research Center of the University of Michigan, Ann Arbor, MI.
Source: U.S. Bureau of the Census, *Historical Statistics of the United States: From Colonial Times to the Present* (Washington, D.C.: U.S. Government Printing Office, 1976), series Q175–186, 717.

Table 7.5. *Installment Credit Outstanding*

Date	Total Installment Credit (current dollars, $ billions)	Automobile Paper (current dollars, $ billions)	Total Installment Credit (2005 real dollars, $ billions)	Automobile Paper (2005 real dollars, $ billions)	Total Installment Credit Per Household (current dollars)	Automobile Paper per Household
1919	$0.80	$0.3	$9.0	$3.4	$33.51	$12.73
1929	3.5	1.4	39.8	15.9	119.13	46.79
1939	4.5	1.5	63.0	21.0	130.87	43.51
1949	11.6	4.6	94.9	37.6	274.76	107.98
1959	39.3	16.4	262.8	109.7	763.04	319.24
1969	98.2	36.6	520.7	194.1	1,588.37	592.22

Notes: The Board of Governors of the Federal Reserve System compiled the data and reported it in its *Supplement to Banking & Monetary Statistics,* section 16 (new), "Consumer Credit," 33, and the *Federal Reserve Bulletin.* Figures are deflated using the consumer price index as reported on the Federal Reserve Bank of Minneapolis web site.

Sources: U.S. Bureau of the Census, *Historical Statistics of the United States: From Colonial Times to the Present* (Washington, D.C.: U.S. Government Printing Office, 1976), series A350, 43; series X 552, 553, 1009; Council of Economic Advisors, *Economic Report of the President, Transmitted to Congress January 1977* (Washington, D.C.: U.S. Government Printing Office, 1977), 241; "What is a Dollar Worth?" Federal Reserve Bank of Minneapolis, http://minneapolisfed.org/Research/data/us/calc/index.cfm, March 12, 2006.

Table 7.6. *Distribution of Auto Loans by Size of Down Payment,*
1925–1965

	Statement Date, End of Year						
	1925	1929	1934	1937	1953	1955	1957
New & Used Cars							
Down Payment under 33 1/3%	19%	8%	18%	23%			
Down Payment over 33 1/3%	81	92	82	77			
New Cars							
Down Payment under 33 1/3%			17	22	30%	52%	60%
Down Payment over 33 1/3%			83	78	70	48	40
Used Cars							
Down Payment under 40%		21					
Down Payment over 40%		79					
Down Payment under 33 1/3%				28	31	38	54
Down Payment over 33 1/3%				72	69	62	46

Source: Geoffrey H. Moore and Philip A. Klein, *The quality of Consumer Instalment Credit,*
National Bureau of Economic Research (New York: Columbia University Press, 1967), 12.

payments shrank. Whereas in 1953 seven in ten contracts carried a down
payment of more than a third of a new car's price, in 1955 half of auto
contracts were written with a down payment of less than a third of the
car's price. For used cars, fifty-four percent of down payments were under
a third of the car's price by 1955 (Table 7.6). Second, lenders lengthened
the duration of contracts. During the 1920s, the vast majority of installment
loans had been written for twelve months or less. In 1934, the time frame
for new and used cars still followed this pattern. By 1937, credit terms had
begun to ease: just twenty-two percent of new car loans and fifty-one percent
of used car loans were written for twelve months or less. Then, after the
wartime interruption, lenders continued to stretch out the duration of loans.
In 1953, eighty percent of new car loans ran from eighteen to twenty-four
months and used car loans from twelve to twenty-four months. In 1957,
forty-four percent of new car loans were repaid over more than a thirty-one-
month period. In 1960, two-thirds of used car loans were written for more
than twenty-five months (Table 7.7). Compared to the 1920s, maturities
had doubled or tripled, while the size of down payments relative to the
total loan had diminished, thereby reducing a car's month-to-month burden
on household budgets. Overall repayments on installment loans averaged
twenty to twenty-two percent of debtors' personal income during the 1950s,
much like the figure in 1935–1936 of twenty-three percent.[41]

[41] Moore and Klein, *The quality of Consumer Instalment Credit,* 21. See also U.S. Board of
  Governors of the Federal Reserve System, *Consumer Instalment Credit,* Part 1, Volume 1,
  "Growth and Import," 135–39.

Table 7.7. *Distribution of Auto Loans by Duration of Loans, 1925–1965*

	Statement Date, End of Year									
	1925	1929	1934	1937	1953	1955	1957	1960	1963	1965
New & Used Cars										
12 months or less	81%	85%	70%	32%						
13+ months	19	15	30	68						
New Cars										
12 months or less			62	22						
13+ months			38	78						
18 months or less				65	17%	9%	6%			
19+ months				35	83	91	94			
24 months or less				95	81	32	20			
25+ months				5	19	68	80			
30 months or less							56	19%	15%	14%
31+ months							44	81	85	86
Used Cars										
12 months or less			85	51	14	17	11			
13+ months			15	49	86	83	89			
24 months or less				99	99	95	65	33	21	21
25+ months				1	1	5	35	67	79	79

Source: Geoffrey H. Moore and Philip A. Klein, *The quality of Consumer Instalment Credit*, National Bureau of Economic Research (New York: Columbia University Press, 1967), 9.

The new credit terms helped sell new and used cars. Noting the forty-five percent increase in automobile credit in 1954 over 1953 (even though auto sales in 1954 dipped below their 1953 level), the *Federal Reserve Bulletin* explained, "credit sales have been stimulated by lower down payments and longer maturities, particularly on new cars."[42] One in four consumer spending units had been involved in an automobile transaction, and sixty percent of new or used car purchases involved credit financing.[43] The use of credit

[42] "Growth of Consumer Instalment Credit," *Federal Reserve Bulletin* 41 (December 1955): 1312–13. See also U.S. Board of Governors of the Federal Reserve System, *Consumer Instalment Credit*, Part 1, Volume 1, "Growth and Import," 130–31.

[43] "1955 Survey of Consumer Finances: Purchases of Durable Goods in 1954," *Federal Reserve Bulletin* 41 (May 1955): 466–67. The Fed designated its primary unit of analysis not the family, but the "spending unit" (SU). Its codebook for the 1955 survey was typical in defining a spending unit as "a group of related people living in the same dwelling unit who pool their incomes for their major items of expense." The vast majority of these spending units were families, but the SU could have been a single individual or an extended family. See also "1955 Survey of Consumer Finances: Technical Appendix," *Federal Reserve Bulletin* 41 (May 1955): 471; and Irving Schweiger, "Size Distribution of Family Income, Saving, and Liquid Asset Holdings in 1945," Folder 565.5, Box 2532, Entry 1, RG 82, NA. The Fed focused on SUs, as it reported in 1947, because "they represent consumer units of economic

increased as family incomes and liquid assets (such as savings accounts) diminished. For 1954, fifty-four percent of spending units with more than $5,000 in annual income took out an auto loan to buy a new car, as compared to seventy percent with less than $5,000 in annual income who relied on installments for their new car purchases. Differences according to liquid assets were more striking. Just thirty percent of spending units with liquid assets of more than $2,000 relied on installment financing, whereas two-thirds of those with liquid assets of $500 to $2,000 took out an auto loan, and eighty-seven percent of those with liquid assets of less than $500 required financing.[44]

I do not argue that credit was the only factor at work in the sale of autos.[45] Aside from credit, family incomes made the purchase of autos possible. In looking at incomes, I make no claim that families were fixed within a specific bracket of the income distribution: Americans moved up and down the income ladder during their lifecycle.[46] Instead, I find that credit remained important for easing the financial burden of automobiles for those families that found themselves on the lower rungs of the income ladder. Some families were on the lower rungs simply because they were young, but many were on the lower rungs as a result of class distinctions, other social hierarchies, illness, injuries, or bouts of unemployment.

What was important was that the liberalized credit helped reduce the auto's financial burden for any family that had access to credit and, as it turned out, families with fewer financial assets tended to take out loans. Consider GM's price ladder. To buy a Cadillac in 1954, shoppers paid the total price up front, in cash, in eighty-nine percent of all cases. For Chevy, forty-five percent of buyers paid the entire price in cash. Buick, Oldsmobile, and Pontiac fell in

---

decisions, actions, and plans better than families (which in some cases contain more than one spending unit) or individuals." "Survey of Consumer Finances, Part I. Expenditures for Durable Goods and Investments," *Federal Reserve Board* 33 (June 1947): 647, 647 n. 1.

[44] A similar pattern applied to used car sales. Of those consumers with liquid assets of $2,000 or more, twenty-two percent used credit financing, whereas fifty-one percent of those with liquid assets of $500 to $1,999 used credit financing and sixty-eight percent of those with fewer than $500 in liquid assets needed an auto loan. The pattern for income was different, as the percentage of credit financing was similar for all income groups in buying used cars. Liquid assets proved a clearer predictor of credit financing, while the nature of income in buying used cars may have had less predictive value because fewer households with incomes below $3,000 owned cars. "1955 Survey of Consumer Finances," *Federal Reserve Bulletin* 41 (May 1955): 466.

[45] Richard Easterlin examined the question of Americans' materialism in his recent collection of essays. See Richard A. Easterlin, *The Reluctant Economist: Perspectives on Economics, Economic History, and Demography* (New York: Cambridge University Press, 2004), 32–53.

[46] One study based on the Survey of Consumer Finances reported significant variations in income in a three-year period. See Ralph B. Bristol, Jr., "Factors Associated with Income Variability," *American Economic Review: Papers and Proceedings of the Seventieth Annual Meeting of the American Economic Association* 48 (May 1958): 279–90. See also Katona, *The Powerful Consumer*, 183–84.

between these two extremes. Ford showed a similar pattern. Nearly seventy-five percent of Lincoln buyers paid the total price in cash, whereas only forty-six percent of Ford buyers did so.[47] For the purchase of new cars, the median ratio of monthly payments to monthly income in 1953 came to thirty percent or more for consumers with an annual income of less than $3,000, twenty-one percent for those with incomes of $3,000 to $4,200, sixteen percent for those with incomes of $4,200 to $6,000, and twelve percent for those with incomes of $6,000 to $12,000. Consumers with incomes in excess of $12,000 devoted six percent of their incomes to installment payments.[48]

In the two decades after World War II, the Big Three automakers marketed brands according to a price ladder that targeted the richest thirty to forty percent of the population. As Detroit hoped, new car buyers were tempted to trade in their existing vehicles before they had worn out. The Fed reported, for instance, that in 1954 one in four new car buyers traded in his or her vehicle at "regular intervals."[49] The average wait time between trades was 3.2 years.[50] These shopping patterns supplied the used cars that, in turn, cascaded to families further down the income ladder. Again, credit for used cars helped dealers sell vehicles, especially to families with smaller incomes or fewer liquid assets.

Although automakers adhered to the basic elements of the marketing strategy articulated by Alfred Sloan for the 1920s – styling, installment credit, and the price pyramid – the quantitative portrait emphasized two changes. First, in contrast to the years from 1910 to 1930, when falling costs and declining prices had triggered the market's expansion, during the 1950s auto prices rose in line with Americans' incomes.[51] Second, the terms for installment loans eased during the postwar years. Thus, although the broad outlines of the Big Three's marketing plan still applied to the immediate postwar years, families faced at least two important changes in the market when buying vehicles. Those changes came about as three institutions – the family, the firm, and the state – shaped the market's maturation in keeping with Detroit's marketing strategy of selling cars that mimicked the skewed distribution of income.

[47] Market Research Division, *U.S. News & World Report* and Benson & Benson, Inc., *The People Buying New Automobiles Today*, 32.

[48] Moore and Klein, *The quality of Consumer Instalment Credit*, 92.

[49] "1955 Survey," *Federal Reserve Bulletin* 41 (May 1955): 466.

[50] The data indicated that sixty-six percent of all cars traded in had been bought within the past three years. Market Research Division, *U.S. News & World Report* and Benson & Benson, Inc., *The People Buying New Automobiles Today*, 29.

[51] The Bureau of Labor Statistics stated, "Probably the most significant factor in the growth of car ownership was a drop of 40 percent in factory-delivered prices of cars" during the 1920s. U.S. Department of Labor, *How American Buying Habits Change* (Washington, D.C.: U.S. Government Printing Office, 1959), 186. On the relationship between prices and technology, see Raff and Trajtenberg, "Quality-Adjusted Prices for the American Automobile Industry: 1906–1940," 71–101.

THE FIRM: PRODUCING CARS

In light of the financial burden imposed by automobile ownership it is worth asking: was the maturation of the U.S. auto market, based on the price ladder and the sale of big, heavy cars, inevitable? One alternative to car ownership was mass transit. In cities with dense populations and good subway systems, car ownership as a form of transportation caught on much more slowly than in other areas of the U.S. In New York, Boston, and Philadelphia, rates of car ownership ranged from thirty-nine to forty-two percent in 1950. By contrast, in the large, but geographically dispersed city of Los Angeles, as well as in smaller cities such as Madison, Wis., and Albuquerque, N.M., rates ranged from seventy-two to seventy-eight percent.[52] By 1960, rates of ownership had increased across the nation, but they still remained lower in cities with good mass transit systems. Whereas fifty percent of New Yorkers and sixty-six percent of Bostonians owned cars, eighty-four percent of the citizens of Los Angeles drove automobiles.[53] Alternatively, the expansion of the automobile market could have been achieved through the sale of small, cheap vehicles designed to match small budgets. At the end of World War II, the Society of Automotive Engineers conducted a survey in which buyers in urban markets reported wanting smaller vehicles.[54] Charles Kettering, as head of GM's research laboratory, had tried to develop a light car during the 1930s. The car encountered numerous technical problems and failed to make the big leap into a marketable product.[55] Shortly after World War II, Ford managers at first supported the creation of an economy car, but then suddenly changed their minds when a survey indicated that consumers wanted big vehicles, in contrast to the opinions obtained by the Society of Automotive Engineers.[56]

[52] Bureau of Labor Statistics, U.S. Department of Labor, *Study of Consumer Expenditures, Incomes and Savings: Statistical Tables, Urban U.S. – 1950*, volume 17 (Philadelphia: University of Pennsylvania, Wharton School of Finance and Commerce, 1957), Table 1–1, 2–3.

[53] Bureau of Labor Statistics, U.S. Department of Labor, "Consumer Expenditures and Income: New York, N.Y., 1960–61," BLS Report No. 237–54 (November 1963), 2; Bureau of Labor Statistics, U.S. Department of Labor, "Consumer Expenditures and Income: Boston, Mass., 1960–61," BLS Report No. 237–57 (February 1964), 2; and Bureau of Labor Statistics, U.S. Department of Labor, "Consumer Expenditures and Income: Los Angeles, Calif., 1960–61," BLS Report No. 237–72 (January 1964), 2. On the building of highways, see for example, Flink, *The Automobile Age*, 358–76; Rose, *Interstate*; and Owen D. Gutfreund, *20th-Century Sprawl: Highways and the Reshaping of the American Landscape* (New York: Oxford University Press, 2004).

[54] Rubenstein, *Making and Selling Cars*, 220.

[55] Stuart W. Leslie, *Boss Kettering: Wizard of General Motors* (New York: Columbia University Press, 1983), 175–80.

[56] Hounshell added that even without going into production, the light car had an important impact on management: "Nevertheless, the idea of a light car remained fixed in some executives' minds and thus intruded into much of the company's long-term planning process." Hounshell, "Planning and Executing 'Automation' at Ford Motor Company, 1945–65: *The Cleveland Engine Plant and Its Consequences*," in *Fordism Transformed: The*

Affordable, economical vehicles did not make serious inroads into the automobile market until the 1960s. At Ford, managers kept up their interest in the light or compact car. Phil Patton noted that for the small Ford Falcon: "Legend had it that Robert McNamara . . . drew up the specifications for the Falcon in church, on the back of a hymn list." It was introduced in 1959.[57] Ford's Mustang also proved enormously popular during the 1960s, capturing the image of youth in an automobile.[58] The most unusual vehicle was the Volkswagen Beetle. The Bug's sales rose from 157,000 in 1960 to 453,000 in 1967, and then peaked at 1.3 million in 1971, at which point James Rubenstein reported that it surpassed "the Model T as the world's best-selling car ever."[59] VW won the hearts of many U.S. consumers with its egg-shaped product and offbeat advertising. Helmut Krone won the VW account for Doyle Dane Bernbach (DDB).[60] The advertiser opted not to mention the Bug's Nazi past. They did not use "German" to describe its engineering. Instead, the advertisements, according to Patton, "tapped into American values" such as "durability, and economy," but also "frugality, integrity of design, . . . and lack of pretense." Americans liked to describe themselves with these values even if they were not Detroit's themes of "power, speed, flight, and luxury."[61] Historian Thomas Frank characterized Detroit cars of the 1950s as "the stuff of technocratic fantasy. Cars were designed and advertised to resemble the exciting hardware of the Cold War: streamlined, finned like airplanes, fitted with elaborate-looking controls, decorated with flashing chrome and abstract representations of rockets or airplanes."[62]

VW's advertising upended Detroit's marketing of a big used car being traded for a big shiny new car. Patton pictured used cars as the first car or the cheap car: the "gospel in Detroit" held "that the real people's car, the inexpensive model, the first car, was a used car. There was no need for small inexpensive cars in America when there were so many large inexpensive used ones."[63] The Bug confused this formula. One ad with a photo of the Beetle read: "After a few years, it starts to look beautiful."[64] DDB complimented readers for keeping the same car, writing, "Ugly is only skin deep." The story of the Kremplers questioned the status-price ladder. After John Glenn walked on the Moon in 1969, DDB ran an advertisement, as Patton

Development of Production Methods in the Automobile Industry, ed. Haruhito Shiomi and Kazuo Wada (New York: Oxford University Press, 1995), 49–86, quote 80 n. 33, 81 n. 34, n. 35.

[57] Ibid., 81 n. 35; and Patton, *Bug*, 100. On the date, see Cross, *An All-Consuming Century*, 182.

[58] Rubenstein, *Making and Selling Cars*, 222.

[59] Ibid., 226–27.   [60] Patton, *Bug*, 92.

[61] Ibid., 71–77, 91–105, quotes 92, 96–97, 104–105.

[62] Frank, *The Conquest of Cool*, 61.   [63] Patton, *Bug*, 100.

[64] The advertisements are pictured in Marcantonio, Abbott, and O'Driscoll, *Is the Bug Dead?* 18, 21, 47.

FIGURE 7.4. Importing VW Bugs, 1962. As an affordable and sturdy vehicle, the Bug offered an important alternative to Detroit's price ladder of brands. Courtesy of the Detroit Public Library, National Automotive History Collection.

recounted, "showing the landing module and the line, 'It's ugly but it gets you there'" (Fig. 7.4).[65]

[65] Patton, *Bug*, 96, 104–105. Frank wrote that while the Big Three had altered their advertising by the mid-1960s, their effort was not to forsake planned obsolescence but instead to find for "annual style changes a more compelling meaning." Frank, *The Conquest of Cool*, 157. On the subject of the market's segmentation, see Cohen, *A Consumers' Republic*, 292–344.

Automakers' marketing strategies were contingent on their production methods. The VW Beetle was unusual, as historian James Flink wrote, because it was "one of the most standardized cars of all time." The major benefit had been lower costs and improved quality (thanks to finer tolerances), but there was also a hitch: to obtain the cost savings, automation required that components "remained basically unchanged from car to car and from model year to model year, such as engines and transmissions." Here the VW Beetle was fortunate. As a standardized car, it permitted extensive automation including "the full automation of body welding and final assembly... between 1953 and 1966."[66] For most vehicles, however, automation ran contrary to their brands' marketing strategies of frequent style changes. In his thorough account of Ford's early experience with automation, David Hounshell seconded this point. Writing that the "horsepower race exposed a major drawback to 'Detroit Automation,'" Hounshell observed that Ford had spent "$236 million for engine manufacturing plants alone" in 1955, and concluded that the firm had paid "a heavy price" in terms of a lack of flexibility in its equipment. Ford's manufacturing executive Charles H. Patterson "continued to preach for greater flexibility in automation" into the 1960s.[67]

That automobiles posed a serious burden for households begs the question: Why did firms raise prices on cars? Why did the 1950s differ from the teens and twenties? One important distinction was labor relations. When the GM sit-down strike of 1936–1937 forced management to collectively bargain, GM's management was not prepared to do so.[68] Caught off-guard, they quickly adjusted. By 1938, management accepted the UAW, provided the auto workers' union, as labor historian Ronald Edsforth explained, quieted "its militant rank and file" and did not interfere with management's "right to hire, fire, promote, and discipline workers."[69] These questions concerned Ford's management as well. The new team of managers assembled by Henry Ford II at the end of World War II found that fear dominated the existing system of labor relations. Wanting to foster better relations, the new team also intended to stop spontaneous strikes which had ballooned to 750 during the war years.[70]

[66] Flink, *The Automobile Age*, 243–44.

[67] Hounshell, "Planning and Executing 'Automation' at Ford Motor Company," 75–76. Thomas J. Sugrue detailed the implications of automation for labor in *The Origins of the Urban Crisis: Race and Inequality in Postwar Detroit* (Princeton, NJ: Princeton University Press, 1996), 130–38, 163–68.

[68] Ronald Edsforth, *Class Conflict and Cultural Consensus: The Making of a Mass Consumer Society in Flint, Michigan* (New Brunswick, NJ: Rutgers University Press, 1987), 164.

[69] Ibid., 192–93.

[70] Hounshell, "Planning and Executing 'Automation' at Ford Motor Company," 56–57. See also Nevins and Hill, *Ford: Decline and Rebirth: 1933–1962*, 306.

GM and Ford executives' chance came in the five years from 1946 to 1950. In 1946, autoworkers launched a major strike against GM. The stakes were high: the union wanted to alter the ways in which management interacted with labor. For instance, the UAW asked for a large increase in pay as a way to redistribute income; they asked that GM open its financial records to reveal whether it could pay workers higher wages; and they requested the firm raise wages but hold the price of cars steady.[71] The distinction between wages and car prices was important, as workers wanted wages to rise thirty percent while keeping car prices constant.[72] Though the UAW secured an 18.5-cent raise for hourly wages, the 1946 agreement failed to achieve its more ambitious demands. Management objected to any control over prices or restrictions on the relation between wages and prices as gross interference with the virtues of free enterprise. GM and other firms got what they wanted: they convinced the Office of Price Administration (OPA) to grant them price increases for vehicles soon after the strike.[73] In 1948, worried about inflation, GM managers proposed cost of living adjustments (COLAs) to wage contracts, and the COLAs were included in a five-year contract signed in 1950.[74] According to historian Nelson Lichtenstein, the clauses raising wages were palatable for management "because this industrial giant faced little effective competition, either foreign or domestic, so it could easily 'administer' any price increases made necessary by the new labor contract."[75]

By the time the Bug had become popular, most households owned vehicles. In other words, the market had matured before small, cheap cars offered a serious alternative to the Big Three's marketing scheme. Automation of production had offered one possible alternative to the existing system of producing and marketing vehicles, but its diffusion was hampered by its requirement for long runs of standardized components – a requirement that

---

[71] Nelson Lichtenstein, "From Corporatism to Collective Bargaining: Organized Labor and the Eclipse of Social Democracy in the Postwar Era," in *The Rise and Fall of the New Deal Order, 1930-1980*, ed. Steve Fraser and Gary Gerstle (Princeton, NJ: Princeton University Press, 1989), 132.

[72] Nelson Lichtenstein, *The Most Dangerous Man in Detroit: Walter Reuther and the Fate of American Labor* (New York: Basic Books, 1995), 229.

[73] Ibid., 239–47. On the role of the OPA in World War II, see Meg Jacobs, *Pocketbook Politics: Economic Citizenship in Twentieth-Century America* (Princeton, NJ: Princeton University Press, 2005), 179–220. For an economic account of price controls, see Hugh Rockoff, *Drastic Measures: A History of Wage and Price Controls in the United States* (New York: Cambridge University Press, 1984); and idem, "The United States: from ploughshares to swords," in *The Economics of World War II*, ed. Mark Hanson (New York: Cambridge University Press, 1998), 81–121. Rockoff discussed the OPA's limited success in controlling prices in "The Response of the Giant Corporations to Wage and Price Controls in World War II," *Journal of Economic History* 41 (March 1981): 123–28. The contest over the OPA at the war's close is recounted in Cohen, *A Consumers' Republic*, 100–109.

[74] Americans in general worried about inflation. See Jacobs, *Pocketbook Politics*, 209–61.

[75] Lichtenstein, "From Corporatism to Collective Bargaining," 141. See also idem, *The Most Dangerous Man in Detroit*, 271–98.

ran into trouble with the horsepower race and annual model changes. The UAW had tried to influence management's pricing policies. Yet, during the Cold War, GM and Ford executives sought to quiet militant organizers; and between 1946 and 1950, hostility to labor took many forms, such as the Taft-Hartley Act's requirement that union officials sign affidavits swearing that they were not Communists.[76] Historian Meg Jacobs wrote of another provision in Taft-Hartley: "the act's advocates fought just as hard to end unions' ability to politicize wages, profits, and prices by subjecting them to public debate. To that end, the law outlawed secondary boycotts and forbid the direct expenditure of union dues in political campaigns."[77] Moreover, the fear of communism had contributed to a "consensus," Thomas Sugrue wrote, that it was "'un-American' to criticize business decisions" or even to "interfere" with management's decisions.[78] Because wages rose through COLAs while prices were not checked, the pressure fell on automobile dealers to sell cars through their usual marketing tools. Dealers, in turn, led the drive to convince officials at the Federal Reserve Board to ease the terms of installment loans.

THE STATE: THE FED'S LIBERALIZED CREDIT TERMS

During World War II and the early postwar years, the Fed focused on consumer credit as part of its effort to control inflation. Officials established a set of regulations, known as Regulation W, to curb installment purchases. Then, after World War II, the Fed initiated two additional periods of credit controls; yet in contrast to the war years, Regulation W inspired protest. Automobile dealers led a "pressure campaign," charging the Fed's credit policies discriminated against low-income consumers.

Under Executive Order 8843, issued on August 9, 1941, the Fed established restrictions on the maximum length of maturities as well as on the minimum down payment required for various goods. In the case of automobiles, buyers were required to make a down payment of one-third of the purchase price and pay off the loan within eighteen months (later modified to fifteen months).[79] Controls went into effect in September 1941 and were removed in November 1947. But with the "inflation threat" looming, President Truman proposed new controls, and Regulation W went back into

---

[76] James T. Patterson summarized provisions of the Taft-Hartley Act in *Grand Expectations: The United States, 1945–1974* (New York: Oxford University Press, 1996), 51. See also Jacobs, *Pocketbook Politics*, 236–38. On the subject of the anti-Communist affidavits, see Lichtenstein, *Most Dangerous Man in Detroit*, 265–70. Edsforth discussed Reuther's tactics in *Class Conflict and Cultural Consensus*, 205–206.

[77] Jacobs, *Pocketbook Politics*, quote 236. See also Cohen, *A Consumers' Republic*, 153.

[78] Sugrue, *Origins of the Urban Crisis*, 7, 156.

[79] U.S. Board of Governors of the Federal Reserve System, *Consumer Instalment Credit*, Part 1, Volume 1, "Growth and Import," 289–96.

operation from September 1948 through June 1949. Its third and last period of operation came during the Korean War. Under the Defense Production Act, the Fed again regulated consumer credit markets from September 1950 through May 1952, and for the period from October 16, 1950 through May 7, 1952, the restrictions were stiff: the Fed continued to require the down payment equal a third of the purchase price (in cash or trade-in) and it restricted maturities on car loans to fifteen or eighteen months.[80]

Dealers protested the second and third phases of the regulation. Linking credit regulation to lost sales, they sent hundreds of letters to the Fed complaining that the regulation should be relaxed or, better still, dismantled. The dealers took particular aim at the distributional consequences of the restrictions on the size of down payments and maturities. In December 1948, a dealer from Salem, Oregon, wrote: "Our lowest priced new car is $2594.00 and Regulation W in its present form eliminates at least 50 percent of our prospective buyers and therefore makes it impossible for us to make sufficient sales to remain in business." Another dealer wrote that, in his farming district, someone "does not buy a car for pleasure – but to go to work and earn a livelihood." He proposed extending the maturity on auto loans from eighteen "to at least 24 months."[81] Again, in 1951 and 1952, dealers protested Regulation W. A Chrysler dealer complained, "Regulation W. created class buying" because it "discriminates against the majority of the people." They need auto transport but "are unable to meet the drastic and limited monthly terms, thus, such persons cannot improve their transportation." Regulation W, he added, "hit the automobile business very hard" and the dealer complained that he and others might well be "squeezed" out of the market. A California dealer repeated this basic point: "Regulation W discriminates against the working man whom it is supposed to protect, because it permits only people of means or with high incomes to purchase new cars, due to the high monthly payments required." By extension, the dealer fretted: "Regulation W works a tremendous hardship on automobile dealers and their employees because of their inability to sell cars under its restrictive terms."[82]

In 1952, a Fed official in Houston observed that dealers for the most part understood the goal of checking inflation. He advised retailers "that there

[80] Ibid., 296–302, especially Table 55, 300.
[81] E. U. Teague to Thomas B. McCabe, Chairman, Board of Governors, December 16, 1948; and George Brown, Freehold Willys, Inc., to Board of Governors, December 16, 1948, both in Folder 502.111, "Automobiles – Pressure Campaign to Permit Longer Maturities," Box 2325, Entry 1, RG 82, NA.
[82] H. W. Robinson, Harry Sommers, Inc., to Walter F. George, no date [stamped May 2, 1952]; and Dick S. Heffern, Secretary Motor Car Dealers Association of Orange County, to Board of Governors of the Federal Reserve System, April 18, 1952, both in Folder 502.111 "Automobiles (Jul 1951–1954) Consumer Durable Goods – Credit Control," Entry 1, Box 2316, RG 82, NA.

was no injustice done with Regulation W when automobiles were in short supply and you could sell all you could get without any extended terms. On both these points most everyone agreed. However, they [the dealers] bring out the fact that automobiles are no longer in short supply and the high prices that cars are now being sold for makes it difficult to sell them on the present market with this limiting control." The official added: "As it now stands, I can't help but agree with them." In other words, the shift from a seller's to a buyer's market had put dealers' own prosperity at risk. Writing in February 1952, the president of Willys-Overland Motors, Inc., observed that "[t]he take-home price of the lowest priced automobile today is in the neighborhood of $2,000, approximately double what it was at the end of the war, and nearly three times what it was before the war." Under the new pricing conditions, he explained, many families could not cover the entire down payment and, even if they could, their monthly payments of "approximately $70 a month" would be too much for their budgets.[83] Neither writer asked why auto prices had risen relative to Americans' incomes. In other words, rather than fault the credit restrictions, dealers or managers could have asked why manufacturers had not established a price ladder of brands so that the price of new vehicles better matched the distribution of Americans' incomes, obviating the need of larger loans with longer maturities.

The Fed lifted Regulation W in the middle of 1952. The next year the economy dipped into a recession, but it revived in late 1954. With the economic rebound in 1955, the volume of installment credit jumped nearly twenty-five percent. The increase captured the attention of Americans and President Eisenhower requested Fed officials to investigate credit markets. To determine whether installment credit had a destabilizing influence on monetary policy or the economy, the Fed conducted a four-part study, paying special attention to automobile paper. In its sections on credit regulation, and again in part III, "Views on Regulation," the Fed recounted the various objections to credit controls, including dealers' complaints about the discriminatory consequences of the minimum down payment requirements and maximum maturities. Fed officials, for the most part, agreed with these complaints: they concluded that the limits for credit controls were felt more by families at the low end of the income distribution (or distribution of liquid assets) rather than farther up the ladder.[84]

[83] Ross Stewart to W. H. Holloway, Federal Reserve Bank of Dallas, April 8, 1952, and Ward M. Canaday, President, Willys-Overland Motors, Inc., February 11, 1952, both in Folder 502.111 "Automobiles (Jul 1951–1954) Consumer Durable Goods – Credit Control," Entry 1, Box 2316, RG 82, NA.

[84] U.S. Board of Governors of the Federal Reserve System, *Consumer Instalment Credit*, Part 1, Volume 1, "Growth and Import," 315–24; and U.S. Board of Governors of the Federal Reserve System, *Consumer Instalment Credit*, Part III, "Views on Regulation," especially 112–34, 168–83.

THE FAMILY: WOMEN'S WORK AND WOMEN'S CREDIT

During the Cold War, policy makers in the U.S. sought to demonstrate the superiority of the U.S. economy to the Soviet system by emphasizing American families' increased consumption.[85] Indeed, according to the Cold War ideology, the U.S. was or was soon to be a classless society thanks to the benefits of consumption. When Vice President Richard Nixon undertook the famous "Kitchen Debate," he argued not only that consumption demonstrated the superiority of capitalism, but claimed as well that women in the U.S. as the family consumer-shoppers were better off than their Soviet counterparts. Historian Elaine Tyler May recalled the debate: "Nixon and Khrushchev revealed some basic assumptions of their two systems.... Khrushchev countered Nixon's boast of comfortable American housewives with pride in productive Soviet female workers: In his country they did not have that 'capitalist attitude toward women.' Nixon clearly did not understand that the Communist system had no use for full-time housewives, for he replied, 'I think that this attitude toward women is universal. What we want is to make easier the life of our housewives.'"[86] U.S. wives enjoyed a higher standard of living than Soviet wives; yet contrary to Nixon's dictum, during these very years, married women with young children joined the paid workforce. Their decisions coincided with changes in family budgets, but also came in the context of segmented labor and credit markets.[87]

One of the most noticeable changes for American families during the postwar years was the move to the suburbs. Suburbs had existed prior to the war and states had funded roads. Yet, after 1945, the federal government encouraged this move and a concomitant surge in auto sales in at least two important ways. First, the Federal Housing Administration along with the Veterans Administration provided low-interest loans for home mortgages and thus encouraged the widespread pattern of families moving to the suburbs and counting on automobiles for transportation. Second, the vast network of highways, facilitated by the 1956 Highway Act, made automobile travel more feasible for households.[88]

[85] Cohen, *A Consumers' Republic*, 124–27. See also the discussion of Elaine Tyler May in *Homeward Bound: American Families in the Cold War Era*, rev. ed. (New York: Basic Books, 1999), 12–18.

[86] May, *Homeward Bound*, 12. See also Cohen, who wrote that postwar consumption "promised the socially progressive end of economic equality without requiring politically progressive means of redistributing existing wealth." Cohen, *A Consumers' Republic*, 125–27, quote 127.

[87] Brown, "Consumption Norms, Work Roles, and Economic Growth, 1918–1980," 47–48.

[88] Rose discusses the Highway Act of 1956 in *Interstate*. See also Mark H. Rose, "Reframing American Highway Politics, 1956–1995," *Journal of Planning History* 2 (August 2003): 212–36. For an account of VA loans, see Jackson, *Crabgrass Frontier*, 195–206. On the diffusion of electrical networks, see Rose, *Cities of Light and Heat*; and Richard F. Hirsh,

A third factor also assisted the move to the suburbs: families reallocated their budgets, spending far less for food and clothing, and to some extent fuel and lighting, and spending much more for transportation plus recreation and insurance. Looking at the example of white laborer households, food's share fell from thirty-four percent in 1935 to twenty-four percent in 1960, and to twenty percent by 1973. The same trend was seen in the other three groups.[89] Among white laborer families, the cost of fuel and lighting claimed six percent of expenditures in 1918, rose to 8.5 percent in 1935, and slipped to between four and five percent in the 1950s and 1960s.[90] As expenditures for household items fell, the purchase of vehicles was made more feasible, but automobiles still posed a large burden on family budgets. Transportation costs, adjusted for inflation, rose sharply through the 1960s. Although real disposable personal income rose fifty-nine percent between 1935 and 1950, white laborers reported nearly a threefold increase in real expenditures on transportation.[91] For white wage earners, real transportation expenditures jumped 2.6 times during this time period. Disposable income per person (adjusted for inflation) rose just fifteen percent during the 1950s, and yet real expenditures for transportation rose by twice that amount for all four groups.[92] It is important to keep in mind that the figures for expenditures on automobiles as a percent of family expenditures were just that, average figures.[93] As rates of auto ownership increased, a larger proportion of families devoted funds to the purchase of new and used vehicles as well as to their upkeep, and so average costs increased.

Power Loss: The Origins of Deregulation and Restructuring in the American Electric Utility System (Cambridge, MA: MIT Press, 1999). See also Cohen, *Making a New Deal*, 273–77. For an assessment of who had access to these resources as well as their distributional consequences, see Cohen, *A Consumers' Republic*. For an account of class distinctions in the suburbs, see Becky M. Nicolaides, *My Blue Heaven: Life and Politics in the Working-Class Suburbs of Los Angeles, 1920-1965* (Chicago: University of Chicago Press, 2002).

[89] Brown, "Consumption Norms, Work Roles, and Economic Growth, 1918–1980," Table 4, 24–25. On the subject of heat and lighting, see also Rose, *Cities of Heat and Light*.

[90] Brown, "Consumption Norms, Work Roles, and Economic Growth, 1918–1980," Table 4, 24–25.

[91] Real auto expenditures are calculated from data in Ibid., Tables 4 and 5, 24–25, 28–29, for real disposable income see 23.

[92] Real auto expenditures are calculated from data in Ibid., Tables 4 and 5, 24–25, 28–29, quote 26.

[93] In its 2001 survey, the Bureau of Labor Statistics made the point: "Because not all consumer units purchased all items during the survey period, the mean expenditures for an item is usually considerably lower than the expenditure by those consumer units that purchased it." Officials gave the example of the purchase of new cars. Because few consumers purchased new vehicles, the average figure reported in the table was $1,628. Yet, "if about 7 percent of the households reported purchasing a new car or truck in 1999, the average expenditure on new cars and trucks for those households would be $23,257." Bureau of Labor Statistics, U.S. Department of Labor, "Consumer Expenditure Survey, 1998–99," *Bulletin* 955 (November 2001): 40.

Families varied in how they earned the money to purchase their cars. Some consumers counted on the higher pay built into the COLA adjustments of union contracts. The so-called "Treaty of Detroit" set the standard for other oligopolistic industries in which union workers received similar pay increases and benefits. Yet, outside oligopolistic markets and even in the automobile industry outside of the Big Three automakers, workers did not receive pay packages on a par with the UAW at GM or Ford. COLAs were rare in most industries, and so the earnings in other parts of the manufacturing sector, such as clothing and retail industries, fell by 1960 to less than sixty-five percent of the autoworkers' average weekly earnings.[94] Although during World War II some labor leaders had promoted an "egalitarian" wage, this objective diminished with the Korean War and post-1965 inflation.[95] Although its settlement with the UAW allowed the Big Three to raise auto prices along with wages for its workers, employees in other segments of the economy were not as well remunerated and thus not as well prepared to finance higher-priced automobiles.[96] A second option for these workers was to take advantage of the longer-term loans, but families could also elect a third option: both husbands and wives, mothers and fathers could work for pay.

Indeed, in the postwar years, growing numbers of wives joined the workforce, even those with children under school age.[97] Between 1950 and 1960, wives with children under age six increased their participation in the workforce from twelve to nineteen percent, and wives with children six years of age or older increased their rates from twenty-eight to thirty-nine percent. By 1973, thirty-three percent of wives with young children and fifty percent of wives with children of school age were in the workforce. Thus, women's added incomes helped to purchase big-ticket items, and offered an alternative to credit financing.[98]

---

[94] Lichtenstein, "From Corporatism to Collective Bargaining," Table 5.1, 145.

[95] Ibid., 144.   [96] Ibid., 145.

[97] May, *Homeward Bound*, 16. Dora L. Costa has reviewed the movement of women into the paid workforce in the United States and compared this development to trends found in other countries. See Dora L. Costa, "From Mill Town to Board Room: The Rise of Women's Paid Labor," *Journal of Economic Perspectives* 14 (Fall 2000): 101–22. See also Brown, "Consumption Norms, Work Roles, and Economic Growth, 1918–1980."

[98] Brown, "Consumption Norms, Work Roles, and Economic Growth, 1918–1980," Table 7, quote 31. Richard Easterlin offered a different account, but a similar timing of the movement of women into the paid workforce in *The Reluctant Economist*, 205–18. As Cohen reported, autoworkers chose lifestyles after the war that reflected their social concerns and not simply their income level. See Cohen, *A Consumers' Republic*, 161–62. In general, see Pierre Bourdieu, *Distinction: A Social Critique of the Judgement of Taste*, trans. Richard Nice (Cambridge, MA: Harvard University Press, 1984). My account of changes within the household facilitating the increased demand for consumer goods is similar to Jan de Vries's account of households during the early modern period. See Jan de Vries, "The Industrial Revolution and the Industrious Revolution," *Journal of Economic History* 54 (June 1994): 249–70.

Women who joined the workforce took jobs typically segregated along gender lines. Lichtenstein put the issue in broad terms: "The weakness of the postwar welfare state and the extreme fragmentation inherent in the American system of industrial relations did much to redivide the American working class into a unionized segment . . . and a still larger stratum, predominantly young, minority, and female, that was left out in the cold."[99] The segmentation applied as well to credit markets. Although dealers pressed the case for easing credit terms so as not to discriminate on the basis of income, neither Fed officials nor retailers questioned credit discrimination associated with race, age, and sex. In these cases, discrimination was not directly linked to the Fed's efforts to stabilize the economy's performance through restrictions on the terms of credit, but was simply found in who had access to credit.

For these numerous consumers, credit markets did not change until the 1970s. Testimony before hearings to pass the 1974 Equal Credit Opportunity Act (ECOA) and the 1976 amended act brought to light a long-standing climate of discrimination. The acts prohibited credit discrimination "on the basis of sex or marital status," as well as "race, color, religion, national origin, age, receipt of income from public assistance programs, and good faith exercise of rights under the Consumer Protection Act of 1968."[100] As one example of credit reforms, the 1974 ECOA banned a common practice among creditors whereby they required women upon marriage to close out their credit accounts and open new accounts in their husbands' names. Thus, unless married women bought cars with cash, the credit for the purchase depended on their husbands' credit record.[101] Speaking before these hearings, Barbara Jordan, Representative from the state of Texas, recalled

---

[99] Lichtenstein, "From Corporatism to Collective Bargaining," 144. Sugrue discussed labor market segmentation in *The Origins of the Urban Crisis*. On the subject of job discrimination, see for example, Claudia Goldin, *Understanding the Gender Gap* (New York: Oxford University Press, 1990); and Pamela Walker Laird, *Pull: Networking and Success since Benjamin Franklin* (Cambridge, MA: Harvard University Press, 2006), 92–136.

[100] "Regulation B: Amendment," *Federal Reserve Bulletin* 63 (January 1973): 89–95, quote 89. Reviewing the amended act, Gail Reizenstein noted that discrimination against the elderly was "the abuse most frequently documented in the hearings held to amend the 1974 Act." Gail R. Reizenstein, "A Fresh Look at the Equal Credit Opportunity Act," *Akron Law Review* 14 (Fall 1980): 219–29, quote 228.

[101] Reizenstein, "A Fresh Look at the Equal Credit Opportunity Act," 216. On the example of married women's credit cards, see Lizabeth Cohen, "From Town Center to Shopping Center: The Reconfiguration of Community Marketplaces in Postwar America," *American Historical Review* 101 (October 1996): 1073–75. See also Cohen, *A Consumers' Republic*, 147–48, 281–83. For an account of the credit discrimination that African Americans faced, see Martha Olney, "When Your Word is Not Enough: Race, Collateral, and Household Credit," *Journal of Economic History* 58 (June 1998): 408–31; and for recent years, Ian Ayres, "Fair Driving: Gender and Race Discrimination in Retail Car Negotiations," *Harvard Law Review* 104 (February 1991): 817–72.

that Will Rogers had found a "solution for traffic jams: keep every car off the road until it was paid for." That cure, she noted, "illustrates the extent to which our economy is dependent upon credit."[102] Women had entered the segmented job market and had been excluded from consumer credit markets at the very time that families reallocated their expenditures and purchased automobiles. Ironically, the very significance of automobiles and the need for credit to purchase them lent support for women and many other groups of consumers demanding passage of the Equal Credit Opportunity Act. With the bill's enactment, a new chapter opened for the Fed: through a set of policies called Regulation B, its officials sought to eliminate numerous unfair lending practices.[103]

CONCLUSION

Between the end of World War II and the mid-1960s, the automobile became entrenched as a daily necessity for the vast majority of Americans. The market's expansion came in part as families reaped the benefits of the postwar prosperity. But this explanation also demands two modifications. First, recognizing the financial burden of automobiles, credit markets had been critical to the auto market's expansion. In contrast to the 1920s, during the 1950s lenders reduced the size of down payments and doubled and then tripled maturities for auto loans. Whereas vehicles imposed a substantially higher financial burden, families made smaller down payments and stretched out the length of the maturities on their loans. Second, not all families counted on postwar bonuses, good union jobs, or liberalized credit terms. The 1950s and 1960s saw the rapid movement of married women, including mothers with young children, into the workforce. Their incomes helped purchase expensive consumables such as automobiles.

This chapter has traced the market's maturation in terms of the consequences, intended or unintended, associated with the firm, the family, and the state. Within U.S. corporations, managers wanted to "stabilize" labor relations, and they included COLAs in their wage agreements with the UAW while raising car prices for the buying public. Automation offered the potential to cut costs and lower car prices, but the technology proved too inflexible to accommodate the marketing strategy of the annual model change.

[102] Statement of Barbara Jordan, *Hearings before the Subcommittee on Consumer Finance, House Committee on Banking and Currency, Relating to Legislation Prohibiting Sex Discrimination in the Granting of Credit*, U.S. House of Representatives, 93rd Cong., 2nd sess., part 1, June 20 and 21, 1974, 472; and Donna Dunkelberger Geck, "Equal Credit: You Can Get There From Here – The Equal Credit Opportunity Act," *North Dakota Law Review* 52 (Winter 1975): 385.

[103] I have found that the best overall treatment of credit discrimination, including a discussion of Regulation B, was National Consumer Law Center, *Credit Discrimination*, 3rd ed. (Boston: National Consumer Law Center, Inc., 2002).

Automakers' pricing policies thus put pressure on dealers to obtain liberalized credit. During these years, as the Fed debated the extent to which the government should control credit markets in its effort to check inflation, dealers charged that credit should not be controlled; rather, they contended, liberalized credit terms should counter the effects of higher car prices. They explicitly linked the new credit terms to the goal of selling cars to Americans on the lower rungs of the income ladder. U.S. families dramatically reallocated their budgets during the 1950s and 1960s as the prices of other goods, such as food and clothing, dropped. As more families devoted a larger proportion of expenditures to items purchased for cash or on credit, more wives joined the workforce. Their earnings offered an alternative to credit financing; for some families, wives' earnings were combined with installment credit to enable the purchase of expensive durables. Thus, the evolution of the firm, the state, and the family had brought about changes that collectively, if unintentionally, worked to expand the auto market in keeping with the price ladder of car brands and the skewed distribution of income.[104]

At least three cultural themes had set their own parameters to the auto market's particular history. One was the fear of communism and the celebration of free enterprise during the Cold War, which underpinned automobile executives' resistance to linking wage rates to the price of their products. A second cultural theme was the set of values associated with the price ladder of brands. To become a successful car import during the 1960s, the Bug had to hide its German past and to assert values – thrift, no-nonsense, whimsy – that challenged the conventional model of marketing U.S. automobiles. The price ladder associated with GM's five brands had played on images of power, speed, comfort, and status, in keeping with the highly skewed distribution of income among U.S. families. This price ladder committed Americans to the sale of the first car as a big used car. "Large and comfortable" was privileged by Detroit over "little and nimble."[105] A third cultural theme concerned the role of housewives in the gender ideology of the Cold War, which celebrated the "freedom" women obtained in the home thanks to the economy's productivity. During these years, the Fed liberalized credit terms. Yet, in spite of the obvious discrimination that women and many other groups of Americans faced in credit markets, officials viewed discrimination simply in terms of income or class. They placed their trust in white male borrowers with low incomes and excluded many others. Thus, the credit markets reinforced a market not oriented to the diversity of consumers, but to families each with a white male head and graded incomes. The upshot was a market that matured

---

[104] While I have focused on the Fed's role in its efforts to curb inflation, other historians have examined gender ideology in periods of deflation. One valuable comparison is found in Mark Metzler, "Woman's Place in Japan's Great Depression: Reflections on the Moral Economy of Deflation," *Journal of Japanese Studies* 30:2 (2004): 315–52.

[105] In general, see Frank, *The Conquest of Cool*; and Patton, *Bug*.

in keeping with the skewed distribution of income and the automakers' marketing strategy of a price ladder of brands. Although the VW Bug and other brands of small cars proved enormously popular during the late 1960s, by then, the automobile had become a required form of transportation for the vast majority of families.

On Labor Day, 2001, the *New York Times* carried an editorial about how Americans spent the dollars they earned. Tracing changes in family budgets during the past century, Jerome Segal testified to the entrenched car culture. Whereas in 1900, most households devoted one or two percent of their expenditures for all transportation, by 1999 they allocated twenty percent of their budgets to transportation, and many dollars went to buying, operating, and maintaining vehicles. Segal observed that Americans worked from January 1 to March 14 just to cover transportation costs, and mused, "No society in history has worked so much just to be able to get around."[106]

[106] Jerome M. Segal, "The Way We Spend Now," *New York Times* (September 3, 2001): A19.

Conclusion

Different problems characterized market relations between consumers and corporations as the automobile market evolved during the twentieth century. In a new market, car buyers and sellers faced the question of who would absorb the social costs of innovation. In a mass market, consumers and the modern corporation negotiated a vehicle's quality and fair pricing mechanisms. In a mature market, buyers and sellers varied in their views of how autos should be distributed in relation to Americans' finances. These market relationships between buyers and sellers were significant, because consumers shaped the modern firm and managers' goals of innovation and growth, just as the structure and power of the modern firm conditioned consumers' welfare.

Recognizing the mutual influence of consumers and firms brings into focus two social patterns through which buyers and sellers encountered each other in the marketplace. First, market actors formed social bonds as a way to promote the market's growth and to lessen tensions (impossible to eliminate fully). As economist Albert Hirschman observed, long-term ties among market participants have been critical to the development of capitalist economies.[1] Hirschman pointed to the work of information economists whose intellectual framework identified ties among suppliers, dealers, customers, and government officials. Still, those bonds resolved conflicts only in part. A second approach has recognized that firms exerted power through market relations by attempting to resolve conflicts in ways suited to their goals of innovation and growth.[2] One measure of the alternating patterns of social bonds and corporate power was the issue of trust. For consumers, trust

---

[1] Albert O. Hirschman, "Rival Interpretations of Market Society: Civilizing, Destructive, or Feeble?" *Journal of Economic Literature* 20 (December 1982): 1463–84. See also Robert W. Gordon, "Macaulay, Macneil, and the Discovery of Solidarity and Power in Contract Law," *Wisconsin Law Review* (May/June 1985): 565–79.

[2] Legal scholars Friedrich Kessler and, more recently, Robert Gordon remind readers of the power firms exerted in their relations with other actors – consumers, dealers, and suppliers. Friedrich Kessler, "Automobile Dealer Franchises: Vertical Integration by Contract," *Yale Law Journal* 66 (July 1957): 1135–90; and Gordon, "Macaulay, Macneil, and the Discovery of Solidarity and Power in Contract Law," 565–79. Kessler and Gordon focused on contracts, but I find that the question of power also applied to other market relations.

was realized in specific forms: the safe design of cars, fair market transactions, and equal access to credit. Yet, faced with conflicting strategies for profitability, managers invited varying degrees of distrust. This problem dated to the start of the market.

In 1900, aspiring entrepreneurs faced the prospect of selling distinctly unreliable and expensive machines to consumers. That the market grew despite this handicap owed much to the first car buyers. They evinced a spirit of risk-taking, often portrayed in cultural terms as male bravado. They also turned for support to other market participants, including fellow drivers, through auto clubs, the press, auto dealers, and suppliers. In other words, although they liked to picture themselves as risk-takers, they also took the prudent step of forming social ties to cope with their rudimentary machines. Their sociability, however, did not fully answer the problem of the vehicle's imperfections. Many car buyers voiced complaints, including suing dealers and manufacturers for several causes that, at root, were prompted by their vehicles' defects. Wanting to expand the market, automakers recognized the need to make their products more reliable, and they formed bonds with suppliers, dealers, and research consultants. Managers also worried about the impact of liability on their new enterprises. Soon after many firms were organized, managers defined mass distribution through a system of franchised car dealers. The sales contract created conditions to foster on-going relations between dealers and manufacturers, but it also blocked consumers' lawsuits because buyers were not in privity of contract with the manufacturer.

MacPherson v. Buick (N.Y. 1916) altered this business landscape. Judge Cardozo held manufacturers accountable for testing and inspecting their products before selling them. His ruling further implied that automakers could not exercise power through their relational ties to deflect liability to suppliers or dealers. It mattered too that *MacPherson* came during the Progressive era. As Americans rethought the risks men and women should face, they in turn reconsidered the extent of power that corporations should exercise in different contexts, including the market for consumer goods. It was not only the court ruling, but also a range of regulatory oversight entities which called on automakers to design safer products. The change of attitudes among Americans and the specific types of public oversight, such as *MacPherson*, put automakers on notice that they needed to better inspect their products. *MacPherson*, it is important to remember, was not all-encompassing. Consumers still faced the difficult task of demonstrating a product's defects. But the court ruling clearly moved away from a climate in which firms could easily impose social costs on buyers.

As the mass market took shape between the mid-1910s and the start of World War II, managers sought consumers' loyalty, but nevertheless engaged in practices that threatened to shortchange consumers in terms of the price and the quality of motor cars. Within the modern corporation, managers established business institutions to make possible a mass market for automobiles. Those institutions now are familiar – the modern research laboratory, the franchised retailer, and the styling department. The business institutions also effected a particular marketing strategy. Again, those elements became familiar in the modern economy – the development of branded goods, a price ladder to correspond with consumers' income levels, the use of advertising and styling (the annual model change) to sell products, and installment credit to close the deal. These changes came with the market's evolution. As Alfred Sloan made clear, four elements defined the mass auto market of the 1920s: the closed body, the annual model change, installment credit, and the used car trade-in. These elements, in turn, posed dilemmas as to how to pursue consumers' loyalty and the firm's profitability. Though engineering a safe product might secure consumers' loyalty, management struck trade-offs between safety and other business goals – notably lower production costs and marketing innovations. Styling automobiles was a critical part of a car's sale, but Sloan's team of managers bargained aesthetic creativity for other concerns, including a car's engineering, cost of production, and ease of service. As for prices, the elements of the mass market for automobiles – the used car trade-in, the annual model change, installment credit – meant that each market transaction entailed a negotiated price so that automakers' gain came at the expense of consumers or dealers. In each of these cases no amount of information gathering (in the form of statistical surveys) could resolve the market-based conflicts between buyers and sellers. Instead, the modern firm's influence vis-à-vis consumers evolved with their market power but also with the intervention of state actors.

The issue of safety prompted a complex response by management which was in part economic, in part cultural. On one hand, the firm's size and power had enabled managers to invest in modern research, but on the other, this voluntary investment fell short of safety goals demanded by oversight entities. Through their ratings, underwriters set higher standards for corporations to meet product safety demands. Professional organizations, notably the Society of Automotive Engineers, promoted standards that could be made uniform across firms, and thus make possible safer products. State regulatory agencies, such as the Conference of Motor Vehicle Administrations, set minimum safety levels and through their enforcement compelled managers to improve their firms' products. These public and private entities represented consumers and formed bonds with managers inside the modern firm to design safer vehicles. But this was not the whole story. Despite the vast array of oversight agencies, product quality in a mass market remained imperfect. One response was management's demand for product liability insurance. A second was management's use of public relations campaigns. GM managers turned to mass media to try to manipulate how Americans thought about automotive technology and safety. PR programs such as the Fisher Body Guild and the Soap Box Derby cultivated positive associations of the automobile with ideas of speed, entertainment, and scientific progress. The programs were especially aimed at young boys and were meant to foster a long-term enthusiasm for this technology as well as the dominant firm. Along with these PR campaigns, automakers sought to define automobile safety through the Automobile Safety Foundation, aiming to focus not on the product's defects but on the streets and consumers' driving patterns.

In the case of design, GM management acknowledged the importance of aesthetics in a mass market when it purchased the Fisher Body Corporation in 1926 and established the Art and Colour Section in 1927. It was not only that the demand for closed bodies rose sharply between 1919 and 1926, but also that management recognized the need to better coordinate design and production. One indication came when GM's leading brand, Cadillac, looked so much like a competitor's brand (Studebaker) that it threatened to undercut the price ladder that was at the core of GM's marketing strategy. By integrating backward, GM gained control over the design process. Yet, GM's investment in styling did not simply promote aesthetic creativity. Instead, Harley Earl made design fit the business parameters of production and engineering. Thus, Earl's streamlined aesthetic was subject to systematic year-to-year alterations as required by the annual model change. Furthermore, because the coming of the all-steel body entailed large capital investments, design served as a competitive weapon. Earl's new styles worked to make rival brands look outdated. Or, in the case of the Cord 810, the small automaker set a new standard for modern auto aesthetics, but it was too costly to sustain against GM's competition.

The franchised car dealer mediated between consumers and management for the sale of each automobile. Their transactions were open to a range of pressures. Management exerted power over dealers when they made them use company financing, thus transferring profits from local businesses to the corporation. Because the coordination of production and distribution was imperfect, managers also pressed dealers to take unwanted cars, especially during the year-end clearance. Dealers, in turn, looked to negotiate better deals with consumers. They packed loans and padded car prices. They operated appraisal bureaus. They worked with management in the 1920s to run company-operated junkyards to remove old cars from the market. The state, through the Federal Trade Commission and the Justice Department, tried to stop unfair business practices – dealers' efforts to limit consumers' price negotiations and management's efforts to force dealers to take unwanted cars. Another answer to the dilemma came from the private sector. In the 1930s, GM managers enlarged dealers' markets and thus eased their pressure on dealers without finding a straightforward solution to the tangled problem of price negotiations.

As the auto's mass market took shape, management faced consumer dilemmas that entailed tradeoffs between improving a vehicle's quality and saving costs, or between pricing policies that profited the manufacturer as opposed to dealers or consumers. Alfred Sloan's autobiography omitted the role of regulatory agencies. It also overlooked the role of advertising and public relations. Including these aspects of the mass market indicated that consumers' loyalty was not secured through the straightforward formula of lower prices and higher quality. Instead, the imperfect process for establishing a vehicle's safe design or setting fair car prices fostered consumers' distrust while nevertheless making possible a mass market.

In the twenty-five years after World War II, the market matured in the sense that automobile ownership was distributed among the vast majority of Americans. I traced the market's maturation in relation to three institutions – the firm, the state, and the family. Inside the modern corporation, managers exerted power in labor relations when they refused the UAW's request to hold steady the price of cars. Instead, they sought to pass on higher labor costs with higher car prices. Automation held the potential to lower costs and thus counter the wage increases, but the technology did not accommodate the annual model change. Instead, automobile prices rose in line with Americans' income, and thus, economic growth did not, by itself, account for the broadening of the automobile market. Even though prices rose, credit facilitated the sale of expensive vehicles and thus played a key role in the market's expansion. The Federal Reserve Board directly shaped credit policy during World War II, and again during the early 1950s, as officials sought to restrict credit terms as part of their fight against inflation. Challenging this policy, automobile dealers framed the problem as discrimination along class lines. They charged that the Fed's credit terms discriminated against families by income, preventing farmers and working-class families with limited incomes from purchasing automobiles. Fed officials accepted this argument. As they liberalized credit terms, they permitted the market to broaden in relation to the family income distribution although leaving unquestioned lenders' restricted definition of creditworthiness. As it turned out, lenders not only defined creditworthiness by financial standards but also in terms of social hierarchies, and thus excluded women and persons of color, as well as Americans of retirement age. The market expanded, but it did so in keeping with a particular picture of American society that privileged families headed by (young) adult white males.

There was an exception to this picture. Aside from the evolution of the firm and the state, changes associated with U.S. families also influenced the development of the automobile market. During these years, many families altered labor patterns as married women, including mothers with children under school age, sought employment in the workforce. Their income provided the funds needed to purchase cars, and yet in entering the workforce, they confronted discrimination in both the credit and labor markets. As the auto market in the U.S. became entrenched during the 1960s, the very significance of automobiles to households and the need to use credit for purchases provided grounds, then, for women to object to patterns of discrimination in credit markets. As the barriers to purchasing automobiles became all the more obvious for women – young and old, married, single, or divorced – the automobile market illustrated the need for credit reform. In 1974, Congress enacted the Equal Credit Opportunity Act and amended it in 1976.

I began this study with the observation that neoclassical economics treats the market in terms of outcomes: the theory explains how demand and supply come together to determine equilibrium prices and quantities. This theory is particularly adept at addressing discrete transactions, which is to say, short-term changes in the market. But this also means that the theory is static. My approach, by contrast, has been to study the market's evolution and I have focused on the theme of trust and power. In a new market, corporations could not win consumers' trust because their products were defective. Instead, small firms exerted power in the market by imposing social costs on car buyers. In a mass market, corporations sought consumers' trust because their market share depended on consumers' loyalty, which is to say, their repeat business. Yet, manufacturers faced dilemmas about how to design vehicles and how to price them. Management exerted power over consumers, for instance, when it tried to shape consumers' attitudes about safety, or when it forced car dealers to take unwanted cars at the year-end clearance. In a mature market, the Big Three automakers through lenders such as GMAC placed their trust in some consumers based on their social characteristics while distrusting others, including women, persons of color, and persons of retirement age. Access to credit was a key variable in defining the market's maturation between 1945 and 1965.

This tension between trust and power prompted the state's intervention as the market evolved. In the new auto market, the prevailing legal context meant firms were able to impose many costs of innovation on consumers. That *MacPherson* held corporations to a higher standard of responsibility for their products' safe design no doubt worked to consumers' benefit. The mass market of the 1920s and 1930s was premised on a reasonably reliable product sold at cheap prices. Yet, consumers' welfare was not determined by the market alone. The quality of their vehicles depended in good part on the regulatory oversight of public and private agencies. Prices too were monitored through the FTC and the Justice Department. And, even with this oversight, the patchwork nature of regulation for monitoring the mechanisms used to establish a product's quality and its price meant that consumers varied in their experiences. Some obtained good bargains, while others paid high prices and drove distinctly unsafe vehicles. In the mature market of the postwar years, the Fed liberalized credit terms and thus facilitated Detroit's marketing strategy of selling large automobiles according to a price pyramid. This strategy nevertheless left open the question of who benefited from the market's expansion. Prevailing attitudes about creditworthiness shaped the market's growth to the benefit of some Americans, while excluding others. Through the Equal Credit Opportunity Act of 1974 and its subsequent amendment, the state changed credit standards and thus provided important benefits for several groups of Americans – women, persons of color, and retired Americans.

In contrast to the static notion of supply intersecting with demand, then, the evolution of the market emphasized the large number of actors who negotiated relations between consumers and corporations. Those actors included the courts, the FTC, the Justice Department, insurance underwriters, state research entities such as the Bureau of Standards, state motor vehicle administrations, and the Federal Reserve Board. Because the automobile was a complex and dangerous technology, the question of safety was not easily answered. Instead, a web of public and private oversight agencies monitored safety. Because of complexities in marketing cars, notably the used car trade-in, consumers never received a clear-cut answer to the question of fair market transactions. In the case of equal access to credit, consumers found the outcome depended on the Fed's enforcement of fair lending practices, as well as on investigations by other government agencies. The history of the U.S. automobile market thus reflected the on-going negotiations among consumers, the modern corporation, and the state over the question of trust and power.

Appendix

Automobile Dealer Agreements and Sales Manager Contracts, 1900–1914

In Chapter 2, I argue that liability for defects represented one important factor in the decisions of managers to rely on the franchise sales contract. I base part of my argument on the analysis of dealer agreements and sales manager contracts. I have tried to locate as many agreements and contracts as possible for the years from 1900 to 1914, and have obtained roughly sixty documents for thirty-two manufacturers. (I also have parts of agreements for a few additional companies.) The most important omission is Buick's dealer franchise agreement for 1909 or 1910 – an item that was not included in the exhibits of either of the two transcripts for *MacPherson*. The 1909 Buick agreement cited in this appendix was typed (not printed), and is unusual compared to other contracts by that date. By contrast, Ford offered the most complete picture. The archives yielded Ford dealer agreements for each year from 1903 (when the firm was organized) through 1914 plus five sales manager contracts for 1905, 1906, and 1909. I have two contracts for Chalmers, Peerless, Pierce, Studebaker, and the White Company, and just one contract for the remaining companies, but fortunately the agreements were distributed evenly throughout this time period.

This appendix lists the sources for each agreement or contract. I add brief comments about a few companies. Unless otherwise noted, information is based on the encyclopedic review of automakers found in *The American Car since 1775*.[1] I report neither information for disputed dealer agreements, such as the Cadillac 1902 agreement, nor data about sales manager contracts in the tables in Chapter 2.

American Electric Vehicle Company (EVC) 1900 agreement, Memorandum of Agreement between the American Electric Vehicle Company and A. F. Neale, December 31, 1900, 6–9, *Neale v. American Electric Vehicle Company*, 186 Mass. 303 (1904), Case No. 2411, Archives and Records Preservation, Supreme Judicial Court, Boston, Mass.

---

[1] Editors of Automobile Quarterly, *The American Car since 1775: the most complete survey of the American automobile ever published*, 2nd ed. (New York: L. Scott Bailey, 1971), especially 138–39, 218–372.

American Locomotive Automobile Company 1912 agreement, Agreement between Eastern Motor Sales Corp. [distributor] and Apperson-Lee Motor Company, October 28, 1912, 24–27, *Eastern Motor Sales Corp. v. Apperson-Lee Motor Co.*, 117 Va. 495 (1912), Records of Supreme Court of Virginia, Virginia State Law Library, Richmond, Va.

Anderson Carriage Company 1907 agreement, Memorandum of agreement between Anderson Carriage Co. and William G. Isbell and George D. Grant, September 19, 1907, Exhibit 1, 183–84, *Isbell v. Anderson Carriage Co.*, 170 Mich. 304 (1912), Records of the Supreme Court of Michigan, University of Michigan Law Library, Ann Arbor, Mich.

Buick Motor Company 1909 letter, F. J. Long, Sales Manager, Buick Motor Company, to D. V. Thompson, January 21, 1909, Exhibit A, 7–8, 1911, *Buick Motor Company v. Thompson*, 138 Ga. 282 (1912), Supreme Court of Georgia, Transcript of Record, Case # A-32325, The Georgia Archives, Morrow, Ga.

Cadillac Motor Car Company 1902 letter (disputed agreement), W. E. Metzger to W. J. Stewart, December 18, 1902, Exhibit 5, 10–11, *Wheaton v. Cadillac Automobile Co.*, 143 Mich. 21 (1906), Records of the Supreme Court of Michigan, University of Michigan Law Library, Ann Arbor, Mich.

Cadillac Automobile Company 1903 sales manager letter, Lem W. Bowen, Secretary, Cadillac Automobile Company, to Wm E. Metzger, December 26, 1903, 7–8, Transcript of Record, *Joslyn v. Cadillac Motor Car Co.*, 177 F. 863 (6th Cir. 1910), Case No. 1998, Records of the U.S. Court of Appeals, RG 276, NA, Chicago.

Cadillac Motor Car Company 1908 agreement, Memorandum of Agreement between Cadillac Motor Car Company and the Utica Motor Car Co., July 22, 1908, Defendant's Exhibit 2, 61–64, *Cadillac Motor Car Co. v. Johnson*, 221 F. 801 (1915), Transcript of Record, Case No. 157, RG 276, NA, N.Y.

Chalmers Motor Company 1914 agreement, blank form, File # 7222-44-1, Box 870, RG 122 BC, NA.

Chalmers-Detroit Motor Company 1909 agreement, Memorandum of Agreement between Chalmers-Detroit Motor Co. and Ogden-Farwell Garage, September 27, 1909, Exhibit 24, 99–110, *State ex. rel. Petition of Pierce-Arrow Motor Car Company, et al. v. Circuit Court of Milwaukee County et al.*, 143 Wis. 282 (1910), Records of the Supreme Court of Wisconsin, Wisconsin State Law Library, Madison, Wis.

Cole Motor Car Co. 1912 agreement, Agreement between the Cole Motor Car Co. and Cole Motor Co. of Texas, Chas. F. Hurst, September 13, 1912, Bill of exceptions, 23–31, *Cole Motor Car Co. v. Hurst et al.*, 228 F. 280 (1915), Transcript of Record, Case No. 2715, Box 421 of 1008, Accession 53-A-21, Location A2602121, National Archives – Southwest Region, Fort Worth, Tex.

Dodge Bros. 1914 agreement, Agreement between the Dodge Brothers and Pegram Motor Car Company, no date [expired June 30, 1915], reprinted in *Ellis v. Dodge Bros.*, 237 F. 860 (N.D. Ga. 1916), 860–63. Note: the Dodge Brothers began producing vehicles in 1914.

Ford Motor Company 1903 agreement, Agreement between Ford Motor Company and C.A. Duerr, August 7, 1903, Exhibit 10, vol. 2, 493–94, *Columbia Motor Car Co. et al. v. C. A. Duerr & Co. et al.*, 184 F. 893 (1st Cir. 1911), Transcript of Record, Case No. 4058–60 (consolidated numbers), RG 276, NA, N.Y.

Ford Motor Company agreements, 1904–1914, File # 7222-68-2, Box 871, RG 122, NA. Note: Officials submitted copies of actual agreements between Ford Motor Company and different dealers as well as blank forms. The company submitted more than one contract for selected years.

Ford Motor Company 1907 agreement, selected clauses, Agreement between Ford Motor Company and E. L. Dildine, December 18, 1907, Petition, 2–6, *Dildine v. Ford Motor Company*, 159 Mo. App. 410 (1911), Records of the Court of Appeals of Missouri, Kansas City, Case No. 9540 (appeal from the Circuit Court of Clinton County), Missouri State Library, Jefferson City, Mo.

Ford Motor Company 1908 agreement (HF), blank form, File L36, Box 2, Acc. 297, HF.

Ford Motor Company 1909 agreement (HF), Dealer's License & Agreement between the Ford Motor Company and Wm. Warnock Co., September 2, 1909, File L36, Box 2, Acc. 297, HF.

Ford Motor Company 1912–13 agreement (HF), Dealer's License & Agreement between the Ford Motor Company and Nichols & Miller, February 20, 1913, Folder 75-14-4, Box 14, Ford Motor Company Legal Records, 1912–31, Acc. 75, HF.

Ford Motor Company 1913–14 agreement (HF), Limited Agency Contract between the Ford Motor Company and F. O. Henizer, October 31, 1913, Folder 75-30-16, Box 30, Acc. 75, HF.

Ford Motor Company 1914–15 agreement (HF), Limited Agency Contract, blank form, Folder 75-39-3, Box 39, Acc. 75, HF.

Ford Motor Company 1905 agreement with H. L. Cunningham (Cleveland branch manager), J. Couzens to H. L. Cunningham, November 8, 1905, Folder 1, Box 1, Acc. 140, HF.

Ford Motor Company 1905 agreement with Thomas Hay (Chicago branch manager), J. Couzens to Thomas Hay, October 30, 1905, Folder 1, Box 1, Acc. 140, HF.

Ford Motor Company 1906 agreement with Thomas Hay (Chicago branch manager), Memorandum of Agreement between Thomas J. Hay and the Ford Motor Company, October 11, 1906, Folder 1, Box 1, Acc. 140, HF.

Ford Motor Company 1909 contract with L. D. Perry (London branch manager), Branch Manager Contract, October 1, 1909, Folder 1, Box 1, Acc. 140, HF.

Ford Motor Company 1905 agreement with Gaston Plantiff, J. Couzens to Gaston Plantiff (New York branch manager), December 29, 1905, Folder 1, Box 1, Acc. 140, HF.

Haynes Automobile Co. 1909 agreement, Agreement between The Haynes Automobile Company and Benjamin H. Goodman, September 1, 1909, Bill of Complaint, 2–6, *Goodman v. Haynes Automobile Co.*, 205 F. 352 (7th Cir. 1913), Transcript of Record, Case No. 1953, RG 276, NA, Chicago.

Hudson 1911 subdealer agreement, Agreement between the Sioux City Auto Company and H. M. Hessenius, July 26, 1911, reprinted in *Hessenius v. Wetmore*, 36 S.D. 157, 153 N.W. 937 (S.D. 1915), 937–39.

Hupp Motor Car Company 1910 agreement, Memorandum of agreement between H. J. Koehler Sporting Goods Company and F. C. Goodyear, August 25, 1910, *Goodyear v. H.J. Koehler Sporting Goods*, 159 A.D. 116 (1913), New York Supreme Court, Appellate Division, First Department, New York State Library, Albany, N.Y.

Inter-state Motor Car Company 1910 agreement, Agreement between Interstate Motor Car Company and W. D. Gile, October 8, 1910, reprinted in *Gile v. Interstate Motor Car Company*, 145 N.W. 732 (N.D. 1914), 733–35.

Jeffery, Thomas B. 1906 agreement, Agreement between Thomas B. Jeffery & Company and the Cedar Rapids Auto & Supply Co., January 20, 1906, Exhibit A, 4–8, *Cedar Rapids Auto & Supply Company v. Thomas B. Jeffery and Company*, 139 Iowa 7 (1908), Records of the Supreme Court of Iowa, Iowa State Law Library, Des Moines, Iowa.

Kissel Motor Car Company 1910 agreement, Agreement between Kissel Motor Car Company and Jerome P. Parker, March 10, 1910, Exhibit A, 14–18, *Parker-Harris Company v. Kissel Motor Car Company*, 165 Wis. 518 (1917), Records of the Supreme Court of Wisconsin, Wisconsin State Law Library, Madison, Wis.

Locomobile Company 1909 agreement, Memorandum of Agreement between the Locomobile Company of America and Schreiber Motor Car Co., July 19, 1909, Exhibit 30, 122–26, *State ex. rel. Petition of Pierce-Arrow Motor Car Company, et al. v. Circuit Court of Milwaukee County et al.*, 143 Wis. 282 (1910), Records of the Supreme Court of Wisconsin, Wisconsin State Law Library, Madison, Wis.

Maxwell Motor Sales Corporation partial 1914 agreement, description of parts of agreement between Herrick & Vandervoort, Maxwell's distributor, and G. Louwein, August 17, 1914, *Maxwell Motor Sales Corporation v. Louwein*, 174 P. 260 (Okla. 1918).

Maxwell 1915 Distributor's Agreement, Agreement between Maxwell Motor Sales Corporation and W. O. Barnes, May 18, 1915, 5–14, *Barnes v. Maxwell Motor Sales Corporation*, 172 Ky. 409, 189 S.W. 444 (1916), Records of the Court of Appeals of Kentucky, Case No. 44884, Kentucky Department for Libraries & Archives, Frankfort, Ky.

Metz Company 1913 agreement, Agreement between the Metz Company and James [Jos.] A. Humphreys, November 5, 1913, Exhibit A, 78–82, *Short v. Metz Company*, 165 Ky. 319 (1915), Records of the Court of Appeals of Kentucky, Kentucky Department for Libraries & Archives, Frankfort, Ky.

Monarch Motor Car Company 1914 sales manager agreement, Agreement between the Monarch Motor Car Co. and Hoover Holton and F. G. Morris, June 22, 1914, Exhibit 1, 2–5, *Holton v. Monarch Motor Car Co.*, 202 Mich. 271 (1918), Records of the Supreme Court of Michigan, University of Michigan Law Library, Ann Arbor, Mich.

Monarch Motor Car Company 1914 sales manager agreement, Agreement between the Monarch Motor Car Co. and Walch Bros., August 9, 1914, Exhibit 2, 104–10, *Holton v. Monarch Motor Car Co.*, 202 Mich. 271 (1918), Records of the Supreme Court of Michigan, University of Michigan Law Library, Ann Arbor, Mich. Note: Exhibits 3 through 11 report contracts similar to Walch's.

Oakland Motor Car Company 1908 agreement, Memorandum of Agreement between the Oakland Motor Car Company and the Indiana Automobile Co., September 16, 1908, Plaintiff's Exhibit 1, 49–51, *Oakland Motor Car Co. v. Indiana Automobile Co.*, 201 F. 499 (7th Cir. 1912), Transcript of Record, Case No. 1891, RG 276, NA, Chicago.

Packard Motor Car Company 1914 agreement, blank form, File # 7222-76-1, Box 872, RG 122, NA.

Peerless 1902 agreement, Memorandum between the Peerless Manufacturing Company and Frederick E. Randall, June 7, 1902, Document 4, 4–6, *Randall v. Peerless Motor Car Company*, 212 Mass. 352 (1912), Archives and Records Preservation, Supreme Judicial Court, Boston, Mass.

Peerless 1903 agreement, Memorandum between the Peerless Motor Car Company and Dr. R. M. Garfield, March 12, 1903, Exhibit A, 9–10, *Garfield v. Peerless Motor Car Company*, 189 Mass. 395 (1908), Massachusetts Reports Papers and Briefs, Volume 189, Social Law Library, Boston, Mass.

Peerless 1905 partial agreement, partial description between plaintiff and defendant for agreement dated January 28, 1905, 1–3, *Schiffman v. Peerless Motor Car Company*, 13 Cal. App. 600 (1910), Court of Appeal of California, Second Appellate District, Civil No. 810, California State Archives, Sacramento, Calif.

Pierce, George N. 1905 agreement, Memorandum of agreement between The George N. Pierce Co. and Banker Brothers Co., October 14, 1905, Exhibit A, 5–7, Banker Brothers Company vs. The Commonwealth of Pennsylvania, *Banker Brothers Company v. Commonwealth of Pennsylvania*, 222 U.S. 210 (1911), U.S. Supreme Court Records & Briefs, Microfilm Reel 872, University of Texas at Austin Law Library, Austin, Tex.

Pierce-Arrow Motor Car Company 1909 agreement, Memorandum of Agreement between the Pierce-Arrow Motor Car Company and American Automobile Company, June 1, 1909, Exhibit 18, 83–87, *State ex. rel. Petition of Pierce-Arrow Motor Car Company, et al. v. Circuit Court of Milwaukee County et al.*, 143 Wis. 282 (1910), Records of the Supreme Court of Wisconsin, Wisconsin State Law Library, Madison, Wis.

Pope Manufacturing Company 1909 agreement, Agreement between The Pope Manufacturing Company and Emil Estberg, May 19, 1909, Exhibit 36, 138–41, *State ex. rel. Petition of Pierce-Arrow Motor Car Company, et al. v. Circuit Court of Milwaukee County et al.*, 143 Wis. 282 (1910), Records of the Supreme Court of Wisconsin, Wisconsin State Law Library, Madison, Wis.

Pullman Motor Car Co. 1911 agreement, Agreement between the Pullman Motor Car Company and the Syracuse Motor Car Co., March 3, 1911, Exhibit A, 16–23, *Syracuse Motor Car Co. v. Pullman Motor Car Co.*, 158 A.D. 95 (1913), Supreme Court of New York, Appellate Division, Fourth Department, New York State Library, Albany, N.Y.

Reid Mfg. Co. 1903 agreement, Agreement between the Reid Mfg. Co. Auto Dept. and the H. B. Day & Co., December 15, 1903, Exhibit 97, 236–38, *Buick Motor Car Co. v. Reid Mfg. Co.*, 150 Mich. 118 (1907), Records of the Supreme Court of Michigan, University of Michigan Law Library, Ann Arbor, Mich.

Reliable Dayton Motor Car Company 1907 agreement, Agreement between Reliable Dayton Motor Car Company and F. E. Sparks, May 28, 1907, Copy of Exhibit A, 27–30, *Sparks v. Reliable Dayton Motor Car Company*, 85 Kan. 29 (1911), Records of the Mitchell district court appealed to the Supreme Court of Kansas, Kansas State Historical Society, Topeka, Kans.

R. E. Olds Co. [Reo] 1906 subdealer agreement, Memorandum of Agreement between E. A. Jenkins Motor Co. and James Cofield, December 10, 1906, Exhibit A, *Cofield v. E. A. Jenkins Motor Co.*, 89 S.C. 419 (1911), Records of Richland County Court of Common Pleas, Judgment Rolls, Case No. 9609

(L40010), South Carolina Department of Archives and History, Columbia, SC. Note: Ransom E. Olds had sold the popular Oldsmobile through the Olds Motor Works, but he subsequently started a new company using his initials in 1904.

Staver Carriage Company selected clauses of 1909 agreement, Agency Agreement between Vincent Bendix and Staver Carriage Company, April 15, 1909, reprinted in *Bendix v. Staver Carriage Company*, 174 Ill. App. 589 (1912), 590–96.

Studebaker E-M-F 1909 agreement, Agreement between Albert Poppenberg and Fred S. Meade, July 15, 1909, Finding of Fact, 6–10, *Meade v. Poppenberg*, 167 A.D. 411, 153 N.Y.S. 182 (1915), Supreme Court, Appellate Division, Fourth Department, New York State Library, Albany, N.Y. Note: Studebaker maintained a contract with Everett-Metzger-Flanders (E-M-F) in 1909.

Studebaker selected clauses of 1911 agreement, partial copy of agreement between Studebaker Corporation of America and George J. Gollmar and LeRoy Messenger, September 1, 1911, Exhibit 3, 29–32, *Studebaker Corporation of America v. George J. Gollmar & LeRoy Messenger (co-partners doing business as Gollmar & Messenger Auto Company)*, 159 Wis. 336 (1915), Records of the Supreme Court of Wisconsin, Wisconsin State Law Library, Madison, Wis.

Studebaker Corporation of America 1914 agreement, blank form, File # 7222-109-1, Box 873, RG 122, NA.

Velie Motor Car Co. 1909 agreement, Agreement between Velie Motor Car Company and Kopmeier Motor Car Co., September 23, 1909, Exhibit A, 6–9, *Velie Motor Car Co. v. Kopmeier Motor Car Co.*, 194 F. 324 (7th Cir. 1912), Transcript of Record, Case No. 1765, RG 276, NA, Chicago.

Wayne Automobile Company 1905 agreement, Agreement between the Wayne Automobile Company and Walter C. Masters & Company, January 16, 1905, Exhibit A, 10–12, *Masters & another v. Wayne Automobile Company & others*, 198 Mass. 25 (1908), Massachusetts Reports Papers and Briefs, Volume 198, Social Law Library, Boston, Mass.

Welch Motor Car Company 1908 agreement, Agreement between the Welch Motor Car Company of Pontiac, Michigan, and Welch Motor Car Company of New York, February 1, 1908, Plaintiff's Exhibit 3, 74–76, and Plaintiff's Exhibit 4, 78–79, *Welch Motor Car Company of New York v. P. Brady & Son Company*, 149 A.D. 945 (1912), Supreme Court of New York, Appellate Division, First Department, New York State Library, Albany, N.Y.

White Sewing Machine Co. 1905 agreement, Articles of Agreement between the White Sewing Machine Company and F. C. Drake & Son, February 23, 1905, Contract Form No. 1, Plaintiff's Exhibit A, 39–41, *Drake and Drake v. White Sewing Machine Company*, 133 A.D. 446 (1909), Supreme Court of New York, Appellate Division, Third Department, New York State Library, Albany, N.Y.

White Co. 1908 agreement, Articles of Agreement between The White Co. and American Motor Car Co., February 1, 1908, Contract Form No. 2, Brief of Evidence, 23–26, *White Company v. American Motor-Car Co.*, 11 Ga. App. 285 (1912), Court of Appeals of Georgia, Case No. 4159, Box 80, The Georgia Archives, Morrow, Ga. Note: The White Sewing Machine Co. renamed itself The White Co.

Index